Praise for *Hands-On Large Language Models*

This is an exceptional guide to the world of language models and their practical applications in industry. Its highly-visual coverage of generative, representational, and retrieval applications of language models empowers readers to quickly understand, use, and refine LLMs. Highly recommended!

—*Nils Reimers, Director of Machine Learning at Cohere | creator of sentence-transformers*

Jay and Maarten have continued their tradition of providing beautifully illustrated and insightful descriptions of complex topics in their new book. Bolstered with working code, timelines, and references to key papers, their book is a valuable resource for anyone looking to understand the main techniques behind how Large Language Models are built.

—*Andrew Ng, founder of DeepLearning.AI*

I can't think of another book that is more important to read right now. On every single page, I learned something that is critical to success in this era of language models.

—*Josh Starmer, StatQuest*

If you're looking to get up to speed in everything regarding LLMs, look no further! In this wonderful book, Jay and Maarten will take you from zero to expert in the history and latest advances in large language models. With very intuitive explanations, great real-life examples, clear illustrations, and comprehensive code labs, this book lifts the curtain on the complexities of transformer models, tokenizers, semantic search, RAG, and many other cutting-edge technologies. A must read for anyone interested in the latest AI technology!

—*Luis Serrano, PhD, Founder and CEO of Serrano Academy*

This book is a must-read for anyone interested in the rapidly-evolving field of generative AI. With a focus on both text and visual embeddings, it's a great blend of algorithmic evolution, theoretical rigor, and practical guidance. Whether you are a student, researcher, or industry professional, this book will equip you with the use cases and solutions needed to level-up your knowledge of generative AI. Well done!

—*Chris Fregly, Principal Solution Architect, Generative AI at AWS*

In the heart of the GenAI revolution, this indispensable guide masterfully balances theory and practice, navigating the vast landscape of large language models to equip readers with the knowledge needed for immediate and transformative impact in the field of AI.

—*Tarun Narayanan Venkatachalam, AI Researcher, University of Washington*

Timely reading to get hands-on experience with language models.

—*Emir Muñoz, Genesys*

Hands-On Large Language Models brings clarity and practical examples to cut through the hype of AI. It provides a wealth of great diagrams and visual aids to supplement the clear explanations. The worked examples and code make concrete what other books leave abstract. The book starts with simple introductory beginnings, and steadily builds in scope. By the final chapters, you will be fine-tuning and building your own large language models with confidence.

—*Leland McInnes, Researcher at the Tutte Institute for Mathematics and Computing*

Finally, a book that not only avoids superficial coverage of large language models but also thoroughly explores the background in a way that is both accessible and engaging. The authors have masterfully created a definitive guide that will remain essential reading despite the fast-paced advancements in the field.

—*Prof. DDr. Roman Egger, CEO of Smartvisions.at and Modul University Vienna*

Hands-On Large Language Models

Language Understanding and Generation

Jay Alammar and Maarten Grootendorst

Beijing • Boston • Farnham • Sebastopol • Tokyo

Hands-On Large Language Models
by Jay Alammar and Maarten Grootendorst

Published by O'Reilly Media, Inc., 1005 Gravenstein Highway North, Sebastopol, CA 95472.

O'Reilly books may be purchased for educational, business, or sales promotional use. Online editions are also available for most titles (*http://oreilly.com*). For more information, contact our corporate/institutional sales department: 800-998-9938 or *corporate@oreilly.com*.

Acquisitions Editor: Nicole Butterfield
Development Editor: Michele Cronin
Production Editor: Ashley Stussy
Copyeditor: Charles Roumeliotis
Proofreader: Kim Cofer
Indexer: BIM Creatives, LLC
Interior Designer: David Futato
Cover Designer: Karen Montgomery
Illustrator: Kate Dullea

September 2024: First Edition

Revision History for the First Edition
2024-09-10: First Release

See *http://oreilly.com/catalog/errata.csp?isbn=9781098150969* for release details.

978-1-098-15096-9

[LSI]

Table of Contents

Part II. Using Pretrained Language Models

Part III. Training and Fine-Tuning Language Models

Preface

Large language models (LLMs) have had a profound and far-reaching impact on the world. By enabling machines to better understand and generate human-like language, LLMs have opened new possibilities in the field of AI and impacted entire industries.

This book provides a comprehensive and highly visual introduction to the world of LLMs, covering both the conceptual foundations and practical applications. From word representations that preceded deep learning to the cutting-edge (at the time of this writing) Transformer architecture, we will explore the history and evolution of LLMs. We delve into the inner workings of LLMs, exploring their architectures, training methods, and fine-tuning techniques. We also examine various applications of LLMs in text classification, clustering, topic modeling, chatbots, search engines, and more.

With its unique blend of intuition-building, applications, and illustrative style, we hope that this book provides the ideal foundation for those looking to explore the exciting world of LLMs. Whether you are a beginner or an expert, we invite you to join us on this journey to start building with LLMs.

An Intuition-First Philosophy

The main goal of this book is to provide an *intuition* into the field of LLMs. The pace of development in the Language AI field is incredibly fast and frustration can build trying to keep up with the latest technologies. Instead, we focus on the fundamentals of LLMs and intend to provide a fun and easy learning process.

To achieve this *intuition-first philosophy* we liberally make use of visual language. Illustrations will help give a visual identity to major concepts and processes involved in the learning process of LLMs.[1] With our illustrative method of storytelling, we want to take you on a journey to this exciting and potentially world-changing field.

Throughout the book, we make a clear distinction between representation and generative language models. Representation models are LLMs that do not generate text but are commonly used for task-specific use cases, like classification, whereas generation models are LLMs that generate text, like GPT models. Although generative models are typically the first thing that comes to mind when thinking about LLMs, there is still much use for representation models. We are also loosely using the word "large" in *large language models* and often elect to simply call them language models as size descriptions are often rather arbitrary and not always indicative of capability.

Prerequisites

This book assumes that you have some experience programming in Python and are familiar with the fundamentals of machine learning. The focus will be on building a strong intuition rather than deriving mathematical equations. As such, illustrations combined with hands-on examples will drive the examples and learning through this book. This book assumes no prior knowledge of popular deep learning frameworks such as PyTorch or TensorFlow nor any prior knowledge of generative modeling.

If you are not familiar with Python, a great place to start is Learn Python (*https://oreil.ly/arcIm*), where you will find many tutorials on the basics of the language. To further ease the learning process, we made all the code available on Google Colab (*https://oreil.ly/kSucO*), a platform where you can run all of the code without the need to install anything locally.

Book Structure

The book is broadly divided into three parts. They are illustrated in Figure P-1 to give you a full view of the book. Note that each chapter can be read independently, so feel free to skim chapters you are already familiar with.

Part I: Understanding Language Models

In Part I of the book, we explore the inner workings of language models both small and large. We start with an overview of the field and common techniques (see Chapter 1) before moving over to two central components of these models, tokenization and embeddings (see Chapter 2). We finish this part of the book with an updated and expanded version of Jay's well-known Illustrated Transformer (*https://oreil.ly/UI4lN*),

1 J. Alammar. "Machine learning research communication via illustrated and interactive web articles." *Beyond Static Papers: Rethinking How We Share Scientific Understanding in ML*. ICLR 2021 Workshop (2021).

which dives into the architecture of these models (see Chapter 3). Many terms and definitions will be introduced that are used throughout the book.

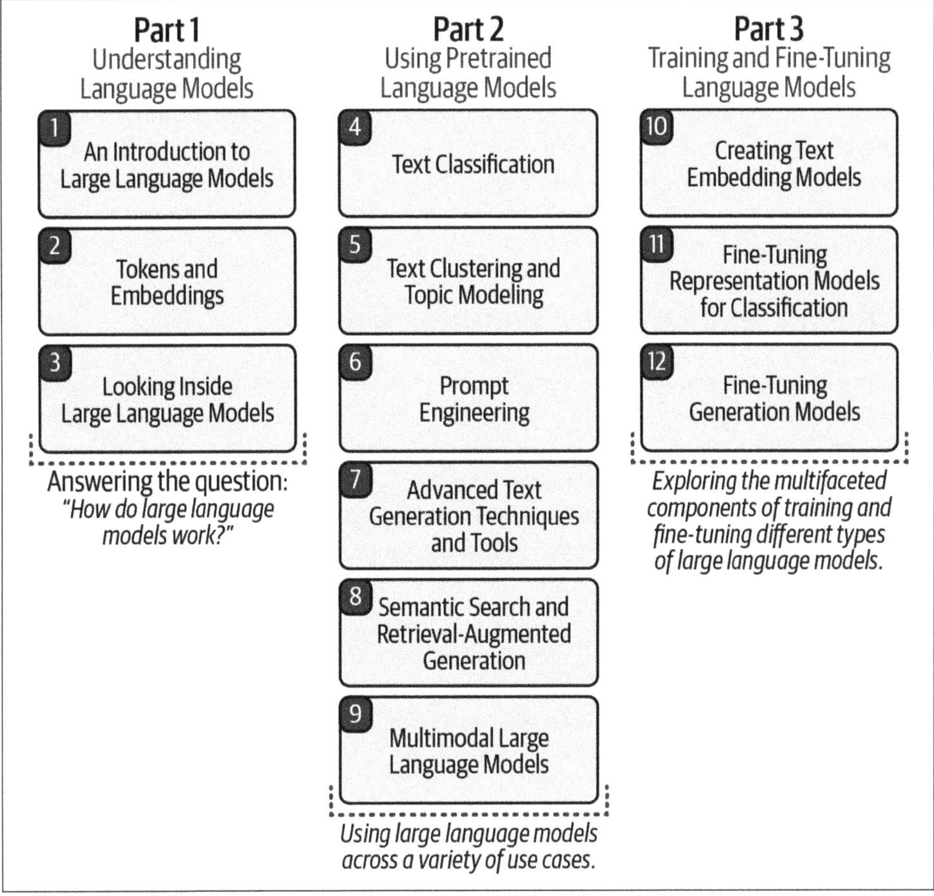

Figure P-1. All parts and chapters of the book.

Part II: Using Pretrained Language Models

In Part II of the book, we explore how LLMs can be used through common use cases. We use pretrained models and demonstrate their capabilities without the need to fine-tune them.

You learn how to use language models for supervised classification (see Chapter 4), text clustering and topic modeling (see Chapter 5), leveraging embedding models for semantic search (see Chapter 6), generating text (see Chapters 7 and 8), and extending the capabilities of text generation to the visual domain (see Chapter 9).

Learning these individual language model capabilities will equip you with the skill set to problem-solve with LLMs and build more and more advanced systems and pipelines.

Part III: Training and Fine-Tuning Language Models

In Part III of the book, we explore advanced concepts through training and fine-tuning all kinds of language models. We will explore how to create and fine-tune an embedding model (see Chapter 10), review how to fine-tune BERT for classification (see Chapter 11), and end the book with several methods for fine-tuning generation models (see Chapter 12).

Hardware and Software Requirements

Running generative models is generally a compute-intensive task that requires a computer with a strong GPU. Since those are not available to every reader, all examples in this book are made to run using an online platform, namely Google Colaboratory (*https://oreil.ly/HQawv*), often shortened to "Google Colab." At the time of writing, this platform allows you to use an NVIDIA GPU (T4) for free to run your code. This GPU has 16 GB of VRAM (which is the memory of your GPU), which is the minimum amount of VRAM we expect for the examples throughout the book.

Not all chapters require a minimum of 16 GB VRAM as some examples, like training and fine-tuning, are more compute-intensive than others, such as prompt engineering. In the repository, you will find the minimum GPU requirements for each chapter.

All code, requirements, and additional tutorials are available in this book's repository (*https://github.com/HandsOnLLM/Hands-On-Large-Language-Models*). If you want to run the examples locally, we recommend access to an NVIDIA GPU with a minimum of 16 GB of VRAM. For a local installation, for example with conda, you can follow this setup to create your environment:

```
conda create -n thellmbook python=3.10
conda activate thellmbook
```

You can install all the necessary dependencies by forking or cloning the repository and then running the following in your newly created Python 3.10 environment:

```
pip install -r requirements.txt
```

API Keys

We use both open source and proprietary models throughout the examples to demonstrate the advantages and disadvantages of both. For the proprietary models, using OpenAI and Cohere's offering, you will need to create a free account:

OpenAI (https://oreil.ly/M4nAa)
: Click "sign up" on the site to create a free account. This account allows you to create an API key, which can be used to access GPT-3.5. Then, go to "API keys" to create a secret key.

Cohere (https://oreil.ly/T63GA)
: Register a free account on the website. Then, go to "API keys" to create a secret key.

Note that with both accounts, rate limits apply and that these free API keys only allow for a limited number of calls per minute. Throughout all examples, we have taken that into account and provided local alternatives if necessary.

For the open source models, you do not need to create an account with the exception of the Llama 2 model in Chapter 2. To use that model, you will need a Hugging Face account:

Hugging Face (https://oreil.ly/_uV3A)
: Click "sign up" on the Hugging Face website to create a free account. Then, in "Settings" go to "Access Tokens" to create a token that you can use to download certain LLMs.

Conventions Used in This Book

The following typographical conventions are used in this book:

Italic
: Indicates new terms, URLs, email addresses, filenames, and file extensions.

`Constant width`
: Used for program listings, as well as within paragraphs to refer to program elements such as variable or function names, databases, data types, environment variables, statements, and keywords.

`Constant width bold`
: Shows commands or other text that should be typed literally by the user.

`Constant width italic`
: Shows text that should be replaced with user-supplied values or by values determined by context.

This element signifies a tip or suggestion.

This element signifies a general note.

Using Code Examples

Supplemental material (code examples, exercises, etc.) is available for download at *https://github.com/HandsOnLLM/Hands-On-Large-Language-Models*.

If you have a technical question or a problem using the code examples, please send email to *support@oreilly.com*.

This book is here to help you get your job done. In general, if example code is offered with this book, you may use it in your programs and documentation. You do not need to contact us for permission unless you're reproducing a significant portion of the code. For example, writing a program that uses several chunks of code from this book does not require permission. Selling or distributing examples from O'Reilly books does require permission. Answering a question by citing this book and quoting example code does not require permission. Incorporating a significant amount of example code from this book into your product's documentation does require permission.

We appreciate, but generally do not require, attribution. An attribution usually includes the title, author, publisher, and ISBN. For example: "*Hands-On Large Language Models* by Jay Alammar and Maarten Grootendorst (O'Reilly). Copyright 2024 Jay Alammar and Maarten Pieter Grootendorst, 978-1-098-15096-9."

If you feel your use of code examples falls outside fair use or the permission given above, feel free to contact us at *permissions@oreilly.com*.

O'Reilly Online Learning

For more than 40 years, *O'Reilly Media* has provided technology and business training, knowledge, and insight to help companies succeed.

Our unique network of experts and innovators share their knowledge and expertise through books, articles, and our online learning platform. O'Reilly's online learning platform gives you on-demand access to live training courses, in-depth learning paths, interactive coding environments, and a vast collection of text and video from O'Reilly and 200+ other publishers. For more information, visit *https://oreilly.com*.

How to Contact Us

Please address comments and questions concerning this book to the publisher:

O'Reilly Media, Inc.
1005 Gravenstein Highway North
Sebastopol, CA 95472
800-889-8969 (in the United States or Canada)
707-827-7019 (international or local)
707-829-0104 (fax)
support@oreilly.com
https://www.oreilly.com/about/contact.html

We have a web page for this book, where we list errata, examples, and any additional information. You can access this page at *https://oreil.ly/hands_on_LLMs_1e*.

For news and information about our books and courses, visit *https://oreilly.com*.

Find us on LinkedIn: *https://linkedin.com/company/oreilly-media*.

Watch us on YouTube: *https://youtube.com/oreillymedia*.

Acknowledgments

Writing this book has been an incredible experience, collaboration, and journey for us.

The field of (large) language models is one of the most dynamic areas in technology today, and within the span of writing this book, we have witnessed extraordinary advancements. Yet, despite the rapid pace of change, the fundamental principles remain strikingly consistent which made the writing process particularly intriguing. We are grateful to have had the opportunity to explore this field in-depth at such a pivotal moment.

Working with our O'Reilly team was incredible! Special thanks to Michele Cronin for her amazing feedback, support, and enthusiasm for this book from day one. We could not have asked for a better editor—you are amazing! Thank you, Nicole Butterfield, for kicking off this book and helping us maintain a structured approach throughout the writing. Thank you to Karen Montgomery for creating our wonderful cover, we love the kangaroo! Big thanks to Kate Dullea for being so patient with us having to go through hundreds of illustrations many times over. The timely early releases by Clare Laylock helped us see our work grow which was a big motivator, thank you. Thanks to Ashley Stussy and Charles Roumeliotis for the development in the final stages of the book and everyone else at O'Reilly who contributed.

Thanks to our amazing crew of technical reviewers. Invaluable feedback was given by Harm Buisman, Emir Muñoz, Luba Elliott, Guarav Chawla, Rafael V. Pierre, Luba Elliott, Tarun Narayanan, Nikhil Buduma, and Patrick Harrison.

Jay

I'd love to extend my deepest gratitude to my family for their unwavering support and inspiration. I would like to specifically acknowledge my parents, Abdullah and Mishael, and my aunts, Hussah and Aljoharah.

I'm grateful to the friends, colleagues, and collaborators who helped me understand and explain the tricky concepts covered in this book as well as to the Cohere folks who cultivate a supporting learning and sharing environment. Thank you to Adrien Morisot, Aidan Gomez, Andy Toulis, Anfal Alatawi, Arash Ahmadian, Bharat Venkitesh, Edward Grefenstette, Ivan Zhang, Joao Araújo, Luis Serrano, Matthias Gallé, Meor Amer, Nick Frosst, Patrick Lewis, Phil Blunsom, Sara Hooker, and Suhas Pai.

I couldn't conceive of this project getting accomplished to the level it has without the extraordinary talent and tireless effort of Maarten, my coauthor. Your ability to repeatedly nail the technical details (from the pinned version of the nth import dependency to the latest in LLM quantization) while weaving some of the world's best visual narratives is absolutely breathtaking.

Lastly, a tip of the hat to the incredible coffee shop scene of Riyadh, Saudi Arabia for supplying me with caffeine and a good place to focus from dawn until midnight. It's where I read most of these papers and worked out my understanding (looking at you, Elixir Bunn).

Maarten

I want to begin by expressing my heartfelt appreciation to my coauthor, Jay. Your insights have made this not only possible but incredibly fulfilling. This journey has been nothing short of amazing and collaborating with you has been an absolute joy.

I want to sincerely thank my wonderful colleagues at IKNL for their continued support throughout this journey. A special mention goes to Harm—our Monday morning coffee breaks discussing this book were a constant source of encouragement.

Thank you to my family and friends for their unwavering support, and to my parents in particular. Pap, despite the challenges you faced, you always found a way to be there for me when I needed it most, thank you. Mam, the conversations we had as aspiring writers were wonderful and motivated me more than you could ever imagine. Thank you both for your endless support and encouragement.

Finally, I am at a loss for words to adequately express my gratitude to my wonderful wife, Ilse. Lieverd, your boundless enthusiasm and patience have been legendary, especially when I droned on about the latest LLM developments for hours on end. You are my greatest support. My apologies to my amazing daughter, Sarah. At just two years old, you already have listened to more about large language models than anyone should have to endure in a lifetime! I promise we'll make up for it with endless playtime and adventures together.

PART I
Understanding Language Models

CHAPTER 1

An Introduction to Large Language Models

Humanity is at an inflection point. From 2012 onwards, developments in building AI systems (using deep neural networks) accelerated so that by the end of the decade, they yielded the first software system able to write articles indiscernible from those written by humans. This system was an AI model called Generative Pre-trained Transformer 2, or GPT-2. 2022 marked the release of ChatGPT, which demonstrated how profoundly this technology was poised to revolutionize how we interact with technology and information. Reaching one million active users in five days and then one hundred million active users in two months, the new breed of AI models started out as human-like chatbots but quickly evolved into a monumental shift in our approach to common tasks, like translation, text generation, summarization, and more. It became an invaluable tool for programmers, educators, and researchers.

The success of ChatGPT was unprecedented and popularized more research into the technology behind it, namely large language models (LLMs). Both proprietary and public models were being released at a steady pace, closing in on, and eventually catching up to the performance of ChatGPT. It is not an exaggeration to state that almost all attention was on LLMs.

As a result, 2023 will always be known, at least to us, as the year that drastically changed our field, Language Artificial Intelligence (Language AI), a field characterized by the development of systems capable of understanding and generating human language.

However, LLMs have been around for a while now and smaller models are still relevant to this day. LLMs are much more than just a single model and there are many other techniques and models in the field of language AI that are worth exploring.

In this book, we aim to give readers a solid understanding of the fundamentals of both LLMs and the field of Language AI in general. This chapter serves as the scaffolding for the rest of the book and will introduce concepts and terms that we will use throughout the chapters.

But mostly, we intend to answer the following questions in this chapter:

- What is Language AI?
- What are large language models?
- What are the common use cases and applications of large language models?
- How can we use large language models ourselves?

What Is Language AI?

The term *artificial intelligence* (AI) is often used to describe computer systems dedicated to performing tasks close to human intelligence, such as speech recognition, language translation, and visual perception. It is the intelligence of software as opposed to the intelligence of humans.

Here is a more formal definition by one of the founders of the artificial intelligence discipline:

> [Artificial intelligence is] the science and engineering of making intelligent machines, especially intelligent computer programs. It is related to the similar task of using computers to understand human intelligence, but AI does not have to confine itself to methods that are biologically observable.
>
> —John McCarthy, 2007[1]

Due to the ever-evolving nature of AI, the term has been used to describe a wide variety of systems, some of which might not truly embody intelligent behavior. For instance, characters in computer games (NPCs [nonplayable characters]) have often been referred to as AI even though many are nothing more than *if-else* statements.

Language AI refers to a subfield of AI that focuses on developing technologies capable of understanding, processing, and generating human language. The term *Language AI* can often be used interchangeably with *natural language processing* (NLP) with the continued success of machine learning methods in tackling language processing problems.

1 J. McCarthy (2007). "What is artificial intelligence?" Retrieved from *https://oreil.ly/C7sja* and *https://oreil.ly/n9X8O*.

We use the term *Language AI* to encompass technologies that technically might not be LLMs but still have a significant impact on the field, like how retrieval systems can give LLMs superpowers (see Chapter 8).

Throughout this book, we want to focus on the models that have had a major role in shaping the field of Language AI. This means exploring more than just LLMs in isolation. That, however, brings us to the question: what are large language models? To begin answering this question in this chapter, let's first explore the history of Language AI.

A Recent History of Language AI

The history of Language AI encompasses many developments and models aiming to represent and generate language, as illustrated in Figure 1-1.

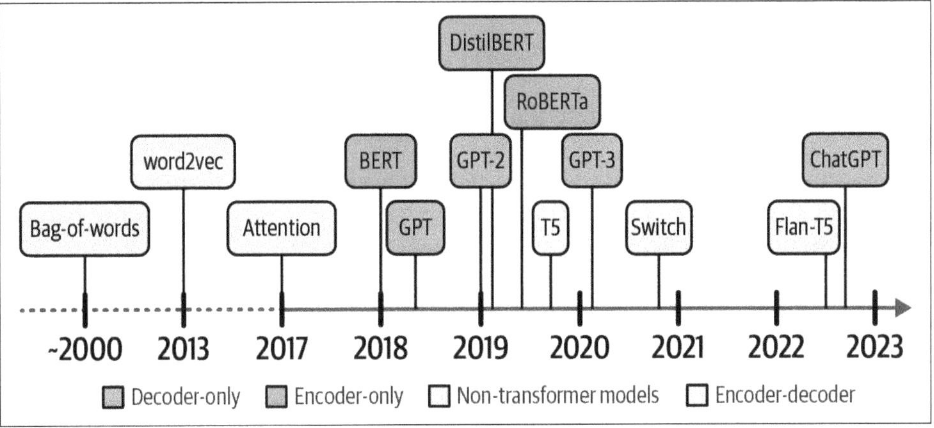

Figure 1-1. A peek into the history of Language AI.

Language, however, is a tricky concept for computers. Text is unstructured in nature and loses its meaning when represented by zeros and ones (individual characters). As a result, throughout the history of Language AI, there has been a large focus on representing language in a structured manner so that it can more easily be used by computers. Examples of these Language AI tasks are provided in Figure 1-2.

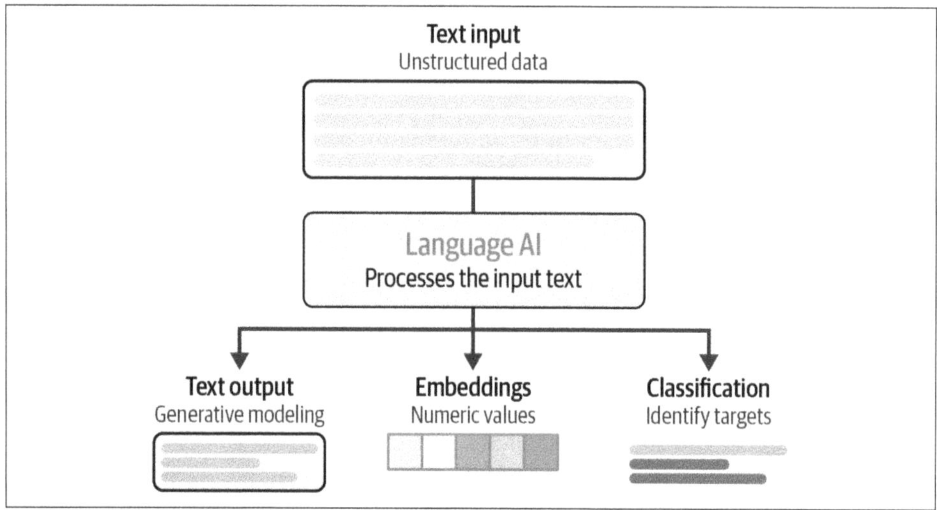

Figure 1-2. Language AI is capable of many tasks by processing textual input.

Representing Language as a Bag-of-Words

Our history of Language AI starts with a technique called bag-of-words, a method for representing unstructured text.[2] It was first mentioned around the 1950s but became popular around the 2000s.

Bag-of-words works as follows: let's assume that we have two sentences for which we want to create numerical representations. The first step of the bag-of-words model is *tokenization*, the process of splitting up the sentences into individual words or subwords (*tokens*), as illustrated in Figure 1-3.

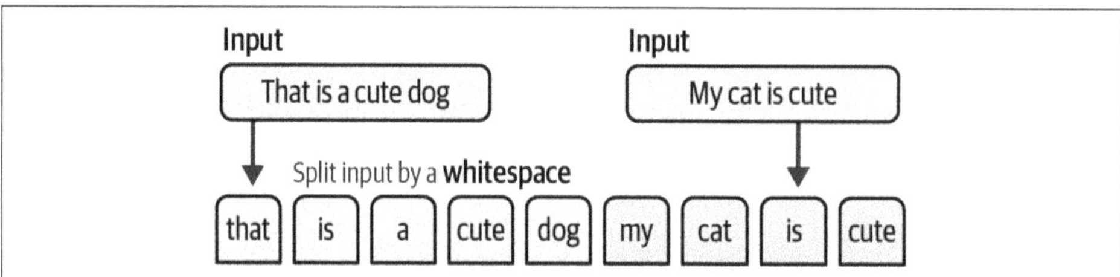

Figure 1-3. Each sentence is split into words (tokens) by splitting on a whitespace.

The most common method for tokenization is by splitting on a whitespace to create individual words. However, this has its disadvantages as some languages, like Mandarin, do not have whitespaces around individual words. In the next chapter, we will

2 Fabrizio Sebastiani. "Machine learning in automated text categorization." *ACM Computing Surveys (CSUR)* 34.1 (2002): 1–47.

go in depth about tokenization and how that technique influences language models. As illustrated in Figure 1-4, after tokenization, we combine all unique words from each sentence to create a vocabulary that we can use to represent the sentences.

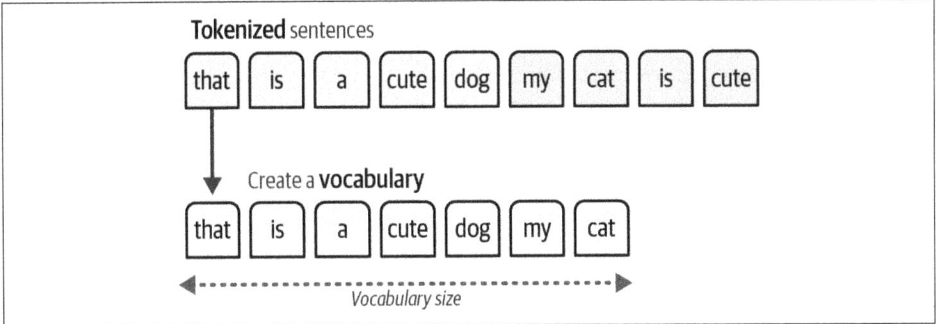

Figure 1-4. A vocabulary is created by retaining all unique words across both sentences.

Using our vocabulary, we simply count how often a word in each sentence appears, quite literally creating a bag of words. As a result, a bag-of-words model aims to create representations of text in the form of numbers, also called vectors or vector representations, observed in Figure 1-5. Throughout the book, we refer to these kinds of models as *representation models*.

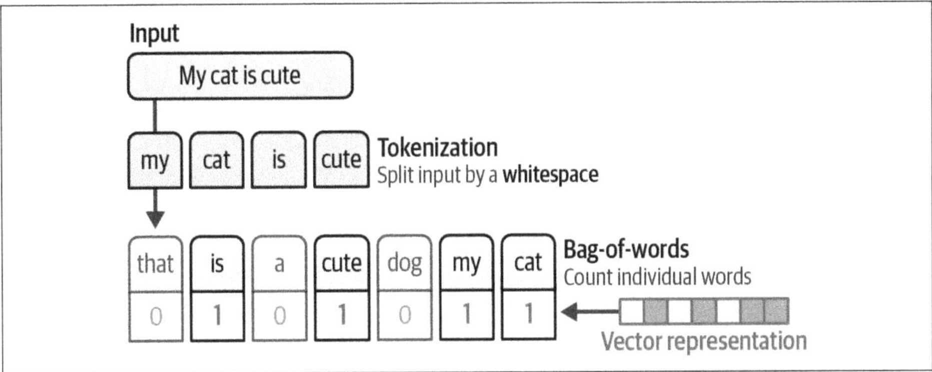

Figure 1-5. A bag-of-words is created by counting individual words. These values are referred to as vector representations.

Although bag-of-words is a classic method, it is by no means completely obsolete. In Chapter 5, we will explore how it can still be used to complement more recent language models.

Better Representations with Dense Vector Embeddings

Bag-of-words, although an elegant approach, has a flaw. It considers language to be nothing more than an almost literal bag of words and ignores the semantic nature, or meaning, of text.

Released in 2013, word2vec was one of the first successful attempts at capturing the meaning of text in *embeddings*.[3] Embeddings are vector representations of data that attempt to capture its meaning. To do so, word2vec learns semantic representations of words by training on vast amounts of textual data, like the entirety of Wikipedia.

To generate these semantic representations, word2vec leverages *neural networks*. These networks consist of interconnected layers of nodes that process information. As illustrated in Figure 1-6, neural networks can have many layers where each connection has a certain weight depending on the input. These weights are often referred to as the *parameters* of the model.

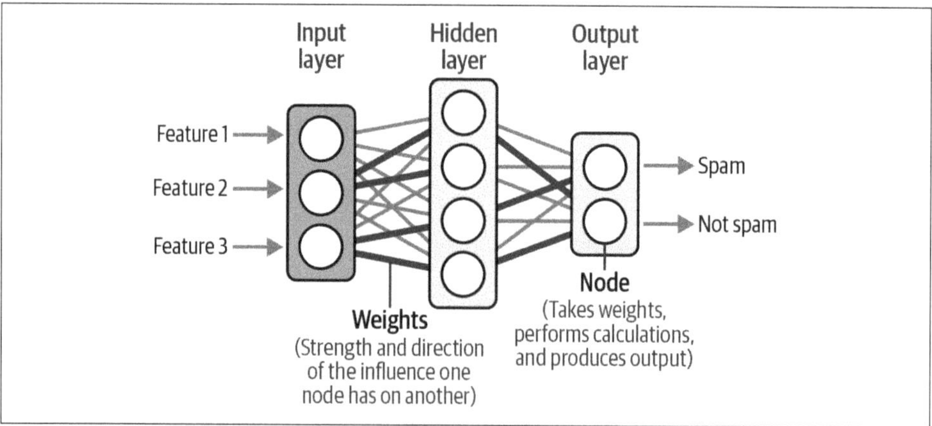

Figure 1-6. A neural network consists of interconnected layers of nodes where each connection is a linear equation.

Using these neural networks, word2vec generates word embeddings by looking at which other words they tend to appear next to in a given sentence. We start by assigning every word in our vocabulary with a vector embedding, say of 50 values for each word initialized with random values. Then in every training step, as illustrated in Figure 1-7, we take pairs of words from the training data and a model attempts to predict whether or not they are likely to be neighbors in a sentence.

3 Tomas Mikolov et al. "Efficient estimation of word representations in vector space." *arXiv preprint arXiv:1301.3781* (2013).

During this training process, word2vec learns the relationship between words and distills that information into the embedding. If the two words tend to have the same neighbors, their embeddings will be closer to one another and vice versa. In Chapter 2, we will look closer at word2vec's training procedure.

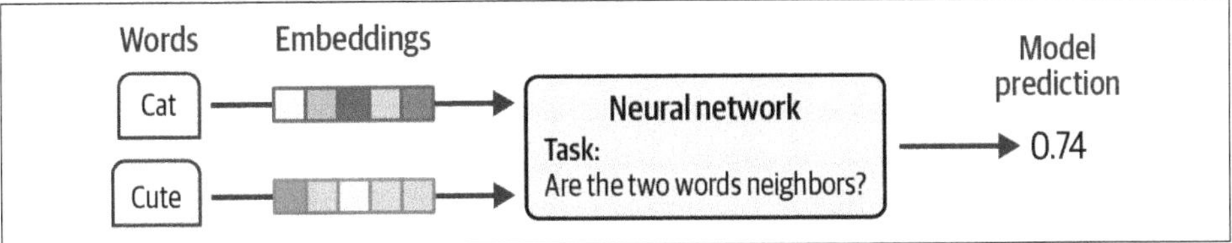

Figure 1-7. A neural network is trained to predict if two words are neighbors. During this process, the embeddings are updated to be in line with the ground truth.

The resulting embeddings capture the meaning of words but what exactly does that mean? To illustrate this phenomenon, let's somewhat oversimplify and imagine we have embeddings of several words, namely "apple" and "baby." Embeddings attempt to capture meaning by representing the properties of words. For instance, the word "baby" might score high on the properties "newborn" and "human" while the word "apple" scores low on these properties.

As illustrated in Figure 1-8, embeddings can have many properties to represent the meaning of a word. Since the size of embeddings is fixed, their properties are chosen to create a mental representation of the word.

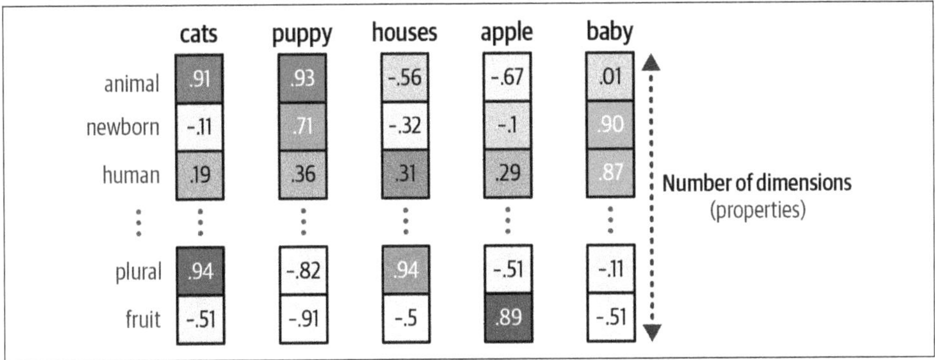

Figure 1-8. The values of embeddings represent properties that are used to represent words. We may oversimplify by imagining that dimensions represent concepts (which they don't), but it helps express the idea.

In practice, these properties are often quite obscure and seldom relate to a single entity or humanly identifiable concept. However, together, these properties make sense to a computer and serve as a good way to translate human language into computer language.

Embeddings are tremendously helpful as they allow us to measure the semantic similarity between two words. Using various distance metrics, we can judge how close one word is to another. As illustrated in Figure 1-9, if we were to compress these embeddings into a two-dimensional representation, you would notice that words with similar meaning tend to be closer. In Chapter 5, we will explore how to compress these embeddings into *n*-dimensional space.

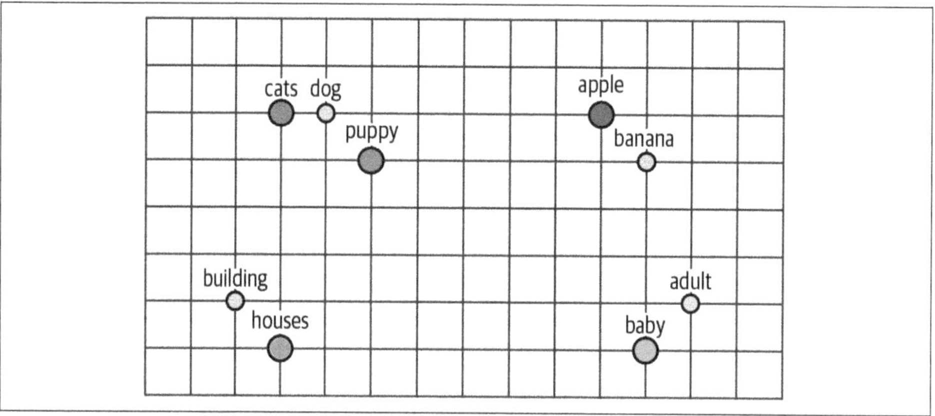

Figure 1-9. Embeddings of words that are similar will be close to each other in dimensional space.

Types of Embeddings

There are many types of embeddings, like word embeddings and sentence embeddings that are used to indicate different levels of abstractions (word versus sentence), as illustrated in Figure 1-10.

Bag-of-words, for instance, creates embeddings at a document level since it represents the entire document. In contrast, word2vec generates embeddings for words only.

Throughout the book, embeddings will take on a central role as they are utilized in many use cases, such as classification (see Chapter 4), clustering (see Chapter 5), and semantic search and retrieval-augmented generation (see Chapter 8). In Chapter 2, we will take our first deep dive into token embeddings.

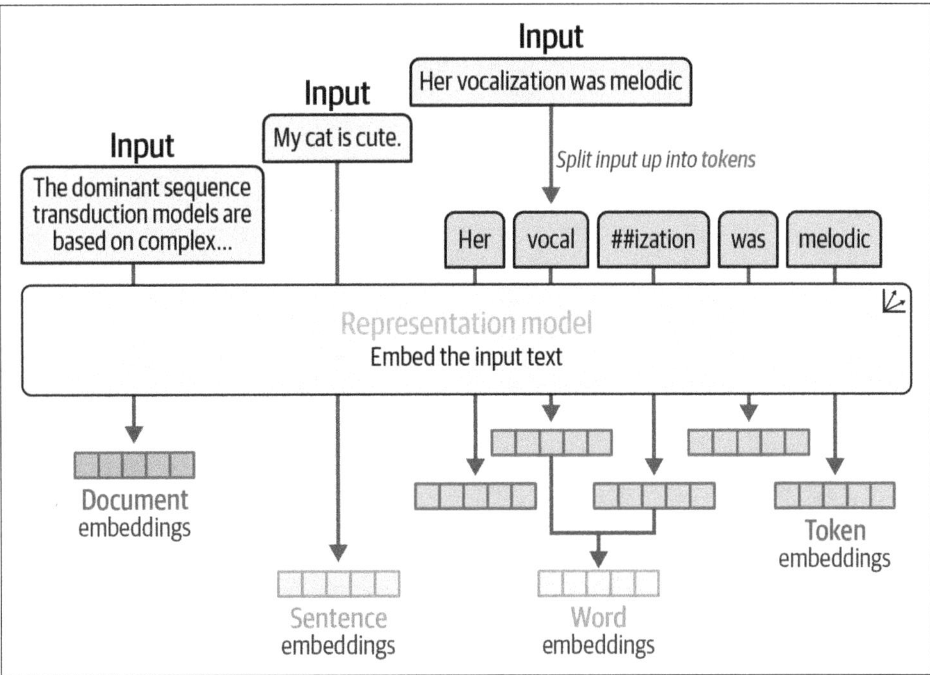

Figure 1-10. Embeddings can be created for different types of input.

Encoding and Decoding Context with Attention

The training process of word2vec creates static, downloadable representations of words. For instance, the word "bank" will always have the same embedding regardless of the context in which it is used. However, "bank" can refer to both a financial bank as well as the bank of a river. Its meaning, and therefore its embeddings, should change depending on the context.

A step in encoding this text was achieved through recurrent neural networks (RNNs). These are variants of neural networks that can model sequences as an additional input.

To do so, these RNNs are used for two tasks, *encoding* or representing an input sentence and *decoding* or generating an output sentence. Figure 1-11 illustrates this concept by showing how a sentence like "I love llamas" gets translated to the Dutch "Ik hou van lama's."

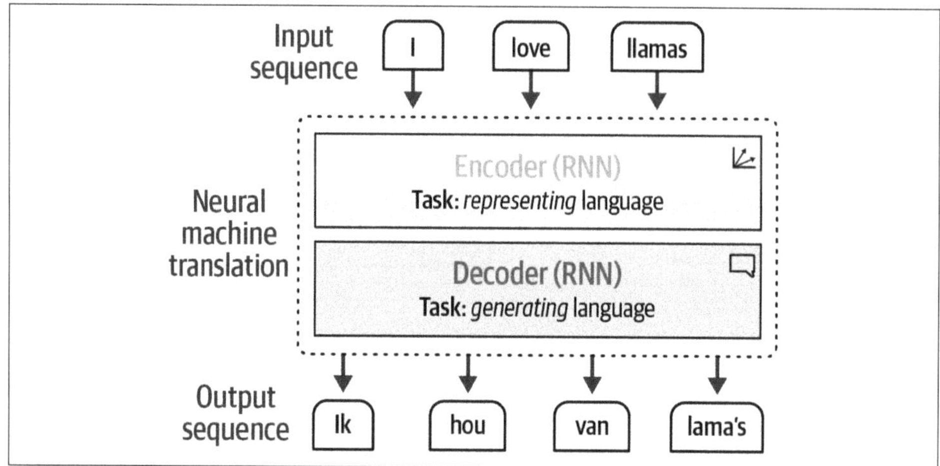

Figure 1-11. Two recurrent neural networks (decoder and encoder) translating an input sequence from English to Dutch.

Each step in this architecture is *autoregressive*. When generating the next word, this architecture needs to consume all previously generated words, as shown in Figure 1-12.

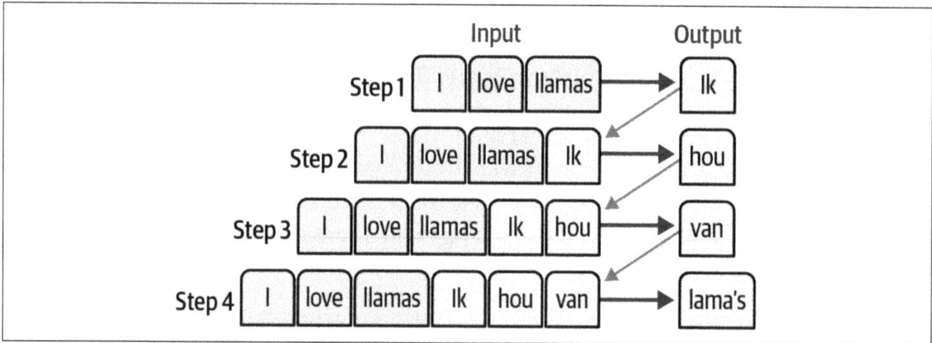

Figure 1-12. Each previous output token is used as input to generate the next token.

The encoding step aims to represent the input as well as possible, generating the context in the form of an embedding, which serves as the input for the decoder. To generate this representation, it takes embeddings as its inputs for words, which means we can use word2vec for the initial representations. In Figure 1-13, we can observe this process. Note how the inputs are processed sequentially, one at a time, as well as the output.

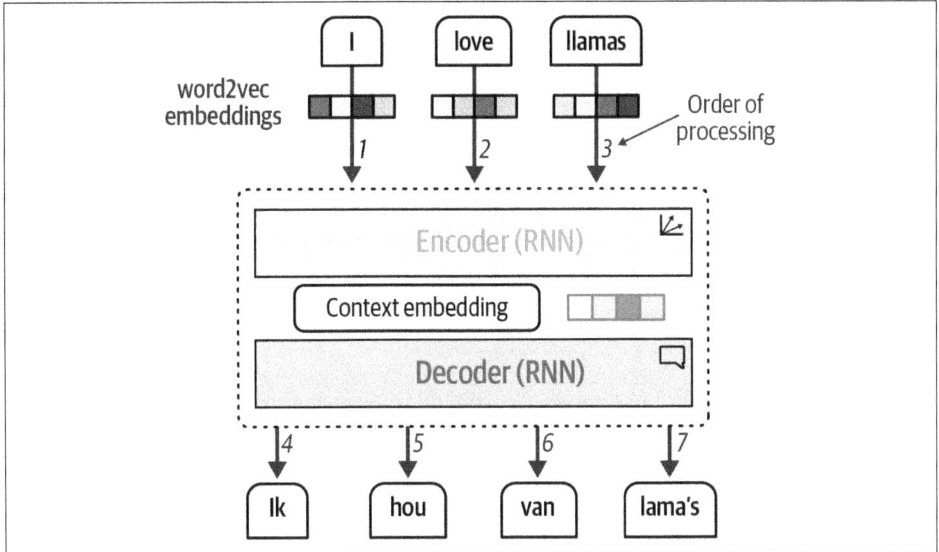

Figure 1-13. Using word2vec embeddings, a context embedding is generated that represents the entire sequence.

This context embedding, however, makes it difficult to deal with longer sentences since it is merely a single embedding representing the entire input. In 2014, a solution called *attention* (*https://oreil.ly/SIDnM*) was introduced that highly improved upon the original architecture.[4] Attention allows a model to focus on parts of the input sequence that are relevant to one another ("attend" to each other) and amplify their signal, as shown in Figure 1-14. Attention selectively determines which words are most important in a given sentence.

For instance, the output word "lama's" is Dutch for "llamas," which is why the attention between both is high. Similarly, the words "lama's" and "I" have lower attention since they aren't as related. In Chapter 3, we will go more in depth on the attention mechanism.

4 Dzmitry Bahdanau, Kyunghyun Cho, and Yoshua Bengio. "Neural machine translation by jointly learning to align and translate." *arXiv preprint arXiv:1409.0473* (2014).

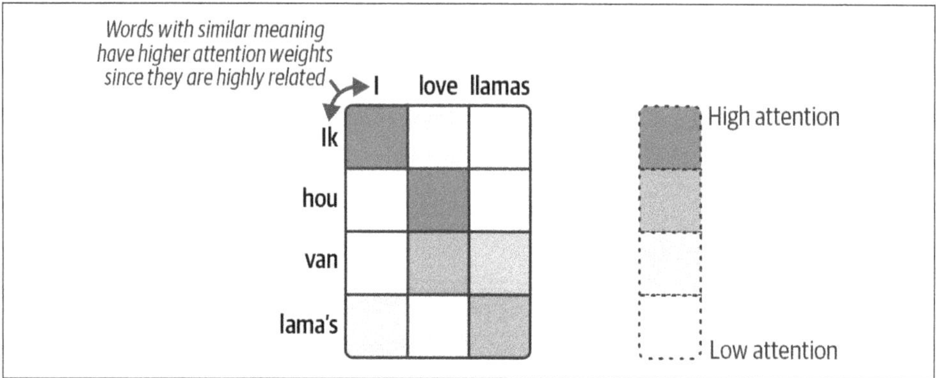

Figure 1-14. Attention allows a model to "attend" to certain parts of sequences that might relate more or less to one another.

By adding these attention mechanisms to the decoder step, the RNN can generate signals for each input word in the sequence related to the potential output. Instead of passing only a context embedding to the decoder, the hidden states of all input words are passed. This process is demonstrated in Figure 1-15.

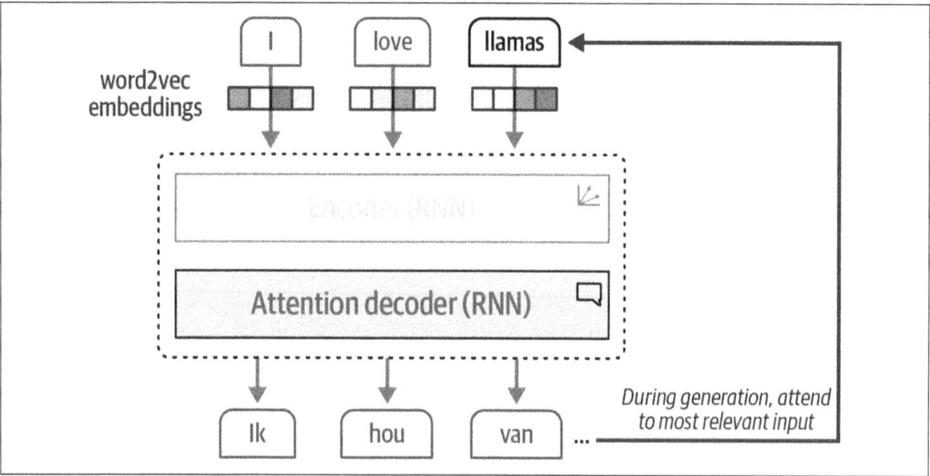

Figure 1-15. After generating the words "Ik," "hou," and "van," the attention mechanism of the decoder enables it to focus on the word "llamas" before it generates the Dutch translation ("lama's").

As a result, during the generation of "Ik hou van lama's," the RNN keeps track of the words it mostly attends to perform the translation. Compared to word2vec, this architecture allows for representing the sequential nature of text and the context in which it appears by "attending" to the entire sentence. This sequential nature, however, precludes parallelization during training of the model.

Attention Is All You Need

The true power of attention, and what drives the amazing abilities of large language models, was first explored in the well-known "Attention is all you need" paper (*https://oreil.ly/KGvIj*) released in 2017.[5] The authors proposed a network architecture called the *Transformer*, which was solely based on the attention mechanism and removed the recurrence network that we saw previously. Compared to the recurrence network, the Transformer could be trained in parallel, which tremendously sped up training.

In the Transformer, encoding and decoder components are stacked on top of each other, as illustrated in Figure 1-16. This architecture remains autoregressive, needing to consume each generated word before creating a new word.

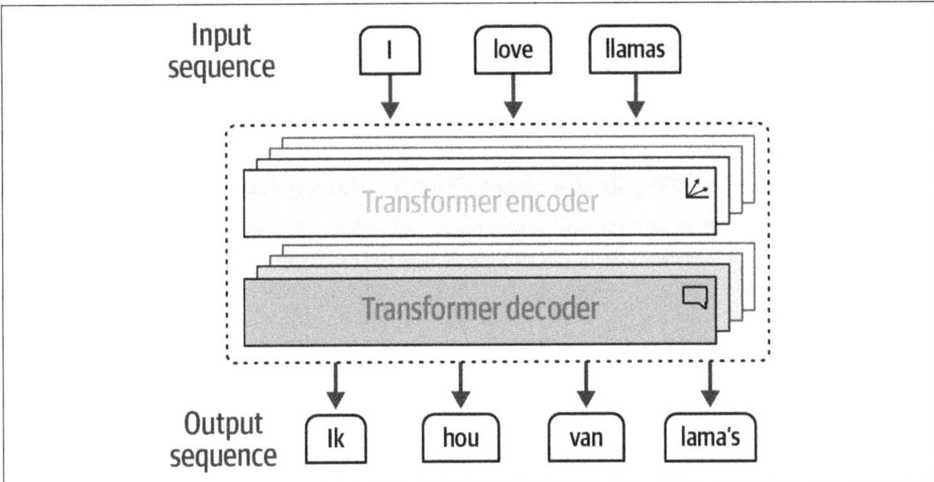

Figure 1-16. The Transformer is a combination of stacked encoder and decoder blocks where the input flows through each encoder and decoder.

Now, both the encoder and decoder blocks would revolve around attention instead of leveraging an RNN with attention features. The encoder block in the Transformer consists of two parts, *self-attention* and a *feedforward neural network*, which are shown in Figure 1-17.

5 Ashish Vaswani et al. "Attention is all you need." *Advances in Neural Information Processing Systems* 30 (2017).

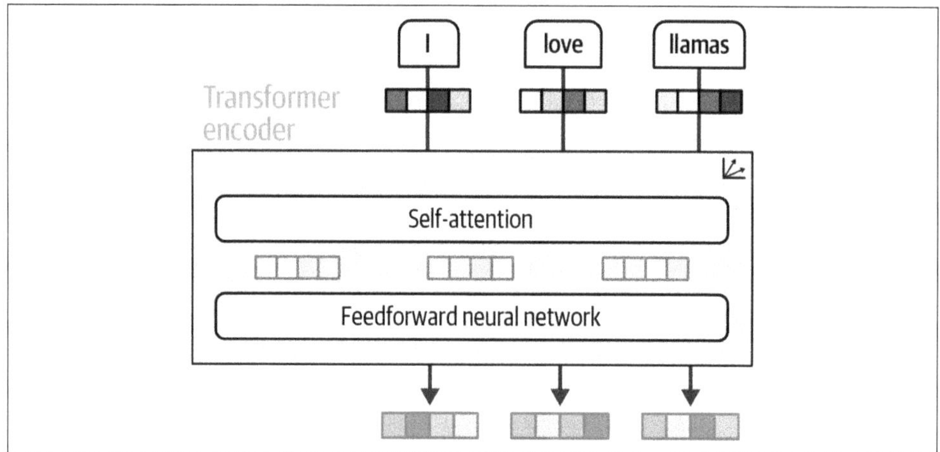

Figure 1-17. An encoder block revolves around self-attention to generate intermediate representations.

Compared to previous methods of attention, self-attention can attend to different positions within a single sequence, thereby more easily and accurately representing the input sequence as illustrated in Figure 1-18. Instead of processing one token at a time, it can be used to look at the entire sequence in one go.

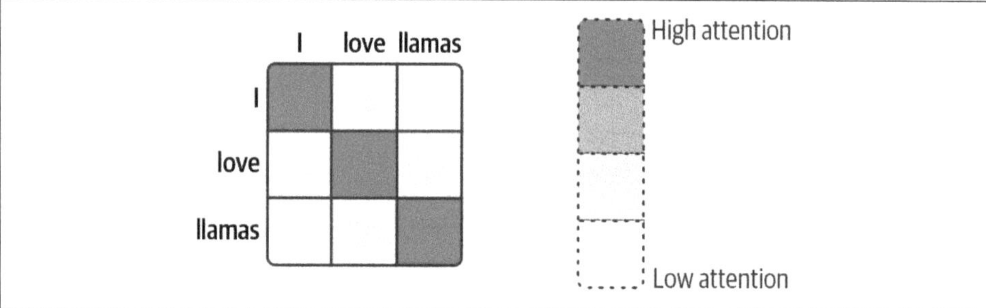

Figure 1-18. Self-attention attends to all parts of the input sequence so that it can "look" both forward and back in a single sequence.

Compared to the encoder, the decoder has an additional layer that pays attention to the output of the encoder (to find the relevant parts of the input). As demonstrated in Figure 1-19, this process is similar to the RNN attention decoder that we discussed previously.

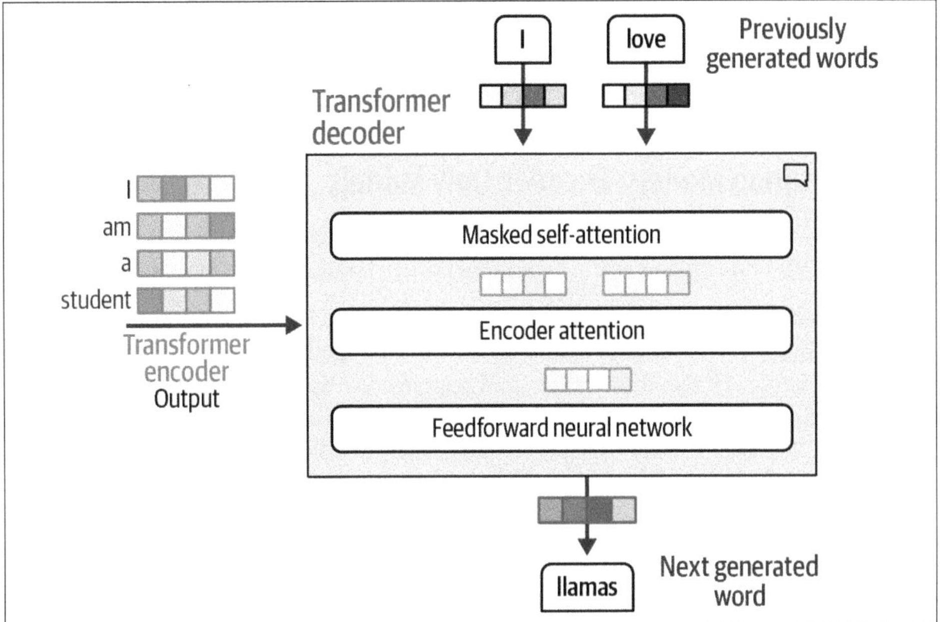

Figure 1-19. The decoder has an additional attention layer that attends to the output of the encoder.

As shown in Figure 1-20, the self-attention layer in the decoder masks future positions so it only attends to earlier positions to prevent leaking information when generating the output.

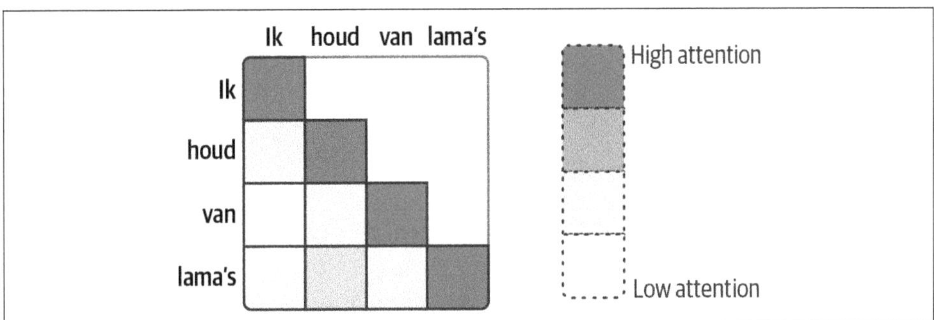

Figure 1-20. Only attend to previous tokens to prevent "looking into the future."

Together, these building blocks create the Transformer architecture and are the foundation of many impactful models in Language AI, such as BERT and GPT-1, which we cover later in this chapter. Throughout this book, most models that we will use are Transformer-based models.

There is much more to the Transformer architecture than what we explored thus far. In Chapters 2 and 3, we will go through the many reasons why Transformer models work so well, including multi-head attention, positional embeddings, and layer normalization.

Representation Models: Encoder-Only Models

The original Transformer model is an encoder-decoder architecture that serves translation tasks well but cannot easily be used for other tasks, like text classification.

In 2018, a new architecture called Bidirectional Encoder Representations from Transformers (BERT) was introduced that could be leveraged for a wide variety of tasks and would serve as the foundation of Language AI for years to come.[6] BERT is an encoder-only architecture that focuses on representing language, as illustrated in Figure 1-21. This means that it only uses the encoder and removes the decoder entirely.

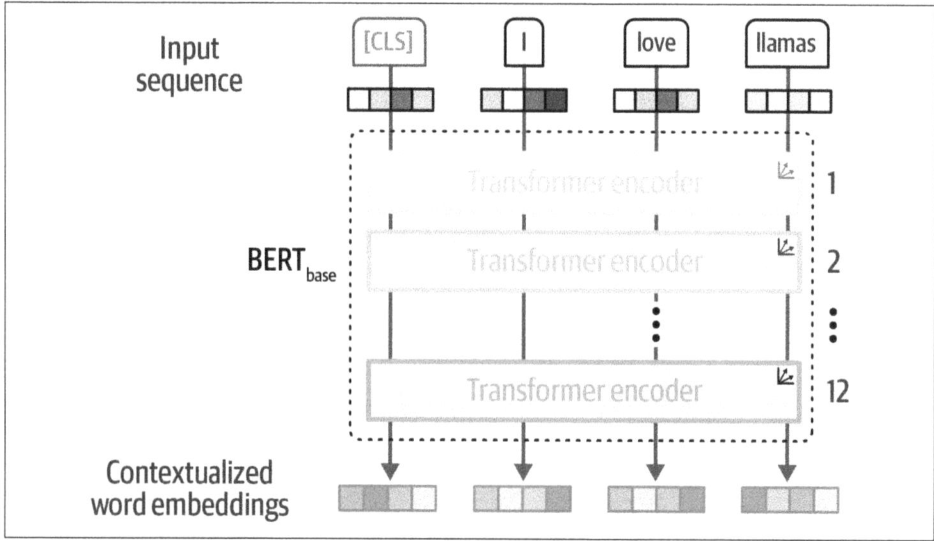

Figure 1-21. The architecture of a BERT base model with 12 encoders.

These encoder blocks are the same as we saw before: self-attention followed by feedforward neural networks. The input contains an additional token, the `[CLS]` or classification token, which is used as the representation for the entire input. Often, we use this `[CLS]` token as the input embedding for fine-tuning the model on specific tasks, like classification.

6 Jacob Devlin et al. "BERT: Pre-training of deep bidirectional transformers for language understanding." *arXiv preprint arXiv:1810.04805* (2018).

Training these encoder stacks can be a difficult task that BERT approaches by adopting a technique called *masked language modeling* (see Chapters 2 and 11). As shown in Figure 1-22, this method masks a part of the input for the model to predict. This prediction task is difficult but allows BERT to create more accurate (intermediate) representations of the input.

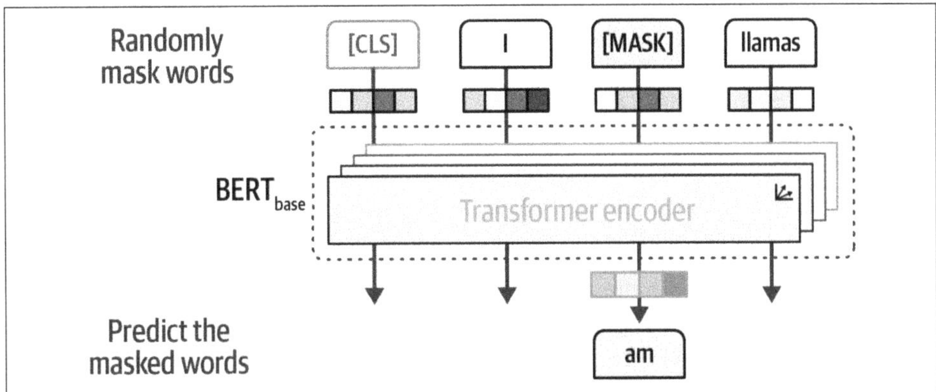

Figure 1-22. Train a BERT model by using masked language modeling.

This architecture and training procedure makes BERT and related architectures incredible at representing contextual language. BERT-like models are commonly used for *transfer learning*, which involves first pretraining it for language modeling and then fine-tuning it for a specific task. For instance, by training BERT on the entirety of Wikipedia, it learns to understand the semantic and contextual nature of text. Then, as shown in Figure 1-23, we can use that *pretrained* model to *fine-tune* it for a specific task, like text classification.

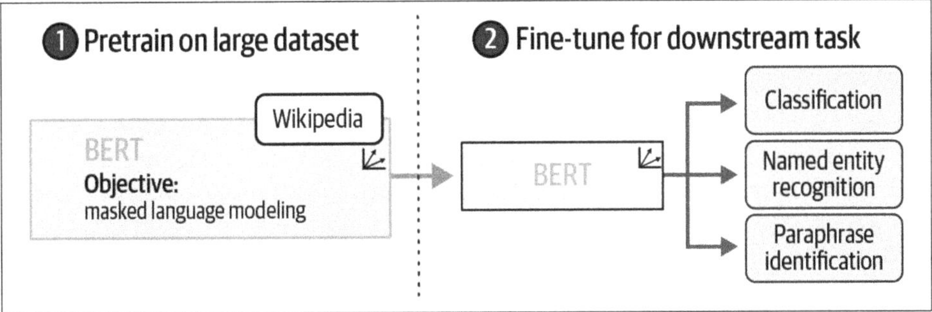

Figure 1-23. After pretraining BERT on masked language model, we fine-tune it for specific tasks.

A huge benefit of pretrained models is that most of the training is already done for us. Fine-tuning on specific tasks is generally less compute-intensive and requires less data. Moreover, BERT-like models generate embeddings at almost every step in their architecture. This also makes BERT models feature extraction machines without the need to fine-tune them on a specific task.

Encoder-only models, like BERT, will be used in many parts of the book. For years, they have been and are still used for common tasks, including classification tasks (see Chapter 4), clustering tasks (see Chapter 5), and semantic search (see Chapter 8).

Throughout the book, we will refer to encoder-only models as *representation models* to differentiate them from decoder-only, which we refer to as *generative models*. Note that the main distinction does not lie between the underlying architecture and the way these models work. Representation models mainly focus on representing language, for instance, by creating embeddings, and typically do not generate text. In contrast, generative models focus primarily on generating text and typically are not trained to generate embeddings.

The distinction between representation and generative models and components will also be shown in most images. Representation models are teal with a small vector icon (to indicate its focus on vectors and embeddings) whilst generative models are pink with a small chat icon (to indicate its generative capabilities).

Generative Models: Decoder-Only Models

Similar to the encoder-only architecture of BERT, a decoder-only architecture was proposed in 2018 to target generative tasks.[7] This architecture was called a Generative Pre-trained Transformer (GPT) for its generative capabilities (it's now known as GPT-1 to distinguish it from later versions). As shown in Figure 1-24, it stacks decoder blocks similar to the encoder-stacked architecture of BERT.

GPT-1 was trained on a corpus of 7,000 books and Common Crawl, a large dataset of web pages. The resulting model consisted of 117 million *parameters*. Each parameter is a numerical value that represents the model's understanding of language.

If everything remains the same, we expect more parameters to greatly influence the capabilities and performance of language models. Keeping this in mind, we saw larger and larger models being released at a steady pace. As illustrated in Figure 1-25, GPT-2 had 1.5 billion parameters[8] and GPT-3 used 175 billion parameters[9] quickly followed.

---

7 Alec Radford et al. "Improving language understanding by generative pre-training" (*https://oreil.ly/8ry5b*), (2018).

8 Alec Radford et al. "Language models are unsupervised multitask learners." *OpenAI Blog* 1.8 (2019): 9.

9 Tom Brown et al. "Language models are few-shot learners." *Advances in Neural Information Processing Systems* 33 (2020): 1877–1901.

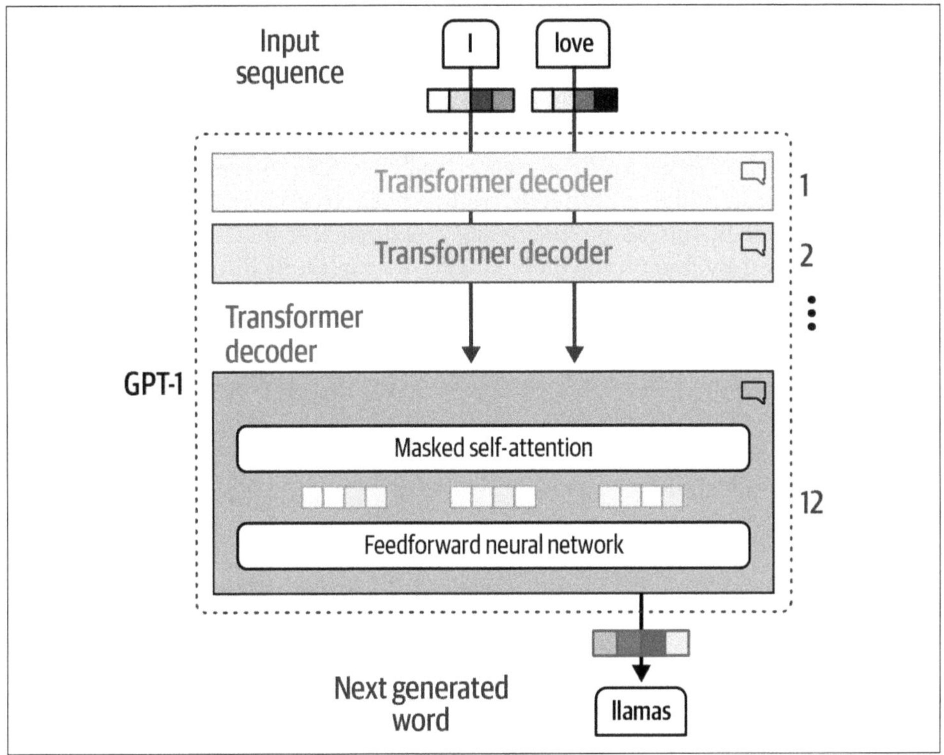

Figure 1-24. The architecture of a GPT-1. It uses a decoder-only architecture and removes the encoder-attention block.

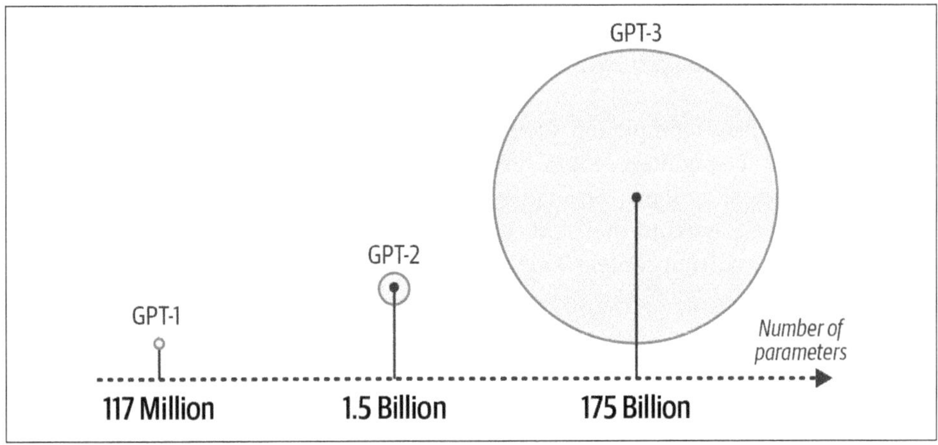

Figure 1-25. GPT models quickly grew in size with each iteration.

These generative decoder-only models, especially the "larger" models, are commonly referred to as *large language models* (LLMs). As we will discuss later in this chapter, the term LLM is not only reserved for generative models (decoder-only) but also representation models (encoder-only).

Generative LLMs, as sequence-to-sequence machines, take in some text and attempt to autocomplete it. Although a handy feature, their true power shone from being trained as a chatbot. Instead of completing a text, what if they could be trained to answer questions? By fine-tuning these models, we can create *instruct* or *chat* models that can follow directions.

As illustrated in Figure 1-26, the resulting model could take in a user query (*prompt*) and output a response that would most likely follow that prompt. As such, you will often hear that generative models are *completion* models.

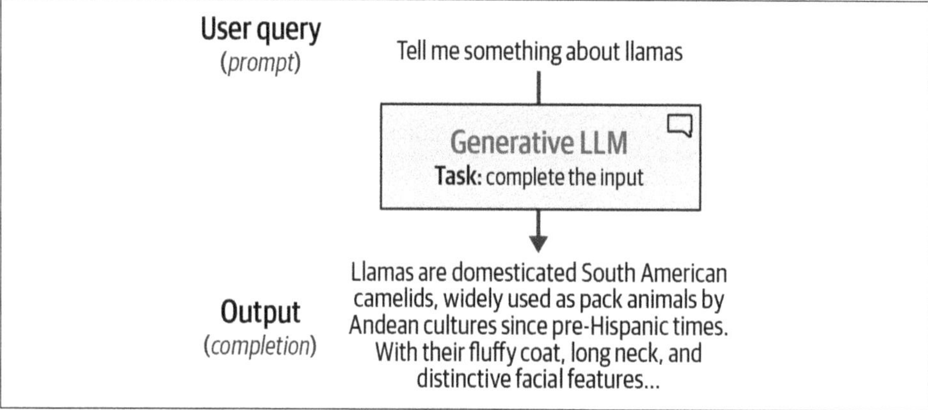

Figure 1-26. Generative LLMs take in some input and try to complete it. With instruct models, this is more than just autocomplete and attempts to answer the question.

A vital part of these completion models is something called the *context length* or *context window*. The context length represents the maximum number of tokens the model can process, as shown in Figure 1-27. A large context window allows entire documents to be passed to the LLM. Note that due to the autoregressive nature of these models, the current context length will increase as new tokens are generated.

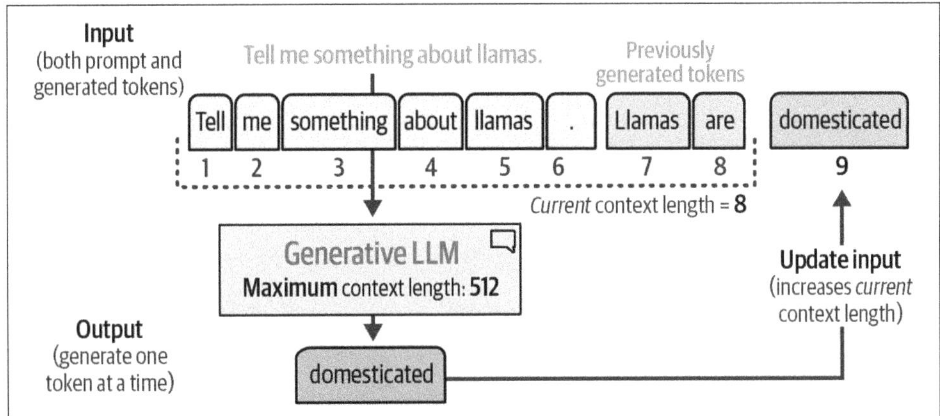

Figure 1-27. The context length is the maximum context an LLM can handle.

The Year of Generative AI

LLMs had a tremendous impact on the field and led some to call 2023 *The Year of Generative AI* with the release, adoption, and media coverage of ChatGPT (GPT-3.5). When we refer to ChatGPT, we are actually talking about the product and not the underlying model. When it was first released, it was powered by the GPT-3.5 LLM and has since then grown to include several more performant variants, such as GPT-4.[10]

GPT-3.5 was not the only model that made its impact in the Year of Generative AI. As illustrated in Figure 1-28, both open source and proprietary LLMs have made their way to the people at an incredible pace. These open source base models are often referred to as *foundation models* and can be fine-tuned for specific tasks, like following instructions.

10 OpenAI, "Gpt-4 technical report." *arXiv preprint arXiv:2303.08774* (2023).

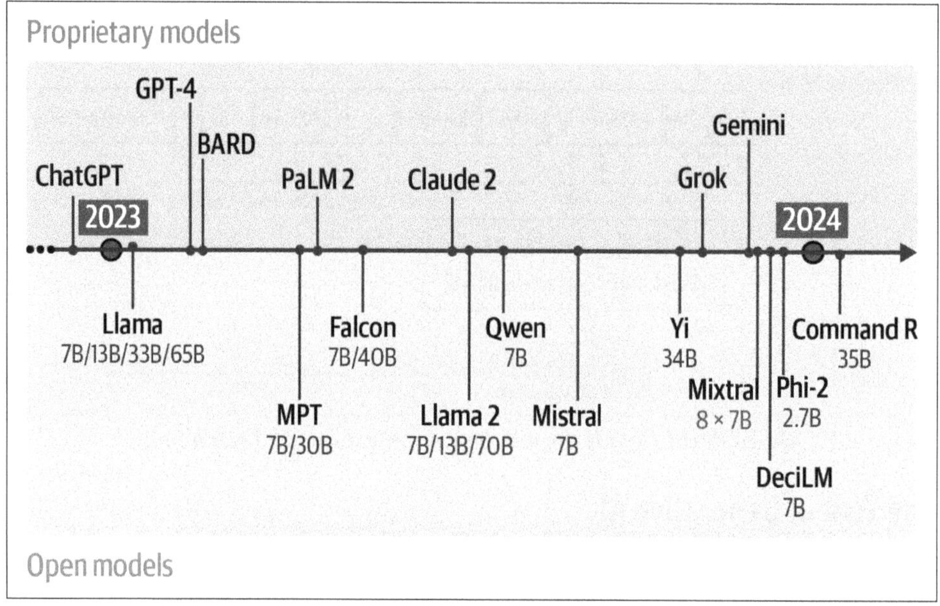

Figure 1-28. A comprehensive view into the Year of Generative AI. Note that many models are still missing from this overview!

Apart from the widely popular Transformer architecture, new promising architectures have emerged such as Mamba[11,12] and RWKV.[13] These novel architectures attempt to reach Transformer-level performance with additional advantages, like larger context windows or faster inference.

These developments exemplify the evolution of the field and showcase 2023 as a truly hectic year for AI. It took all we had to just keep up with the many developments, both within and outside of Language AI.

As such, this book explores more than just the latest LLMs. We will explore how other models, such as embedding models, encoder-only models, and even bag-of-words can be used to empower LLMs.

11 Albert Gu and Tri Dao. "Mamba: Linear-time sequence modeling with selective state spaces." *arXiv preprint arXiv:2312.00752* (2023).

12 See "A Visual Guide to Mamba and State Space Models" (*https://oreil.ly/ikVmy*) for an illustrated and visual guide to Mamba as an alternative to the Transformer architecture.

13 Bo Peng et al. "RWKV: Reinventing RNNs for the transformer era." *arXiv preprint arXiv:2305.13048* (2023).

The Moving Definition of a "Large Language Model"

In our travels through the recent history of Language AI, we observed that primarily generative decoder-only (Transformer) models are commonly referred to as *large language models*. Especially if they are considered to be "large." In practice, this seems like a rather constrained description!

What if we create a model with the same capabilities as GPT-3 but 10 times smaller? Would such a model fall outside the "large" language model categorization?

Similarly, what if we released a model as big as GPT-4 that can perform accurate text classification but does not have any generative capabilities? Would it still qualify as a large "language model" if its primary function is not language generation, even though it still represents text?

The problem with these kinds of definitions is that we exclude capable models. What name we give one model or the other does not change how it behaves.

Since the definition of the term "large language model" tends to evolve with the release of new models, we want to be explicit in what it means for this book. "Large" is arbitrary and what might be considered a large model today could be small tomorrow. There are currently many names for the same thing and to us, "large language models" are also models that do not generate text and can be run on consumer hardware.

As such, aside from covering generative models, this book will also cover models with fewer than 1 billion parameters that do not generate text. We will explore how other models, such as embedding models, representation models, and even bag-of-words can be used to empower LLMs.

The Training Paradigm of Large Language Models

Traditional machine learning generally involves training a model for a specific task, like classification. As shown in Figure 1-29, we consider this to be a one-step process.

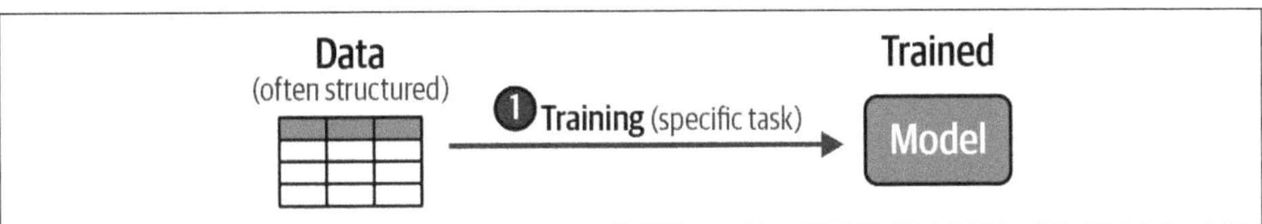

Figure 1-29. Traditional machine learning involves a single step: training a model for a specific target task, like classification or regression.

Creating LLMs, in contrast, typically consists of at least two steps:

Language modeling
: The first step, called *pretraining*, takes the majority of computation and training time. An LLM is trained on a vast corpus of internet text allowing the model to learn grammar, context, and language patterns. This broad training phase is not yet directed toward specific tasks or applications beyond predicting the next word. The resulting model is often referred to as a *foundation model* or *base model*. These models generally do not follow instructions.

Fine-tuning
: The second step, *fine-tuning* or sometimes *post-training*, involves using the previously trained model and further training it on a narrower task. This allows the LLM to adapt to specific tasks or to exhibit desired behavior. For example, we could fine-tune a base model to perform well on a classification task or to follow instructions. It saves massive amounts of resources because the pretraining phase is quite costly and generally requires data and computing resources that are out of the reach of most people and organizations. For instance, Llama 2 has been trained on a dataset containing 2 trillion tokens.[14] Imagine the compute necessary to create that model! In Chapter 12, we will go over several methods for fine-tuning foundation models on your dataset.

Any model that goes through the first step, pretraining, we consider a *pretrained model*, which also includes fine-tuned models. This two-step approach of training is visualized in Figure 1-30.

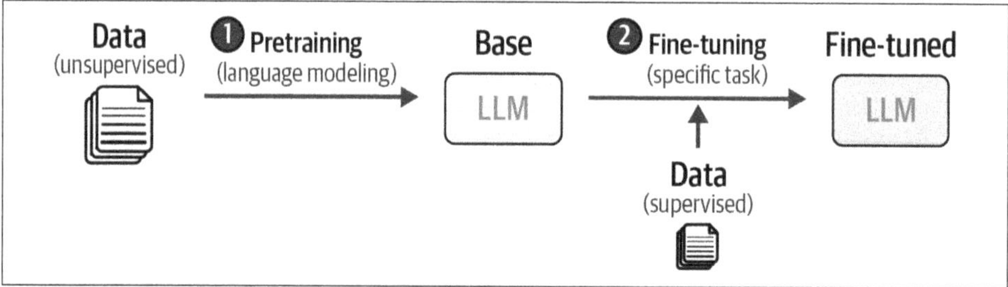

Figure 1-30. Compared to traditional machine learning, LLM training takes a multistep approach.

Additional fine-tuning steps can be added to further align the model with the user's preferences, as we will explore in Chapter 12.

14 Hugo Touvron et al. "Llama 2: Open foundation and fine-tuned chat models." *arXiv preprint arXiv:2307.09288* (2023).

Large Language Model Applications: What Makes Them So Useful?

The nature of LLMs makes them suitable for a wide range of tasks. With text generation and prompting, it almost seems as if your imagination is the limit. To illustrate, let's explore some common tasks and techniques:

Detecting whether a review left by a customer is positive or negative
: This is (supervised) classification and can be handled with both encoder- and decoder-only models either with pretrained models (see Chapter 4) or by fine-tuning models (see Chapter 11).

Developing a system for finding common topics in ticket issues
: This is (unsupervised) classification for which we have no predefined labels. We can leverage encoder-only models to perform the classification itself and decoder-only models for labeling the topics (see Chapter 5).

Building a system for retrieval and inspection of relevant documents
: A major component of language model systems is their ability to add external resources of information. Using semantic search, we can build systems that allow us to easily access and find information for an LLM to use (see Chapter 8). Improve your system by creating or fine-tuning a custom embedding model (see Chapter 12).

Constructing an LLM chatbot that can leverage external resources, such as tools and documents
: This is a combination of techniques that demonstrates how the true power of LLMs can be found through additional components. Methods such as prompt engineering (see Chapter 6), retrieval-augmented generation (see Chapter 8), and fine-tuning an LLM (see Chapter 12) are all pieces of the LLM puzzle.

Constructing an LLM capable of writing recipes based on a picture showing the products in your fridge
: This is a multimodal task where the LLM takes in an image and reasons about what it sees (see Chapter 9). LLMs are being adapted to other modalities, such as Vision, which opens a wide variety of interesting use cases.

LLM applications are incredibly satisfying to create since they are partially bounded by the things you can imagine. As these models grow more accurate, using them in practice for creative use cases such as role-playing and writing children's books simply becomes more and more fun.

Responsible LLM Development and Usage

The impact of LLMs has been and likely continues to be significant due to their widespread adoption. As we explore the incredible capabilities of LLMs it is important to keep their societal and ethical implications in mind. Several key points to consider:

Bias and fairness
: LLMs are trained on large amounts of data that might contain biases. LLMs might learn from these biases, start to reproduce them, and potentially amplify them. Since the data on which LLMs are trained are seldom shared, it remains unclear what potential biases they might contain unless you try them out.

Transparency and accountability
: Due to LLMs' incredible capabilities, it is not always clear when you are talking with a human or an LLM. As such, the usage of LLMs when interacting with humans can have unintended consequences when there is no human in the loop. For instance, LLM-based applications used in the medical field might be regulated as medical devices since they could affect a patient's well-being.

Generating harmful content
: An LLM does not necessarily generate ground-truth content and might confidently output incorrect text. Moreover, they can be used to generate fake news, articles, and other misleading sources of information.

Intellectual property
: Is the output of an LLM your intellectual property or that of the LLM's creator? When the output is similar to a phrase in the training data, does the intellectual property belong to the author of that phrase? Without access to the training data it remains unclear when copyrighted material is being used by the LLM.

Regulation
: Due to the enormous impact of LLMs, governments are starting to regulate commercial applications. An example is the European AI Act (*https://oreil.ly/nYgi5*), which regulates the development and deployment of foundation models including LLMs.

As you develop and use LLMs, we want to stress the importance of ethical considerations and urge you to learn more about the safe and responsible use of LLMs and AI systems in general.

Limited Resources Are All You Need

The compute resources that we have referenced several times thus far generally relate to the GPU(s) you have available on your system. A powerful GPU (graphics card) will make both training and using LLMs much more efficient and faster.

In choosing a GPU, an important component is the amount of VRAM (video random-access memory) you have available. This refers to the amount of memory you have available on your GPU. In practice, the more VRAM you have the better. The reason for this is that some models simply cannot be used at all if you do not have sufficient VRAM.

Because training and fine-tuning LLMs can be an expensive process, GPU-wise, those without a powerful GPU have often been referred to as the GPU-poor. This illustrates the battle for computing resources to train these huge models. To create the Llama 2 family of models, for example, Meta used A100-80 GB GPUs. Assuming renting such a GPU would cost $1.50/hr, the total costs of creating these models would exceed $5,000,000![15]

Unfortunately, there is no single rule to determine exactly how much VRAM you need for a specific model. It depends on the model's architecture and size, compression technique, context size, backend for running the model, etc.

This book is for the GPU-poor! We will use models that users can run without the most expensive GPU(s) available or a big budget. To do so, we will make all the code available in Google Colab instances. At the time of writing, a free instance of Google Colab will net you a T4 GPU with 16 GB VRAM, which is the minimum amount of VRAM that we suggest.

Interfacing with Large Language Models

Interfacing with LLMs is a vital component of not only using them but also developing an understanding of their inner workings. Due to the many developments in the field, there has been an abundance of techniques, methods, and packages for communicating with LLMs. Throughout the book, we intend to explore the most common techniques for doing so, including using both proprietary (closed source) and publicly available open models.

Proprietary, Private Models

Closed source LLMs are models that do not have their weights and architecture shared with the public. They are developed by specific organizations with their underlying code being kept secret. Examples of such models include OpenAI's GPT-4 and Anthropic's Claude. These proprietary models are generally backed by significant commercial support and have been developed and integrated within their services.

15 The models were trained for 3,311,616 GPU hours (*https://oreil.ly/PSbVT*), which refers to the amount of time it takes to train a model on a GPU, multiplied by the number of GPUs available.

You can access these models through an interface that communicates with the LLM, called an API (application programming interface), as illustrated in Figure 1-31. For instance, to use ChatGPT in Python you can use OpenAI's package (*https://oreil.ly/Vx1m3*) to interface with the service without directly accessing it.

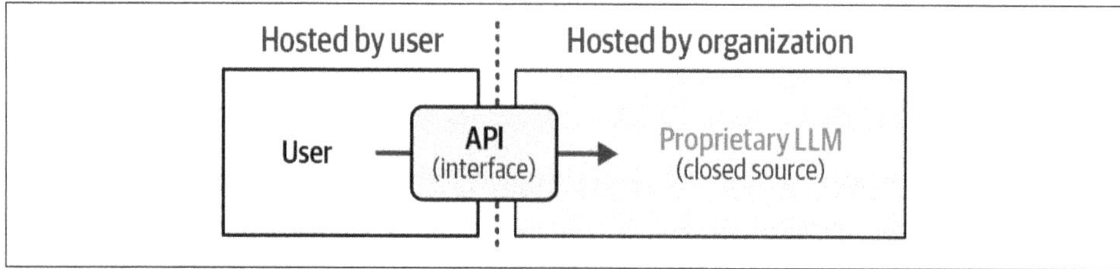

Figure 1-31. Closed source LLMs are accessed by an interface (API). As a result, details of the LLM itself, including its code and architecture are not shared with the user.

A huge benefit of proprietary models is that the user does not need to have a strong GPU to use the LLM. The provider takes care of hosting and running the model and generally has more computing available. There is no expertise necessary concerning hosting and using the model, which lowers the barrier to entry significantly. Moreover, these models tend to be more performant than their open source counterparts due to the significant investment from these organizations.

A downside to this is that it can be a costly service. The provider manages the risk and costs of hosting the LLM, which often translates to a paid service. Moreover, since there is no direct access to the model, there is no method to fine-tune it yourself. Lastly, your data is shared with the provider, which is not desirable in many common use cases, such as sharing patient data.

Open Models

Open LLMs are models that share their weights and architecture with the public to use. They are still developed by specific organizations but often share their code for creating or running the model locally—with varying levels of licensing that may or may not allow commercial usage of the model. Cohere's Command R, the Mistral models, Microsoft's Phi, and Meta's Llama models are all examples of open models.

There are ongoing discussions as to what truly represents an open source model. For instance, some publicly shared models have a permissive commercial license, which means that the model cannot be used for commercial purposes. For many, this is not the true definition of open source, which states that using these models should not have any restrictions. Similarly, the data on which a model is trained as well as its source code are seldom shared.

You can download these models and use them on your device as long as you have a powerful GPU that can handle these kinds of models, as shown in Figure 1-32.

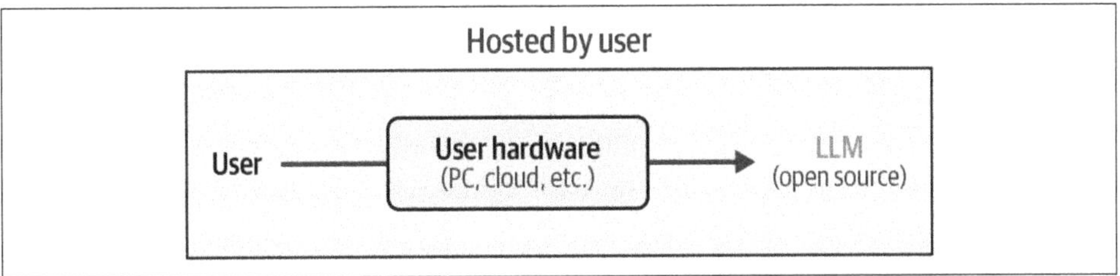

Figure 1-32. Open source LLMs are directly by the user. As a result, details of the LLM itself including its code and architecture are shared with the user.

A major advantage of these local models is that you, the user, have complete control over the model. You can use the model without depending on the API connection, fine-tune it, and run sensitive data through it. You are not dependent on any service and have complete transparency of the processes that lead to the output of the model. This benefit is enhanced by the large communities that enable these processes, such as Hugging Face (*https://oreil.ly/-G52Z*), demonstrating the possibilities of collaborative efforts.

A downside is that you need powerful hardware to run these models and even more when training or fine-tuning them. Moreover, it requires specific knowledge to set up and use these models (which we will cover throughout this book).

We generally prefer using open source models wherever we can. The freedom this gives to play around with options, explore the inner workings, and use the model locally arguably provides more benefits than using proprietary LLMs.

Open Source Frameworks

Compared to closed source LLMs, open source LLMs require you to use certain packages to run them. In 2023, many different packages and frameworks were released that, each in their own way, interact with and make use of LLMs. Wading through hundreds upon hundreds of potentially worthwhile frameworks is not the most enjoyable experience.

As a result, you might even miss your favorite framework in this book!

Instead of attempting to cover every LLM framework in existence (there are too many, and they continue to grow in number), we aim to provide you with a solid foundation for leveraging LLMs. The idea is that after reading this book, you can easily pick up most other frameworks as they all work in a very similar manner.

The intuition that we attempt to realize is an important component of this. If you have an intuitive understanding of not only LLMs but also using them in practice with common frameworks, branching out to others should be a straightforward task.

More specifically, we focus on backend packages. These are packages without a GUI (graphical user interface) that are created for efficiently loading and running any LLM on your device, such as llama.cpp (*https://oreil.ly/g2QVa*), LangChain (*https://oreil.ly/fE7P3*), and the core of many frameworks, Hugging Face Transformers (*https://oreil.ly/uvKQD*).

We will mostly cover frameworks for interacting with large language models through code. Although it helps you learn the fundamentals of these frameworks, sometimes you just want a ChatGPT-like interface with a local LLM. Fortunately, there are many incredible frameworks that allow for this. A few examples include text-generation-webui (*https://oreil.ly/hYb_C*), KoboldCpp (*https://oreil.ly/x08L2*), and LM Studio (*https://oreil.ly/dLJXI*).

Generating Your First Text

An important component of using language models is selecting them. The main source for finding and downloading LLMs is the Hugging Face Hub (*https://oreil.ly/tQobb*). Hugging Face is the organization behind the well-known Transformers package, which for years has driven the development of language models in general. As the name implies, the package was built on top of the `transformers` framework (*https://oreil.ly/AV-gJ*) that we discussed in "A Recent History of Language AI" on page 5.

At the time of writing, you will find more than 800,000 models on Hugging Face's platform for many different purposes, from LLMs and computer vision models to models that work with audio and tabular data. Here, you can find almost any open source LLM.

Although we will explore all kinds of models throughout this book, let's start our first lines of code with a generative model. The main generative model we use throughout the book is Phi-3-mini, which is a relatively small (3.8 billion parameters) but quite performant model.[16] Due to its small size, the model can be run on devices with less than 8 GB of VRAM. If you perform quantization, a type of compression that we will further discuss in Chapters 7 and 12, you can use even less than 6 GB of VRAM. Moreover, the model is licensed under the MIT license, which allows the model to be used for commercial purposes without constraints!

16 Marah Abdin et al. "Phi-3 technical report: A highly capable language model locally on your phone." *arXiv preprint arXiv:2404.14219* (2024).

Keep in mind that new and improved LLMs are frequently released. To ensure this book remains current, most examples are designed to work with any LLM. We'll also highlight different models in the repository associated with this book for you to try out.

Let's get started! When you use an LLM, two models are loaded:

- The generative model itself
- Its underlying tokenizer

The tokenizer is in charge of splitting the input text into tokens before feeding it to the generative model. You can find the tokenizer and model on the Hugging Face site (*https://oreil.ly/lkdG-*) and only need the corresponding IDs to be passed. In this case, we use "microsoft/Phi-3-mini-4k-instruct" as the main path to the model.

We can use `transformers` to load both the tokenizer and model. Note that we assume you have an NVIDIA GPU (`device_map="cuda"`) but you can choose a different device instead. If you do not have access to a GPU you can use the free Google Colab notebooks we made available in the repository of this book:

```
from transformers import AutoModelForCausalLM, AutoTokenizer

# Load model and tokenizer
model = AutoModelForCausalLM.from_pretrained(
    "microsoft/Phi-3-mini-4k-instruct",
    device_map="cuda",
    torch_dtype="auto",
    trust_remote_code=True,
)
tokenizer = AutoTokenizer.from_pretrained("microsoft/Phi-3-mini-4k-instruct")
```

Running the code will start downloading the model and depending on your internet connection can take a couple of minutes.

Although we now have enough to start generating text, there is a nice trick in transformers that simplifies the process, namely `transformers.pipeline`. It encapsulates the model, tokenizer, and text generation process into a single function:

```
from transformers import pipeline

# Create a pipeline
generator = pipeline(
    "text-generation",
    model=model,
    tokenizer=tokenizer,
    return_full_text=False,
    max_new_tokens=500,
    do_sample=False
)
```

The following parameters are worth mentioning:

`return_full_text`
: By setting this to `False`, the prompt will not be returned but merely the output of the model.

`max_new_tokens`
: The maximum number of tokens the model will generate. By setting a limit, we prevent long and unwieldy output as some models might continue generating output until they reach their context window.

`do_sample`
: Whether the model uses a sampling strategy to choose the next token. By setting this to `False`, the model will always select the next most probable token. In Chapter 6, we explore several sampling parameters that invoke some creativity in the model's output.

To generate our first text, let's instruct the model to tell a joke about chickens. To do so, we format the prompt in a list of dictionaries where each dictionary relates to an entity in the conversation. Our role is that of "user" and we use the "content" key to define our prompt:

```
# The prompt (user input / query)
messages = [
    {"role": "user", "content": "Create a funny joke about chickens."}
]

# Generate output
output = generator(messages)
print(output[0]["generated_text"])
```

```
Why don't chickens like to go to the gym? Because they can't crack the egg-
sistence of it!
```

And that is it! The first text generated in this book was a decent joke about chickens.

Summary

In this first chapter of the book, we delved into the revolutionary impact LLMs have had on the Language AI field. It has significantly changed our approach to tasks such as translation, classification, summarization, and more. Through a recent history of Language AI, we explored the fundamentals of several types of LLMs, from a simple bag-of-words representation to more complex representations using neural networks.

We discussed the attention mechanism as a step toward encoding context within models, a vital component of what makes LLMs so capable. We touched on two main categories of models that use this incredible mechanism: representation models (encoder-only) like BERT and generative models (decoder-only) like the GPT family of models. Both categories are considered large language models throughout this book.

Overall, the chapter provided an overview of the landscape of Language AI, including its applications, societal and ethical implications, and the resources needed to run such models. We ended by generating our first text using Phi-3, a model that will be used throughout the book.

In the next two chapters, you will learn about some underlying processes. We start by exploring tokenization and embeddings in Chapter 2, two often underestimated but vital components of the Language AI field. What follows in Chapter 3 is an in-depth look into language models where you will discover the precise methods used for generating text.

CHAPTER 2
Tokens and Embeddings

Tokens and embeddings are two of the central concepts of using large language models (LLMs). As we've seen in the first chapter, they're not only important to understanding the history of Language AI, but we cannot have a clear sense of how LLMs work, how they're built, and where they will go in the future without a good sense of tokens and embeddings, as we can see in Figure 2-1.

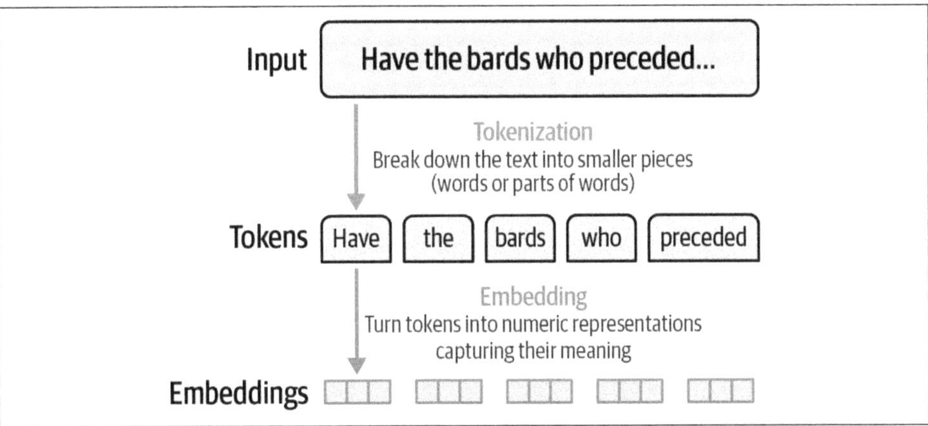

Figure 2-1. Language models deal with text in small chunks called tokens. For the language model to compute language, it needs to turn tokens into numeric representations called embeddings.

In this chapter, we look more closely at what tokens are and the tokenization methods used to power LLMs. We will then dive into the famous word2vec embedding method that preceded modern-day LLMs and see how it's extending the concept of token embeddings to build commercial recommendation systems that power a lot of the apps you use. Finally, we go from token embeddings into *sentence* or *text* embeddings, where a whole sentence or document can have one vector that represents it—enabling applications like semantic search and topic modeling that we see in Part II of this book.

LLM Tokenization

The way the majority of people interact with language models, at the time of this writing, is through a web playground that presents a chat interface between the user and a language model. You may notice that a model does not produce its output response all at once; it actually generates one token at a time.

But tokens aren't only the output of a model, they're also the way in which the model sees its inputs. A text prompt sent to the model is first broken down into tokens, as we'll now see.

How Tokenizers Prepare the Inputs to the Language Model

Viewed from the outside, generative LLMs take an input prompt and generate a response, as we can see in Figure 2-2.

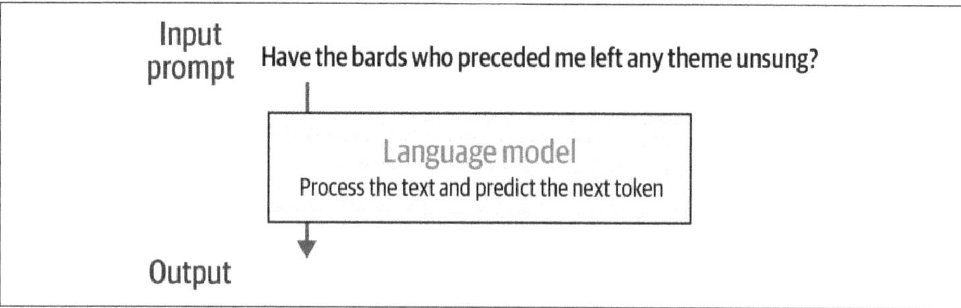

Figure 2-2. High-level view of a language model and its input prompt.

Before the prompt is presented to the language model, however, it first has to go through a tokenizer that breaks it into pieces. You can find an example showing the tokenizer of GPT-4 on the OpenAI Platform (*https://oreil.ly/ovUWO*). If we feed it the input text, it shows the output in Figure 2-3, where each token is shown in a different color.

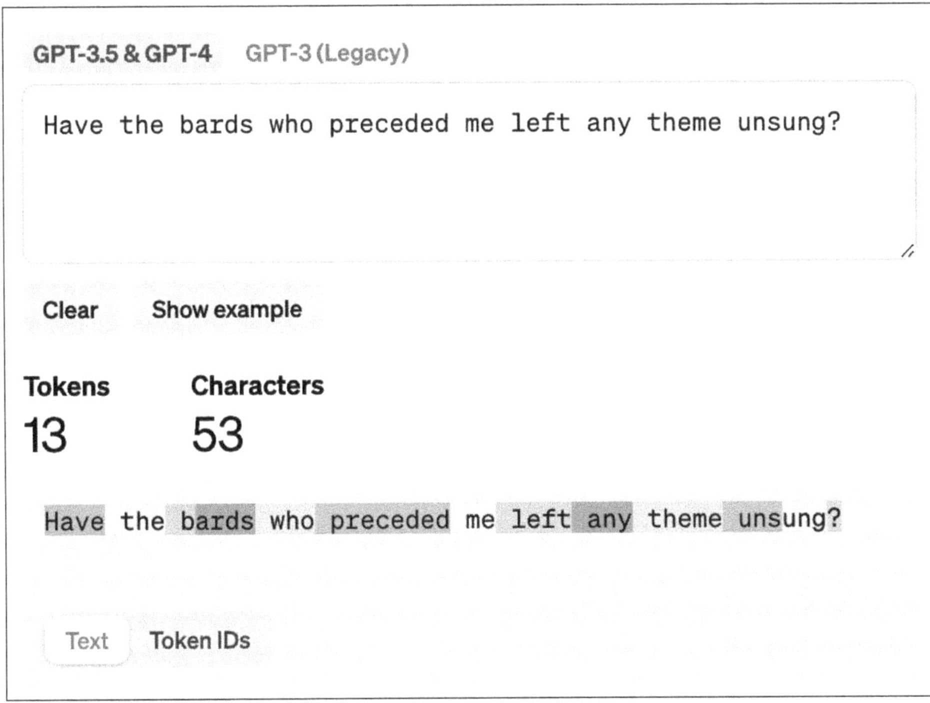

Figure 2-3. A tokenizer breaks down text into words or parts of words before the model processes the text. It does so according to a specific method and training procedure (from https://oreil.ly/ovUWO).

Let's look at a code example and interact with these tokens ourselves. Here we'll be downloading an LLM and seeing how to tokenize the input before generating text with the LLM.

Downloading and Running an LLM

Let's start by loading our model and its tokenizer as we've done in Chapter 1:

```
from transformers import AutoModelForCausalLM, AutoTokenizer

# Load model and tokenizer
model = AutoModelForCausalLM.from_pretrained(
    "microsoft/Phi-3-mini-4k-instruct",
    device_map="cuda",
    torch_dtype="auto",
    trust_remote_code=True,
)
tokenizer = AutoTokenizer.from_pretrained("microsoft/Phi-3-mini-4k-instruct")
```

We can then proceed to the actual generation. We first declare our prompt, then tokenize it, then pass those tokens to the model, which generates its output. In this case, we're asking the model to only generate 20 new tokens:

```
prompt = "Write an email apologizing to Sarah for the tragic gardening mishap.
Explain how it happened.<|assistant|>"

# Tokenize the input prompt
input_ids = tokenizer(prompt, return_tensors="pt").input_ids.to("cuda")

# Generate the text
generation_output = model.generate(
  input_ids=input_ids,
  max_new_tokens=20
)

# Print the output
print(tokenizer.decode(generation_output[0]))
```

Output:

```
<s> Write an email apologizing to Sarah for the tragic gardening mishap.
Explain how it happened.<|assistant|> Subject: My Sincere Apologies for the
Gardening Mishap

Dear
```

The text in bold is the 20 tokens generated by the model.

Looking at the code, we can see that the model does not in fact receive the text prompt. Instead, the tokenizers processed the input prompt, and returned the information the model needed in the variable `input_ids`, which the model used as its input.

Let's print `input_ids` to see what it holds inside:

```
tensor([[ 1, 14350, 385, 4876, 27746, 5281, 304, 19235, 363, 278, 25305, 293,
16423, 292, 286, 728, 481, 29889, 12027, 7420, 920, 372, 9559, 29889, 32001]],
device='cuda:0')
```

This reveals the inputs that LLMs respond to, a series of integers as shown in Figure 2-4. Each one is the unique ID for a specific token (character, word, or part of a word). These IDs reference a table inside the tokenizer containing all the tokens it knows.

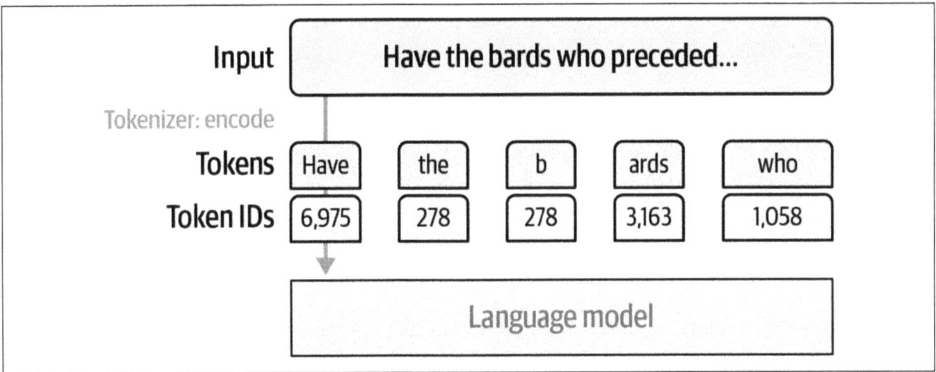

Figure 2-4. A tokenizer processes the input prompt and prepares the actual input into the language model: a list of token IDs. The specific token IDs in the figure are just demonstrative.

If we want to inspect those IDs, we can use the tokenizer's decode method to translate the IDs back into text that we can read:

```
for id in input_ids[0]:
   print(tokenizer.decode(id))
```

This prints (each token is on a separate line):

```
<s>
Write
an
email
apolog
izing
to
Sarah
for
the
trag
ic
garden
ing
m
ish
```

```
ap
.
Exp
lain
how
it
happened
.
<|assistant|>
```

This is how the tokenizer broke down our input prompt. Notice the following:

- The first token is ID 1 (`<s>`), a special token indicating the beginning of the text.
- Some tokens are complete words (e.g., *Write*, *an*, *email*).
- Some tokens are parts of words (e.g., *apolog*, *izing*, *trag*, *ic*).
- Punctuation characters are their own token.

Notice how the space character does not have its own token. Instead, partial tokens (like "izing" and "ic") have a special hidden character at their beginning that indicates that they're connected with the token that precedes them in the text. Tokens without that special character are assumed to have a space before them.

On the output side, we can also inspect the tokens generated by the model by printing the `generation_output` variable. This shows the input tokens as well as the output tokens (we'll highlight the new tokens in bold):

```
tensor([[ 1, 14350, 385, 4876, 27746, 5281, 304, 19235, 363, 278,
25305, 293, 16423, 292, 286, 728, 481, 29889, 12027, 7420,
920, 372, 9559, 29889, 32001, 3323, 622, 29901, 1619, 317,
3742, 406, 6225, 11763, 363, 278, 19906, 292, 341, 728,
481, 13, 13, 29928, 799]], device='cuda:0')
```

This shows us the model generated the token 3323, `'Sub'`, followed by token 622, `'ject'`. Together they formed the word `'Subject'`. They were then followed by token 29901, which is the colon `':'`...and so on. Just like on the input side, we need the tokenizer on the output side to translate the token ID into the actual text. We do that using the tokenizer's decode method. We can pass it an individual token ID or a list of them:

```
print(tokenizer.decode(3323))
print(tokenizer.decode(622))
print(tokenizer.decode([3323, 622]))
print(tokenizer.decode(29901))
```

This outputs:

```
Sub

ject

Subject

:
```

How Does the Tokenizer Break Down Text?

There are three major factors that dictate how a tokenizer breaks down an input prompt.

First, at model design time, the creator of the model chooses a tokenization method. Popular methods include byte pair encoding (BPE) (widely used by GPT models) and WordPiece (used by BERT). These methods are similar in that they aim to optimize an efficient set of tokens to represent a text dataset, but they arrive at it in different ways.

Second, after choosing the method, we need to make a number of tokenizer design choices like vocabulary size and what special tokens to use. More on this in "Comparing Trained LLM Tokenizers" on page 46.

Third, the tokenizer needs to be trained on a specific dataset to establish the best vocabulary it can use to represent that dataset. Even if we set the same methods and parameters, a tokenizer trained on an English text dataset will be different from another trained on a code dataset or a multilingual text dataset.

In addition to being used to process the input text into a language model, tokenizers are used on the output of the language model to turn the resulting token ID into the output word or token associated with it, as Figure 2-5 shows.

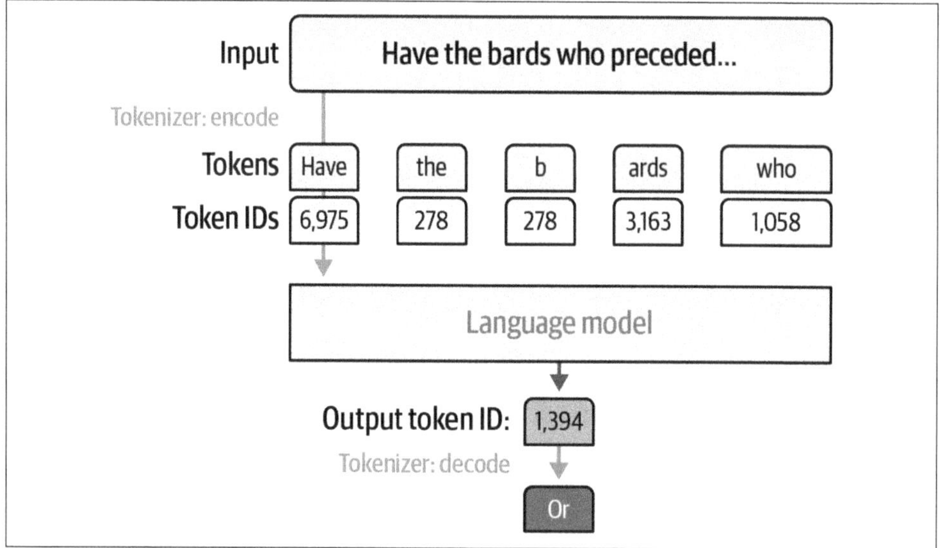

Figure 2-5. Tokenizers are also used to process the output of the model by converting the output token ID into the word or token associated with that ID.

Word Versus Subword Versus Character Versus Byte Tokens

The tokenization scheme we just discussed is called *subword tokenization*. It's the most commonly used tokenization scheme but not the only one. The four notable ways to tokenize are shown in Figure 2-6. Let's go over them:

Word tokens
: This approach was common with earlier methods like word2vec but is being used less and less in NLP. Its usefulness, however, led it to be used outside of NLP for use cases such as recommendation systems, as we'll see later in the chapter.

  One challenge with word tokenization is that the tokenizer may be unable to deal with new words that enter the dataset after the tokenizer was trained. This also results in a vocabulary that has a lot of tokens with minimal differences between them (e.g., apology, apologize, apologetic, apologist). This latter challenge is resolved by subword tokenization as it has a token for *apolog*, and then suffix tokens (e.g., *-y*, *-ize*, *-etic*, *-ist*) that are common with many other tokens, resulting in a more expressive vocabulary.

Subword tokens
: This method contains full and partial words. In addition to the vocabulary expressivity mentioned earlier, another benefit of the approach is its ability to represent new words by breaking down the new token into smaller characters, which tend to be a part of the vocabulary.

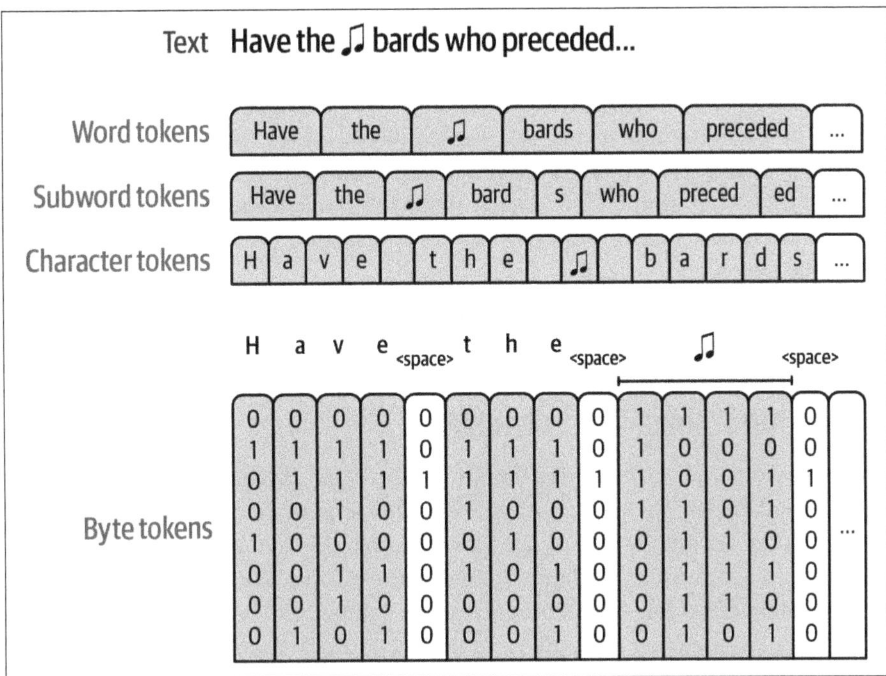

Figure 2-6. There are multiple methods of tokenization that break down the text to different sizes of components (words, subwords, characters, and bytes).

Character tokens

This is another method that can deal successfully with new words because it has the raw letters to fall back on. While that makes the representation easier to tokenize, it makes the modeling more difficult. Where a model with subword tokenization can represent "play" as one token, a model using character-level tokens needs to model the information to spell out "p-l-a-y" in addition to modeling the rest of the sequence.

Subword tokens present an advantage over character tokens in the ability to fit more text within the limited context length of a Transformer model. So with a model with a context length of 1,024, you may be able to fit about three times as much text using subword tokenization than using character tokens (subword tokens often average three characters per token).

Byte tokens

One additional tokenization method breaks down tokens into the individual bytes that are used to represent unicode characters. Papers like "CANINE: Pre-training an efficient tokenization-free encoder for language representation" (*https://oreil.ly/eP-wq*) outline methods like this, which are also called "tokenization-free encoding." Other works like "ByT5: Towards a token-free future with pre-trained byte-to-byte models" (*https://oreil.ly/a-pqF*) show that this can be a competitive method, especially in multilingual scenarios.

One distinction to highlight here: some subword tokenizers also include bytes as tokens in their vocabulary as the final building block to fall back to when they encounter characters they can't otherwise represent. The GPT-2 and RoBERTa tokenizers do this, for example. This doesn't make them tokenization-free byte-level tokenizers, because they don't use these bytes to represent everything, only a subset, as we'll see in the next section.

If you want to go deeper into tokenizers, they are discussed in more detail in *Designing Large Language Model Applications*.

Comparing Trained LLM Tokenizers

We've pointed out earlier three major factors that dictate the tokens that appear within a tokenizer: the tokenization method, the parameters and special tokens we use to initialize the tokenizer, and the dataset the tokenizer is trained on. Let's compare and contrast a number of actual, trained tokenizers to see how these choices change their behavior. This comparison will show us that newer tokenizers have changed their behavior to improve model performance, and we'll also see how specialized models (like code generation models, for example) often need specialized tokenizers.

We'll use a number of tokenizers to encode the following text:

```
text = """

English and CAPITALIZATION

🎵鸟
show_tokens False None elif == >= else: two tabs:"		" Three tabs: "			"

12.0*50=600

"""
```

This will allow us to see how each tokenizer deals with a number of different kinds of tokens:

- Capitalization.
- Languages other than English.
- Emojis.
- Programming code with keywords and whitespaces often used for indentation (in languages like Python for example).

- Numbers and digits.
- Special tokens. These are unique tokens that have a role other than representing text. They include tokens that indicate the beginning of the text, or the end of the text (which is the way the model signals to the system that it has completed this generation), or other functions as we'll see.

Let's go from older to newer tokenizers to see how they tokenize this text and what that might say about the language model. We'll tokenize the text, and then print each token with a color background color using this function:

```
colors_list = [
    '102;194;165', '252;141;98', '141;160;203',
    '231;138;195', '166;216;84', '255;217;47'
]

def show_tokens(sentence, tokenizer_name):
    tokenizer = AutoTokenizer.from_pretrained(tokenizer_name)
    token_ids = tokenizer(sentence).input_ids
    for idx, t in enumerate(token_ids):
        print(
            f'\x1b[0;30;48;2;{colors_list[idx % len(colors_list)]}m' +
            tokenizer.decode(t) +
            '\x1b[0m',
            end=' '
        )
```

BERT base model (uncased) (2018)

Link to the model on the HuggingFace model hub (*https://oreil.ly/gQK_N*)

Tokenization method: WordPiece, introduced in "Japanese and Korean voice search" (*https://oreil.ly/4nE6b*):

Vocabulary size: 30,522

Special tokens:

`unk_token [UNK]`
: An unknown token that the tokenizer has no specific encoding for.

`sep_token [SEP]`
: A separator that enables certain tasks that require giving the model two texts (in these cases, the model is called a cross-encoder). One example is reranking, as we'll see in Chapter 8.

`pad_token [PAD]`
: A padding token used to pad unused positions in the model's input (as the model expects a certain length of input, its context-size).

`cls_token [CLS]`
: A special classification token for classification tasks, as we'll see in Chapter 4.

`mask_token [MASK]`
: A masking token used to hide tokens during the training process.

Tokenized text:

```
[CLS] english and capital ##ization [UNK] [UNK] show _ token ##s false none
eli ##f = = > = else : two tab ##s : " " three tab ##s : " " 12 . 0 * 50 = 600 [SEP]
```

BERT was released in two major flavors: cased (where the capitalization is kept) and uncased (where all capital letters are first turned into small cap letters). With the uncased (and more popular) version of the BERT tokenizer, we notice the following:

- The newline breaks are gone, which makes the model blind to information encoded in newlines (e.g., a chat log when each turn is in a new line).
- All the text is in lowercase.
- The word "capitalization" is encoded as two subtokens: `capital ##ization`. The `##` characters are used to indicate this token is a partial token connected to the token that precedes it. This is also a method to indicate where the spaces are, as it is assumed tokens without `##` in front have a space before them.
- The emoji and Chinese characters are gone and replaced with the `[UNK]` special token indicating an "unknown token."

BERT base model (cased) (2018)

Link to the model on the HuggingFace model hub (*https://oreil.ly/nvFOZ*)

Tokenization method: WordPiece

Vocabulary size: 28,996

Special tokens: Same as the uncased version

Tokenized text:

```
[CLS] English and CA ##PI ##TA ##L ##I ##Z ##AT ##ION [UNK] [UNK] show _ token
##s F ##als ##e None el ##if = = > = else : two ta ##bs : " " Three ta ##bs : " "
12 . 0 * 50 = 600 [SEP]
```

The cased version of the BERT tokenizer differs mainly in including uppercase tokens.

- Notice how "CAPITALIZATION" is now represented as eight tokens: `CA ##PI ##TA ##L ##I ##Z ##AT ##ION`.

- Both BERT tokenizers wrap the input within a starting [CLS] token and a closing [SEP] token. [CLS] and [SEP] are utility tokens used to wrap the input text and they serve their own purposes. [CLS] stands for classification as it's a token used at times for sentence classification. [SEP] stands for separator, as it's used to separate sentences in some applications that require passing two sentences to a model (For example, in Chapter 8, we will use a [SEP] token to separate the text of the query and a candidate result.)

GPT-2 (2019)

Link to the model on the HuggingFace model hub (*https://oreil.ly/hhJ-I*)

Tokenization method: Byte pair encoding (BPE), introduced in "Neural machine translation of rare words with subword units" (*https://oreil.ly/qCxr4*).

Vocabulary size: 50,257

Special tokens: <|endoftext|>

English and CAP ITAL IZ ATION

� � � � � �

show _ t ok ens False None el if == >= else : two tabs :" " Three tabs : " "

12 . 0 * 50 = 600

With the GPT-2 tokenizer, we notice the following:

- The newline breaks are represented in the tokenizer.
- Capitalization is preserved, and the word "CAPITALIZATION" is represented in four tokens.
- The 🎶鸟 characters are now represented by multiple tokens each. While we see these tokens printed as the � character, they actually stand for different tokens. For example, the 🎶 emoji is broken down into the tokens with token IDs 8582, 236, and 113. The tokenizer is successful in reconstructing the original character from these tokens. We can see that by printing `tokenizer.decode([8582, 236, 113])`, which prints out 🎶.
- The two tabs are represented as two tokens (token number 197 in that vocabulary) and the four spaces are represented as three tokens (number 220) with the final space being a part of the token for the closing quote character.
- The two tabs are represented as two tokens (token number 197 in that vocabulary) and the four spaces are represented as three tokens (number 220) with the final space being a part of the token for the closing quote character.

What is the significance of whitespace characters? These are important for models to understand or generate code. A model that uses a single token to represent four consecutive whitespace characters is more tuned to a Python code dataset. While a model can live with representing it as four different tokens, it does make the modeling more difficult as the model needs to keep track of the indentation level, which often leads to worse performance. This is an example of where tokenization choices can help the model improve on a certain task.

Flan-T5 (2022)

Tokenization method: Flan-T5 (*https://oreil.ly/cmWPA*) uses a tokenizer implementation called SentencePiece, introduced in "SentencePiece: A simple and language independent subword tokenizer and detokenizer for neural text processing" (*https://oreil.ly/2aNI5*), which supports BPE and the *unigram language model* (described in "Subword regularization: Improving neural network translation models with multiple subword candidates" (*https://oreil.ly/B4WiL*)).

Vocabulary size: 32,100

Special tokens:

- `unk_token <unk>`
- `pad_token <pad>`

Tokenized text:

```
English and CA PI TAL IZ ATION <unk> <unk> show _ to ken s Fal s e None e l if = = >
= else : two tab s : " " Three tab s : " " 12. 0 * 50 = 600 </s>
```

The Flan-T5 family of models use the SentencePiece method. We notice the following:

- No newline or whitespace tokens; this would make it challenging for the model to work with code.
- The emoji and Chinese characters are both replaced by the <unk> token, making the model completely blind to them.

GPT-4 (2023)

Tokenization method: BPE

Vocabulary size: A little over 100,000

Special tokens:

- <|endoftext|>
- Fill in the middle tokens. These three tokens enable the LLM to generate a completion given not only the text before it but also considering the text after it. This method is explained in more detail in the paper "Efficient training of language models to fill in the middle" (*https://oreil.ly/7S7ZZ*); its exact details are beyond the scope of this book. These special tokens are:
  - <|fim_prefix|>
  - <|fim_middle|>
  - <|fim_suffix|>

Tokenized text:

```
English and CAPITAL IZATION

� � � � � �

show _tokens False None elif == >= else : two tabs :"    " Three tabs : "        "

12 . 0 * 50 = 600
```

The GPT-4 tokenizer behaves similarly to its ancestor, the GPT-2 tokenizer. Some differences are:

- The GPT-4 tokenizer represents the four spaces as a single token. In fact, it has a specific token for every sequence of whitespaces up to a list of 83 whitespaces.
- The Python keyword `elif` has its own token in GPT-4. Both this and the previous point stem from the model's focus on code in addition to natural language.
- The GPT-4 tokenizer uses fewer tokens to represent most words. Examples here include "CAPITALIZATION" (two tokens versus four) and "tokens" (one token versus three).
- Refer back to what we said about the GPT-2 tokenizer with regards to the Ł tokens.

StarCoder2 (2024)

StarCoder2 (*https://oreil.ly/hBZ9V*) is a 15-billion parameter model focused on generating code described in the paper "StarCoder 2 and the stack v2: The next generation" (*https://oreil.ly/k4b-T*), which continues the work from the original StarCoder described in "StarCoder: May the source be with you!" (*https://oreil.ly/RJmCn*).

Tokenization method: Byte pair encoding (BPE)

Vocabulary size: 49,152

Example special tokens:

- `<|endoftext|>`
- Fill in the middle tokens:
  - `<fim_prefix>`
  - `<fim_middle>`
  - `<fim_suffix>`
  - `<fim_pad>`
- When representing code, managing the context is important. One file might make a function call to a function that is defined in a different file. So the model needs some way of being able to identify code that is in different files in the same code repository, while making a distinction between code in different repos. That's why StarCoder2 uses special tokens for the name of the repository and the filename:
  - `<filename>`
  - `<reponame>`
  - `<gh_stars>`

Tokenized text:

```
English and CAPITAL IZATION

� � � � �

show _ tokens False None elif == >= else : two tabs :"  " Three tabs : "   "

1 2 . 0 * 5 0 = 6 0 0
```

This is an encoder that focuses on code generation:

- Similar to GPT-4, it encodes the list of whitespaces as a single token.
- A major difference here to everything we've seen so far is that each digit is assigned its own token (so 600 becomes `6 0 0`). The hypothesis here is that this would lead to better representation of numbers and mathematics. In GPT-2, for example, the number 870 is represented as a single token. But 871 is represented as two tokens (`8` and `71`). You can intuitively see how that might be confusing to the model and how it represents numbers.

Galactica

The Galactica model (*https://oreil.ly/I6IXt*) described in "Galactica: A large language model for science" (*https://oreil.ly/gWRzV*) is focused on scientific knowledge and is trained on many scientific papers, reference materials, and knowledge bases. It pays extra attention to tokenization that makes it more sensitive to the nuances of the dataset it's representing. For example, it includes special tokens for citations, reasoning, mathematics, amino acid sequences, and DNA sequences.

Tokenization method: Byte pair encoding (BPE)

Vocabulary size: 50,000

Special tokens:

- `<s>`
- `<pad>`
- `</s>`
- `<unk>`
- References: Citations are wrapped within the two special tokens:
  - `[START_REF]`
  - `[END_REF]`
  - One example of usage from the paper is: `Recurrent neural networks, long short-term memory [START_REF]Long Short-Term Memory, Hochreiter[END_REF]`
- Step-by-step reasoning:
  - `<work>` is an interesting token that the model uses for chain-of-thought reasoning.

Tokenized text:

`English and CAP ITAL IZATION`

`� � � � � � �`

`show _ tokens False None elif == > = else : two t abs : " " Three t abs : " "`

`1 2 . 0 * 5 0 = 6 0 0`

The Galactica tokenizer behaves similar to StarCoder2 in that it has code in mind. It also encodes whitespaces in the same way: assigning a single token to sequences of whitespace of different lengths. It differs in that it also does that for tabs, though. So from all the tokenizers we've seen so far, it's the only one that assigns a single token to the string made up of two tabs (`'\t\t'`).

Phi-3 (and Llama 2)

The Phi-3 model (*https://oreil.ly/GI-xn*) we look at in this book reuses the tokenizer of Llama 2 (*https://oreil.ly/fezbc*) yet adds a number of special tokens.

Tokenization method: Byte pair encoding (BPE)

Vocabulary size: 32,000

Special tokens:

- `<|endoftext|>`
- Chat tokens: As chat LLMs rose to popularity in 2023, the conversational nature of LLMs started to be a leading use case. Tokenizers have been adapted to this direction by the addition of tokens that indicate the turns in a conversation and the roles of each speaker. These special tokens include:
  - `<|user|>`
  - `<|assistant|>`
  - `<|system|>`

We can now recap our tour by looking at all these examples side by side:

BERT base model (uncased)	[CLS] english and capital ##ization [UNK] [UNK] show _ token ##s false none eli ##f = = > = else : two tab ##s : " " three tab ##s : " " 12 . 0 * 50 = 600 [SEP]
BERT base model (cased)	[CLS] English and CA ##PI ##TA ##L ##I ##Z ##AT ##ION [UNK] [UNK] show _ token ##s F ##als ##e None el ##if = = > = else : two ta ##bs : " " Three ta ##bs : " " 12 . 0 * 50 = 600 [SEP]
GPT-2	English and CAP ITAL IZ ATION � � � � � � show _ t ok ens False None el if == >= else : two tabs :" " Three tabs : " " 12 . 0 * 50 = 600
FLAN-T5	English and CA PI TAL IZ ATION <unk> <unk> show _ to ken s Fal s e None e l if = = > = else : two tab s : " " Three tab s : " " 12. 0 * 50 = 600 </s>
GPT-4	English and CAPITAL IZATION � � � � � � show _tokens False None elif == >= else : two tabs :" " Three tabs : " " 12 . 0 * 50 = 600
StarCoder	English and CAPITAL IZATION � � � � � show _ tokens False None elif == >= else : two tabs :" " Three tabs : " " 1 2 . 0 * 5 0 = 6 0 0

Galactica	English and CAP ITAL IZATION � � � � � � � show _ tokens False None elif == > = else : two t abs : " " Three t abs : " " 1 2 . 0 * 5 0 = 6 0 0
Phi-3 and Llama 2	<s> English and C AP IT AL IZ ATION � � � � � � � show _ to kens False None elif == >= else : two tabs :" " Three tabs : " " 1 2 . 0 * 5 0 = 6 0 0

Tokenizer Properties

The preceding guided tour of trained tokenizers showed a number of ways in which actual tokenizers differ from each other. But what determines their tokenization behavior? There are three major groups of design choices that determine how the tokenizer will break down text: the tokenization method, the initialization parameters, and the domain of the data the tokenizer targets.

Tokenization methods

As we've seen, there are a number of tokenization methods with byte pair encoding (BPE) being the more popular one. Each of these methods outlines an algorithm for how to choose an appropriate set of tokens to represent a dataset. You can find a great overview of all these methods on the Hugging Face page that summarizes tokenizers (*https://oreil.ly/-vbn0*).

Tokenizer parameters

After choosing a tokenization method, an LLM designer needs to make some decisions about the parameters of the tokenizer. These include:

Vocabulary size
: How many tokens to keep in the tokenizer's vocabulary? (30K and 50K are often used as vocabulary size values, but more and more we're seeing larger sizes like 100K.)

Special tokens
: What special tokens do we want the model to keep track of? We can add as many of these as we want, especially if we want to build an LLM for special use cases. Common choices include:

  - Beginning of text token (e.g., <s>)
  - End of text token
  - Padding token

- Unknown token
- CLS token
- Masking token

Aside from these, the LLM designer can add tokens that help better model the domain of the problem they're trying to focus on, as we've seen with Galactica's `<work>` and `[START_REF]` tokens.

Capitalization
: In languages such as English, how do we want to deal with capitalization? Should we convert everything to lowercase? (Name capitalization often carries useful information, but do we want to waste token vocabulary space on all-caps versions of words?)

The domain of the data

Even if we select the same method and parameters, tokenizer behavior will be different based on the dataset it was trained on (before we even start model training). The tokenization methods mentioned previously work by optimizing the vocabulary to represent a specific dataset. From our guided tour we've seen how that has an impact on datasets like code and multilingual text.

For code, for example, we've seen that a text-focused tokenizer may tokenize the indentation spaces like this (we'll highlight some tokens in color):

```
def add_numbers(a, b):
...."""Add the two numbers `a` and `b`."""
....return a + b
```

This may be suboptimal for a code-focused model. Code-focused models are often improved by making different tokenization choices:

```
def add_numbers(a, b):
...."""Add the two numbers `a` and `b`."""
....return a + b
```

These tokenization choices make the model's job easier and thus its performance has a higher probability of improving.

You can find a more detailed tutorial on training tokenizers in the Tokenizers section of the Hugging Face course (*https://oreil.ly/4Gfbi*) and in *Natural Language Processing with Transformers, Revised Edition*.

Token Embeddings

Now that we understand tokenization, we have solved one part of the problem of representing language to a language model. In this sense, language is a sequence of tokens. And if we train a good-enough model on a large-enough set of tokens, it starts to capture the complex patterns that appear in its training dataset:

- If the training data contains a lot of English text, that pattern reveals itself as a model capable of representing and generating the English language.
- If the training data contains factual information (Wikipedia, for example), the model would have the ability to generate some factual information (see the following note).

The next piece of the puzzle is finding the best numerical representation for these tokens that the model can use to calculate and properly model the patterns in the text. These patterns reveal themselves to us as a model's coherence in a specific language, or capability to code, or any of the growing list of capabilities we expect from language models.

As we've seen in Chapter 1, that is what embeddings are. They are the numeric representation space utilized to capture the meanings and patterns in language.

Oops: Achieving a good threshold of language coherence and better-than-average factual generation, however, starts to present a new problem. Some users start to trust the model's fact generation ability (e.g., at the beginning of 2023 some language models were being dubbed "Google killers" (*https://oreil.ly/U8QvX*)). It didn't take long for advanced users to recognize that generation models alone aren't reliable search engines. This led to the rise of retrieval-augmented generation (RAG), which combines search and LLMs. We cover RAG in more detail in Chapter 8.

A Language Model Holds Embeddings for the Vocabulary of Its Tokenizer

After a tokenizer is initialized and trained, it is then used in the training process of its associated language model. This is why a pretrained language model is linked with its tokenizer and can't use a different tokenizer without training.

The language model holds an embedding vector for each token in the tokenizer's vocabulary, as we can see in Figure 2-7. When we download a pretrained language model, a portion of the model is this embeddings matrix holding all of these vectors.

Before the beginning of the training process, these vectors are randomly initialized like the rest of the model's weights, but the training process assigns them the values that enable the useful behavior they're trained to perform.

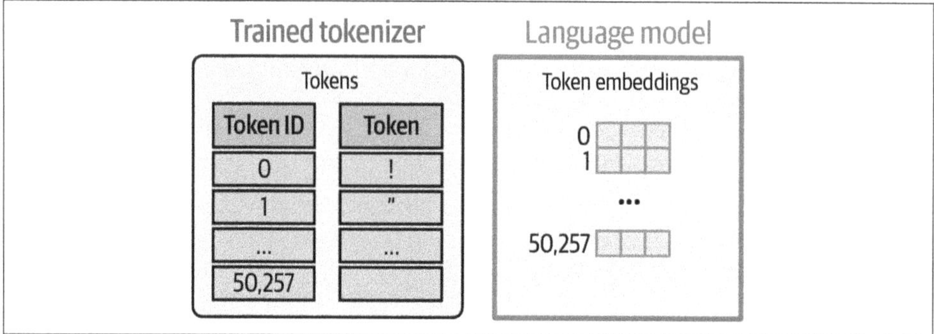

Figure 2-7. A language model holds an embedding vector associated with each token in its tokenizer.

Creating Contextualized Word Embeddings with Language Models

Now that we've covered token embeddings as the input to a language model, let's look at how language models can *create* better token embeddings. This is one of the primary ways to use language models for text representation. This empowers applications like named-entity recognition or extractive text summarization (which summarizes a long text by highlighting the most important parts of it, instead of generating new text as a summary).

Instead of representing each token or word with a static vector, language models create contextualized word embeddings (shown in Figure 2-8) that represent a word with a different token based on its context. These vectors can then be used by other systems for a variety of tasks. In addition to the text applications we mentioned in the previous paragraph, these contextualized vectors, for example, are what powers AI image generation systems like DALL·E, Midjourney, and Stable Diffusion, for example.

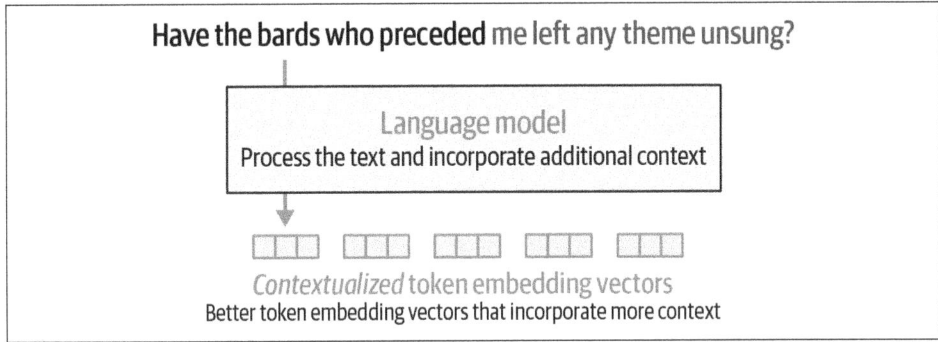

Figure 2-8. Language models produce contextualized token embeddings that improve on raw, static token embeddings.

Let's look at how we can generate contextualized word embeddings; the majority of this code should be familiar to you by now:

```
from transformers import AutoModel, AutoTokenizer

# Load a tokenizer
tokenizer = AutoTokenizer.from_pretrained("microsoft/deberta-base")

# Load a language model
model = AutoModel.from_pretrained("microsoft/deberta-v3-xsmall")

# Tokenize the sentence
tokens = tokenizer('Hello world', return_tensors='pt')

# Process the tokens
output = model(**tokens)[0]
```

The model we're using here is called DeBERTa v3, which at the time of writing is one of the best-performing language models for token embeddings while being small and highly efficient. It is described in the paper "DeBERTaV3: Improving DeBERTa using ELECTRA-style pre-training gradient-disentangled embedding sharing" (*https://oreil.ly/3Piya*).

This code downloads a pretrained tokenizer and model, then uses them to process the string "Hello world". The output of the model is then saved in the output variable. Let's inspect that variable by first printing its dimensions (we expect it to be a multidimensional array):

```
output.shape
```

This prints out:

```
torch.Size([1, 4, 384])
```

Skipping the first dimension, we can read this as four tokens, each one embedded in a vector of 384 values. The first dimension is the batch dimension used in cases (like training) when we want to send multiple input sentences to the model at the same time (they're processed at the same time, which speeds up the process).

But what are these four vectors? Did the tokenizer break the two words into four tokens, or is something else happening here? We can use what we've learned about tokenizers to inspect them:

```
for token in tokens['input_ids'][0]:
    print(tokenizer.decode(token))
```

This prints out:

```
[CLS]
Hello
world
[SEP]
```

This particular tokenizer and model operate by adding the `[CLS]` and `[SEP]` tokens to the beginning and end of a string.

Our language model has now processed the text input. The result of its output is the following:

```
tensor([[
[-3.3060, -0.0507, -0.1098, ..., -0.1704, -0.1618, 0.6932],
[ 0.8918, 0.0740, -0.1583, ..., 0.1869, 1.4760, 0.0751],
[ 0.0871, 0.6364, -0.3050, ..., 0.4729, -0.1829, 1.0157],
[-3.1624, -0.1436, -0.0941, ..., -0.0290, -0.1265, 0.7954]
]], grad_fn=<NativeLayerNormBackward0>)
```

This is the raw output of a language model. The applications of large language models build on top of outputs like this.

We recap the input tokenization and resulting outputs of a language model in Figure 2-9. Technically, the switch from token IDs into raw embeddings is the first step that occurs inside a language model.

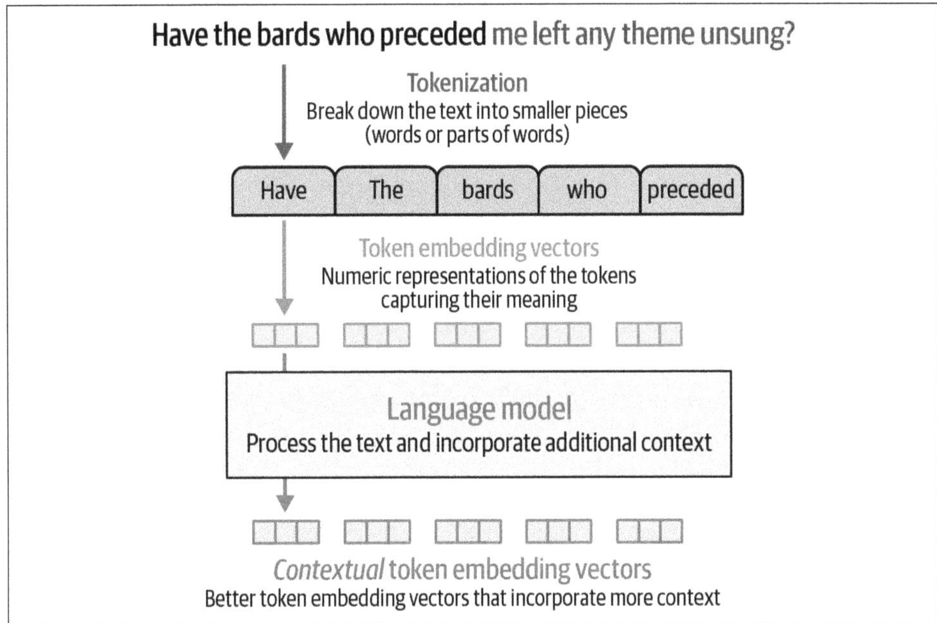

Figure 2-9. A language model operates on raw, static embeddings as its input and produces contextual text embeddings.

A visual like this is essential for the next chapter when we start to look at how Transformer-based LLMs work.

Text Embeddings (for Sentences and Whole Documents)

While token embeddings are key to how LLMs operate, a number of LLM applications require operating on entire sentences, paragraphs, or even text documents. This has led to special language models that produce text embeddings—a single vector that represents a piece of text longer than just one token.

We can think of text embedding models as taking a piece of text and ultimately producing a single vector that represents that text and captures its meaning in some useful form. Figure 2-10 shows that process.

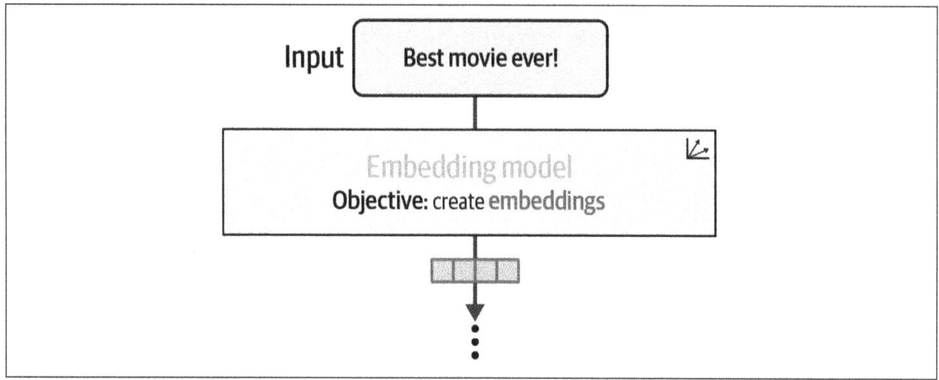

Figure 2-10. In step 1, we use the embedding model to extract the features and convert the input text to embeddings.

There are multiple ways of producing a *text* embedding vector. One of the most common ways is to average the values of all the *token* embeddings produced by the model. Yet high-quality text embedding models tend to be trained specifically for text embedding tasks.

We can produce text embeddings with `sentence-transformers` (*https://oreil.ly/Tlt3e*), a popular package for leveraging pretrained embedding models.[1] The package, like `transformers` in the previous chapter, can be used to load publicly available models. To illustrate creating embeddings, we use the all-mpnet-base-v2 model (*https://oreil.ly/EwDyX*). Note that in Chapter 4, we will further explore how you can choose an embedding model for your task.

```
from sentence_transformers import SentenceTransformer

# Load model
model = SentenceTransformer("sentence-transformers/all-mpnet-base-v2")

# Convert text to text embeddings
vector = model.encode("Best movie ever!")
```

The number of values, or the dimensions, of the embedding vector depends on the underlying embedding model. Let's explore that for our model:

```
vector.shape
```

```
(768,)
```

1 Nils Reimers and Iryna Gurevych. "Sentence-BERT: Sentence embeddings using Siamese BERT-networks." *arXiv preprint arXiv:1908.10084* (2019).

This sentence is now encoded in this one vector with a dimension of 768 numerical values. In Part II of this book, once we start looking at applications, we'll start to see the immense usefulness of these text embeddings vectors in powering everything from categorization to semantic search to RAG.

Word Embeddings Beyond LLMs

Embeddings are useful even outside of text and language generation. Embeddings, or assigning meaningful vector representations to objects, turns out to be useful in many domains, including recommender engines and robotics. In this section, we'll look at how to use pretrained word2vec embeddings and touch on how the method creates word embeddings. Seeing how word2vec is trained will prime you to learn about contrastive training in Chapter 10. Then in the following section, we'll see how those embeddings can be used for recommendation systems.

Using pretrained Word Embeddings

Let's look at how we can download pretrained word embeddings (like word2vec or GloVe) using the Gensim library (*https://oreil.ly/M8wi8*):

```
import gensim.downloader as api

# Download embeddings (66MB, glove, trained on wikipedia, vector size: 50)
# Other options include "word2vec-google-news-300"
# More options at https://github.com/RaRe-Technologies/gensim-data
model = api.load("glove-wiki-gigaword-50")
```

Here, we've downloaded the embeddings of a large number of words trained on Wikipedia. We can then explore the embedding space by seeing the nearest neighbors of a specific word, "king" for example:

```
model.most_similar([model['king']], topn=11)
```

This outputs:

```
[('king', 1.0000001192092896),
('prince', 0.8236179351806641),
('queen', 0.7839043140411377),
('ii', 0.7746230363845825),
('emperor', 0.7736247777938843),
('son', 0.766719400882721),
('uncle', 0.7627150416374207),
('kingdom', 0.7542161345481873),
('throne', 0.7539914846420288),
('brother', 0.7492411136627197),
('ruler', 0.7434253692626953)]
```

The Word2vec Algorithm and Contrastive Training

The word2vec algorithm described in the paper "Efficient estimation of word representations in vector space" (*https://oreil.ly/nLDeS*) is described in detail in The Illustrated Word2vec (*https://oreil.ly/ybd-K*). The central ideas are condensed here as we build on them when discussing one method for creating embeddings for recommendation engines in the following section.

Just like LLMs, word2vec is trained on examples generated from text. Let's say, for example, we have the text "Thou shalt not make a machine in the likeness of a human mind" from the *Dune* novels by Frank Herbert. The algorithm uses a sliding window to generate training examples. We can, for example, have a window size two, meaning that we consider two neighbors on each side of a central word.

The embeddings are generated from a classification task. This task is used to train a neural network to predict if words commonly appear in the same context or not (*context* here means in many sentences in the training dataset we're modeling). We can think of this as a neural network that takes two words and outputs 1 if they tend to appear in the same context, and 0 if they do not.

In the first position for the sliding window, we can generate four training examples, as we can see in Figure 2-11.

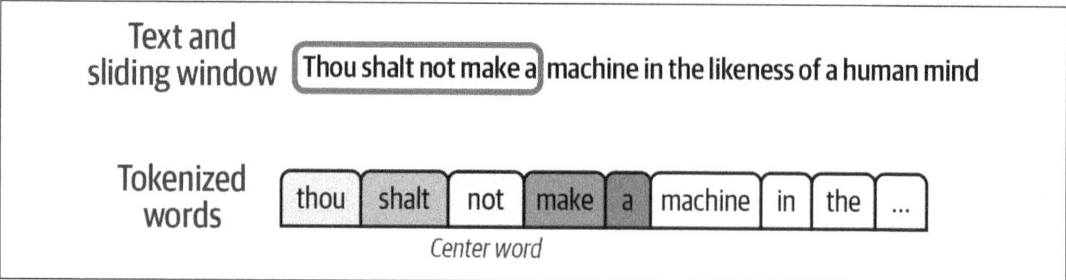

Figure 2-11. A sliding window is used to generate training examples for the word2vec algorithm to later predict if two words are neighbors or not.

In each of the produced training examples, the word in the center is used as one input, and each of its neighbors is a distinct second input in each training example. We expect the final trained model to be able to classify this neighbor relationship and output 1 if the two input words it receives are indeed neighbors. These training examples are visualized in Figure 2-12.

	Word 1	Word 2	Target
Training examples	Not	thou	1
	Not	shalt	1
	Not	make	1
	Not	a	1

Figure 2-12. Each generated training example shows a pair of neighboring words.

If, however, we have a dataset of only a target value of 1, then a model can cheat and ace it by outputting 1 all the time. To get around this, we need to enrich our training dataset with examples of words that are not typically neighbors. These are called negative examples and are shown in Figure 2-13.

Word 1	Word 2	Target	
not	thou	1	Positive examples
not	shalt	1	
not	make	1	
not	a	1	
thou	apothecary	0	Negative examples
not	sublime	0	
make	def	0	
a	playback	0	

Figure 2-13. We need to present our models with negative examples: words that are not usually neighbors. A better model is able to better distinguish between the positive and negative examples.

It turns out that we don't have to be too scientific in how we choose the negative examples. A lot of useful models result from the simple ability to detect positive examples from randomly generated examples (inspired by an important idea called *noise-contrastive estimation* and described in "Noise-contrastive estimation: A new estimation principle for unnormalized statistical models" (*https://oreil.ly/BkBVt*)). So in this case, we get random words and add them to the dataset and indicate that they are not neighbors (and thus the model should output 0 when it sees them).

With this, we've seen two of the main concepts of word2vec (Figure 2-14): skip-gram, the method of selecting neighboring words, and negative sampling, adding negative examples by random sampling from the dataset.

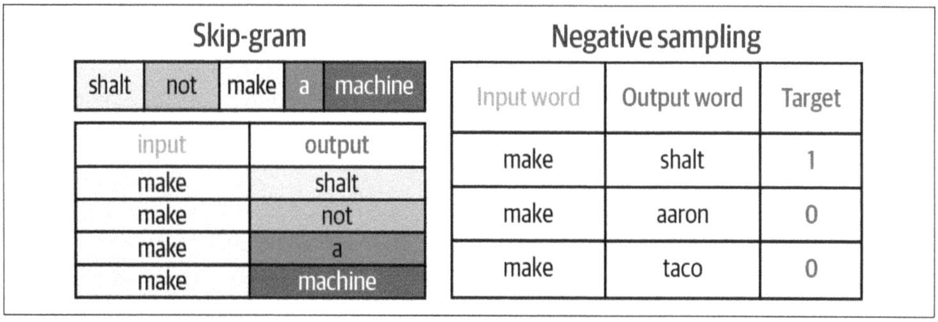

Figure 2-14. Skip-gram and negative sampling are two of the main ideas behind the word2vec algorithm and are useful in many other problems that can be formulated as token sequence problems.

We can generate millions and even billions of training examples like this from running text. Before proceeding to train a neural network on this dataset, we need to make a couple of tokenization decisions, which, just like we've seen with LLM tokenizers, include how to deal with capitalization and punctuation and how many tokens we want in our vocabulary.

We then create an embedding vector for each token, and randomly initialize them, as can be seen in Figure 2-15. In practice, this is a matrix of dimensions `vocab_size x embedding_dimensions`.

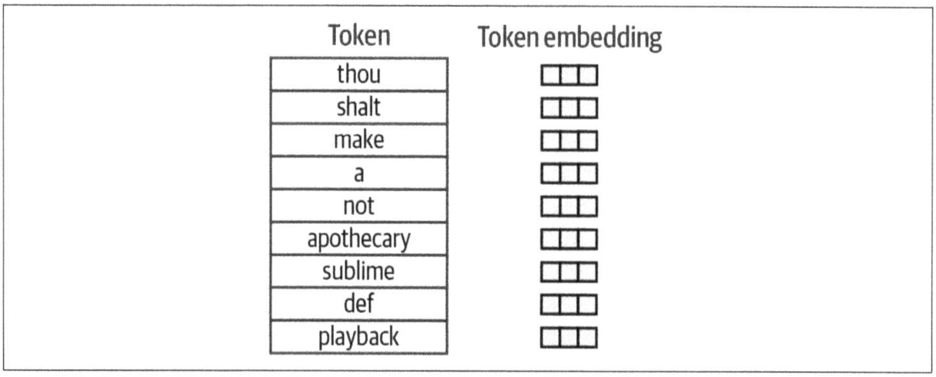

Figure 2-15. A vocabulary of words and their starting, random, uninitialized embedding vectors.

A model is then trained on each example to take in two embedding vectors and predict if they're related or not. We can see what this looks like in Figure 2-16.

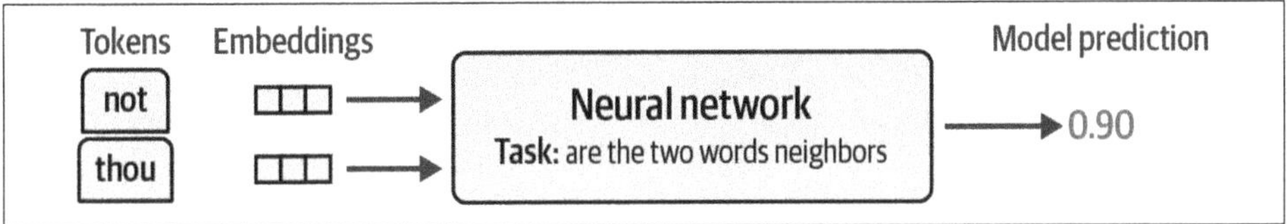

Figure 2-16. A neural network is trained to predict if two words are neighbors. It updates the embeddings in the training process to produce the final, trained embeddings.

Based on whether its prediction was correct or not, the typical machine learning training step updates the embeddings so that the next time the model is presented with those two vectors, it has a better chance of being more correct. And by the end of the training process, we have better embeddings for all the tokens in our vocabulary.

This idea of a model that takes two vectors and predicts if they have a certain relation is one of the most powerful ideas in machine learning, and time after time has proven to work very well with language models. This is why we're dedicating Chapter 10 to this concept and how it optimizes language models for specific tasks (like sentence embeddings and retrieval).

The same idea is also central to bridging modalities like text and images, which is key to AI image generation models, as we'll see in Chapter 9 on multimodal models. In that formulation, a model is presented with an image and a caption, and it should predict whether that caption describes the image or not.

Embeddings for Recommendation Systems

As we've mentioned, the concept of embeddings is useful in so many other domains. In industry, it's widely used for recommendation systems, for example.

Recommending Songs by Embeddings

In this section we'll use the word2vec algorithm to embed songs using human-made music playlists. Imagine if we treated each song as we would a word or token, and we treated each playlist like a sentence. These embeddings can then be used to recommend similar songs that often appear together in playlists.

The dataset (*https://oreil.ly/A-AK6*) we'll use was collected by Shuo Chen from Cornell University. It contains playlists from hundreds of radio stations around the US. Figure 2-17 demonstrates this dataset.

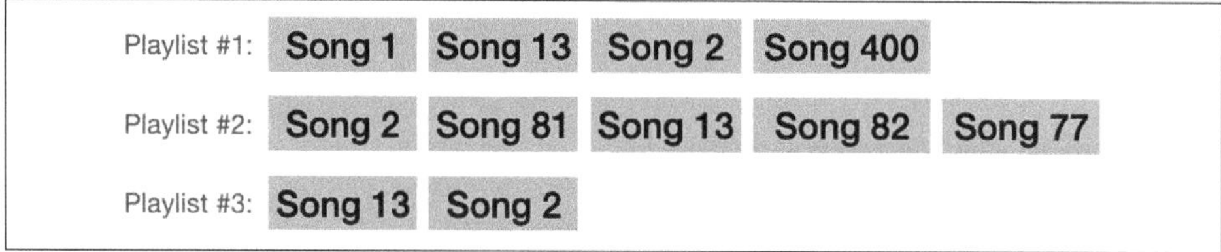

Figure 2-17. For song embeddings that capture song similarity we'll use a dataset made up of a collection of playlists, each containing a list of songs.

Let's demonstrate the end product before we look at how it's built. So let's give it a few songs and see what it recommends in response.

Let's start by giving it Michael Jackson's "Billie Jean," the song with ID 3822:

```
# We will define and explore this function in detail below
print_recommendations(3822)
```

id	Title	artist
4181	Kiss	Prince & The Revolution
12749	Wanna Be Startin' Somethin'	Michael Jackson
1506	The Way You Make Me Feel	Michael Jackson
3396	Holiday	Madonna
500	Don't Stop 'Til You Get Enough	Michael Jackson

That looks reasonable. Madonna, Prince, and other Michael Jackson songs are the nearest neighbors.

Let's step away from pop and into rap, and see the neighbors of 2Pac's "California Love":

```
print_recommendations(842)
```

id	Title	artist
413	If I Ruled the World (Imagine That) (w\/ Lauryn Hill)	Nas
196	I'll Be Missing You	Puff Daddy & The Family
330	Hate It or Love It (w\/ 50 Cent)	The Game
211	Hypnotize	The Notorious B.I.G.
5788	Drop It Like It's Hot (w\/ Pharrell)	Snoop Dogg

Another quite reasonable list! Now that we know it works, let's see how to build such a system.

Training a Song Embedding Model

We'll start by loading the dataset containing the song playlists as well as each song's metadata, such as its title and artist:

```
import pandas as pd
from urllib import request

# Get the playlist dataset file
data = request.urlopen('https://storage.googleapis.com/maps-premium/data
set/yes_complete/train.txt')

# Parse the playlist dataset file. Skip the first two lines as
# they only contain metadata
lines = data.read().decode("utf-8").split('\n')[2:]

# Remove playlists with only one song
playlists = [s.rstrip().split() for s in lines if len(s.split()) > 1]

# Load song metadata
songs_file = request.urlopen('https://storage.googleapis.com/maps-premium/data
set/yes_complete/song_hash.txt')
songs_file = songs_file.read().decode("utf-8").split('\n')
songs = [s.rstrip().split('\t') for s in songs_file]
songs_df = pd.DataFrame(data=songs, columns = ['id', 'title', 'artist'])
songs_df = songs_df.set_index('id')
```

Now that we've saved them, let's inspect the `playlists` list. Each element inside it is a playlist containing a list of song IDs:

```
print( 'Playlist #1:\n ', playlists[0], '\n')
print( 'Playlist #2:\n ', playlists[1])
```

```
Playlist #1: ['0', '1', '2', '3', '4', '5', ..., '43']
Playlist #2: ['78', '79', '80', '3', '62', ..., '210']
```

Let's train the model:

```
from gensim.models import Word2Vec

# Train our Word2Vec model
model = Word2Vec(
    playlists, vector_size=32, window=20, negative=50, min_count=1, workers=4
)
```

That takes a minute or two to train and results in embeddings being calculated for each song that we have. Now we can use those embeddings to find similar songs exactly as we did earlier with words:

```
song_id = 2172

# Ask the model for songs similar to song #2172
model.wv.most_similar(positive=str(song_id))
```

This outputs:

```
[('2976', 0.9977465271949768),
 ('3167', 0.9977430701255798),
 ('3094', 0.9975950717926025),
 ('2640', 0.9966474175453186),
 ('2849', 0.9963167905807495)]
```

That is the list of the songs whose embeddings are most similar to song 2172.

In this case, the song is:

```
print(songs_df.iloc[2172])
```

```
title Fade To Black
artist Metallica
Name: 2172 , dtype: object
```

This results in recommendations that are all in the same heavy metal and hard rock genre:

```
import numpy as np

def print_recommendations(song_id):
    similar_songs = np.array(
        model.wv.most_similar(positive=str(song_id),topn=5)
    )[:,0]
    return  songs_df.iloc[similar_songs]

# Extract recommendations
print_recommendations(2172)
```

id	Title	artist
11473	Little Guitars	Van Halen
3167	Unchained	Van Halen
5586	The Last in Line	Dio
5634	Mr. Brownstone	Guns N' Roses
3094	Breaking the Law	Judas Priest

Summary

In this chapter, we have covered LLM tokens, tokenizers, and useful approaches to using token embeddings. This prepares us to start looking closer at language models in the next chapter, and also opens the door to learn about how embeddings are used beyond language models.

We explored how tokenizers are the first step in processing input to an LLM, transforming raw textual input into token IDs. Common tokenization schemes include breaking text down into words, subword tokens, characters, or bytes, depending on the specific requirements of a given application.

A tour of real-world pretrained tokenizers (from BERT to GPT-2, GPT-4, and other models) showed us areas where some tokenizers are better (e.g., preserving information like capitalization, newlines, or tokens in other languages) and other areas where tokenizers are just different from each other (e.g., how they break down certain words).

Three of the major tokenizer design decisions are the tokenizer algorithm (e.g., BPE, WordPiece, SentencePiece), tokenization parameters (including vocabulary size, special tokens, capitalization, treatment of capitalization and different languages), and the dataset the tokenizer is trained on.

Language models are also creators of high-quality contextualized token embeddings that improve on raw static embeddings. Those contextualized token embeddings are what's used for tasks including named-entity recognition (NER), extractive text summarization, and text classification. In addition to producing token embeddings, language models can produce text embeddings that cover entire sentences or even documents. This empowers plenty of applications that will be shown in Part II of this book covering language model applications

Before LLMs, word embedding methods like word2vec, GloVe, and fastText were popular. In language processing, this has largely been replaced with contextualized word embeddings produced by language models. The word2vec algorithm relies on two main ideas: skip-gram and negative sampling. It also uses contrastive training similar to the type we'll see in Chapter 10.

Embeddings are useful for creating and improving recommender systems as we discussed in the music recommender we built from curated song playlists.

In the next chapter, we will take a deep dive into the process after tokenization: how does an LLM process these tokens and generate text? We will look at some of the main intuitions of how LLMs that use the Transformer architecture work.

CHAPTER 3

Looking Inside Large Language Models

Now that we have a sense of tokenization and embeddings, we're ready to dive deeper into the language model and see how it works. In this chapter, we'll look at some of the main intuitions of how Transformer language models work. Our focus will be on text generation models so we get a deeper sense for generative LLMs in particular.

We'll be looking at both the concepts and some code examples that demonstrate them. Let's start by loading a language model and getting it ready for generation by declaring a pipeline. In your first read, feel free to skip the code and focus on grasping the concepts involved. Then in a second read, the code will get you to start applying these concepts.

```
import torch
from transformers import AutoModelForCausalLM, AutoTokenizer, pipeline

# Load model and tokenizer
tokenizer = AutoTokenizer.from_pretrained("microsoft/Phi-3-mini-4k-instruct")

model = AutoModelForCausalLM.from_pretrained(
    "microsoft/Phi-3-mini-4k-instruct",
    device_map="cuda",
    torch_dtype="auto",
    trust_remote_code=True,
)

# Create a pipeline
generator = pipeline(
    "text-generation",
    model=model,
    tokenizer=tokenizer,
    return_full_text=False,
    max_new_tokens=50,
    do_sample=False,
)
```

An Overview of Transformer Models

Let's begin our exploration with a high-level overview of the model, and then we'll see how later work has improved upon the Transformer model since its introduction in 2017.

The Inputs and Outputs of a Trained Transformer LLM

The most common picture of understanding the behavior of a Transformer LLM is to think of it as a software system that takes in text and generates text in response. Once a large enough text-in-text-out model is trained on a large enough high-quality dataset, it becomes able to generate impressive and useful outputs. Figure 3-1 shows one such model used to author an email.

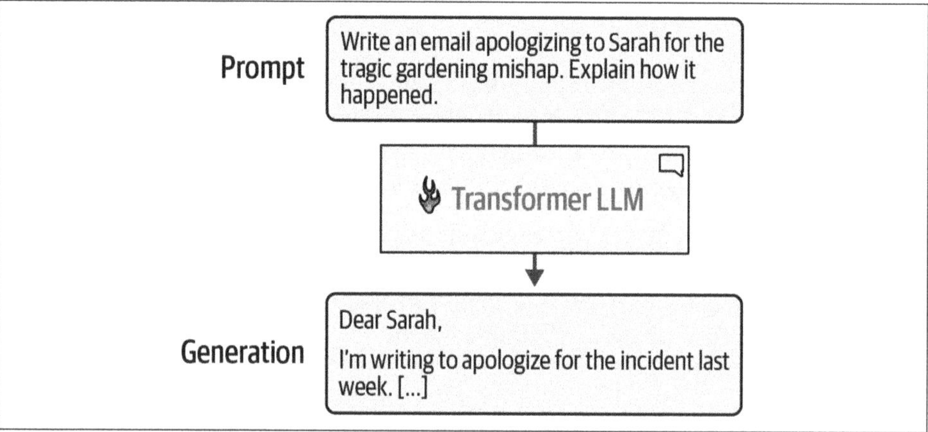

Figure 3-1. At a high level of abstraction, Transformer LLMs take a text prompt and output generated text.

The model does not generate the text all in one operation; it actually generates one token at a time. Figure 3-2 shows four steps of token generation in response to the input prompt. Each token generation step is one forward pass through the model (that's machine-learning speak for the inputs going into the neural network and flowing through the computations it needs to produce an output on the other end of the computation graph).

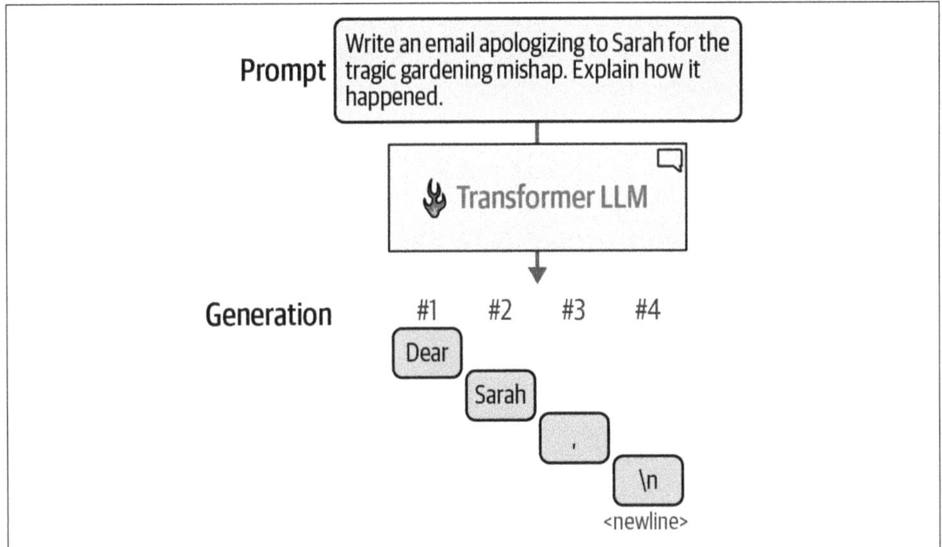

Figure 3-2. Transformer LLMs generate one token at a time, not the entire text at once.

After each token generation, we tweak the input prompt for the next generation step by appending the output token to the end of the input prompt. We can see this in Figure 3-3.

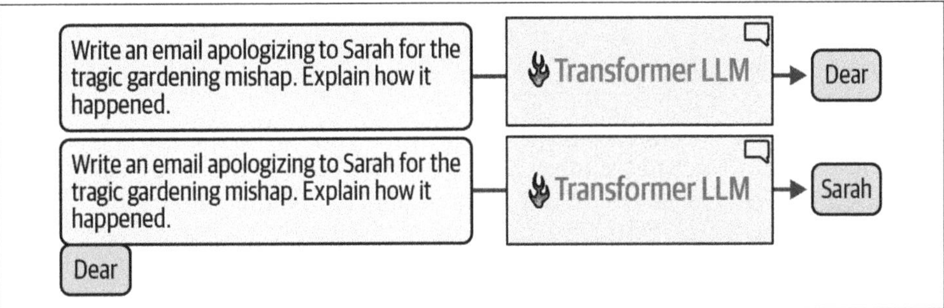

Figure 3-3. An output token is appended to the prompt, then this new text is presented to the model again for another forward pass to generate the next token.

This gives us a more accurate picture of the model as it is simply predicting the next token based on an input prompt. Software around the neural network basically runs it in a loop to sequentially expand the generated text until completion.

There's a specific word used in machine learning to describe models that consume their earlier predictions to make later predictions (e.g., the model's first generated token is used to generate the second token). They're called *autoregressive* models. That is why you'll hear text generation LLMs being called autoregressive models. This is often used to differentiate text generation models from text representation models like BERT, which are not autoregressive.

This autoregressive, token-by-token generation is what happens under the hood when we generate text with the LLM like we see here:

```
prompt = "Write an email apologizing to Sarah for the tragic gardening mishap.
Explain how it happened."

output = generator(prompt)

print(output[0]['generated_text'])
```

This generates the text:

```
Solution 1:

Subject: My Sincere Apologies for the Gardening Mishap

Dear Sarah,

I hope this message finds you well. I am writing to express my deep
```

We can see the model begin to write the email starting with the subject. It stopped abruptly because it reached the token limit we established by setting `max_new_tokens` to 50 tokens. If we increase that, it will continue until concluding the email.

The Components of the Forward Pass

In addition to the loop, two key internal components are the tokenizer and the language modeling head (LM head). Figure 3-4 shows where these components lie in the system. We saw in the previous chapter how tokenizers break down the text into a sequence of token IDs that then become the input to the model.

The tokenizer is followed by the neural network: a stack of Transformer blocks that do all of the processing. That stack is then followed by the LM head, which translates the output of the stack into probability scores for what the most likely next token is.

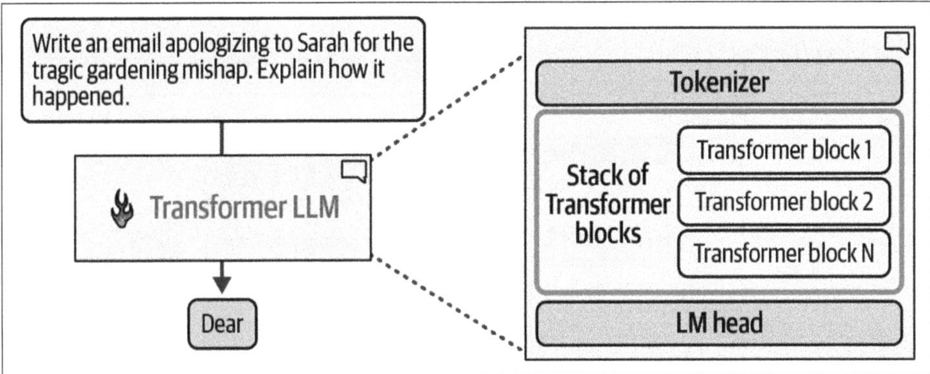

Figure 3-4. A Transformer LLM is made up of a tokenizer, a stack of Transformer blocks, and a language modeling head.

Recall from Chapter 2 that the tokenizer contains a table of tokens—the tokenizer's *vocabulary*. The model has a vector representation associated with each of these tokens in the vocabulary (token embeddings). Figure 3-5 shows both the vocabulary and associated token embeddings for a model with a vocabulary of 50,000 tokens.

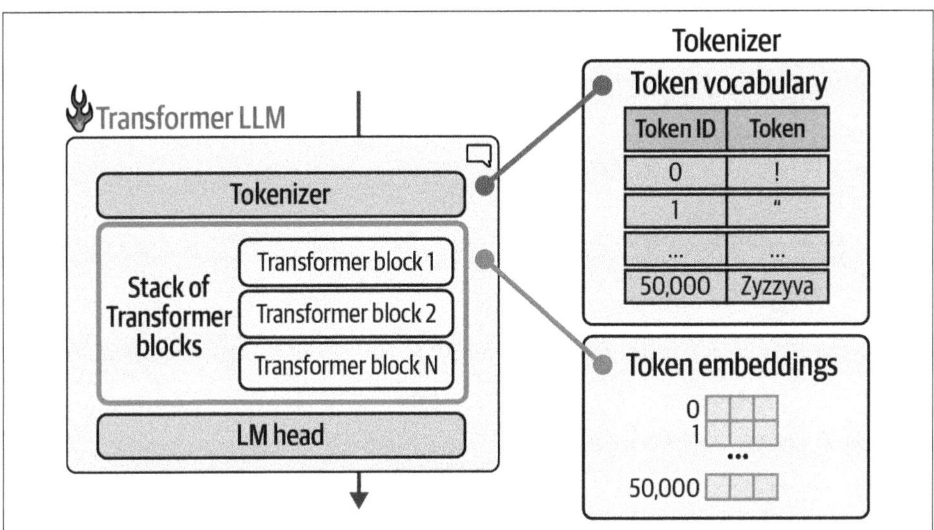

Figure 3-5. The tokenizer has a vocabulary of 50,000 tokens. The model has token embeddings associated with those embeddings.

The flow of the computation follows the direction of the arrow from top to bottom. For each generated token, the process flows once through each of the Transformer blocks in the stack in order, then to the LM head, which finally outputs the probability distribution for the next token, seen in Figure 3-6.

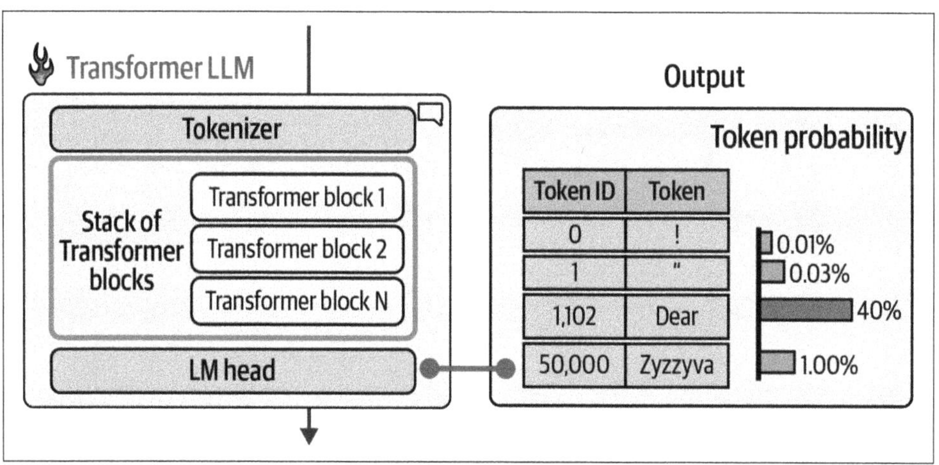

Figure 3-6. At the end of the forward pass, the model predicts a probability score for each token in the vocabulary.

The LM head is a simple neural network layer itself. It is one of multiple possible "heads" to attach to a stack of Transformer blocks to build different kinds of systems. Other kinds of Transformer heads include sequence classification heads and token classification heads.

We can display the order of the layers by simply printing out the model variable. For this model, we have:

```
Phi3ForCausalLM(
  (model): Phi3Model(
    (embed_tokens): Embedding(32064, 3072, padding_idx=32000)
    (embed_dropout): Dropout(p=0.0, inplace=False)
    (layers): ModuleList(
      (0-31): 32 x Phi3DecoderLayer(
        (self_attn): Phi3Attention(
          (o_proj): Linear(in_features=3072, out_features=3072, bias=False)
          (qkv_proj): Linear(in_features=3072, out_features=9216, bias=False)
          (rotary_emb): Phi3RotaryEmbedding()
        )
        (mlp): Phi3MLP(
          (gate_up_proj): Linear(in_features=3072, out_features=16384,
bias=False)
          (down_proj): Linear(in_features=8192, out_features=3072, bias=False)
          (activation_fn): SiLU()
        )
        (input_layernorm): Phi3RMSNorm()
        (resid_attn_dropout): Dropout(p=0.0, inplace=False)
        (resid_mlp_dropout): Dropout(p=0.0, inplace=False)
        (post_attention_layernorm): Phi3RMSNorm()
      )
    )
    (norm): Phi3RMSNorm()
  )
  (lm_head): Linear(in_features=3072, out_features=32064, bias=False)
)
```

Looking at this structure, we can notice the following highlights:

- This shows us the various nested layers of the model. The majority of the model is labeled `model`, followed by `lm_head`.
- Inside the `Phi3Model` model, we see the embeddings matrix `embed_tokens` and its dimensions. It has 32,064 tokens each with a vector size of 3,072.
- Skipping the dropout layer for now, we can see the next major component is the stack of Transformer decoder layers. It contains 32 blocks of type `Phi3DecoderLayer`.
- Each of these Transformer blocks includes an attention layer and a feedforward neural network (also known as an `mlp` or multilevel perceptron). We'll cover these in more detail later in the chapter.
- Finally, we see the `lm_head` taking a vector of size 3,072 and outputting a vector equivalent to the number of tokens the model knows. That output is the probability score for each token that helps us select the output token.

Choosing a Single Token from the Probability Distribution (Sampling/Decoding)

At the end of processing, the output of the model is a probability score for each token in the vocabulary, as we saw previously in Figure 3-6. The method of choosing a single token from the probability distribution is called the *decoding strategy*. Figure 3-7 shows how this leads to picking the token "Dear" in one example.

The easiest decoding strategy would be to always pick the token with the highest probability score. In practice, this doesn't tend to lead to the best outputs for most use cases. A better approach is to add some randomness and sometimes choose the second or third highest probability token. The idea here is to basically *sample* from the probability distribution based on the probability score, as the statisticians would say.

What this means for the example in Figure 3-7 is that if the token "Dear" has a 40% probability of being the next token, then it has a 40% chance of being picked (instead of greedy search, which would pick it directly for having the highest score). So with this method, all the other tokens have a chance of being picked according to their score.

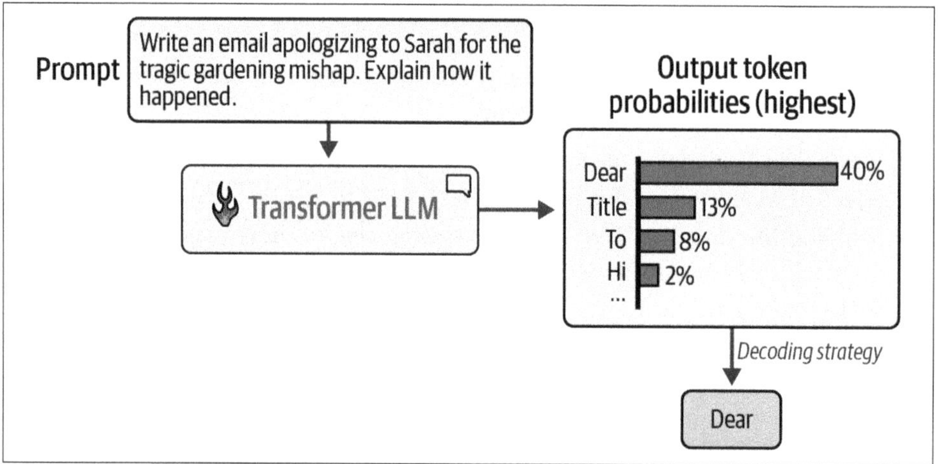

Figure 3-7. The tokens with the highest probability after the model's forward pass. Our decoding strategy decides which of the tokens to output by sampling based on the probabilities.

Choosing the highest scoring token every time is called *greedy decoding*. It's what happens if you set the temperature parameter to zero in an LLM. We cover the concept of temperature in Chapter 6.

Let's look more closely at the code that demonstrates this process. In this code block, we pass the input tokens through the model, and then `lm_head`:

```
prompt = "The capital of France is"

# Tokenize the input prompt
input_ids = tokenizer(prompt, return_tensors="pt").input_ids

# Tokenize the input prompt
input_ids = input_ids.to("cuda")

# Get the output of the model before the lm_head
model_output = model.model(input_ids)

# Get the output of the lm_head
lm_head_output = model.lm_head(model_output[0])
```

Now, `lm_head_output` is of the shape [1, 6, 32064]. We can access the token probability scores for the last generated token using `lm_head_output[0,-1]`, which uses the index 0 across the batch dimension; the index –1 gets us the last token in the sequence. This is now a list of probability scores for all 32,064 tokens. We can get the top scoring token ID, and then decode it to arrive at the text of the generated output token:

```
token_id = lm_head_output[0,-1].argmax(-1)
tokenizer.decode(token_id)
```

In this case this turns out to be:

```
Paris
```

Parallel Token Processing and Context Size

One of the most compelling features of Transformers is that they lend themselves better to parallel computing than previous neural network architectures in language processing. In text generation, we get a first glance at this when looking at how each token is processed. We know from the previous chapter that the tokenizer will break down the text into tokens. Each of these input tokens then flows through its own computation path (that's a good first intuition, at least). We can see these individual processing tracks or streams in Figure 3-8.

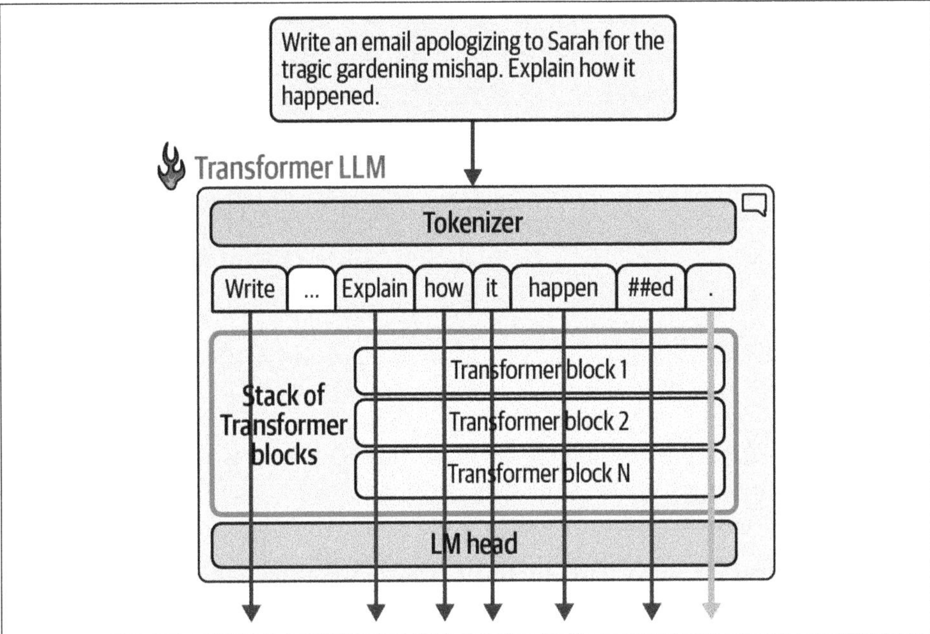

Figure 3-8. Each token is processed through its own stream of computation (with some interaction between them in attention steps, as we'll later see).

Current Transformer models have a limit for how many tokens they can process at once. That limit is called the model's context length. A model with 4K context length can only process 4K tokens and would only have 4K of these streams.

Each of the token streams starts with an input vector (the embedding vector and some positional information; we'll discuss positional embeddings later in the chapter). At the end of the stream, another vector emerges as the result of the model's processing, as shown in Figure 3-9.

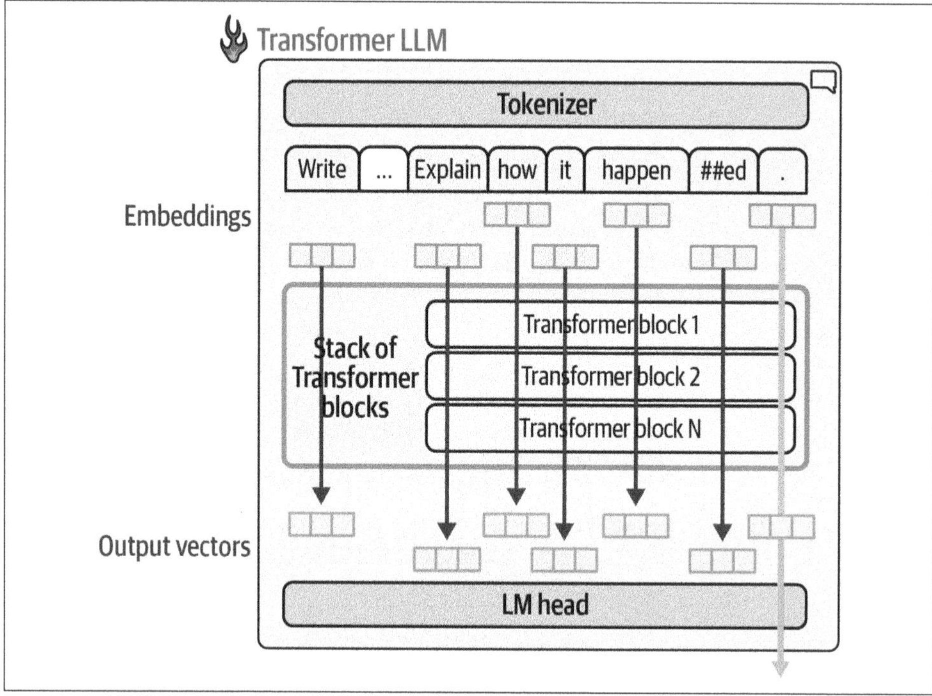

Figure 3-9. Each processing stream takes a vector as input and produces a final resulting vector of the same size (often referred to as the model dimension).

For text generation, only the output result of the last stream is used to predict the next token. That output vector is the only input into the LM head as it calculates the probabilities of the next token.

You may wonder why we go through the trouble of calculating all the token streams if we're discarding the outputs of all but the last token. The answer is that the calculations of the previous streams are required and used in calculating the final stream. Yes, we're not using their final output vector, but we use earlier outputs (in each Transformer block) in the Transformer block's attention mechanism.

If you're following along with the code examples, recall that the output of `lm_head` was of the shape [1, 6, 32064]. That was because the input to it was of the shape [1, 6, 3072], which is a batch of one input string, containing six tokens, each of them represented by a vector of size 3,072 corresponding to the output vectors after the stack of Transformer blocks.

We can access these matrices and view their dimensions by printing:

```
model_output[0].shape
```

This outputs:

```
torch.Size([1, 6, 3072])
```

Similarly, we can print the output of the LM head:

```
lm_head_output.shape
```

This outputs:

```
torch.Size([1, 6, 32064])
```

Speeding Up Generation by Caching Keys and Values

Recall that when generating the second token, we simply append the output token to the input and do another forward pass through the model. If we give the model the ability to cache the results of the previous calculation (especially some of the specific vectors in the attention mechanism), we no longer need to repeat the calculations of the previous streams. This time the only needed calculation is for the last stream. This is an optimization technique called the keys and values (kv) cache (*https://oreil.ly/1q45J*) and it provides a significant speedup of the generation process. Keys and values are some of the central components of the attention mechanism, as we'll see later in this chapter.

Figure 3-10 shows how when generating the second token, only one processing stream is active as we cache the results of the previous streams.

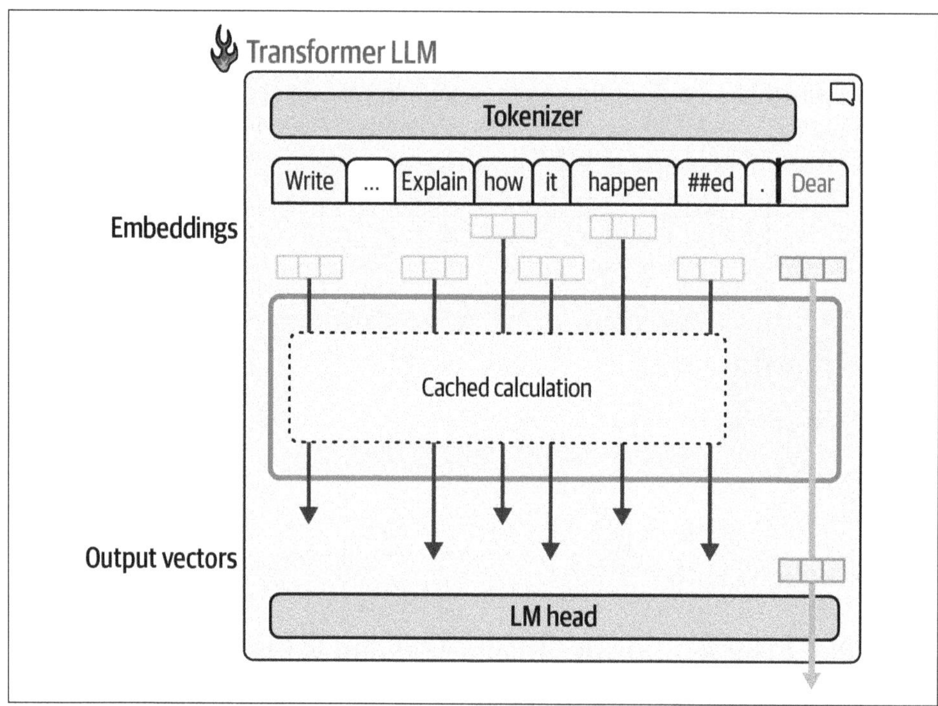

Figure 3-10. When generating text, it's important to cache the computation results of previous tokens instead of repeating the same calculation over and over again.

In Hugging Face Transformers, cache is enabled by default. We can disable it by setting `use_cache` to `False`. We can see the difference in speed by asking for a long generation, and timing the generation with and without caching:

```
prompt = "Write a very long email apologizing to Sarah for the tragic gardening
mishap. Explain how it happened."
# Tokenize the input prompt
input_ids = tokenizer(prompt, return_tensors="pt").input_ids
input_ids = input_ids.to("cuda")
```

Then we time how long it takes to generate 100 tokens with caching. We can use the `%%timeit` magic command in Jupyter or Colab to time how long the execution takes (it runs the command several times and gets the average):

```
%%timeit -n 1
# Generate the text
generation_output = model.generate(
  input_ids=input_ids,
  max_new_tokens=100,
  use_cache=True
)
```

On a Colab with a T4 GPU, this comes to 4.5 seconds. How long would that take if we disable the cache, however?

```
%%timeit -n 1
# Generate the text
generation_output = model.generate(
  input_ids=input_ids,
  max_new_tokens=100,
  use_cache=False
)
```

This comes out to 21.8 seconds. A dramatic difference. In fact, from a user experience standpoint, even the four-second generation time tends to be a long time to wait for a user that's staring at a screen and waiting for an output from the model. This is one reason why LLM APIs stream the output tokens as the model generates them instead of waiting for the entire generation to be completed.

Inside the Transformer Block

We can now talk about where the vast majority of processing happens: the Transformer blocks. As Figure 3-11 shows, Transformer LLMs are composed of a series Transformer blocks (often in the range of six in the original Transformer paper, to over a hundred in many large LLMs). Each block processes its inputs, then passes the results of its processing to the next block.

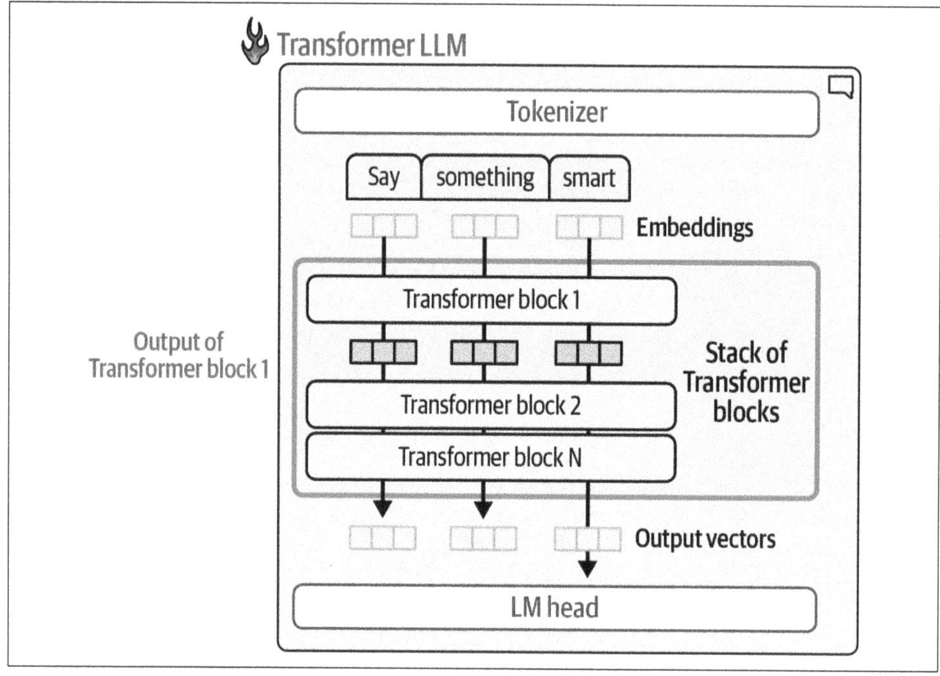

Figure 3-11. The bulk of the Transformer LLM processing happens inside a series of Transformer blocks, each handing the result of its processing as input to the subsequent block.

A Transformer block (Figure 3-12) is made up of two successive components:

1. *The attention layer* is mainly concerned with incorporating relevant information from other input tokens and positions
2. *The feedforward layer* houses the majority of the model's processing capacity

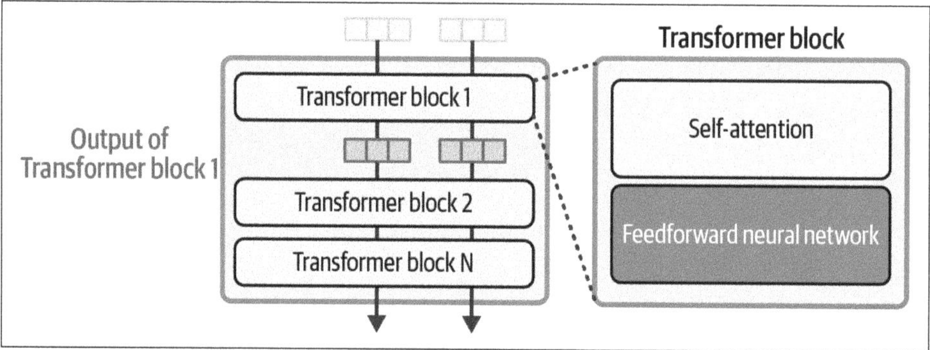

Figure 3-12. A Transformer block is made up of a self-attention layer and a feedforward neural network.

The feedforward neural network at a glance

A simple example giving the intuition of the feedforward neural network would be if we pass the simple input "The Shawshank" to a language model, with the expectation that it will generate "Redemption" as the most probable next word (in reference to the film from 1994).

The feedforward neural network (collectively in all the model layers) is the source of this information, as Figure 3-13 shows. When the model was successfully trained to model a massive text archive (which included many mentions of "The Shawshank Redemption"), it learned and stored the information (and behaviors) that make it succeed at this task.

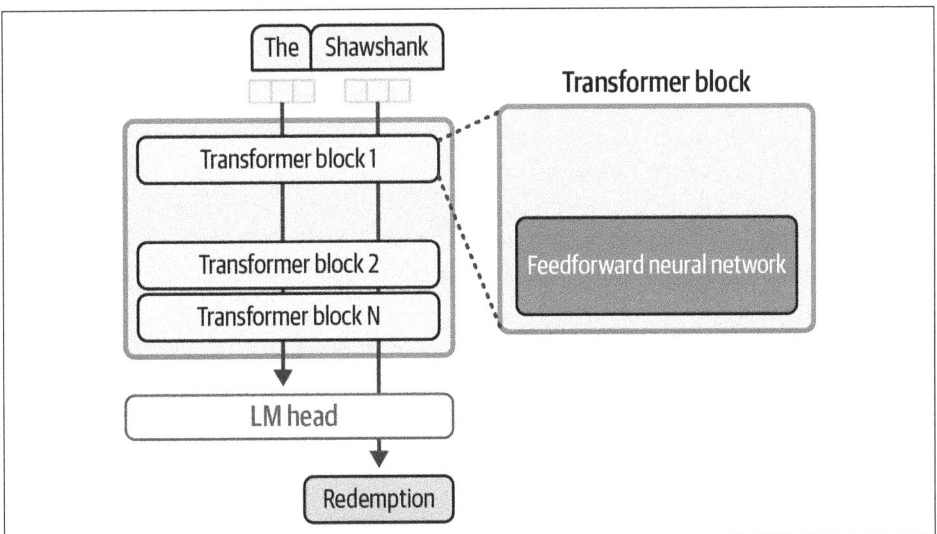

Figure 3-13. The feedforward neural network component of a Transformer block likely does the majority of the model's memorization and interpolation.

For an LLM to be successfully trained, it needs to memorize a lot of information. But it is not simply a large database. Memorization is only one ingredient in the recipe of impressive text generation. The model is able to use this same machinery to interpolate between data points and more complex patterns to be able to generalize—which means doing well on inputs it hadn't seen in the past and were not in its training dataset.

When you use a modern commercial LLM, the outputs you get are not the ones mentioned earlier in the strict meaning of a "language model." Passing "The Shawshank" to a chat LLM like GPT-4 produces an output:

```
"The Shawshank Redemption" is a 1994 film directed
by Frank Darabont and is based on the novella "Rita
Hayworth and Shawshank Redemption" written by Stephen
King. ...etc.
```

This is because raw language models (like GPT-3) are difficult for people to properly utilize. This is why the language model is then trained on instruction-tuning and human preference and feedback fine-tuning to match people's expectations of what the model should output.

The attention layer at a glance

Context is vital in order to properly model language. Simple memorization and interpolation based on the previous token can only take us so far. We know that because this was one of the leading approaches to build language models before neural networks (see Chapter 3, "N-gram Language Models" of *Speech and Language Processing* (*https://oreil.ly/9onN8*) by Daniel Jurafsky and James H. Martin).

Attention is a mechanism that helps the model incorporate context as it's processing a specific token. Think of the following prompt:

> "The dog chased the squirrel because **it**"

For the model to predict what comes after "it," it needs to know what "it" refers to. Does it refer to the dog or the squirrel?

In a trained Transformer LLM, the attention mechanism makes that determination. Attention adds information from the context into the representation of the "it" token. We can see a simple version of that in Figure 3-14.

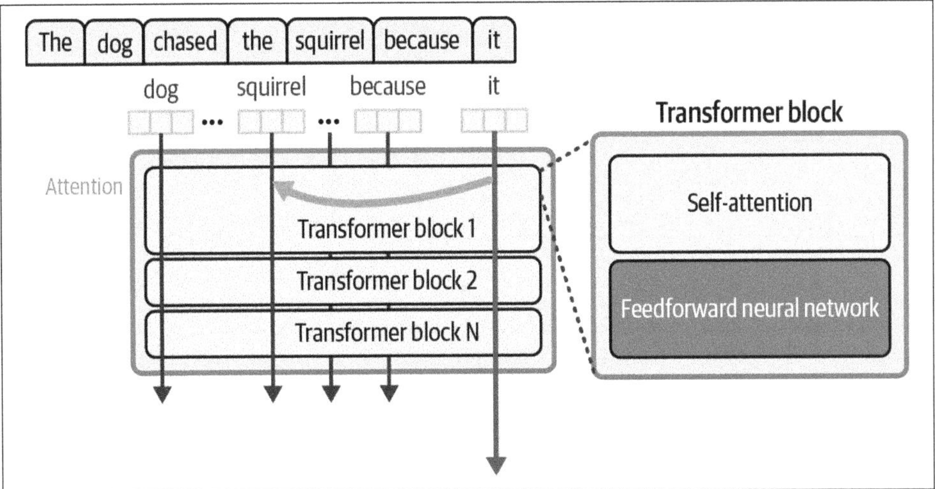

Figure 3-14. The self-attention layer incorporates relevant information from previous positions that help process the current token.

The model does that based on the patterns seen and learned from the training dataset. Perhaps previous sentences also give more clues, like, for example, referring to the dog as "she" thus making it clear that "it" refers to the squirrel.

Attention is all you need

It is worth diving deeper into the attention mechanism. The most stripped-down version of the mechanism is shown in Figure 3-15. It shows multiple token positions going into the attention layer; the final one is the one being currently processed (the pink arrow). The attention mechanism operates on the input vector at that position. It incorporates relevant information from the context into the vector it produces as the output for that position.

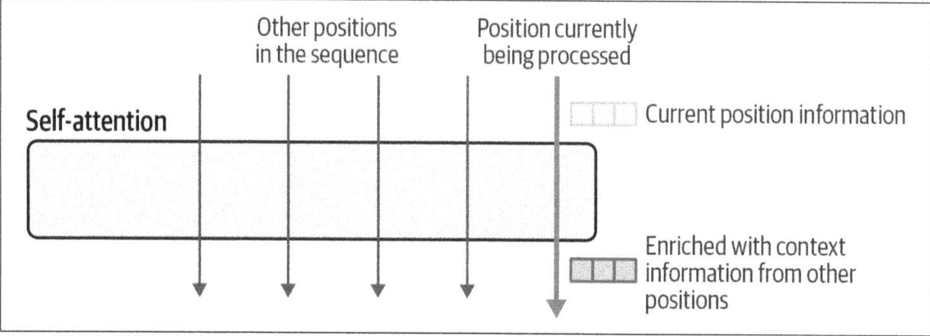

Figure 3-15. A simplified framing of attention: an input sequence and a current position being processed. As we're mainly concerned with this position, the figure shows an input vector and an output vector that incorporates information from the previous elements in the sequence according to the attention mechanism.

Two main steps are involved in the attention mechanism:

1. A way to score how relevant each of the previous input tokens are to the current token being processed (in the pink arrow).
2. Using those scores, we combine the information from the various positions into a single output vector.

Figure 3-16 shows these two steps.

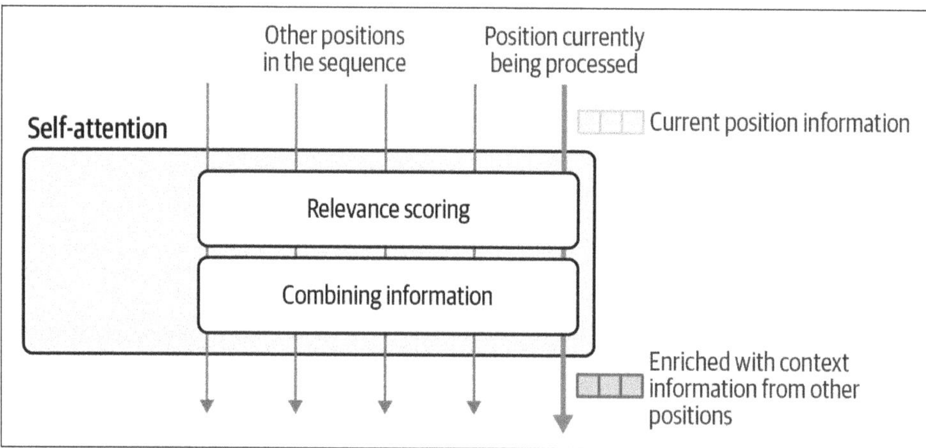

Figure 3-16. Attention is made up of two major steps: relevance scoring for each position, then a step where we combine the information based on those scores.

To give the Transformer more extensive attention capability, the attention mechanism is duplicated and executed multiple times in parallel. Each of these parallel applications of attention is conducted into an *attention head*. This increases the model's capacity to model complex patterns in the input sequence that require paying attention to different patterns at once.

Figure 3-17 shows the intuition of how attention heads run in parallel with a preceding step of splitting information and a later step of combining the results of all the heads.

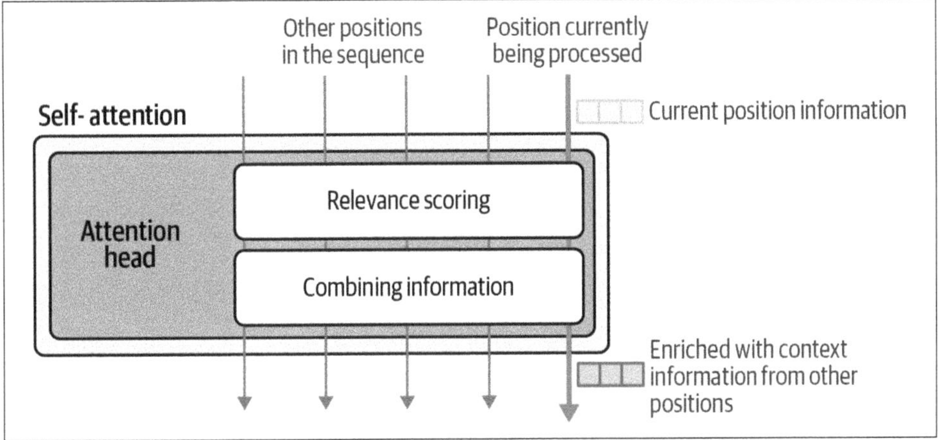

Figure 3-17. We get better LLMs by doing attention multiple times in parallel, increasing the model's capacity to attend to different types of information.

How attention is calculated

Let's look at how attention is calculated inside a single attention head. Before we start the calculation, let's observe the following as the starting position:

- The attention layer (of a generative LLM) is processing attention for a single position.
- The inputs to the layer are:
  - The vector representation of the current position or token
  - The vector representations of the previous tokens
- The goal is to produce a new representation of the current position that incorporates relevant information from the previous tokens:
  - For example, if we're processing the last position in the sentence "Sarah fed the cat because it," we want "it" to represent the cat—so attention bakes in "cat information" from the cat token.

- The training process produces three projection matrices that produce the components that interact in this calculation:
  - — A query projection matrix
  - — A key projection matrix
  - — A value projection matrix

Figure 3-18 shows the starting position for all of these components before the attention calculations start. For simplicity, let's look at only one attention head because the other heads have identical calculations but with their individual projection matrices.

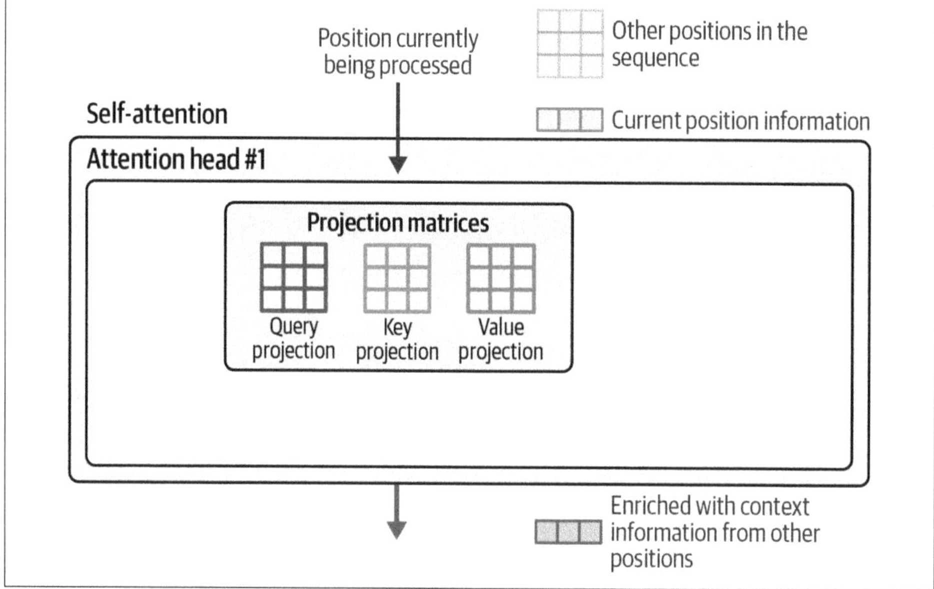

Figure 3-18. Before starting the self-attention calculation, we have the inputs to the layer and projection matrices for queries, keys, and values.

Attention starts by multiplying the inputs by the projection matrices to create three new matrices. These are called the queries, keys, and values matrices. These matrices contain the information of the input tokens projected to three different spaces that help carry out the two steps of attention:

1. Relevance scoring
2. Combining information

Figure 3-19 shows these three new matrices, and how the bottom row of all three matrices is associated with the current position while the rows above it are associated with the previous positions.

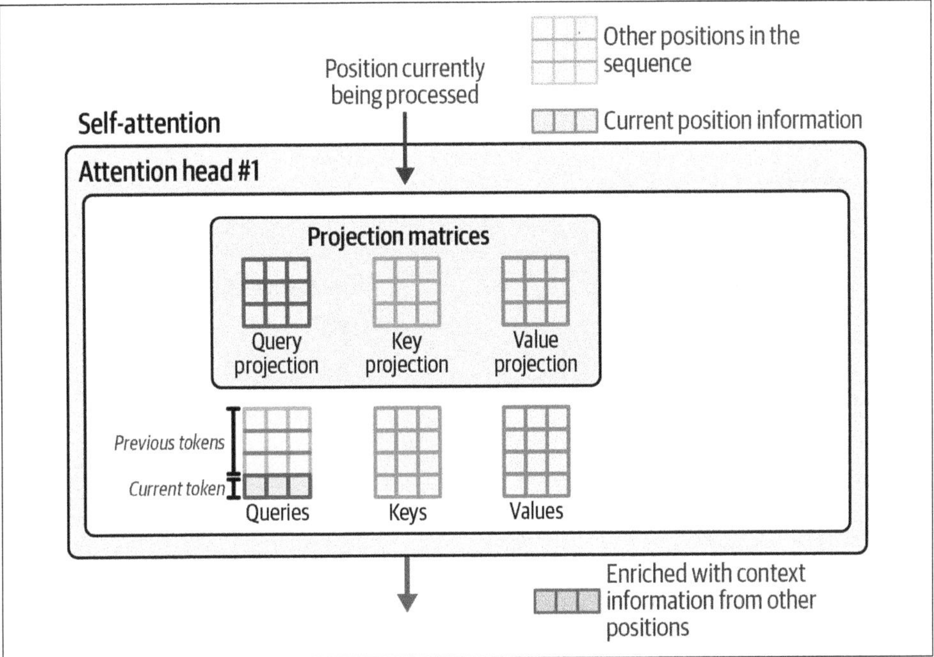

Figure 3-19. Attention is carried out by the interaction of the queries, keys, and values matrices. Those are produced by multiplying the layer's inputs with the projection matrices.

Self-attention: Relevance scoring

In a generative Transformer, we're generating one token at a time. This means we're processing one position at a time. So the attention mechanism here is only concerned with this one position, and how information from other positions can be pulled in to inform this position.

The relevance scoring step of attention is conducted by multiplying the query vector of the current position with the keys matrix. This produces a score stating how relevant each previous token is. Passing that by a softmax operation normalizes these scores so they sum up to 1. Figure 3-20 shows the relevance score resulting from this calculation.

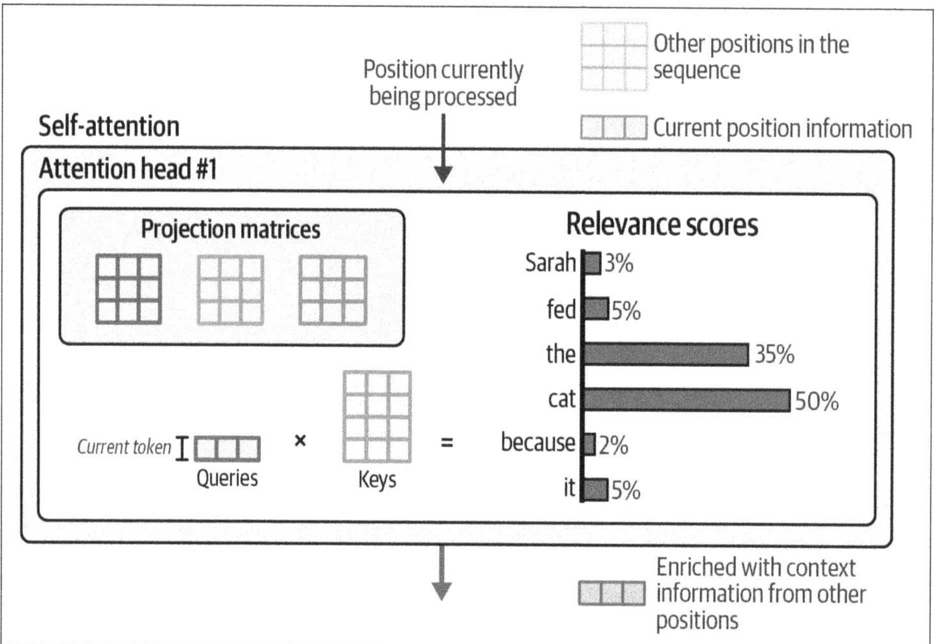

Figure 3-20. Scoring the relevance of previous tokens is accomplished by multiplying the query associated with the current position with the keys matrix.

Self-attention: Combining information

Now that we have the relevance scores, we multiply the value vector associated with each token by that token's score. Summing up those resulting vectors produces the output of this attention step, as we see in Figure 3-21.

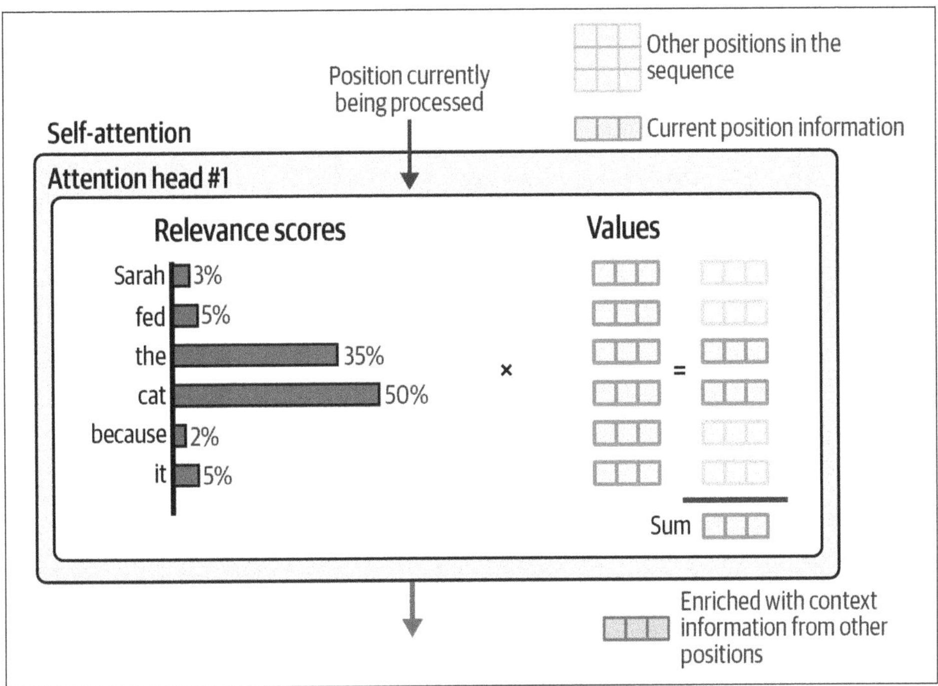

Figure 3-21. Attention combines the relevant information of previous positions by multiplying their relevance scores by their respective value vectors.

Recent Improvements to the Transformer Architecture

Since the release of the Transformer architecture, much work has been done to improve it and create better models. This spans training on larger datasets and optimizations for the training process and learning rates to use, but it also extends to the architecture itself. At the time of writing, a lot of the ideas of the original Transformer stand unchanged. There are a few architectural ideas that have proved to be valuable. They contribute to the performance of more recent Transformer models like Llama 2. In this final section of the chapter, we go over a number of the important recent developments of the Transformer architecture.

More Efficient Attention

The area that gets the most focus from the research community is the attention layer of the Transformer. This is because the attention calculation is the most computationally expensive part of the process.

Local/sparse attention

As Transformers started getting larger, ideas like sparse attention ("Generating long sequences with sparse transformers" (*https://oreil.ly/V1xqH*)) and sliding window attention ("Longformer: The long-document transformer" (*https://oreil.ly/uUKtU*)) provided improvements for the efficiency of the attention calculation. Sparse attention limits the context of previous tokens that the model can attend to, as we can see in Figure 3-22.

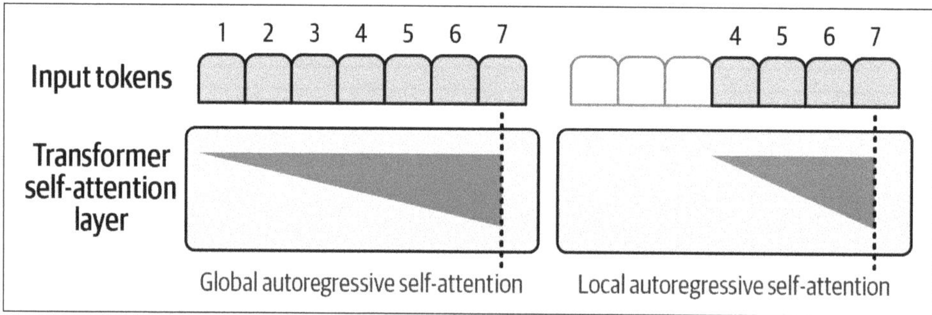

Figure 3-22. Local attention boosts performance by only paying attention to a small number of previous positions.

One model that incorporates such a mechanism is GPT-3. But it does not use that for all the Transformer blocks—the quality of the generation would vastly degrade if the model could only see a small number of previous tokens. The GPT-3 architecture interweaved full-attention and efficient-attention Transformer blocks. So the Transformer blocks alternate between full attention (e.g., blocks 1 and 3) and sparse attention (e.g., blocks 2 and 4).

To demonstrate different kinds of attention, review Figure 3-23, which shows how different attention mechanisms work. Each figure shows which previous tokens (light blue) can be attended to when processing the current token (in dark blue).

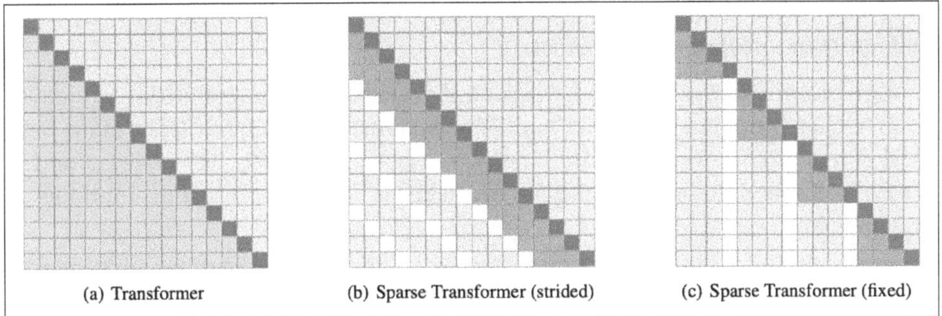

Figure 3-23. Full attention versus sparse attention. Figure 3-24 explains the coloring. (Source: "Generating long sequences with sparse transformers" (https://oreil.ly/0ap7A).)

Each row corresponds to a token being processed. The color coding indicates which tokens the model is able to pay attention to while it's processing the token in the dark blue cell. Figure 3-24 describes this with more clarity.

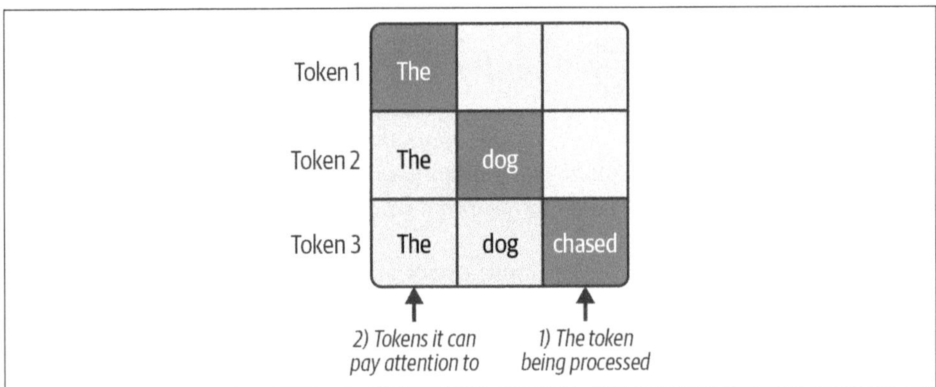

Figure 3-24. Attention figures show which token is being processed, and which previous tokens an attention mechanism allows it to attend to.

This figure also shows the autoregressive nature of decoder Transformer blocks (which make up most text generation models); they can only pay attention to previous tokens. Contrast this to BERT, which can pay attention to both sides (hence the B in BERT stands for bidirectional).

Multi-query and grouped-query attention

A more recent efficient attention tweak to the Transformer is grouped-query attention ("GQA: Training generalized multi-query transformer models from multi-head checkpoints" (*https://oreil.ly/gY2oF*)), which is used by models like Llama 2 and 3. Figure 3-25 shows these different types of attention, and the next section continues to explain them.

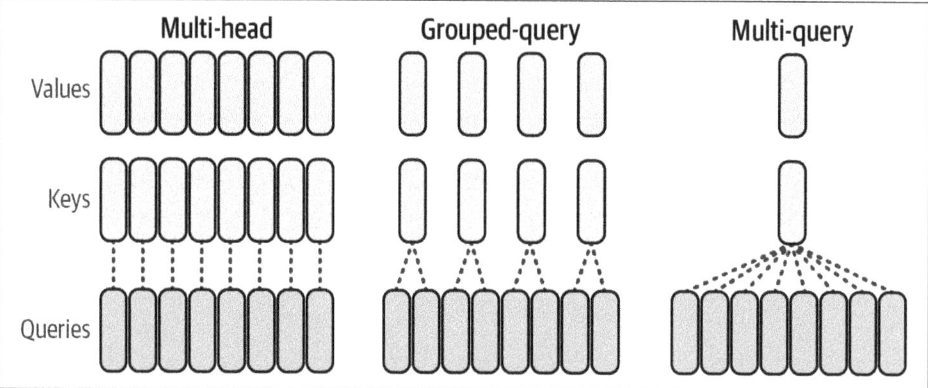

Figure 3-25. A comparison of different kinds of attention: the original multi-head, grouped-query attention, and multi-query attention (source: "Fast transformer decoding: One write-head is all you need" (https://oreil.ly/2mTiE)).

Grouped-query attention builds on multi-query attention ("Fast transformer decoding: One write-head is all you need" (*https://oreil.ly/jrZeM*)). These methods improve inference scalability of larger models by reducing the size of the matrices involved.

Optimizing attention: From multi-head to multi-query to grouped query

Earlier in the chapter we showed how the Transformer paper described multi-headed attention. The Illustrated Transformer (*https://oreil.ly/5dOd8*) discusses in detail how the queries, keys, and values matrices are used to conduct the attention operation. Figure 3-26 shows how each "attention head" has its own distinct query, key, and value matrices calculated for a given input.

The way that multi-query attention optimizes this is to share the keys and values matrices between all the heads. So the only unique matrices for each head would be the queries matrices, as we can see in Figure 3-27.

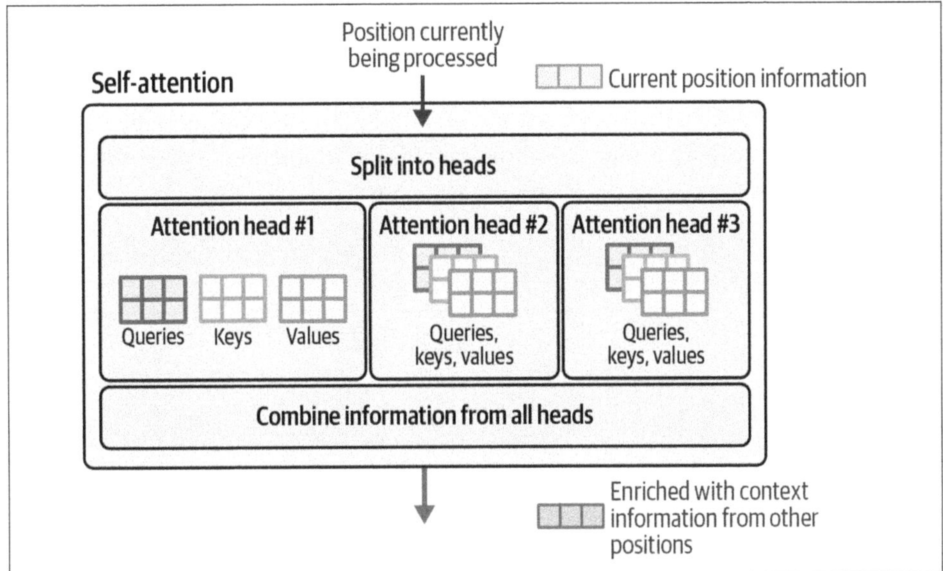

Figure 3-26. Attention is conducted using matrices of queries, keys, and values. In multi-head attention, each head has a distinct version of each of these matrices.

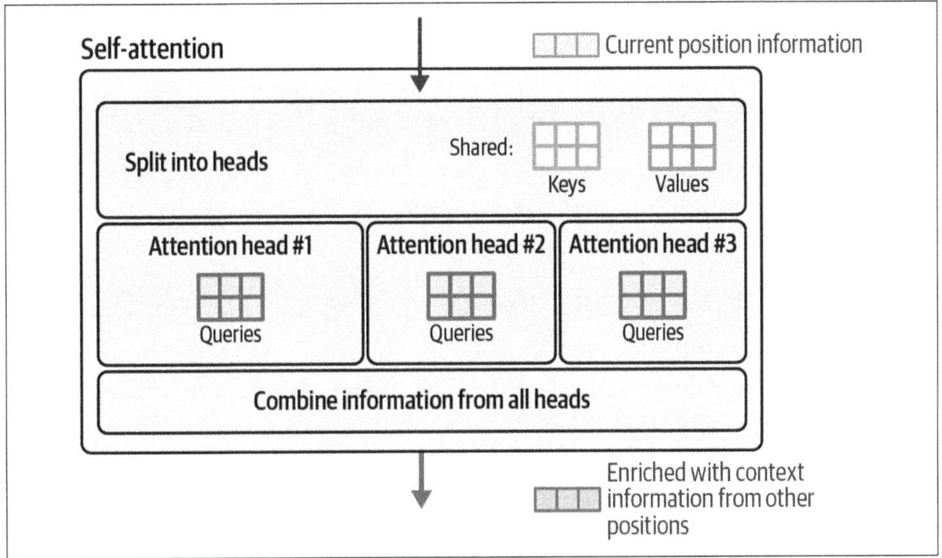

Figure 3-27. Multi-query attention presents a more efficient attention mechanism by sharing the keys and values matrices across all the attention heads.

As model sizes grow, however, this optimization can be too punishing and we can afford to use a little more memory to improve the quality of the models. This is where grouped-query attention comes in. Instead of cutting the number of keys and values matrices to one of each, it allows us to use more (but less than the number of heads). Figure 3-28 shows these groups and how each group of attention heads shares keys and values matrices.

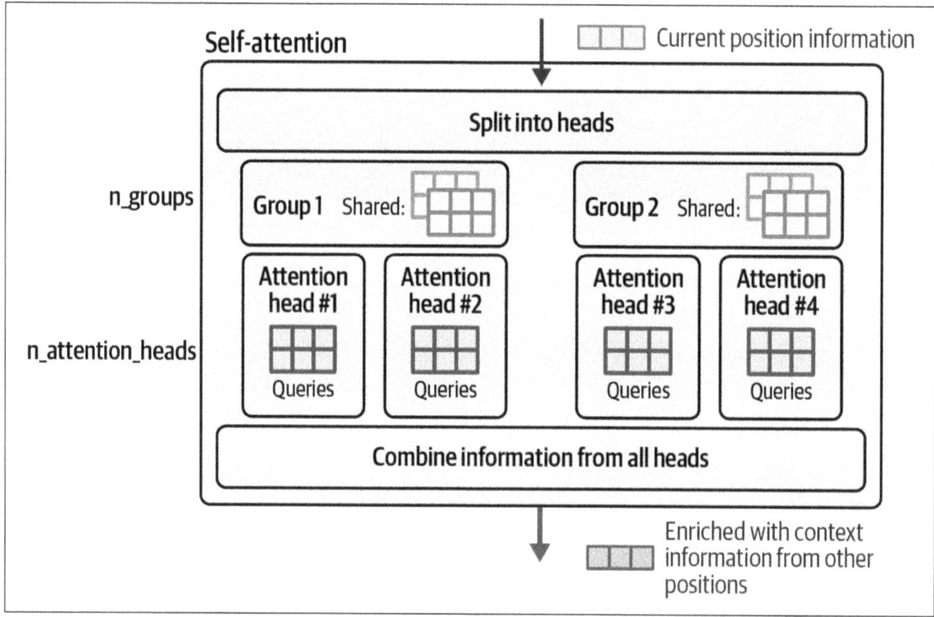

Figure 3-28. Grouped-query attention sacrifices a little bit of the efficiency of multi-query attention in return for a large improvement in quality by allowing multiple groups of shared key/value matrices; each group has its respective set of attention heads.

Flash Attention

Flash Attention is a popular method and implementation that provides significant speedups for both training and inference of Transformer LLMs on GPUs. It speeds up the attention calculation by optimizing what values are loaded and moved between a GPU's shared memory (SRAM) and high bandwidth memory (HBM). It is described in detail in the papers "FlashAttention: Fast and memory-efficient exact attention with IO-awareness" (*https://oreil.ly/r98GH*) and the subsequent "FlashAttention-2: Faster attention with better parallelism and work partitioning" (*https://oreil.ly/PkGg1*).

The Transformer Block

Recall that the two major components of a Transformer block are an attention layer and a feedforward neural network. A more detailed view of the block would also reveal the residual connections and layer-normalization operations that we can see in Figure 3-29.

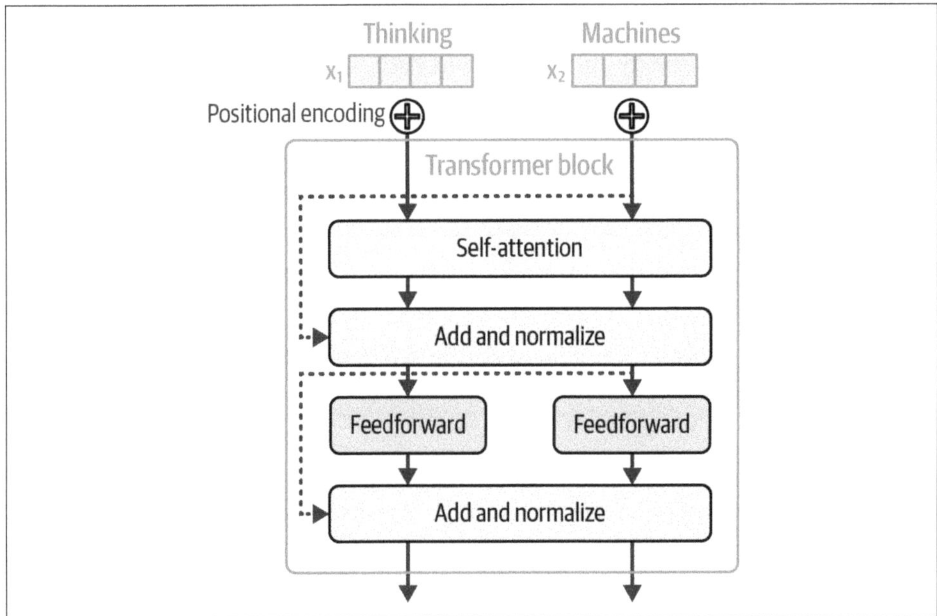

Figure 3-29. A Transformer block from the original Transformer paper.

The latest Transformer models at the time of this writing still retain the major components, yet make a number of tweaks as we can see in Figure 3-30.

One of the differences we see in this version of the Transformer block is that normalization happens prior to attention and the feedforward layers. This has been reported to reduce the required training time (read: "On layer normalization in the Transformer architecture" (*https://oreil.ly/uYkft*)). Another improvement in normalization here is using RMSNorm, which is simpler and more efficient than the LayerNorm used in the original Transformer (read: "Root mean square layer normalization" (*https://oreil.ly/GHLSM*)). Lastly, instead of the original Transformer's ReLU activation function, newer variants like SwiGLU (described in "GLU Variants Improve Transformer" (*https://oreil.ly/ikugL*)) are now more common.

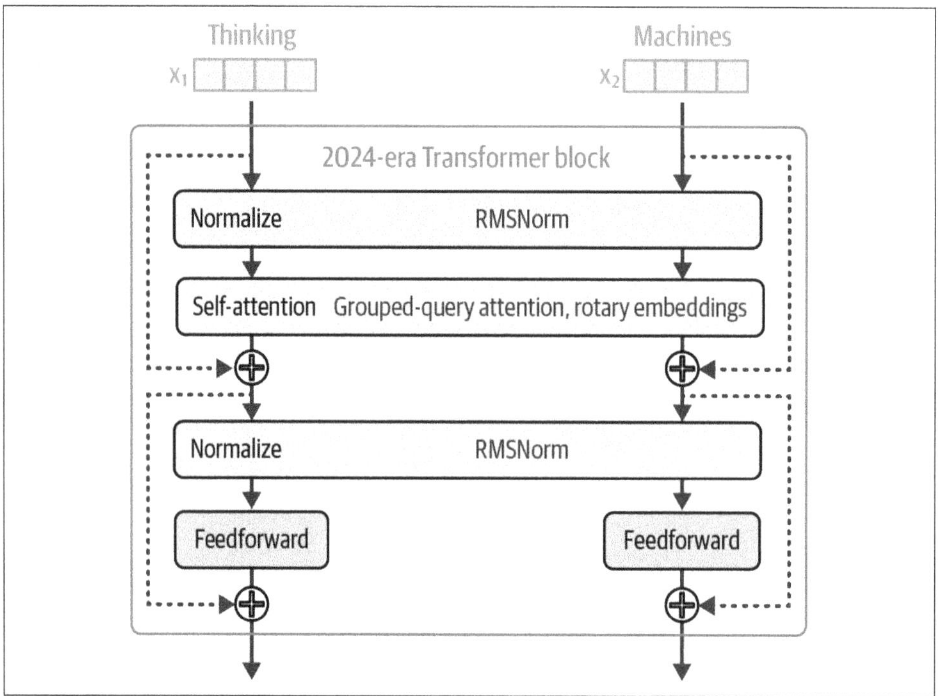

Figure 3-30. The Transformer block of a 2024-era Transformer like Llama 3 features some tweaks like pre-normalization and an attention optimized with grouped-query attention and rotary embeddings.

Positional Embeddings (RoPE)

Positional embeddings have been a key component since the original Transformer. They enable the model to keep track of the order of tokens/words in a sequence/sentence, which is an indispensable source of information in language. From the many positional encoding schemes proposed in the past years, rotary positional embeddings (or "RoPE," introduced in "RoFormer: Enhanced Transformer with rotary position embedding" (*https://oreil.ly/A5cEn*)) is especially important to point out.

The original Transformer paper and some of the early variants had absolute positional embeddings that, in essence, marked the first token as position 1, the second as position 2...etc. These could either be static methods (where the positional vectors are generated using geometric functions) or learned (where the model training assigns them their values during the learning process). Some challenges arise from such methods when we scale up models, which requires us to find ways to improve their efficiency.

For example, one challenge in efficiently training models with large context is that a lot of documents in the training set are much shorter than that context. It would be inefficient to allocate the entire, say, 4K context to a short 10-word sentence. So during model training, documents are packed together into each context in the training batch, as Figure 3-31 shows.

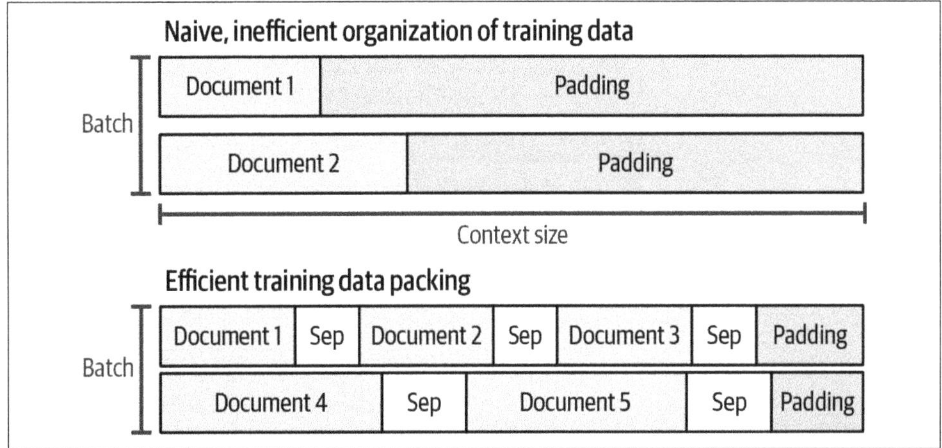

Figure 3-31. Packing is the process of efficiently organizing short training documents into the context. It includes grouping multiple documents in a single context while minimizing the padding at the end of the context.

Learn more about packing by reading "Efficient sequence packing without cross-contamination: Accelerating large language models without impacting performance" (*https://oreil.ly/Zgiy0*) and watching the great visuals in "Introducing packed BERT for 2X training speed-up in natural language processing" (*https://oreil.ly/xMbZr*).

Positional embedding methods have to adapt to this and other practical considerations. If Document 50, for example, starts at position 50, then we'd be misinforming the model if we tell it that that first token is number 50 and that would affect its performance (because it would assume there's previous context while in reality the earlier tokens belong to a different and unrelated document the model should ignore).

Instead of the static, absolute embeddings that are added in the beginning of the forward pass, rotary embeddings are a method to encode positional information in a way that captures absolute and relative token position information. It is based on the idea of rotating vectors in their embeddings space. In the forward pass, they are added in the attention step, as Figure 3-32 shows.

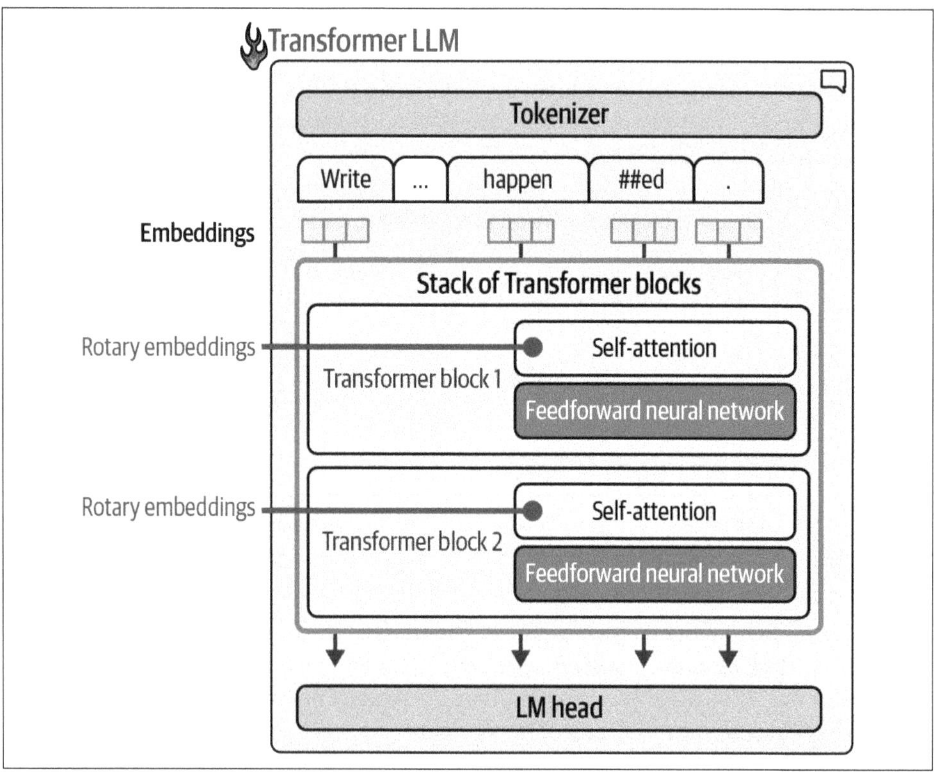

Figure 3-32. Rotary embeddings are applied in the attention step, not at the start of the forward pass.

During the attention process, the positional information is mixed in specifically to the queries and keys matrices just before we multiply them for relevance scoring, as we can see in Figure 3-33.

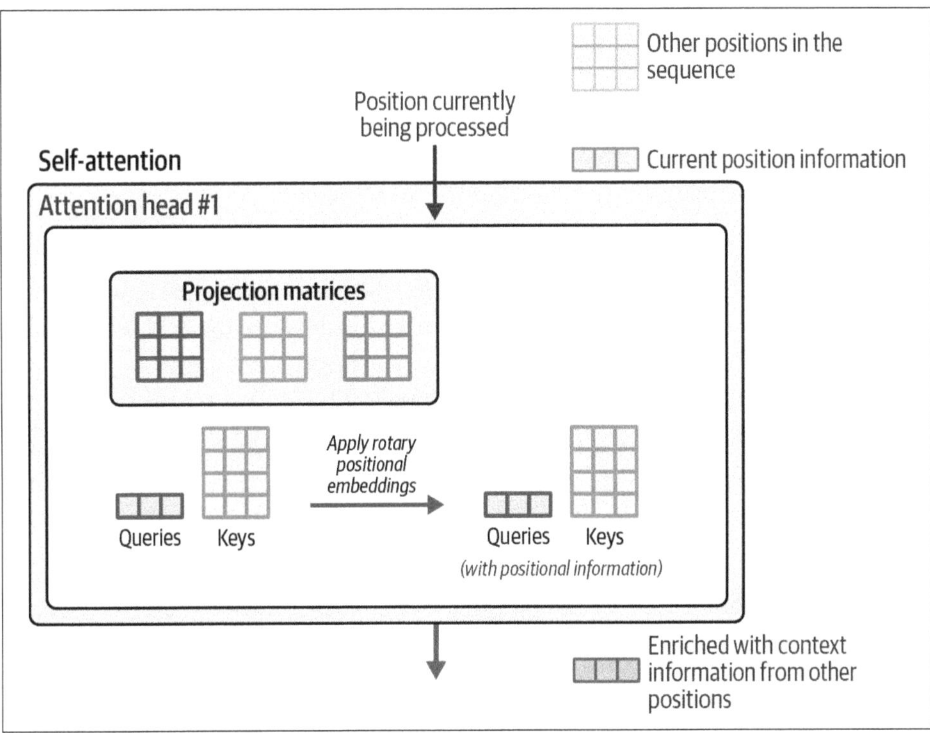

Figure 3-33. Rotary positional embeddings are added to the representation of tokens just before the relevance scoring step in self-attention.

Other Architectural Experiments and Improvements

Many tweaks of the Transformer are proposed and researched on a continuous basis. "A Survey of Transformers" (*https://oreil.ly/3SrG4*) highlights a few of the main directions. Transformer architectures are also constantly adapted to domains beyond LLMs. Computer vision is an area where a lot of Transformer architecture research is happening (see: "Transformers in vision: A survey" (*https://oreil.ly/35CES*) and "A survey on vision transformer" (*https://oreil.ly/0zEbq*)). Other domains include robotics (see "Open X-Embodiment: Robotic learning datasets and RT-X models" (*https://oreil.ly/SXAuB*)) and time series (see "Transformers in time series: A survey" (*https://oreil.ly/p9duV*)).

Summary

In this chapter we discussed the main intuitions of Transformers and recent developments that enable the latest Transformer LLMs. We went over many new concepts, so let's break down the key concepts that we discussed in this chapter:

- A Transformer LLM generates *one token at a time.*
- That output token is *appended to the prompt*, then this updated prompt is presented to the model again for another forward pass to generate the next token.
- The *three major components* of the Transformer LLM are the tokenizer, a stack of Transformer blocks, and a language modeling head.
- The tokenizer contains the *token vocabulary* for the model. The model has *token embeddings* associated with those tokens. Breaking the text into tokens and then using the embeddings of these tokens is the first step in the token generation process.
- The forward pass flows through all the stages once, *one by one.*
- Near the end of the process, the LM head scores the *probabilities of the next possible token.* Decoding strategies inform which actual token to pick as the output for this generation step (sometimes it's the most probable next token, but not always).
- One reason the Transformer excels is its ability to process tokens in parallel. Each of the input tokens flow into their *individual tracks or streams of processing.* The number of streams is the model's "context size" and this represents the max number of tokens the model can operate on.
- Because Transformer LLMs loop to generate the text one token at a time, it's a good idea to *cache* the processing results of each step so we don't duplicate the processing effort (these results are stored as various matrices within the layers).
- The majority of processing happens within *Transformer blocks.* These are made up of two components. One of them is the *feedforward neural network,* which is able to store information and make predictions and interpolations from data it was trained on.
- The second major component of a Transformer block is the *attention* layer. Attention incorporates contextual information to allow the model to better capture the nuance of language.
- Attention happens in two major steps: (1) scoring relevance and (2) combining information.

- A Transformer attention layer conducts several attention operations in parallel, each occurring inside an *attention head*, and their outputs are aggregated to make up the output of the attention layer.
- Attention can be accelerated via sharing the keys and values matrices between all heads, or groups of heads (*grouped-query attention*).
- Methods like *Flash Attention* speed up the attention calculation by optimizing how the operation is done on the different memory systems of a GPU.

Transformers continue to see new developments and proposed tweaks to improve them in different scenarios, including language models and other domains and applications.

In Part II of the book, we will cover some of these practical applications of LLMs. In Chapter 4, we start with text classification, a common task in Language AI. This next chapter serves as an introduction to applying both generative and representation models.

PART II

Using Pretrained Language Models

CHAPTER 4

Text Classification

A common task in natural language processing is classification. The goal of the task is to train a model to assign a label or class to some input text (see Figure 4-1). Classifying text is used across the world for a wide range of applications, from sentiment analysis and intent detection to extracting entities and detecting language. The impact of language models, both representative and generative, on classification cannot be understated.

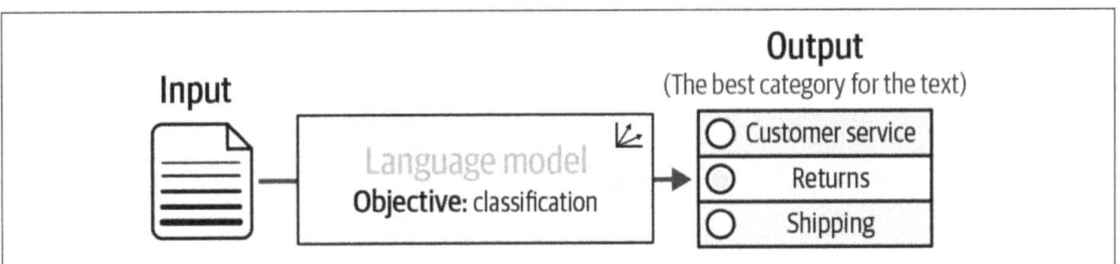

Figure 4-1. Using a language model to classify text.

In this chapter, we will discuss several ways to use language models for classifying text. It will serve as an accessible introduction to using language models that already have been trained. Due to the broad field of text classification, we will discuss several techniques and use them to explore the field of language models:

- "Text Classification with Representation Models" on page 113 demonstrates the flexibility of nongenerative models for classification. We will cover both task-specific models and embedding models.
- "Text Classification with Generative Models" on page 127 is an introduction to generative language models as most of them can be used for classification. We will cover both an open source as well as a closed source language model.

In this chapter, we will focus on leveraging pretrained language models, models that already have been trained on large amounts of data that can be used for classifying text. As illustrated in Figure 4-2, we will examine both representation and language models and explore their differences.

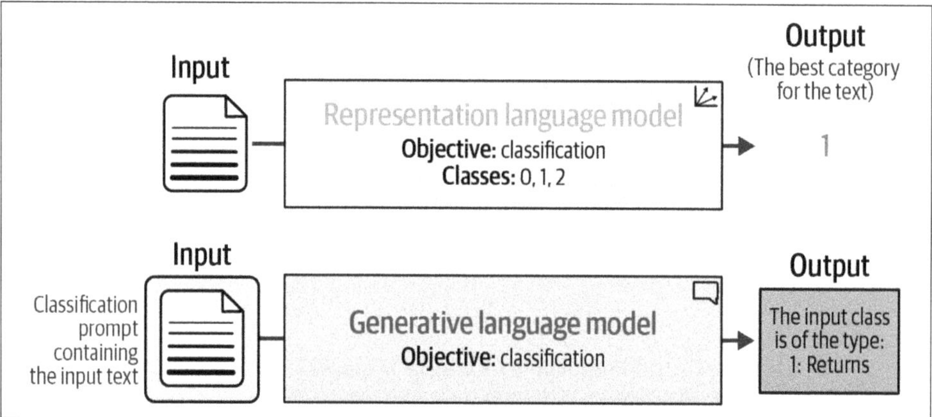

Figure 4-2. Although both representation and generative models can be used for classification, their approaches differ.

This chapter serves as an introduction to a variety of language models, both generative and nongenerative. We will encounter common packages for loading and using these models.

Although this book focuses on LLMs, it is highly advised to compare these examples against classic, but strong baselines such as representing text with TF-IDF and training a logistic regression classifier on top of that.

The Sentiment of Movie Reviews

You can find the data we use to explore techniques for classifying text on the Hugging Face Hub, a platform for hosting models but also data (*https://oreil.ly/ndroe*). We will use the well-known "rotten_tomatoes" dataset (*https://oreil.ly/44-1y*) to train and evaluate our models.[1] It contains 5,331 positive and 5,331 negative movie reviews from Rotten Tomatoes.

To load this data, we make use of the `datasets` package, which will be used throughout the book:

1 Bo Pang and Lillian Lee. "Seeing stars: Exploiting class relationships for sentiment categorization with respect to rating scales." *arXiv preprint cs/0506075* (2005).

```
from datasets import load_dataset

# Load our data
data = load_dataset("rotten_tomatoes")
data
```

```
DatasetDict({
    train: Dataset({
        features: ['text', 'label'],
        num_rows: 8530
    })
    validation: Dataset({
        features: ['text', 'label'],
        num_rows: 1066
    })
    test: Dataset({
        features: ['text', 'label'],
        num_rows: 1066
    })
})
```

The data is split up into *train*, *test*, and *validation* splits. Throughout this chapter, we will use the train split when we train a model and the test split for validating the results. Note that the additional validation split can be used to further validate generalization if you used the train and test splits to perform hyperparameter tuning.

Let's take a look at some examples in our train split:

```
data["train"][0, -1]
```

```
{'text': ['the rock is destined to be the 21st century\'s new " conan " and
that he\'s going to make a splash even greater than arnold schwarzenegger ,
jean-claud van damme or steven segal .',
  'things really get weird , though not particularly scary : the movie is all
portent and no content .'],
  'label': [1, 0]}
```

These short reviews are either labeled as positive (1) or negative (0). This means that we will focus on binary sentiment classification.

Text Classification with Representation Models

Classification with pretrained representation models generally comes in two flavors, either using a task-specific model or an embedding model. As we explored in the previous chapter, these models are created by fine-tuning a foundation model, like BERT, on a specific downstream task as illustrated in Figure 4-3.

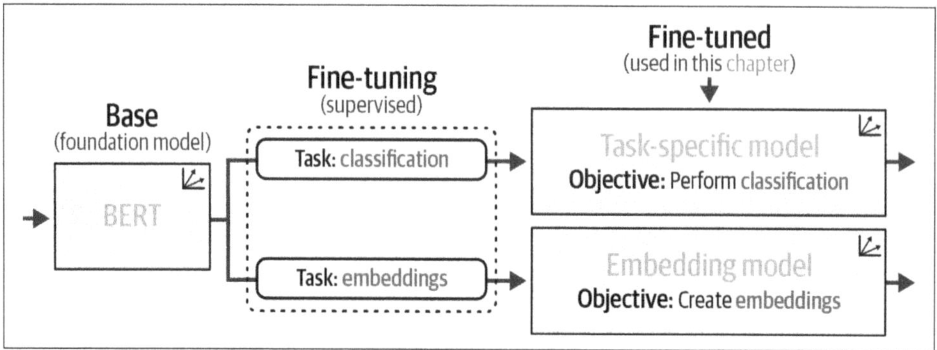

Figure 4-3. A foundation model is fine-tuned for specific tasks; for instance, to perform classification or generate general-purpose embeddings.

A task-specific model is a representation model, such as BERT, trained for a specific task, like sentiment analysis. As we explored in Chapter 1, an embedding model generates general-purpose embeddings that can be used for a variety of tasks not limited to classification, like semantic search (see Chapter 8).

The process of fine-tuning a BERT model for classification is covered in Chapter 11 while creating an embedding model is covered in Chapter 10. In this chapter, we keep both models *frozen* (nontrainable) and only use their output as shown in Figure 4-4.

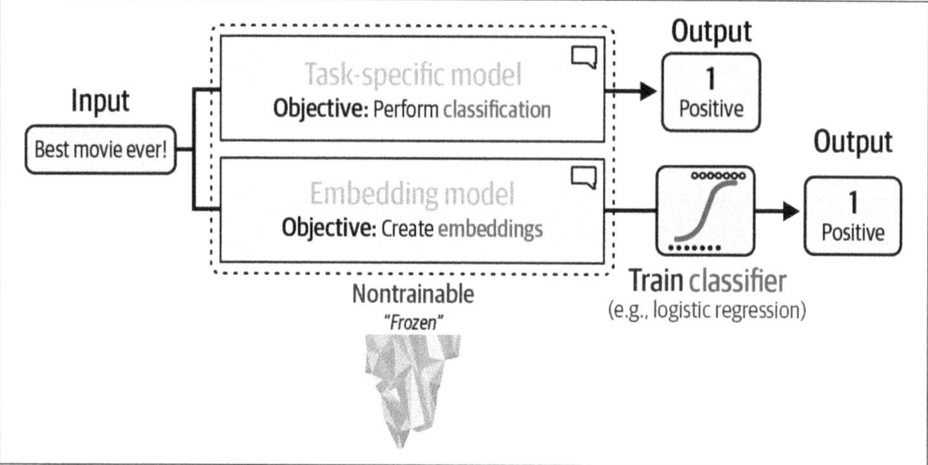

Figure 4-4. Perform classification directly with a task-specific model or indirectly with general-purpose embeddings.

We will leverage pretrained models that others have already fine-tuned for us and explore how they can be used to classify our selected movie reviews.

Model Selection

Choosing the right models is not as straightforward as you might think with over 60,000 models on the Hugging Face Hub for text classification (*https://oreil.ly/IPWTY*) and more than 8,000 models that generate embeddings (*https://oreil.ly/yviVH*) at the moment of writing. Moreover, it's crucial to select a model that fits your use case and consider its language compatibility, the underlying architecture, size, and performance.

Let's start with the underlying architecture. As we explored in Chapter 1, BERT, a well-known encoder-only architecture, is a popular choice for creating task-specific and embedding models. While generative models, like the GPT family, are incredible models, encoder-only models similarly excel in task-specific use cases and tend to be significantly smaller in size.

Over the years, many variations of BERT have been developed, including RoBERTa,[2] DistilBERT,[3] ALBERT,[4] and DeBERTa,[5] each trained in various contexts. You can find an overview of some well-known BERT-like models in Figure 4-5.

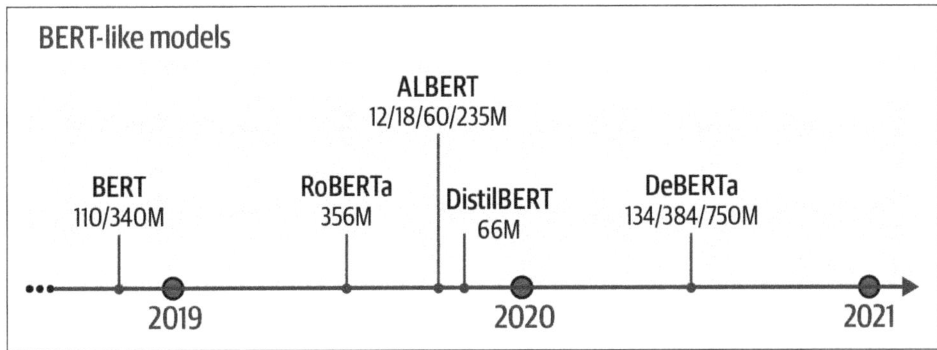

Figure 4-5. A timeline of common BERT-like model releases. These are considered foundation models and are mostly intended to be fine-tuned on a downstream task.

Selecting the right model for the job can be a form of art in itself. Trying thousands of pretrained models that can be found on Hugging Face's Hub is not feasible so we

2 Yinhan Liuet et al. "RoBERTa: A robustly optimized BERT pretraining approach." *arXiv preprint arXiv:1907.11692* (2019).

3 Victor Sanh et al. "DistilBERT, a distilled version of BERT: smaller, faster, cheaper and lighter." *arXiv preprint arXiv:1910.01108* (2019).

4 Zhenzhong Lan et al. "ALBERT: A lite BERT for self-supervised learning of language representations." *arXiv preprint arXiv:1909.11942* (2019).

5 Pengcheng He et al. "DeBERTa: Decoding-enhanced BERT with disentangled attention." *arXiv preprint arXiv:2006.03654* (2020).

need to be efficient with the models that we choose. Having said that, several models are great starting points and give you an idea of the base performance of these kinds of models. Consider them solid baselines:

- BERT base model (uncased) (*https://oreil.ly/nq_GM*)
- RoBERTa base model (*https://oreil.ly/rz4dQ*)
- DistilBERT base model (uncased) (*https://oreil.ly/ieLs3*)
- DeBERTa base model (*https://oreil.ly/wN8yl*)
- bert-tiny (*https://oreil.ly/HLRPn*)
- ALBERT base v2 (*https://oreil.ly/Mw93z*)

For the task-specific model, we are choosing the Twitter-RoBERTa-base for Sentiment Analysis (*https://oreil.ly/HmvFk*) model. This is a RoBERTa model fine-tuned on tweets for sentiment analysis. Although this was not trained specifically for movie reviews, it is interesting to explore how this model generalizes.

When selecting models to generate embeddings from, the MTEB leaderboard (*https://oreil.ly/mUVXD*) is a great place to start. It contains open and closed source models benchmarked across several tasks. Make sure to not only take performance into account. The importance of inference speed should not be underestimated in real-life solutions. As such, we will use sentence-transformers/all-mpnet-base-v2 (*https://oreil.ly/3pozB*) as the embedding throughout this section. It is a small but performant model.

Using a Task-Specific Model

Now that we have selected our task-specific representation model, let's start by loading our model:

```
from transformers import pipeline

# Path to our HF model
model_path = "cardiffnlp/twitter-roberta-base-sentiment-latest"

# Load model into pipeline
pipe = pipeline(
    model=model_path,
    tokenizer=model_path,
    return_all_scores=True,
    device="cuda:0"
)
```

As we load our model, we also load the *tokenizer*, which is responsible for converting input text into individual tokens, as illustrated in Figure 4-6. Although that parameter is not needed as it is loaded automatically, it illustrates what is happening under the hood.

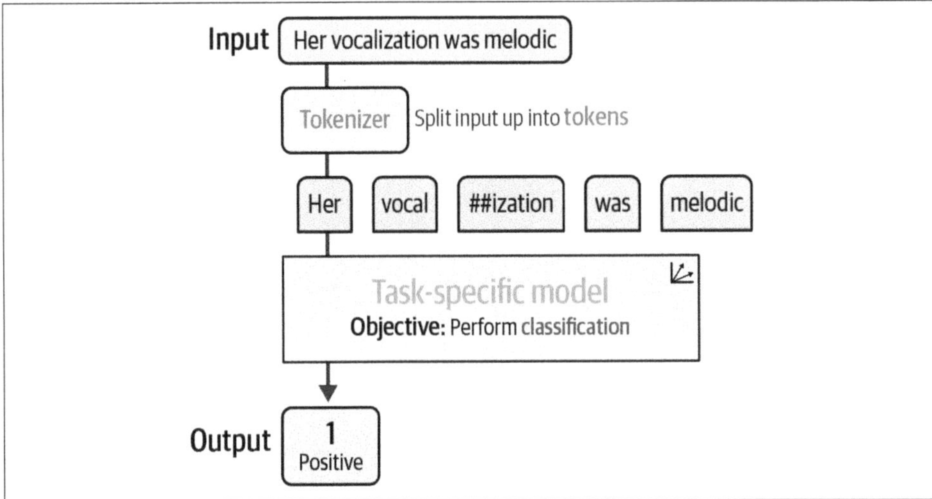

Figure 4-6. An input sentence is first fed to a tokenizer before it can be processed by the task-specific model.

These tokens are at the core of most language models, as explored in depth in Chapter 2. A major benefit of these tokens is that they can be combined to generate representations even if they were not in the training data, as shown in Figure 4-7.

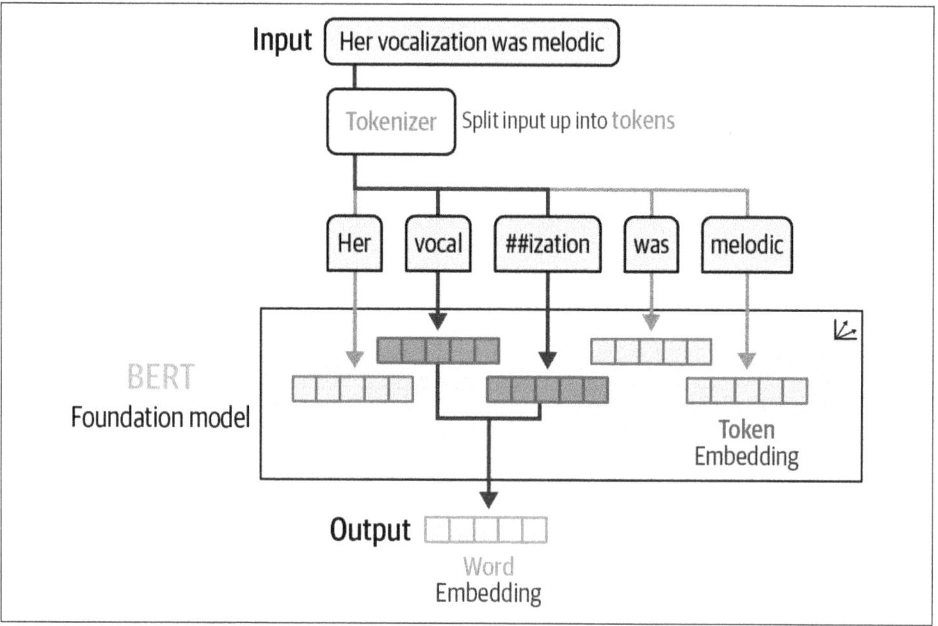

Figure 4-7. By breaking down an unknown word into tokens, word embeddings can still be generated.

After loading all the necessary components, we can go ahead and use our model on the test split of our data:

```
import        as
from      import tqdm
from                                  import KeyDataset

# Run inference
y_pred = []
for output in tqdm(pipe(KeyDataset(data["test"], "text")),
total=len(data["test"])):
    negative_score = output[0]["score"]
    positive_score = output[2]["score"]
    assignment = np.argmax([negative_score, positive_score])
    y_pred.append(assignment)
```

Now that we have generated our predictions, all that is left is evaluation. We create a small function that we can easily use throughout this chapter:

```
from                 import classification_report

def evaluate_performance(y_true, y_pred):
    """Create and print the classification report"""
    performance = classification_report(
        y_true, y_pred,
        target_names=["Negative Review", "Positive Review"]
```

```
)
print(performance)
```

Next, let's create our classification report:

```
evaluate_performance(data["test"]["label"], y_pred)
```

```
                 precision    recall  f1-score   support

Negative Review       0.76      0.88      0.81       533
Positive Review       0.86      0.72      0.78       533

       accuracy                           0.80      1066
      macro avg       0.81      0.80      0.80      1066
   weighted avg       0.81      0.80      0.80      1066
```

To read the resulting classification report, let's first start by exploring how we can identify correct and incorrect predictions. There are four combinations depending on whether we predict something correctly (True) versus incorrectly (False) and whether we predict the correct class (Positive) versus incorrect class (Negative). We can illustrate these combinations as a matrix, commonly referred to as a *confusion matrix*, in Figure 4-8.

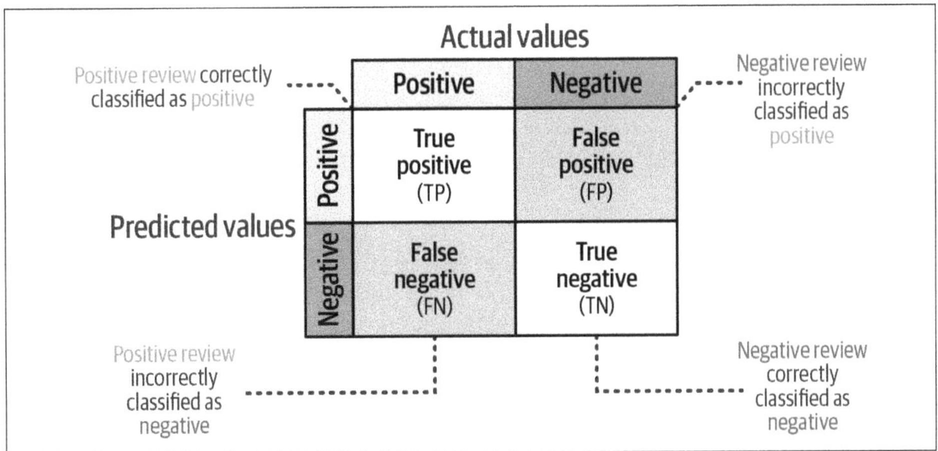

Figure 4-8. The confusion matrix describes four types of predictions we can make.

Using the confusion matrix, we can derive several formulas to describe the quality of the model. In the previously generated classification report we can see four such methods, namely *precision*, *recall*, *accuracy*, and the *F1 score:*

- *Precision* measures how many of the items found are relevant, which indicates the accuracy of the relevant results.
- *Recall* refers to how many relevant classes were found, which indicates its ability to find all relevant results.

- *Accuracy* refers to how many correct predictions the model makes out of all predictions, which indicates the overall correctness of the model.
- The *F1 score* balances both precision and recall to create a model's overall performance.

These four metrics are illustrated in Figure 4-9, which describes them using the aforementioned classification report.

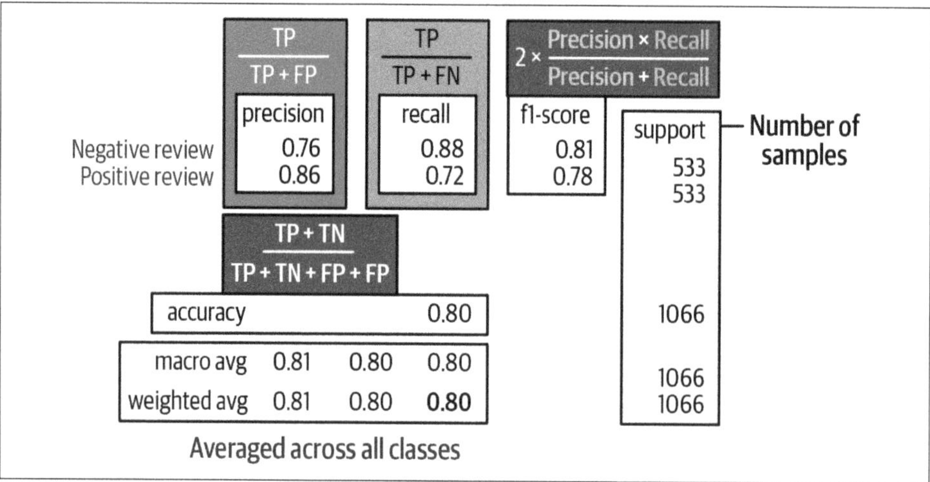

Figure 4-9. The classification report describes several metrics for evaluating a model's performance.

We will consider the weighted average of the F1 score throughout the examples in this book to make sure each class is treated equally. Our pretrained BERT model gives us an F1 score of 0.80 (we are reading this from the *weighted avg* row and the *f1-score* column), which is great for a model not trained specifically on our domain data!

To improve the performance of our selected model, we could do a few different things including selecting a model trained on our domain data, movie reviews in this case, like DistilBERT base uncased finetuned SST-2 (*https://oreil.ly/7-zVj*). We could also shift our focus to another flavor of representation models, namely embedding models.

Classification Tasks That Leverage Embeddings

In the previous example, we used a pretrained task-specific model for sentiment analysis. However, what if we cannot find a model that was pretrained for this specific task? Do we need to fine-tune a representation model ourselves? The answer is no!

There might be times when you want to fine-tune the model yourself if you have sufficient computing available (see Chapter 11). However, not everyone has access to extensive computing. This is where general-purpose embedding models come in.

Supervised Classification

Unlike the previous example, we can perform part of the training process ourselves by approaching it from a more classical perspective. Instead of directly using the representation model for classification, we will use an embedding model for generating features. Those features can then be fed into a classifier, thereby creating a two-step approach as shown in Figure 4-10.

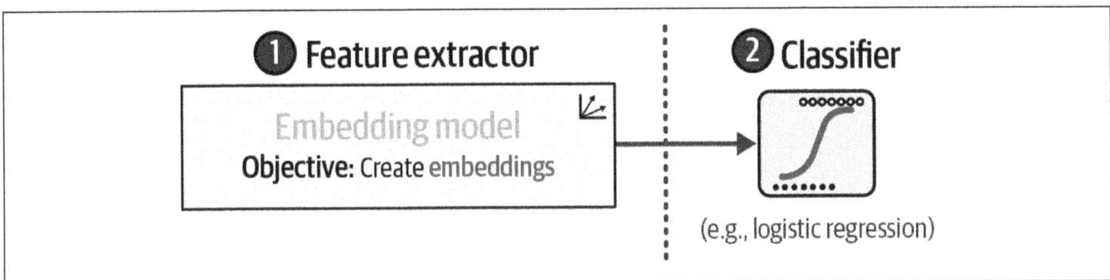

Figure 4-10. The feature extraction step and classification steps are separated.

A major benefit of this separation is that we do not need to fine-tune our embedding model, which can be costly. In contrast, we can train a classifier, like a logistic regression, on the CPU instead.

In the first step, we convert our textual input to embeddings using the embedding model as shown in Figure 4-11. Note that this model is similarly kept *frozen* and is not updated during the training process.

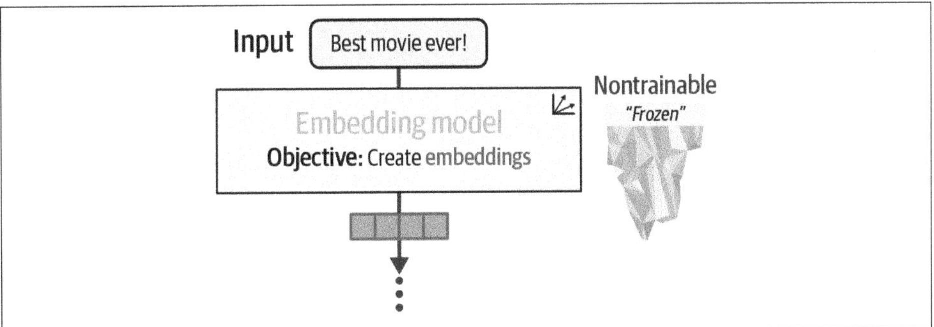

Figure 4-11. In step 1, we use the embedding model to extract the features and convert the input text to embeddings.

We can perform this step with `sentence-transformer`, a popular package for leveraging pretrained embedding models.[6] Creating the embeddings is straightforward:

```
from sentence_transformers import SentenceTransformer

# Load model
model = SentenceTransformer("sentence-transformers/all-mpnet-base-v2")

# Convert text to embeddings
train_embeddings = model.encode(data["train"]["text"], show_progress_bar=True)
test_embeddings = model.encode(data["test"]["text"], show_progress_bar=True)
```

As we covered in Chapter 1, these embeddings are numerical representations of the input text. The number of values, or dimension, of the embedding depends on the underlying embedding model. Let's explore that for our model:

```
train_embeddings.shape
```

```
(8530, 768)
```

This shows that each of our 8,530 input documents has an embedding dimension of 768 and therefore each embedding contains 768 numerical values.

In the second step, these embeddings serve as the input features to the classifier illustrated in Figure 4-12. The classifier is trainable and not limited to logistic regression and can take on any form as long as it performs classification.

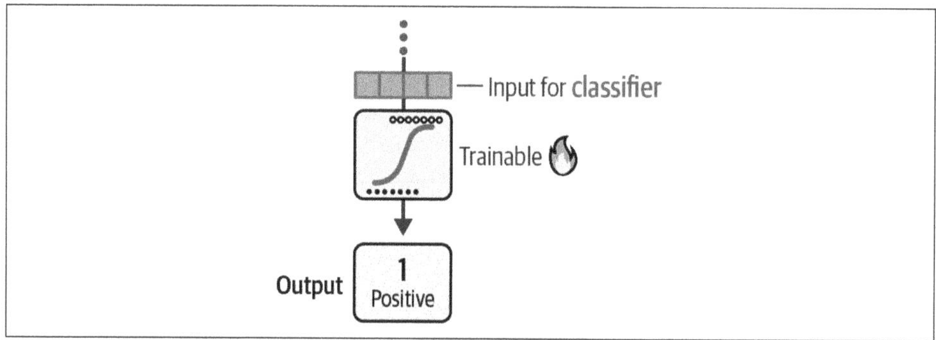

Figure 4-12. Using the embeddings as our features, we train a logistic regression model on our training data.

We will keep this step straightforward and use a logistic regression as the classifier. To train it, we only need to use the generated embeddings together with our labels:

6 Nils Reimers and Iryna Gurevych. "Sentence-BERT: Sentence embeddings using Siamese BERT-networks." *arXiv preprint arXiv:1908.10084* (2019).

```
from sklearn.linear_model import LogisticRegression

# Train a logistic regression on our train embeddings
clf = LogisticRegression(random_state=42)
clf.fit(train_embeddings, data["train"]["label"])
```

Next, let's evaluate our model:

```
# Predict previously unseen instances
y_pred = clf.predict(test_embeddings)
evaluate_performance(data["test"]["label"], y_pred)
```

```
                 precision    recall  f1-score   support

Negative Review       0.85      0.86      0.85       533
Positive Review       0.86      0.85      0.85       533

       accuracy                           0.85      1066
      macro avg       0.85      0.85      0.85      1066
   weighted avg       0.85      0.85      0.85      1066
```

By training a classifier on top of our embeddings, we managed to get an F1 score of 0.85! This demonstrates the possibilities of training a lightweight classifier while keeping the underlying embedding model frozen.

In this example, we used `sentence-transformers` to extract our embeddings, which benefits from a GPU to speed up inference. However, we can remove this GPU dependency by using an external API to create the embeddings. Popular choices for generating embeddings are Cohere's and OpenAI's offerings. As a result, this would allow the pipeline to run entirely on the CPU.

What If We Do Not Have Labeled Data?

In our previous example, we had labeled data that we could leverage, but this might not always be the case in practice. Getting labeled data is a resource-intensive task that can require significant human labor. Moreover, is it actually worthwhile to collect these labels?

To test this, we can perform zero-shot classification, where we have no labeled data to explore whether the task seems feasible. Although we know the definition of the labels (their names), we do not have labeled data to support them. Zero-shot classification attempts to predict the labels of input text even though it was not trained on them, as shown in Figure 4-13.

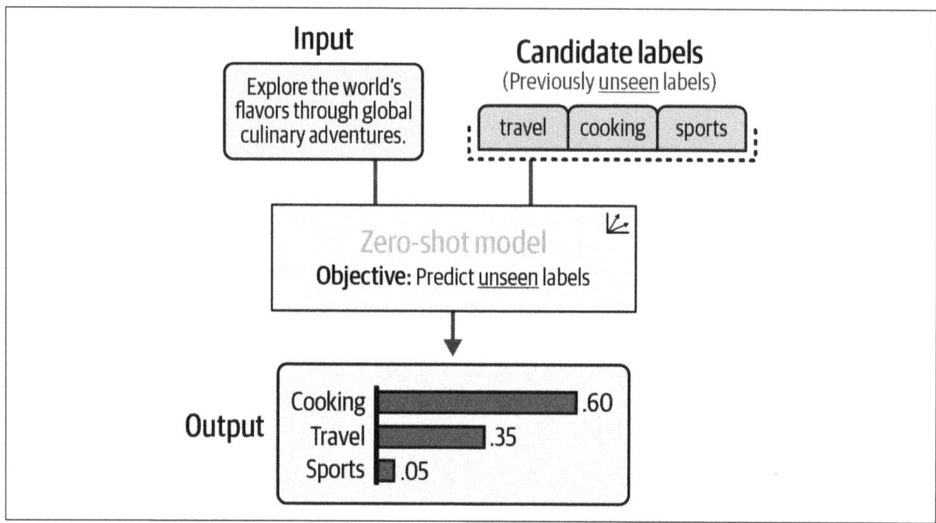

Figure 4-13. In zero-shot classification, we have no labeled data, only the labels themselves. The zero-shot model decides how the input is related to the candidate labels.

To perform zero-shot classification with embeddings, there is a neat trick that we can use. We can describe our labels based on what they should represent. For example, a negative label for movie reviews can be described as "This is a negative movie review." By describing and embedding the labels and documents, we have data that we can work with. This process, as illustrated in Figure 4-14, allows us to generate our own target labels without the need to actually have any labeled data.

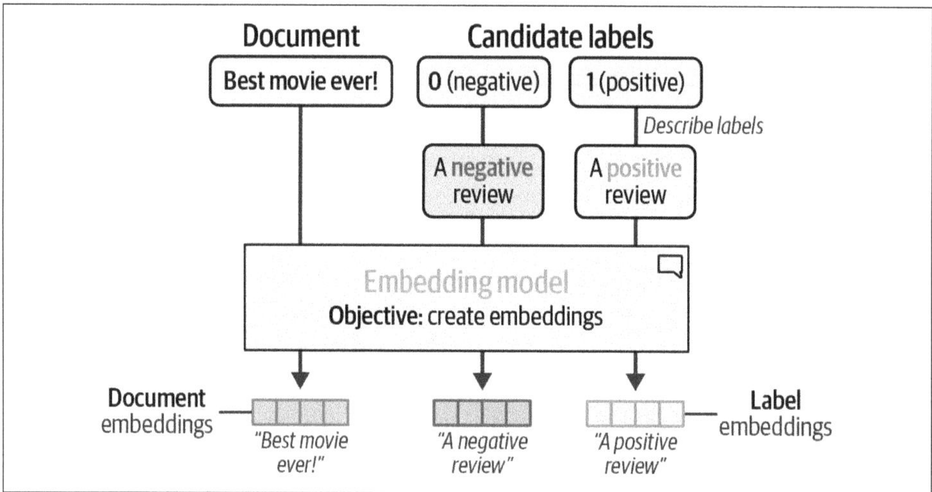

Figure 4-14. To embed the labels, we first need to give them a description, such as "a negative movie review." This can then be embedded through sentence-transformers.

We can create these label embeddings using the `.encode` function as we did earlier:

```
# Create embeddings for our labels
label_embeddings = model.encode(["A negative review",  "A positive review"])
```

To assign labels to documents, we can apply cosine similarity to the document label pairs. This is the cosine of the angle between vectors, which is calculated through the dot product of the embeddings and divided by the product of their lengths, as illustrated in Figure 4-15.

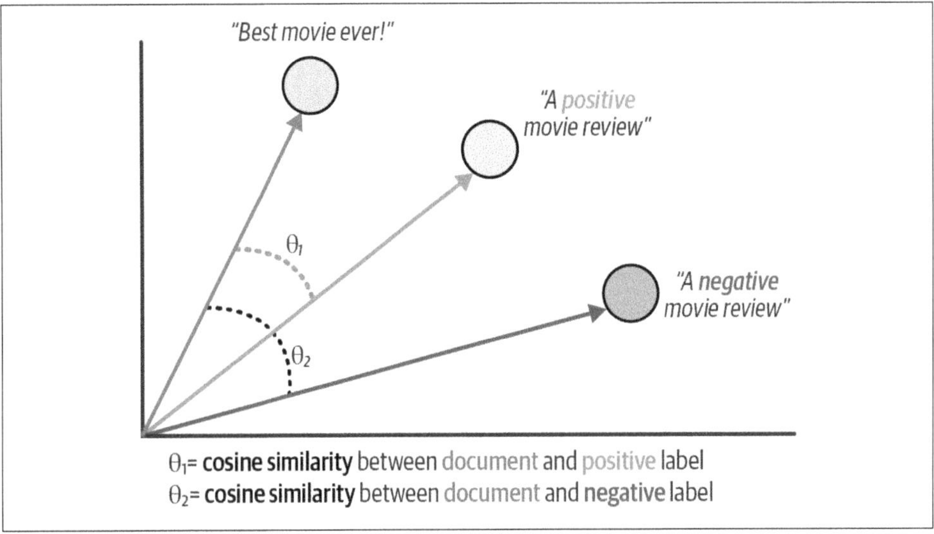

Figure 4-15. The cosine similarity is the angle between two vectors or embeddings. In this example, we calculate the similarity between a document and the two possible labels, positive and negative.

We can use cosine similarity to check how similar a given document is to the description of the candidate labels. The label with the highest similarity to the document is chosen as illustrated in Figure 4-16.

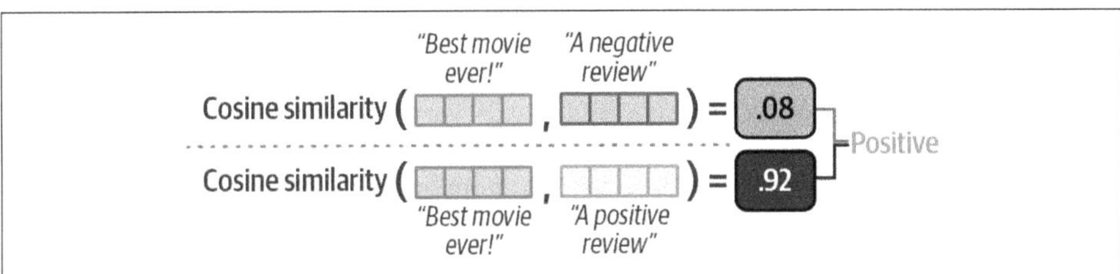

Figure 4-16. After embedding the label descriptions and the documents, we can use cosine similarity for each label document pair.

To perform cosine similarity on the embeddings, we only need to compare the document embeddings with the label embeddings and get the best matching pairs:

```
from sklearn.metrics.pairwise import cosine_similarity

# Find the best matching label for each document
sim_matrix = cosine_similarity(test_embeddings, label_embeddings)
y_pred = np.argmax(sim_matrix, axis=1)
```

And that is it! We only needed to come up with names for our labels to perform our classification tasks. Let's see how well this method works:

```
evaluate_performance(data["test"]["label"], y_pred)
```

```
                 precision    recall  f1-score   support

Negative Review       0.78      0.77      0.78       533
Positive Review       0.77      0.79      0.78       533

       accuracy                           0.78      1066
      macro avg       0.78      0.78      0.78      1066
   weighted avg       0.78      0.78      0.78      1066
```

If you are familiar with zero-shot classification (*https://oreil.ly/jpayB*) with Transformer-based models, you might wonder why we choose to illustrate this with embeddings instead. Although natural language inference models are amazing for zero-shot classification, the example here demonstrates the flexibility of embeddings for a variety of tasks. As you will see throughout the book, embeddings can be found in most Language AI use cases and are often an underestimated but incredibly vital component.

An F1 score of 0.78 is quite impressive considering we did not use any labeled data at all! This just shows how versatile and useful embeddings are, especially if you are a bit creative with how they are used.

Let's put that creativity to the test. We decided upon "A negative/positive review" as the name of our labels but that can be improved. Instead, we can make them a bit more concrete and specific toward our data by using "A very negative/positive movie review" instead. This way, the embedding will capture that it is a movie review and will focus a bit more on the extremes of the two labels. Try it out and explore how it affects the results.

Text Classification with Generative Models

Classification with generative language models, such as OpenAI's GPT models, works a bit differently from what we have done thus far. These models take as input some text and generative text and are thereby aptly named sequence-to-sequence models. This is in stark contrast to our task-specific model, which outputs a class instead, as illustrated in Figure 4-17.

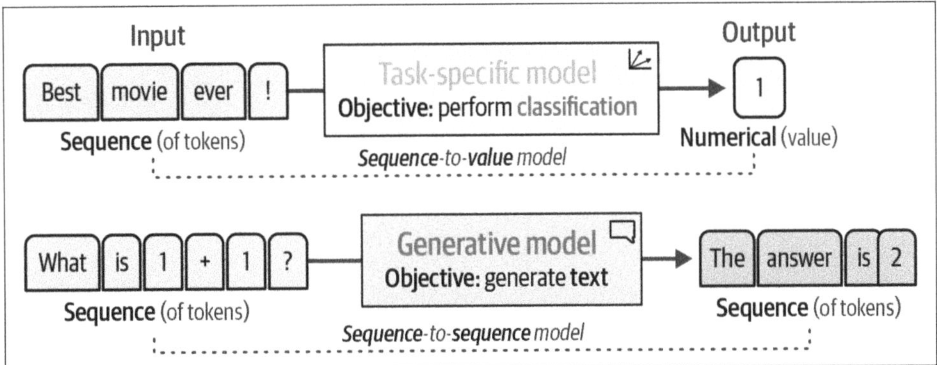

Figure 4-17. A task-specific model generates numerical values from sequences of tokens while a generative model generates sequences of tokens from sequences of tokens.

These generative models are generally trained on a wide variety of tasks and usually do not perform your use case out of the box. For instance, if we give a generative model a movie review without any context, it has no idea what to do with it.

Instead, we need to help it understand the context and guide it toward the answers that we are looking for. As demonstrated in Figure 4-18, this guiding process is done mainly through the instruction, or *prompt*, that you give such a model. Iteratively improving your prompt to get your preferred output is called *prompt engineering*.

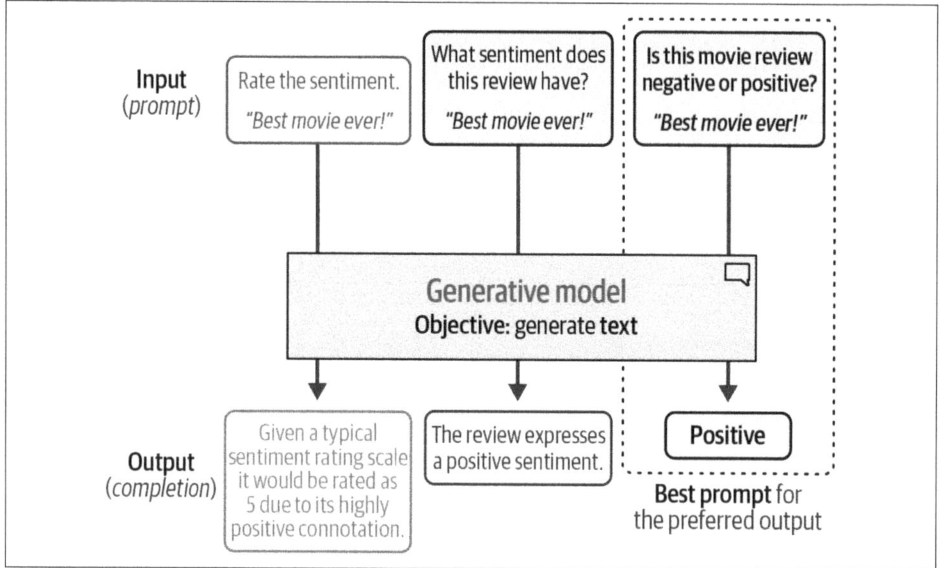

Figure 4-18. Prompt engineering allows prompts to be updated to improve the output generated by the model.

In this section, we will demonstrate how we can leverage different types of generative models to perform classification without our Rotten Tomatoes dataset.

Using the Text-to-Text Transfer Transformer

Throughout this book, we will explore mostly encoder-only (representation) models like BERT and decoder-only (generative) models like ChatGPT. However, as discussed in Chapter 1, the original Transformer architecture actually consists of an encoder-decoder architecture. Like the decoder-only models, these encoder-decoder models are sequence-to-sequence models and generally fall in the category of generative models.

An interesting family of models that leverage this architecture is the Text-to-Text Transfer Transformer or T5 model. Illustrated in Figure 4-19, its architecture is similar to the original Transformer where 12 decoders and 12 encoders are stacked together.[7]

7 Colin Raffel et al. "Exploring the limits of transfer learning with a unified text-to-text transformer." *The Journal of Machine Learning Research* 21.1 (2020): 5485–5551.

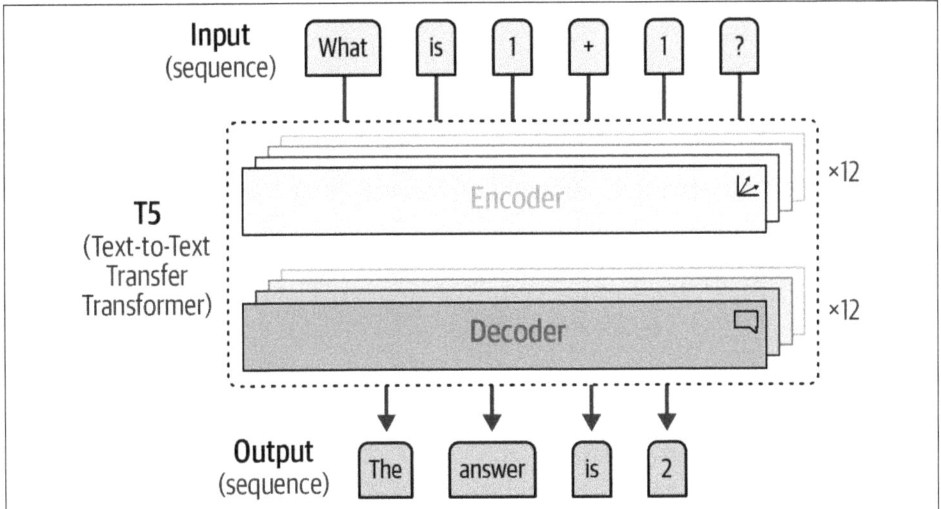

Figure 4-19. The T5 architecture is similar to the original Transformer model, a decoder-encoder architecture.

With this architecture, these models were first pretrained using masked language modeling. In the first step of training, illustrated in Figure 4-20, instead of masking individual tokens, sets of tokens (or *token spans*) were masked during pretraining.

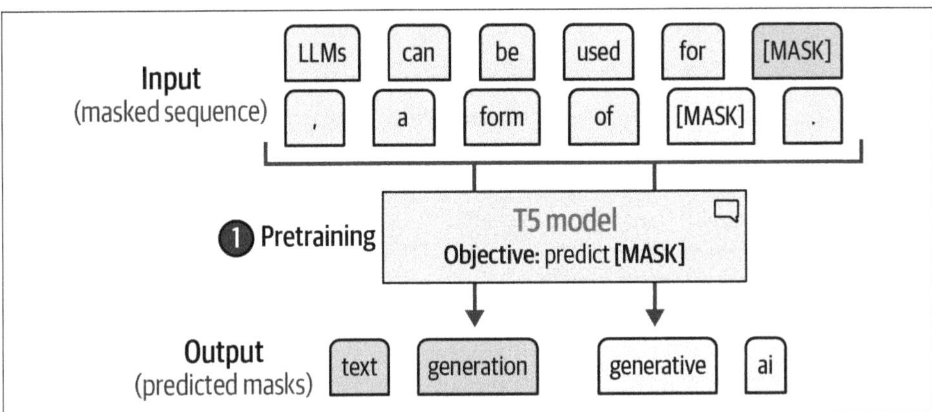

Figure 4-20. In the first step of training, namely pretraining, the T5 model needs to predict masks that could contain multiple tokens.

The second step of training, namely fine-tuning the base model, is where the real magic happens. Instead of fine-tuning the model for one specific task, each task is converted to a sequence-to-sequence task and trained simultaneously. As illustrated in Figure 4-21, this allows the model to be trained on a wide variety of tasks.

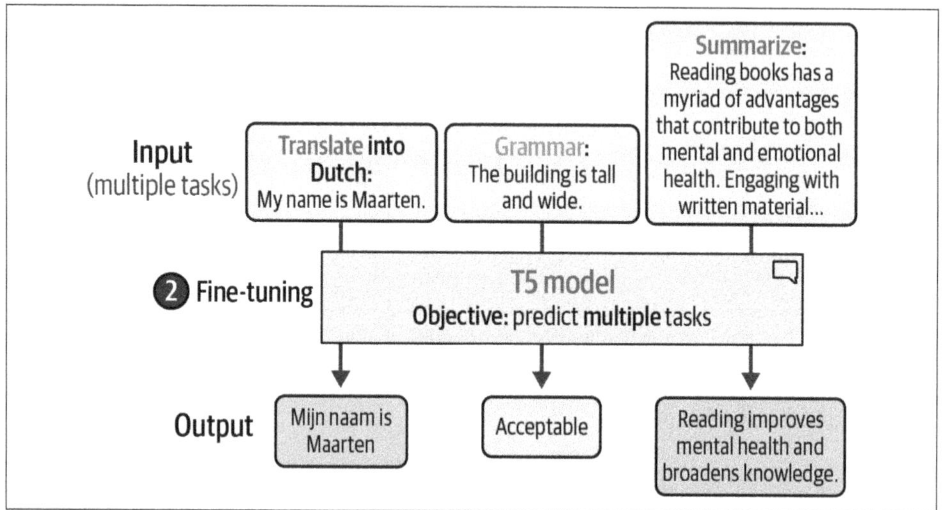

Figure 4-21. By converting specific tasks to textual instructions, the T5 model can be trained on a variety of tasks during fine-tuning.

This method of fine-tuning was extended in the paper "Scaling instruction-finetuned language models" (*https://oreil.ly/yl9Et*), which introduced more than a thousand tasks during fine-tuning that more closely follow instructions as we know them from GPT models.[8] This resulted in the Flan-T5 family of models that benefit from this large variety of tasks.

To use this pretrained Flan-T5 model for classification, we will start by loading it through the `"text2text-generation"` task, which is generally reserved for these encoder-decoder models:

```
# Load our model
pipe = pipeline(
    "text2text-generation",
    model="google/flan-t5-small",
    device="cuda:0"
)
```

The Flan-T5 model comes in various sizes (flan-t5-small/base/large/xl/xxl) and we will use the smallest to speed things up a bit. However, feel free to play around with larger models to see if you can improve the results.

Compared to our task-specific model, we cannot just give the model some text and hope it will output the sentiment. Instead, we will have to instruct the model to do so.

8 Hyung Won Chung et al. "Scaling instruction-finetuned language models." *arXiv preprint arXiv:2210.11416* (2022).

Thus, we prefix each document with the prompt "Is the following sentence positive or negative?":

```
# Prepare our data
prompt = "Is the following sentence positive or negative? "
data = data.map(lambda example: {"t5": prompt + example['text']})
data
```

```
DatasetDict({
    train: Dataset({
        features: ['text', 'label', 't5'],
        num_rows: 8530
    })
    validation: Dataset({
        features: ['text', 'label', 't5'],
        num_rows: 1066
    })
    test: Dataset({
        features: ['text', 'label', 't5'],
        num_rows: 1066
    })
})
```

After creating our updated data, we can run the pipeline similar to the task-specific example:

```
# Run inference
y_pred = []
for output in tqdm(pipe(KeyDataset(data["test"], "t5")),
total=len(data["test"])):
    text = output[0]["generated_text"]
    y_pred.append(0 if text == "negative" else 1)
```

Since this model generates text, we did need to convert the textual output to numerical values. The output word "negative" was mapped to 0 whereas "positive" was mapped to 1.

These numerical values now allow us to test the quality of the model in the same way we have done before:

```
evaluate_performance(data["test"]["label"], y_pred)
```

```
                 precision    recall  f1-score   support

Negative Review       0.83      0.85      0.84       533
Positive Review       0.85      0.83      0.84       533

       accuracy                           0.84      1066
      macro avg       0.84      0.84      0.84      1066
   weighted avg       0.84      0.84      0.84      1066
```

With an F1 score of 0.84, it is clear this Flan-T5 model is an amazing first look into the capabilities of generative models.

ChatGPT for Classification

Although we focus throughout the book on open source models, another major component of the Language AI field is closed sourced models; in particular, ChatGPT.

Although the underlying architecture of the original ChatGPT model (GPT-3.5) is not shared, we can assume from its name that it is based on the decoder-only architecture that we have seen in the GPT models thus far.

Fortunately, OpenAI shared an overview of the training procedure (*https://oreil.ly/-yf84*) that involved an important component, namely preference tuning. As illustrated in Figure 4-22, OpenAI first manually created the desired output to an input prompt (instruction data) and used that data to create a first variant of its model.

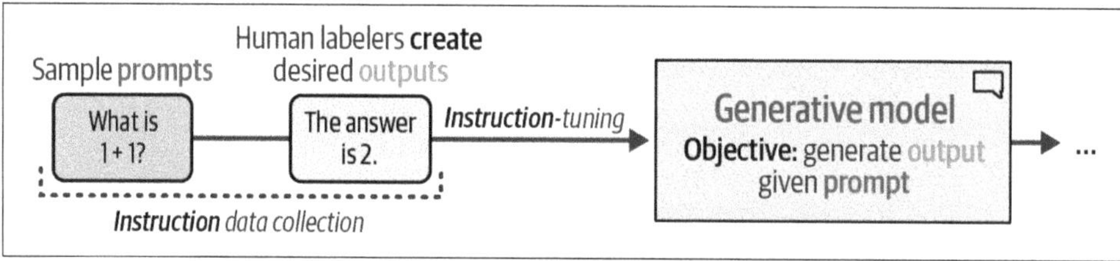

Figure 4-22. Manually labeled data consisting of an instruction (prompt) and output was used to perform fine-tuning (instruction-tuning).

OpenAI used the resulting model to generate multiple outputs that were manually ranked from best to worst. As shown in Figure 4-23, this ranking demonstrates a preference for certain outputs (preference data) and was used to create its final model, ChatGPT.

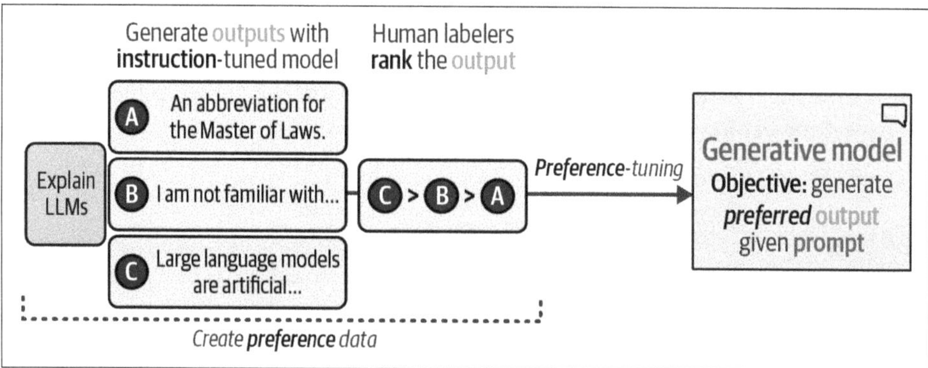

Figure 4-23. Manually ranked preference data was used to generate the final model, ChatGPT.

A major benefit of using preference data over instruction data is the nuance it represents. By demonstrating the difference between a good and better output the generative model learns to generate text that resembles human preference. In Chapter 12, we will explore how these fine-tuning and preference-tuning methodologies work and how you can perform them yourself.

The process of using a closed sourced model is quite different from the open sourced examples we have seen thus far. Instead of loading the model, we can access the model through OpenAI's API.

Before we go into the classification example, you will first need to create a free account on *https://oreil.ly/AEXvA* and create an API key here: *https://oreil.ly/lrTXl*. After doing so, you can use your API to communicate with OpenAI's servers.

We can use this key to create a client:

```
import openai

# Create client
client = openai.OpenAI(api_key="YOUR_KEY_HERE")
```

Using this client, we create the `chatgpt_generation` function, which allows us to generate some text based on a specific prompt, input document, and the selected model:

```
def chatgpt_generation(prompt, document, model="gpt-3.5-turbo-0125"):
    """Generate an output based on a prompt and an input document."""
    messages=[
        {
            "role": "system",
            "content": "You are a helpful assistant."
            },
        {
            "role": "user",
            "content":   prompt.replace("[DOCUMENT]", document)
            }
    ]
    chat_completion = client.chat.completions.create(
      messages=messages,
      model=model,
      temperature=0
    )
    return chat_completion.choices[0].message.content
```

Next, we will need to create a template to ask the model to perform the classification:

```
# Define a prompt template as a base
prompt = """Predict whether the following document is a positive or negative
movie review:

[DOCUMENT]

If it is positive return 1 and if it is negative return 0. Do not give any
other answers.
"""

# Predict the target using GPT
document = "unpretentious , charming , quirky , original"
chatgpt_generation(prompt, document)
```

This template is merely an example and can be changed however you want. For now, we kept it as simple as possible to illustrate how to use such a template.

Before you use this over a potentially large dataset, it is important to always keep track of your usage. External APIs such as OpenAI's offering can quickly become costly if you perform many requests. At the time of writing, running our test dataset using the "gpt-3.5-turbo-0125" model costs 3 cents, which is covered by the free account, but this might change in the future.

When dealing with external APIs, you might run into rate limit errors. These appear when you call the API too often as some APIs might limit the rate with which you can use it per minute or hour.

To prevent these errors, we can implement several methods for retrying the request, including something referred to as *exponential backoff*. It performs a short sleep each time we hit a rate limit error and then retries the unsuccessful request. Whenever it is unsuccessful again, the sleep length is increased until the request is successful or we hit a maximum number of retries.

To use it with OpenAI, there is a great guide (*https://oreil.ly/ZH4Uo*) that can help you get started.

Next, we can run this for all reviews in the test dataset to get its predictions. You can skip this if you want to save your (free) credits for other tasks.

```
# You can skip this if you want to save your (free) credits
predictions = [
    chatgpt_generation(prompt, doc) for doc in tqdm(data["test"]["text"])
]
```

Like the previous example, we need to convert the output from strings to integers to evaluate its performance:

```
# Extract predictions
y_pred = [int(pred) for pred in predictions]

# Evaluate performance
evaluate_performance(data["test"]["label"], y_pred)
```

```
                 precision    recall  f1-score   support

Negative Review       0.87      0.97      0.92       533
Positive Review       0.96      0.86      0.91       533

       accuracy                           0.91      1066
      macro avg       0.92      0.91      0.91      1066
   weighted avg       0.92      0.91      0.91      1066
```

The F1 score of 0.91 already gives a glimpse into the performance of the model that brought generative AI to the masses. However, since we do not know what data the model was trained on, we cannot easily use these kinds of metrics for evaluating the model. For all we know, it might have actually been trained on our dataset!

In Chapter 12, we will explore how we can evaluate both open source and closed source models on more generalized tasks.

Summary

In this chapter, we discussed many different techniques for performing a wide variety of classification tasks, from fine-tuning your entire model to no tuning at all! Classifying textual data is not as straightforward as it may seem on the surface and there is an incredible amount of creative techniques for doing so.

In this chapter, we explored text classification using both generative and representation language models. Our goal was to assign a label or class to input text for the classification of a review's sentiment.

We explored two types of representation models, a task-specific model and an embedding model. The task-specific model was pretrained on a large dataset specifically for sentiment analysis and showed us that pretrained models are a great technique for classifying documents. The embedding model was used to generate multipurpose embeddings that we used as the input to train a classifier.

Similarly, we explored two types of generative models, an open source encoder-decoder model (Flan-T5) and a closed source decoder-only model (GPT-3.5). We used these generative models in text classification without requiring specific (additional) training on domain data or labeled datasets.

In the next chapter, we will continue with classification but focus instead on unsupervised classification. What can we do if we have textual data without any labels? What information can we extract? We will focus on clustering our data as well as naming the clusters with topic modeling techniques.

CHAPTER 5

Text Clustering and Topic Modeling

Although supervised techniques, such as classification, have reigned supreme over the last few years in the industry, the potential of unsupervised techniques such as text clustering cannot be understated.

Text clustering aims to group similar texts based on their semantic content, meaning, and relationships. As illustrated in Figure 5-1, the resulting clusters of semantically similar documents not only facilitate efficient categorization of large volumes of unstructured text but also allow for quick exploratory data analysis.

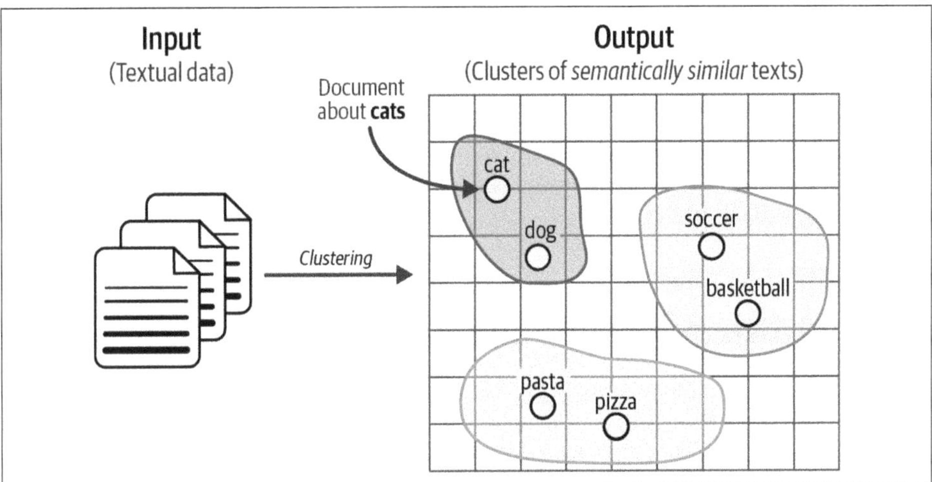

Figure 5-1. Clustering unstructured textual data.

The recent evolution of language models, which enable contextual and semantic representations of text, has enhanced the effectiveness of text clustering. Language is more than a bag of words, and recent language models have proved to be quite capable of capturing that notion. Text clustering, unbound by supervision, allows for creative solutions and diverse applications, such as finding outliers, speedup labeling, and finding incorrectly labeled data.

Text clustering has also found itself in the realm of topic modeling, where we want to discover (abstract) topics that appear in large collections of textual data. As shown in Figure 5-2, we generally describe a topic using keywords or keyphrases and, ideally, have a single overarching label.

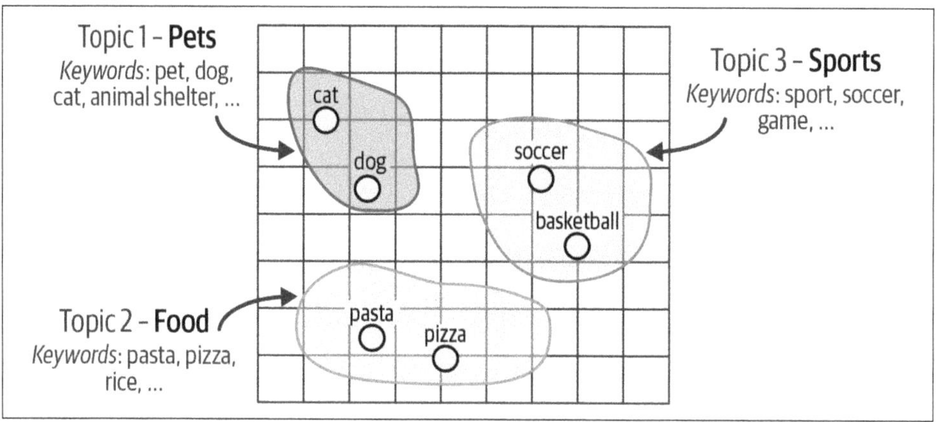

Figure 5-2. Topic modeling is a way to give meaning to clusters of textual documents.

In this chapter, we will first explore how to perform clustering with embedding models and then transition to a text-clustering-inspired method of topic modeling, namely BERTopic.

Text clustering and topic modeling have an important role in this book as they explore creative ways to combine a variety of different language models. We will explore how combining encoder-only (embeddings), decoder-only (generative), and even classical methods (bag-of-words) can result in amazing new techniques and pipelines.

ArXiv's Articles: Computation and Language

Throughout this chapter, we will be running clustering and topic modeling algorithms on ArXiv articles. ArXiv (*https://oreil.ly/ece40*) is an open-access platform for scholarly articles, mostly in the fields of computer science, mathematics, and physics. We will explore articles in the field of Computation and Language to keep with the theme of this book. The dataset (*https://oreil.ly/Lz2dq*) contains 44,949 abstracts between 1991 and 2024 from ArXiv's cs.CL (*https://oreil.ly/-xlSS*) (Computation and Language) section.

We load the data and create separate variables for the abstracts, titles, and years of each article:

```
# Load data from Hugging Face
from datasets import load_dataset
dataset = load_dataset("maartengr/arxiv_nlp")["train"]

# Extract metadata
abstracts = dataset["Abstracts"]
titles = dataset["Titles"]
```

A Common Pipeline for Text Clustering

Text clustering allows for discovering patterns in data that you may or may not be familiar with. It allows for getting an intuitive understanding of the task, for example, a classification task, but also of its complexity. As a result, text clustering can become more than just a quick method for exploratory data analysis.

Although there are many methods for text clustering, from graph-based neural networks to centroid-based clustering techniques, a common pipeline that has gained popularity involves three steps and algorithms:

1. Convert the input documents to embeddings with an *embedding model*.
2. Reduce the dimensionality of embeddings with a *dimensionality reduction model*.
3. Find groups of semantically similar documents with a *cluster model*.

Embedding Documents

The first step is to convert our textual data to embeddings, as illustrated in Figure 5-3. Recall from previous chapters that embeddings are numerical representations of text that attempt to capture its meaning.

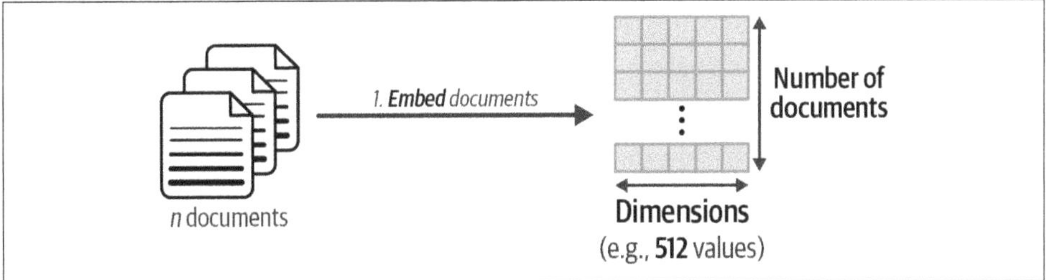

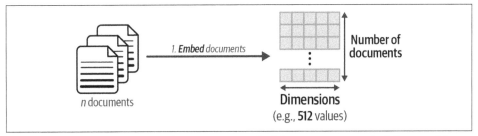

Figure 5-3. Step 1: We convert documents to embeddings using an embedding model.

Choosing embedding models optimized for semantic similarity tasks is especially important for clustering as we attempt to find groups of semantically similar documents. Fortunately, most embedding models at the time of writing focus on just that, semantic similarity.

As we did in the previous chapter, we will use the MTEB leaderboard (*https://oreil.ly/XFrbO*) to select an embedding model. We will need an embedding model that has a decent score on clustering tasks but also is small enough to run quickly. Instead of using the "sentence-transformers/all-mpnet-base-v2" model we used in the previous chapter, we use the "thenlper/gte-small" (*https://oreil.ly/h-Gkg*) model instead. It is a more recent model that outperforms the previous model on clustering tasks and due to its small size is even faster for inference. However, feel free to play around with newer models that have been released since!

```
from sentence_transformers import SentenceTransformer

# Create an embedding for each abstract
embedding_model = SentenceTransformer("thenlper/gte-small")
embeddings = embedding_model.encode(abstracts, show_progress_bar=True)
```

Let's check how many values each document embedding contains:

```
# Check the dimensions of the resulting embeddings
embeddings.shape
```

```
(44949, 384)
```

Each embedding has 384 values that together represent the semantic representation of the document. You can view these embeddings as the features that we want to cluster.

Reducing the Dimensionality of Embeddings

Before we cluster the embeddings, we will first need to take their high dimensionality into account. As the number of dimensions increases, there is an exponential growth in the number of possible values within each dimension. Finding all subspaces within each dimension becomes increasingly complex.

As a result, high-dimensional data can be troublesome for many clustering techniques as it gets more difficult to identify meaningful clusters. Instead, we can make use of dimensionality reduction. As illustrated in Figure 5-4, this technique allows us to reduce the size of the dimensional space and represent the same data with fewer dimensions. Dimensionality reduction techniques aim to preserve the global structure of high-dimensional data by finding low-dimensional representations.

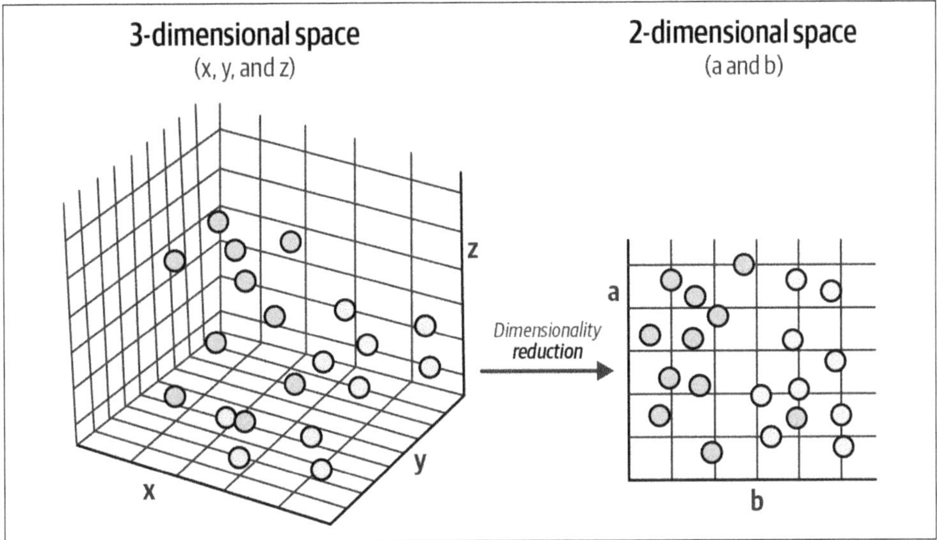

Figure 5-4. Dimensionality reduction allows data in high-dimensional space to be compressed to a lower-dimensional representation.

Note that this is a compression technique and that the underlying algorithm is not arbitrarily removing dimensions. To help the cluster model create meaningful clusters, the second step in our clustering pipeline is therefore dimensionality reduction, as shown in Figure 5-5.

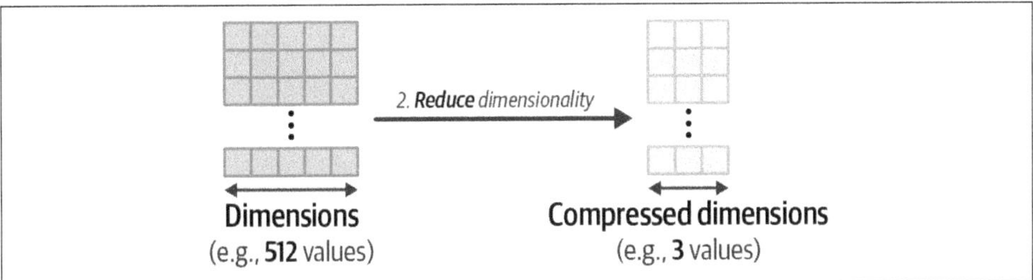

Figure 5-5. Step 2: The embeddings are reduced to a lower-dimensional space using dimensionality reduction.

Well-known methods for dimensionality reduction are Principal Component Analysis (PCA)[1] and Uniform Manifold Approximation and Projection (UMAP).[2] For this

1 Harold Hotelling. "Analysis of a complex of statistical variables into principal components." *Journal of Educational Psychology* 24.6 (1933): 417.

2 Leland McInnes, John Healy, and James Melville. "UMAP: Uniform Manifold Approximation and Projection for dimension reduction." *arXiv preprint arXiv:1802.03426* (2018).

pipeline, we are going with UMAP as it tends to handle nonlinear relationships and structures a bit better than PCA.

Dimensionality reduction techniques, however, are not flawless. They do not perfectly capture high-dimensional data in a lower-dimensional representation. Information will always be lost with this procedure. There is a balance between reducing dimensionality and keeping as much information as possible.

To perform dimensionality reduction, we need to instantiate our UMAP class and pass the generated embeddings to it:

```
from umap import UMAP

# We reduce the input embeddings from 384 dimensions to 5 dimensions
umap_model = UMAP(
    n_components=5, min_dist=0.0, metric='cosine', random_state=42
)
reduced_embeddings = umap_model.fit_transform(embeddings)
```

We can use the `n_components` parameter to decide the shape of the lower-dimensional space, namely 5 dimensions. Generally, values between 5 and 10 work well to capture high-dimensional global structures.

The `min_dist` parameter is the minimum distance between embedded points. We are setting this to 0 as that generally results in tighter clusters. We set `metric` to `'cosine'` as Euclidean-based methods have issues dealing with high-dimensional data.

Note that setting a `random_state` in UMAP will make the results reproducible across sessions but will disable parallelism and therefore slow down training.

Cluster the Reduced Embeddings

The third step is to cluster the reduced embeddings, as illustrated in Figure 5-6.

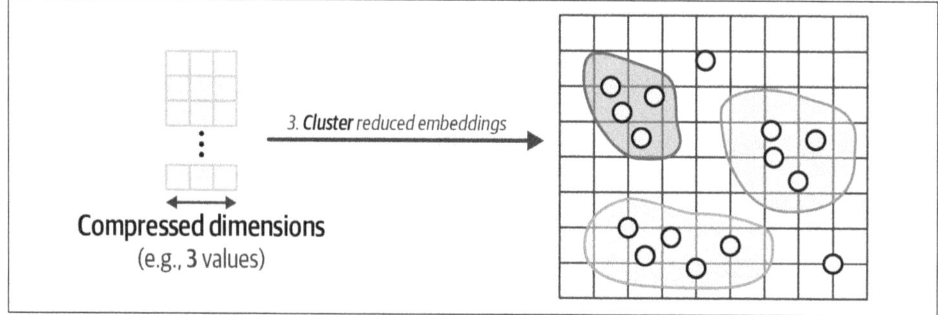

Figure 5-6. Step 3: We cluster the documents using the embeddings with reduced dimensionality.

Although a common choice is a centroid-based algorithm like k-means, which requires a set of clusters to be generated, we do not know the number of clusters beforehand. Instead, a density-based algorithm freely calculates the number of clusters and does not force all data points to be part of a cluster, as illustrated in Figure 5-7.

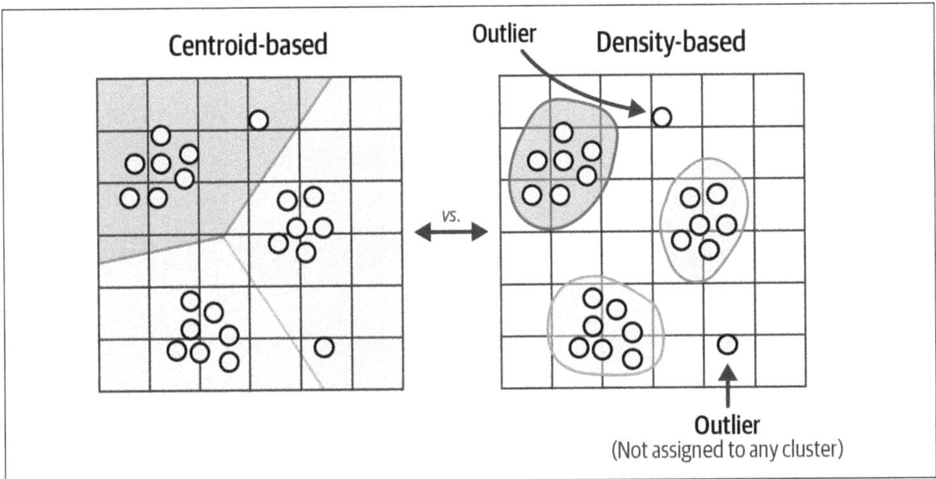

Figure 5-7. The clustering algorithm not only impacts how clusters are generated but also how they are viewed.

A common density-based model is Hierarchical Density-Based Spatial Clustering of Applications with Noise (HDBSCAN).[3] HDBSCAN is a hierarchical variation of a clustering algorithm called DBSCAN that allows for dense (micro)-clusters to be found without having to explicitly specify the number of clusters.[4] As a density-based method, HDBSCAN can also detect *outliers* in the data, which are data points that do not belong to any cluster. These outliers will not be assigned or forced to belong to any cluster. In other words, they are ignored. Since ArXiv articles might contain some niche papers, using a model that detects outliers could be helpful.

As with the previous packages, using HDBSCAN is straightforward. We only need to instantiate the model and pass our reduced embeddings to it:

3 Leland McInnes, John Healy, and Steve Astels. "hdbscan: Hierarchical density based clustering." *J. Open Source Softw.* 2.11 (2017): 205.

4 Martin Ester et al. "A density-based algorithm for discovering clusters in large spatial databases with noise." *KDD'96*, Aug. 1996: 226–231.

```
from hdbscan import HDBSCAN

# We fit the model and extract the clusters
hdbscan_model = HDBSCAN(
    min_cluster_size=50, metric="euclidean", cluster_selection_method="eom"
).fit(reduced_embeddings)
clusters = hdbscan_model.labels_

# How many clusters did we generate?
len(set(clusters))
```

```
156
```

With HDBSCAN, we generated 156 clusters in our dataset. To create more clusters, we will need to reduce the value of `min_cluster_size` as it represents the minimum size that a cluster can take.

Inspecting the Clusters

Now that we have generated our clusters, we can inspect each cluster manually and explore the assigned documents to get an understanding of its content. For example, let us take a few random documents from cluster 0:

```
import numpy as np

# Print first three documents in cluster 0
cluster = 0
for index in np.where(clusters==cluster)[0][:3]:
    print(abstracts[index][:300] + "... \n")
```

```
This works aims to design a statistical machine translation from English text
to American Sign Language (ASL). The system is based on Moses tool with some
modifications and the results are synthesized through a 3D avatar for
interpretation. First, we translate the input text to gloss, a written fo...

Researches on signed languages still strongly dissociate lin- guistic issues
related on phonological and phonetic aspects, and gesture studies for
recognition and synthesis purposes. This paper focuses on the imbrication of
motion and meaning for the analysis, synthesis and evaluation of sign lang...

Modern computational linguistic software cannot produce important aspects of
sign language translation. Using some researches we deduce that the majority of
automatic sign language translation systems ignore many aspects when they
generate animation; therefore the interpretation lost the truth inf...
```

From these documents, it seems that this cluster contains documents mostly about translation from and to sign language, interesting!

We can take this one step further and attempt to visualize our results instead of going through all documents manually. To do so, we will need to reduce our document embeddings to two dimensions, as that allows us to plot the documents on an x/y plane:

```
import pandas as pd

# Reduce 384-dimensional embeddings to two dimensions for easier visualization
reduced_embeddings = UMAP(
    n_components=2, min_dist=0.0, metric="cosine", random_state=42
).fit_transform(embeddings)

# Create dataframe
df = pd.DataFrame(reduced_embeddings, columns=["x", "y"])
df["title"] = titles
df["cluster"] = [str(c) for c in clusters]

# Select outliers and non-outliers (clusters)
to_plot = df.loc[df.cluster != "-1", :]
outliers = df.loc[df.cluster == "-1", :]
```

We also created a dataframe for our clusters (`clusters_df`) and for the outliers (`outliers_df`) separately since we generally want to focus on the clusters and highlight those.

Using any dimensionality reduction technique for visualization purposes creates information loss. It is merely an approximation of what our original embeddings look like. Although it is informative, it might push clusters together and drive them further apart than they actually are. Human evaluation, inspecting the clusters ourselves, is therefore a key component of cluster analysis!

To generate a static plot, we will use the well-known plotting library, `matplotlib`:

```
import matplotlib.pyplot as plt

# Plot outliers and non-outliers separately
plt.scatter(outliers_df.x, outliers_df.y, alpha=0.05, s=2, c="grey")
plt.scatter(
    clusters_df.x, clusters_df.y, c=clusters_df.cluster.astype(int),
    alpha=0.6, s=2, cmap="tab20b"
)
plt.axis("off")
```

As we can see in Figure 5-8, it tends to capture major clusters quite well. Note how clusters of points are colored in the same color, indicating that HDBSCAN put them in a group together. Since we have a large number of clusters, the plotting library cycles the colors between clusters, so don't think that all green points are one cluster, for example.

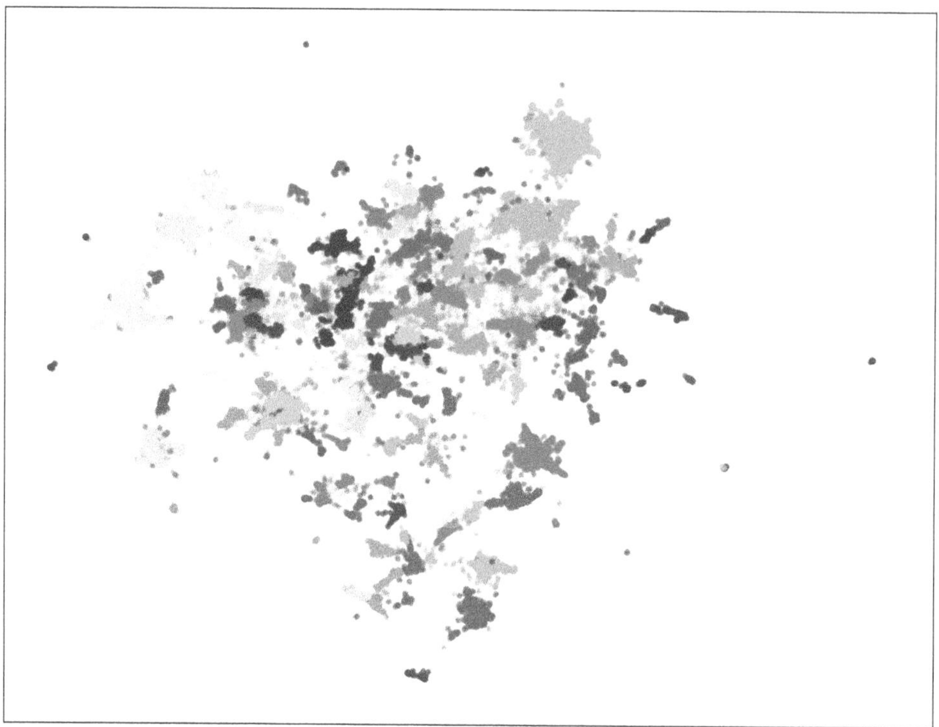

Figure 5-8. The generated clusters (colored) and outliers (gray) are represented as a 2D visualization.

This is visually appealing but does not yet allow us to see what is happening inside the clusters. Instead, we can extend this visualization by going from text clustering to topic modeling.

From Text Clustering to Topic Modeling

Text clustering is a powerful tool for finding structure among large collections of documents. In our previous example, we could manually inspect each cluster and identify them based on their collection of documents. For instance, we explored a cluster that contained documents about sign language. We could say that the *topic* of that cluster is "sign language."

This idea of finding themes or latent topics in a collection of textual data is often referred to as *topic modeling*. Traditionally, it involves finding a set of keywords or phrases that best represent and capture the meaning of the topic, as we illustrate in Figure 5-9.

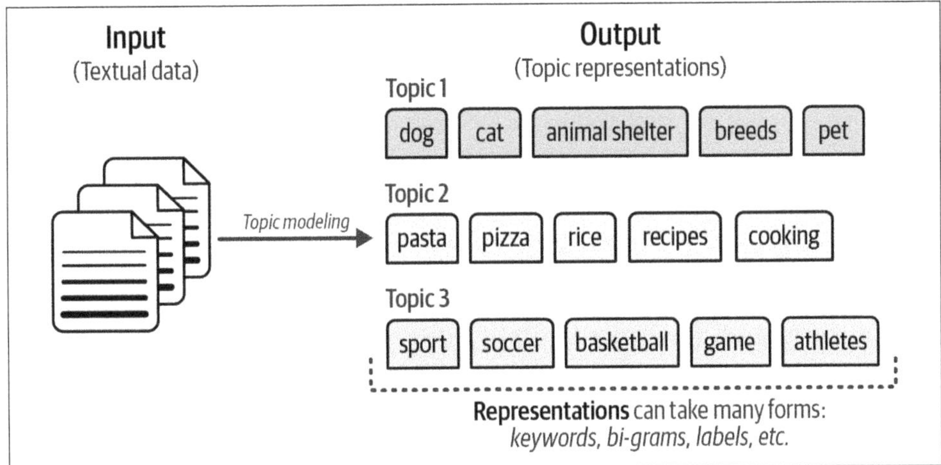

Figure 5-9. Traditionally, topics are represented by a number of keywords but can take other forms.

Instead of labeling a topic as "sign language," these techniques use keywords such as "sign," "language," and "translation" to describe the topic. As such, this does not give a single label to a topic and instead requires the user to understand the meaning of the topic through those keywords.

Classic approaches, like latent Dirichlet allocation, assume that each topic is characterized by a probability distribution of words in a corpus's vocabulary.[5] Figure 5-10 demonstrates how each word in a vocabulary is scored against its relevance to each topic.

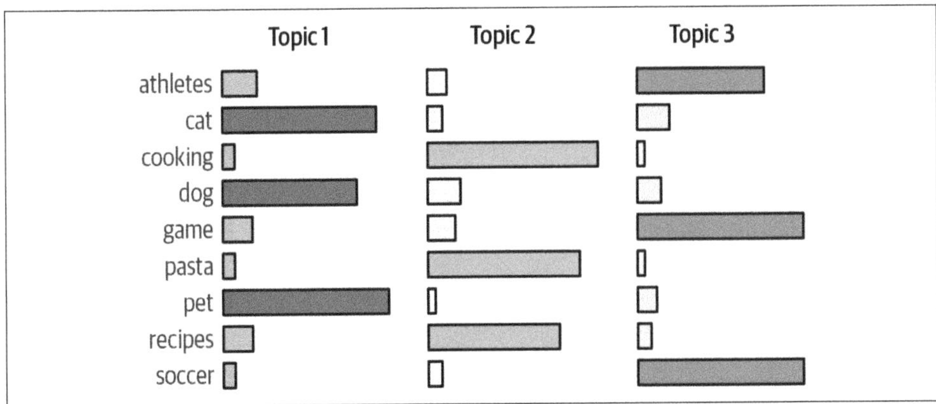

Figure 5-10. Keywords are extracted based on their distribution over a single topic.

5 David M. Blei, Andrew Y. Ng, and Michael I. Jordan. "Latent Dirichlet allocation." *Journal of Machine Learning Research* 3. Jan (2003): 993–1022.

These approaches generally use a bag-of-words technique for the main features of the textual data, which does not take the context nor the meaning of words and phrases into account. In contrast, our text clustering example does take both into account as it relies on Transformer-based embeddings that are optimized for semantic similarity and contextual meaning through attention.

In this section, we will extend text clustering into the realm of topic modeling through a highly modular text clustering and topic modeling framework, namely BERTopic.

BERTopic: A Modular Topic Modeling Framework

BERTopic is a topic modeling technique that leverages clusters of semantically similar texts to extract various types of topic representations.[6] The underlying algorithm can be thought of in two steps.

First, as illustrated in Figure 5-11, we follow the same procedure as we did before in our text clustering example. We embed documents, reduce their dimensionality, and finally cluster the reduced embedding to create groups of semantically similar documents.

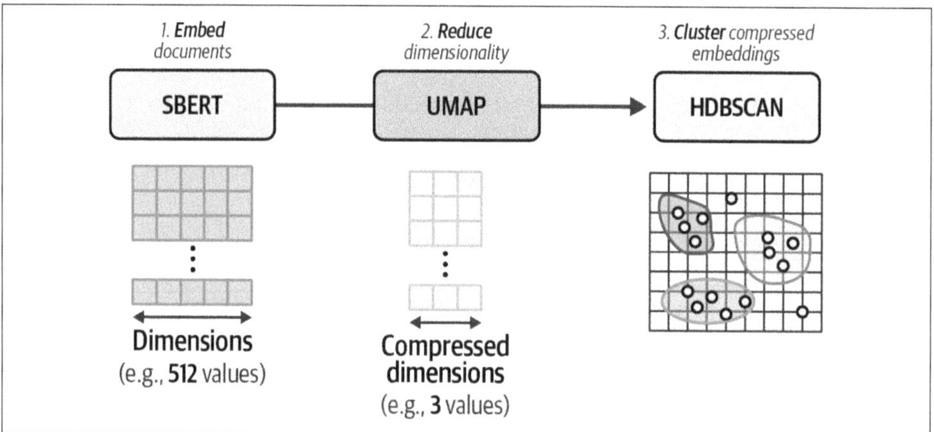

Figure 5-11. The first part of BERTopic's pipeline is to create clusters of semantically similar documents.

Second, it models a distribution over words in the corpus's vocabulary by leveraging a classic method, namely bag-of-words. The bag-of-words, as we discussed briefly in Chapter 1 and illustrate in Figure 5-12, does exactly what its name implies, counting

6 Maarten Grootendorst. "BERTopic: Neural topic modeling with a class-based TF-IDF procedure." *arXiv preprint arXiv:2203.05794* (2022).

the number of times each word appears in a document. The resulting representation could be used to extract the most frequent words inside a document.

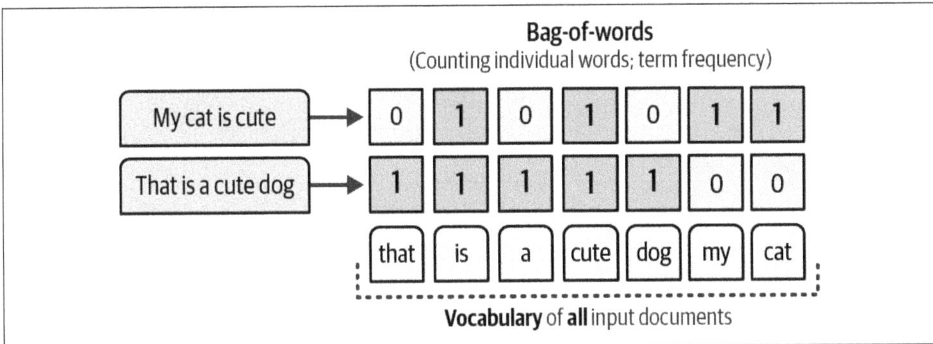

Figure 5-12. A bag-of-words counts the number of times each word appears inside a document.

There are two caveats, however. First, this is a representation on a document level and we are interested in a cluster-level perspective. To address this, the frequency of words is calculated within the entire cluster instead of only the document, as illustrated in Figure 5-13.

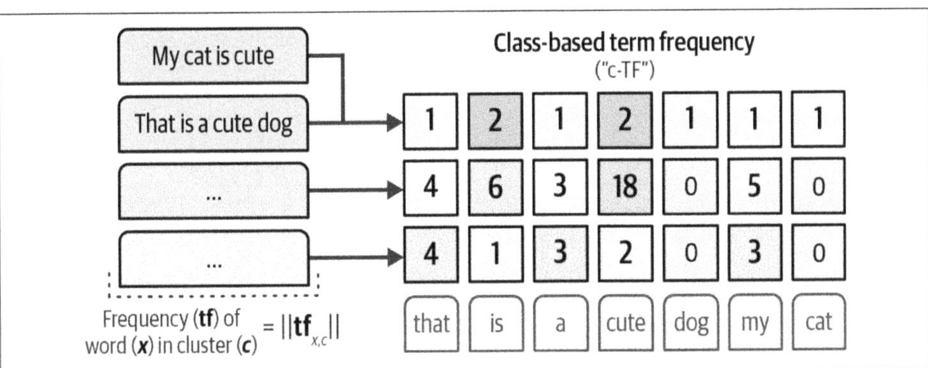

Figure 5-13. Generating c-TF by counting the frequency of words per cluster instead of per document.

Second, stop words like "the" and "I" tend to appear often in documents and provide little meaning to the actual documents. BERTopic uses a class-based variant of term frequency–inverse document frequency (c-TF-IDF) to put more weight on words that are more meaningful to a cluster and put less weight on words that are used across all clusters.

Each word in the bag-of-words, the c-TF in c-TF-IDF, is multiplied by the IDF value of each word. As shown in Figure 5-14, the IDF value is calculated by taking the logarithm of the average frequency of all words across all clusters divided by the total frequency of each word.

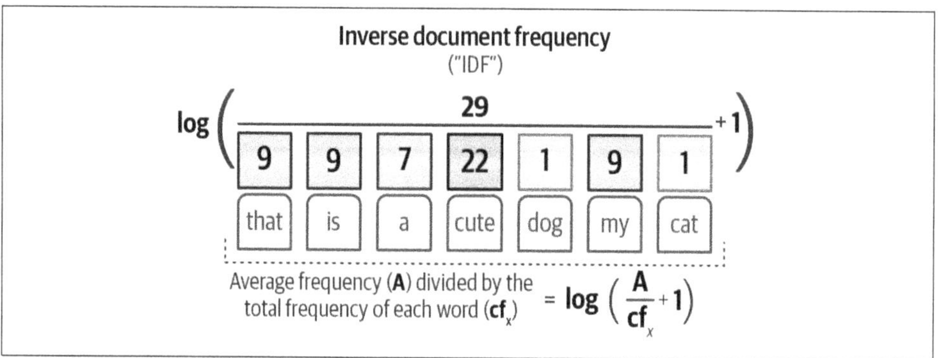

Figure 5-14. Creating a weighting scheme.

The result is a weight ("IDF") for each word that we can multiply with their frequency ("c-TF") to get the weighted values ("c-TF-IDF").

This second part of the procedure, as shown in Figure 5-15, allows for generating a distribution over words as we have seen before. We can use scikit-learn's `CountVectorizer` to generate the bag-of-words (or term frequency) representation. Here, each cluster is considered a topic that has a specific ranking of the corpus's vocabulary.

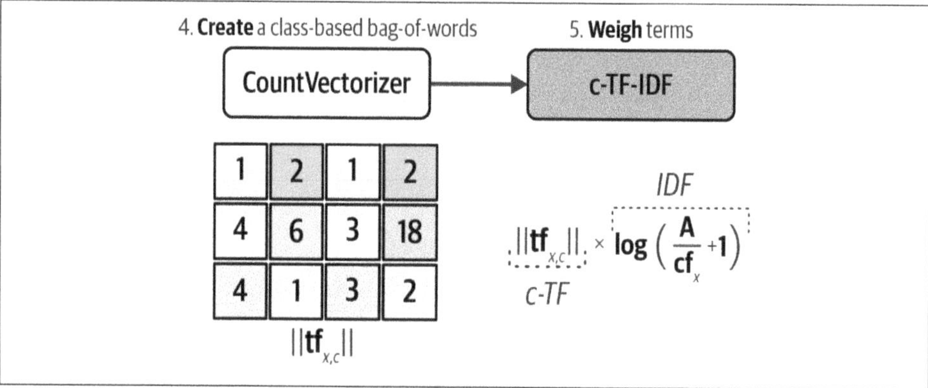

*Figure 5-15. The second part of BERTopic's pipeline is representing the topics: the calculation of the weight of term *x* in a class *c*.*

Putting the two steps together, clustering and representing topics, results in the full pipeline of BERTopic, as illustrated in Figure 5-16. With this pipeline, we can cluster semantically similar documents and from the clusters generate topics represented by several keywords. The higher a word's weight in a topic, the more representative it is of that topic.

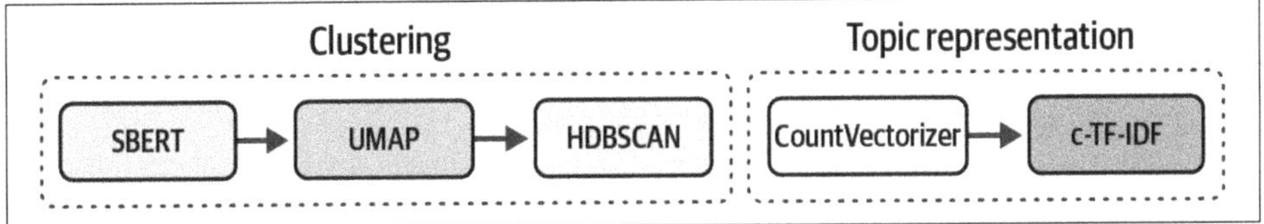

Figure 5-16. The full pipeline of BERTopic, roughly, consists of two steps, clustering and topic representation.

A major advantage of this pipeline is that the two steps, clustering and topic representation, are largely independent of one another. For instance, with c-TF-IDF, we are not dependent on the models used in clustering the documents. This allows for significant modularity throughout every component of the pipeline. And as we will explore later in this chapter, it is a great starting point to fine-tune the topic representations.

As illustrated in Figure 5-17, although `sentence-transformers` is used as the default embedding model, we can swap it with any other embedding technique. The same applies to all other steps. If you do not want outliers generated with HDBSCAN, you can use k-means instead.

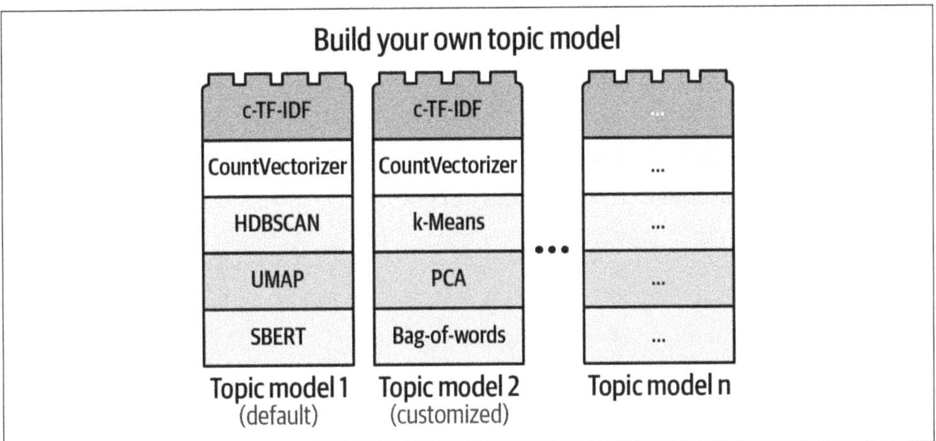

Figure 5-17. The modularity of BERTopic is a key component and allows you to build your own topic model however you want.

You can think of this modularity as building with Lego blocks; each part of the pipeline is completely replaceable with another, similar algorithm. Through this modularity, newly released models can be integrated within its architecture. As the field of Language AI grows, so does BERTopic!

The Modularity of BERTopic

The modularity of BERTopic has another advantage: it allows it to be used and adapted to different use cases using the same base model. For instance, BERTopic supports a wide variety of algorithmic variants:

- Guided topic modeling
- (Semi-)supervised topic modeling
- Hierarchical topic modeling
- Dynamic topic modeling
- Multimodal topic modeling
- Multi-aspect topic modeling
- Online and incremental topic modeling
- Zero-shot topic modeling
- Etc.

The modularity and algorithmic flexibility are the foundation of the author's aim to make BERTopic the one-stop-shop for topic modeling. You can find a full overview of its capabilities in the documentation (*https://oreil.ly/XKxJE*) or the repository (*https://oreil.ly/-iPzP*).

To run BERTopic with our ArXiv dataset, we can use our previously defined models and embeddings (although it is not mandatory):

```
from bertopic import BERTopic

# Train our model with our previously defined models
topic_model = BERTopic(
    embedding_model=embedding_model,
    umap_model=umap_model,
    hdbscan_model=hdbscan_model,
    verbose=True
).fit(abstracts, embeddings)
```

Let us start by exploring the topics that were created. The `get_topic_info()` method is useful to get a quick description of the topics that we found:

```
topic_model.get_topic_info()
```

Topic	Count	Name	Representation
-1	14520	-1_the_of_and_to	[the, of, and, to, in, we, that, language, for...
0	2290	0_speech_asr_recognition_end	[speech, asr, recognition, end, acoustic, spea...
1	1403	1_medical_clinical_biomedical_patient	[medical, clinical, biomedical, patient, healt...
2	1156	2_sentiment_aspect_analysis_reviews	[sentiment, aspect, analysis, reviews, opinion...
3	986	3_translation_nmt_machine_neural	[translation, nmt, machine, neural, bleu, engl...
...	...	...	...
150	54	150_coherence_discourse_paragraph_text	[coherence, discourse, paragraph, text, cohesi...
151	54	151_prompt_prompts_optimization_prompting	[prompt, prompts, optimization, prompting, llm...
152	53	152_sentence_sts_embeddings_similarity	[sentence, sts, embeddings, similarity, embedd...
153	53	153_counseling_mental_health_therapy	[counseling, mental, health, therapy, psychoth...
154	50	154_backdoor_attacks_attack_triggers	[backdoor, attacks, attack, triggers, poisoned...

Each of these topics is represented by several keywords, which are concatenated with a "_" in the `Name` column. This `Name` column allows us to quickly get a feeling of what the topic is about as it shows the four keywords that best represent it.

You might also have noticed that the very first topic is labeled -1. That topic contains all documents that could not be fitted within a topic and are considered outliers. This is a result of the clustering algorithm, HDBSCAN, which does not force all points to be clustered. To remove outliers, we could either use a non-outlier algorithm like k-means or use BERTopic's `reduce_outliers()` function to reassign the outliers to topics.

We can inspect individual topics and explore which keywords best represent them with the `get_topic` function. For example, topic 0 contains the following keywords:

```
topic_model.get_topic(0)
```

```
[('speech', 0.028177697715245358),
 ('asr', 0.018971184497453525),
 ('recognition', 0.013457745472471012),
 ('end', 0.00980445092749381),
 ('acoustic', 0.009452082794507863),
 ('speaker', 0.0068822647060204885),
 ('audio', 0.006807649923681604),
 ('the', 0.0063343444687017645),
 ('error', 0.006320144717019838),
 ('automatic', 0.006290216996043161)]
```

For example, topic 0 contains the keywords "speech," "asr," and "recognition." Based on these keywords, it seems that the topic is about automatic speech recognition (ASR).

We can use the `find_topics()` function to search for specific topics based on a search term. Let's search for a topic about topic modeling:

```
topic_model.find_topics("topic modeling")
```

```
([22, -1, 1, 47, 32],
 [0.95456535, 0.91173744, 0.9074769, 0.9067007, 0.90510106])
```

This returns that topic 22 has a relatively high similarity (0.95) with our search term. If we then inspect the topic, we can see that it is indeed a topic about topic modeling:

```
topic_model.get_topic(22)
```

```
[('topic', 0.06634619076655907),
 ('topics', 0.035308535091932707),
 ('lda', 0.016386314730705634),
 ('latent', 0.013372311924864435),
 ('document', 0.012973600191120576),
 ('documents', 0.012383715497143821),
 ('modeling', 0.011978375291037142),
 ('dirichlet', 0.010078277589545706),
 ('word', 0.008505619415413312),
 ('allocation', 0.007930890698168108)]
```

Although we know that this topic is about topic modeling, let's see if the BERTopic abstract is also assigned to this topic:

```
topic_model.topics_[titles.index("BERTopic: Neural topic modeling with a class-
based TF-IDF procedure")]
```

```
22
```

It is! These functionalities allow us to quickly find the topics that we are interested in.

The modularity of BERTopic gives you a lot of choices, which can be overwhelming. For that purpose, the author created a best practices guide (*https://oreil.ly/IsP1k*) that goes through common practices to speed up training, improve representations, and more.

To make exploration of the topics a bit easier, we can look back at our text clustering example. There, we created a static visualization to see the general structure of the created topic. With BERTopic, we can create an interactive variant that allows us to quickly explore which topics exist and which documents they contain.

Doing so requires us to use the two-dimensional embeddings, `reduced_embeddings`, that we created with UMAP. Moreover, when we hover over documents, we will show the title instead of the abstract to quickly get an understanding of the documents in a topic:

```
# Visualize topics and documents
fig = topic_model.visualize_documents(
    titles,
    reduced_embeddings=reduced_embeddings,
    width=1200,
    hide_annotations=True
)

# Update fonts of legend for easier visualization
fig.update_layout(font=dict(size=16))
```

As we can see in Figure 5-18, this interactive plot quickly gives us a sense of the created topics. You can zoom in to view individual documents or double-click a topic on the righthand side to only view it.

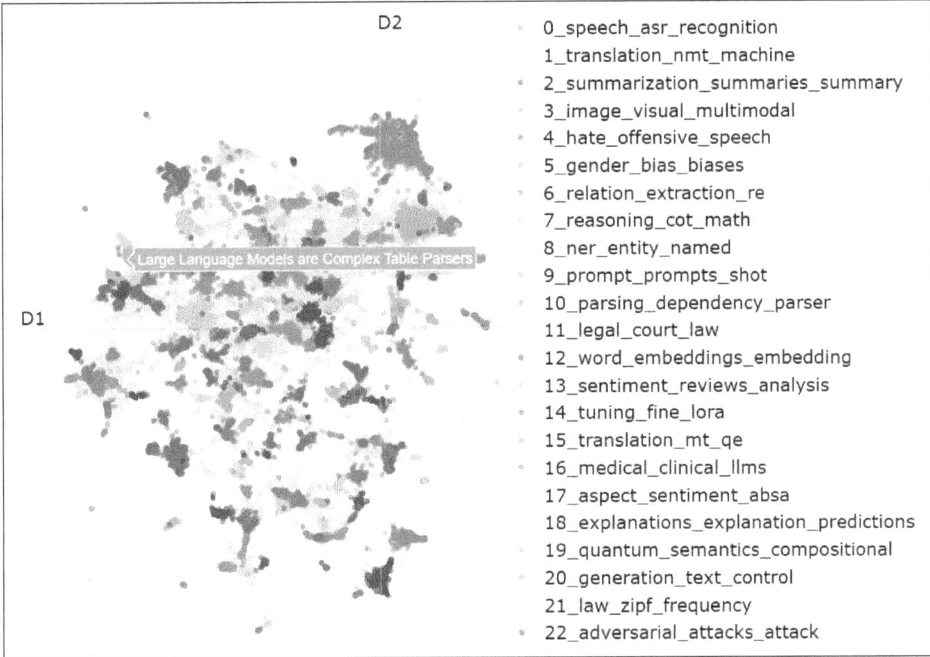

Figure 5-18. The output when we visualize documents and topics.

There is a wide range of visualization options in BERTopic. There are three that are worthwhile to explore to get an idea of the relationships between topics:

```
# Visualize barchart with ranked keywords
topic_model.visualize_barchart()

# Visualize relationships between topics
```

```
topic_model.visualize_heatmap(n_clusters=30)

# Visualize the potential hierarchical structure of topics
topic_model.visualize_hierarchy()
```

Adding a Special Lego Block

The pipeline in BERTopic that we have explored thus far, albeit fast and modular, has a disadvantage: it still represents a topic through a bag-of-words without taking into account semantic structures.

The solution is to leverage the strength of the bag-of-words representation, which is its speed to generate a meaningful representation. We can use this first meaningful representation and tweak it using more powerful but slower techniques, like embedding models. As shown in Figure 5-19, we can rerank the initial distribution of words to improve the resulting representation. Note that this idea of reranking an initial set of results is a main staple in neural search, a subject that we cover in Chapter 8.

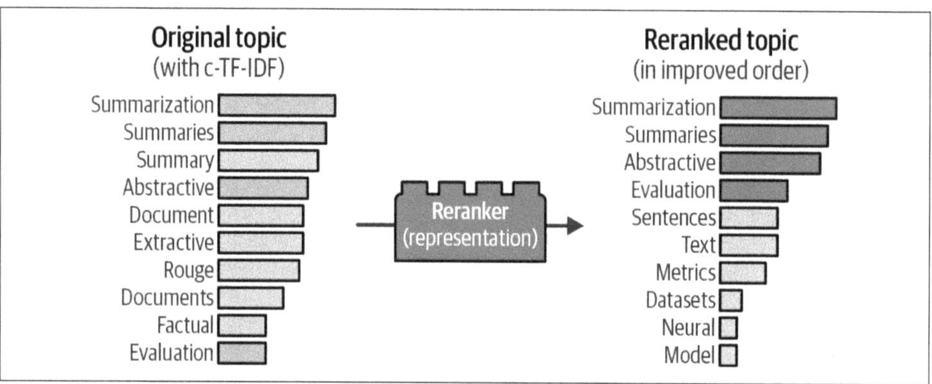

Figure 5-19. Fine-tune the topic representations by reranking the original c-TF-IDF distributions.

As a result, we can design a new Lego block, as shown in Figure 5-20, that takes in this first topic representation and spits out an improved representation.

In BERTopic, such reranker models are referred to as *representation models*. A major benefit of this approach is that the optimization of topic representations only needs to be done as many times as we have topics. For instance, if we have millions of documents and a hundred topics, the representation block only needs to be applied once for every topic instead of for every document.

As shown in Figure 5-21, a wide variety of representation blocks have been designed for BERTopic that allows you to fine-tune the representations. The representation block can even be stacked multiple times to fine-tune representations using different methodologies.

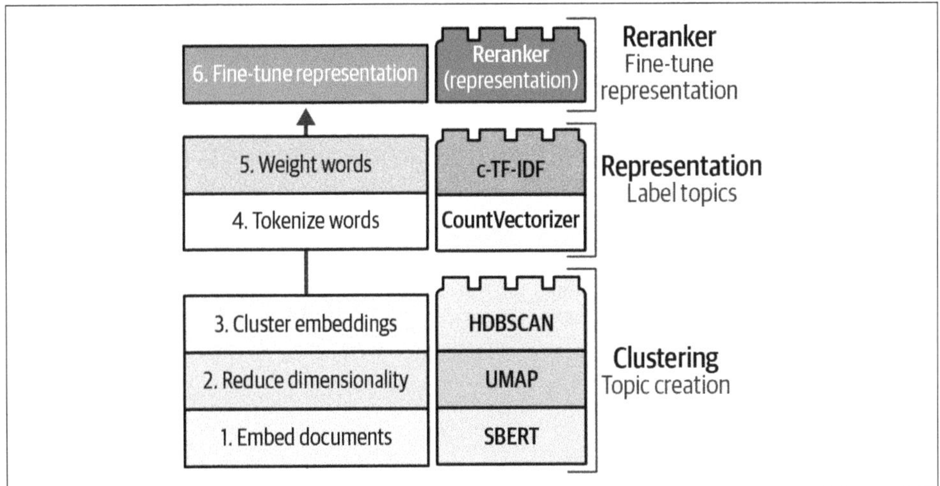

Figure 5-20. The reranker (representation) block sits on top of the c-TF-IDF representation.

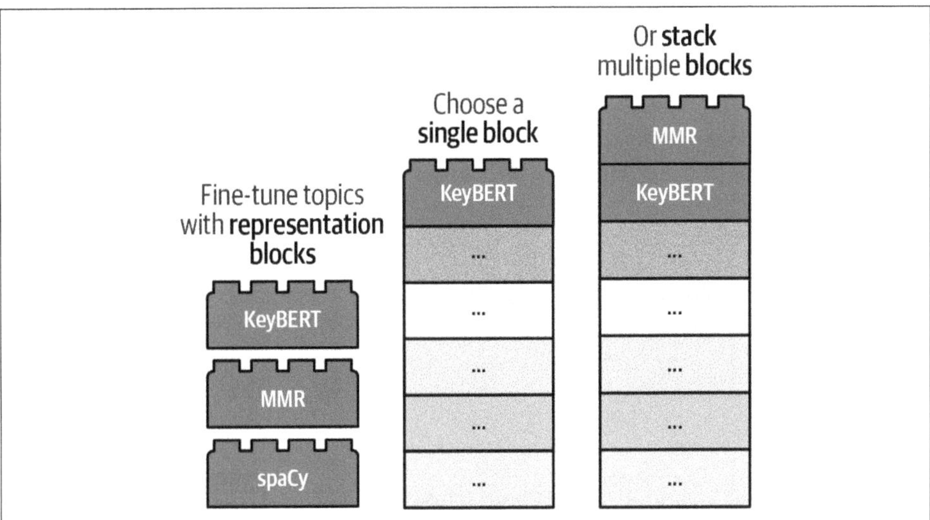

Figure 5-21. After applying the c-TF-IDF weighting, topics can be fine-tuned with a wide variety of representation models, many of which are large language models.

Before we explore how we can use these representation blocks, we first need to do two things. First, we are going to save our original topic representations so that it will be much easier to compare with and without representation models:

```
# Save original representations
from copy import deepcopy
original_topics = deepcopy(topic_model.topic_representations_)
```

Second, let's create a short wrapper that we can use to quickly visualize the differences in topic words to compare with and without representation models:

```
def topic_differences(model, original_topics, nr_topics=5):
    """Show the differences in topic representations between two models """
    df = pd.DataFrame(columns=["Topic", "Original", "Updated"])
    for topic in range(nr_topics):

        # Extract top 5 words per topic per model
        og_words = " | ".join(list(zip(*original_topics[topic]))[0][:5])
        new_words = " | ".join(list(zip(*model.get_topic(topic)))[0][:5])
        df.loc[len(df)] = [topic, og_words, new_words]

    return df
```

KeyBERTInspired

The first representation block that we are going to explore is KeyBERTInspired. KeyBERTInspired is, as you might have guessed, a method inspired by the keyword extraction package, KeyBERT (*https://oreil.ly/_SZU7*).[7] KeyBERT extracts keywords from texts by comparing word and document embeddings through cosine similarity.

BERTopic uses a similar approach. KeyBERTInspired uses c-TF-IDF to extract the most representative documents per topic by calculating the similarity between a document's c-TF-IDF values and those of the topic they correspond to. As shown in Figure 5-22, the average document embedding per topic is calculated and compared to the embeddings of candidate keywords to rerank the keywords.

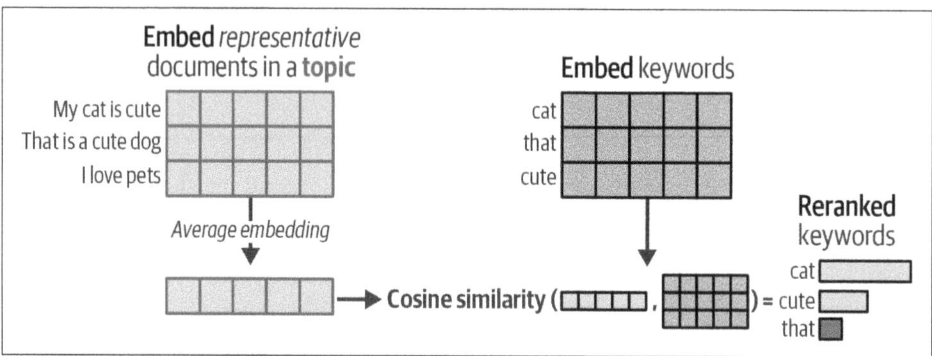

Figure 5-22. KeyBERTInspired representation model procedure.

Due to the modular nature of BERTopic, we can update our initial topic representations with KeyBERTInspired without needing to perform the dimensionality reduction and clustering steps:

7 Maarten Grootendorst. "KeyBERT: Minimal keyword extraction with BERT." (2020).

```
from bertopic.representation import KeyBERTInspired

# Update our topic representations using KeyBERTInspired
representation_model = KeyBERTInspired()
topic_model.update_topics(abstracts, representation_model=representation_model)

# Show topic differences
topic_differences(topic_model, original_topics)
```

Topic	Original	Updated
0	speech | asr | recognition | end | acoustic	speech | encoder | phonetic | language | trans...
1	medical | clinical | biomedical | patient | he...	nlp | ehr | clinical | biomedical | language
2	sentiment | aspect | analysis | reviews | opinion	aspect | sentiment | aspects | sentiments | cl...
3	translation | nmt | machine | neural | bleu	translation | translating | translate | transl...
4	summarization | summaries | summary | abstract...	summarization | summarizers | summaries | summ...

The updated model shows that the topics are easier to read compared to the original model. It also demonstrates the downside of using embedding-based techniques. Words in the original model, like *nmt* (topic 3), which stands for neural machine translation, are removed as the model could not properly represent the entity. For domain experts, these abbreviations are highly informative.

Maximal marginal relevance

With c-TF-IDF and the previously shown KeyBERTInspired techniques, we still have significant redundancy in the resulting topic representations. For instance, having both the words "summaries" and "summary" in a topic representation introduces redundancy as they are quite similar.

We can use maximal marginal relevance (MMR) to diversify our topic representations. The algorithm attempts to find a set of keywords that are diverse from one another but still relate to the documents they are compared to. It does so by embedding a set of candidate keywords and iteratively calculating the next best keyword to add. Doing so requires setting a diversity parameter, which indicates how diverse keywords need to be.

In BERTopic, we use MMR to go from a set of initial keywords, let's say 30, to a smaller but more diverse set of keywords, let's say 10. It filters out redundant words and only keeps words that contribute something new to the topic representation.

Doing so is rather straightforward:

```
from bertopic.representation import MaximalMarginalRelevance

# Update our topic representations to MaximalMarginalRelevance
representation_model = MaximalMarginalRelevance(diversity=0.2)
topic_model.update_topics(abstracts, representation_model=representation_model)

# Show topic differences
topic_differences(topic_model, original_topics)
```

Topic	Original	Updated
0	speech | asr | recognition | end | acoustic	speech | asr | error | model | training
1	medical | clinical | biomedical | patient | he...	clinical | biomedical | patient | healthcare |...
2	sentiment | aspect | analysis | reviews | opinion	sentiment | analysis | reviews | absa | polarity
3	translation | nmt | machine | neural | bleu	translation | nmt | bleu | parallel | multilin...
4	summarization | summaries | summary | abstract...	summarization | document | extractive | rouge ...

The resulting topics demonstrate more diversity in their representations. For instance, topic 4 only shows one "summary"-like word and instead adds other words that might contribute more to the overall representation.

Both KeyBERTInspired and MMR are amazing techniques for improving the first set of topic representations. KeyBERTInspired especially tends to remove nearly all stop words since it focuses on the semantic relationships between words and documents.

The Text Generation Lego Block

The representation block in BERTopic has been acting as a reranking block in our previous examples. However, as we already explored in the previous chapter, generative models have great potential for a wide variety of tasks.

We can use generative models in BERTopic quite efficiently by following a part of the reranking procedure. Instead of using a generative model to identify the topic of all documents, of which there can potentially be millions, we will use the model to generate a label for our topic. As illustrated in Figure 5-23, instead of generating or reranking keywords, we ask the model to generate a short label based on keywords that were previously generated and a small set of representative documents.

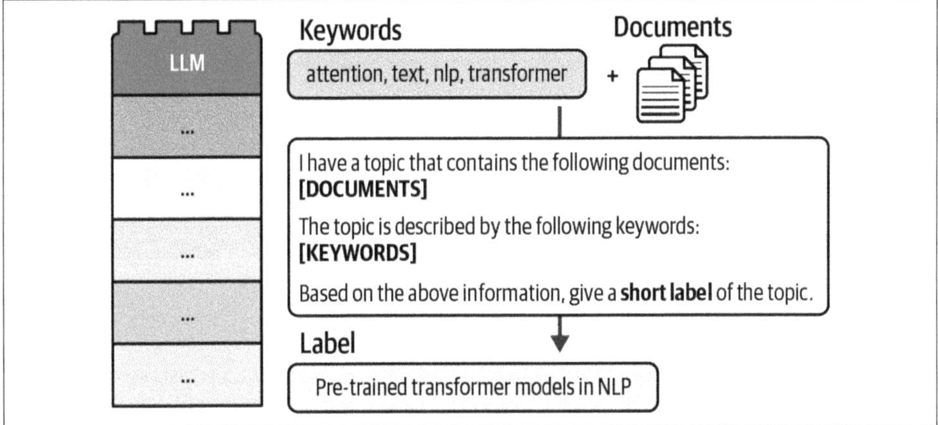

Figure 5-23. Use text generative LLMs and prompt engineering to create labels for topics from keywords and documents related to each topic.

There are two components to the illustrated prompt. First, the documents that are inserted using the `[DOCUMENTS]` tag are a small subset of documents, typically four, that best represent the topic. The documents with the highest cosine similarity of their c-TF-IDF values with those of the topic are selected. Second, the keywords that make up a topic are also passed to the prompt and referenced using the `[KEYWORDS]` tag. The keywords could be generated by c-TF-IDF or any of the other representations we discussed thus far.

As a result, we only need to use the generative model once for every topic, of which there could be potentially hundreds, instead of once for each document, of which there could potentially be millions. There are many generative models that we can choose from, both open source and proprietary. Let's start with a model that we have explored in the previous chapter, the Flan-T5 model.

We create a prompt that works well with the model and use it in BERTopic through the `representation_model` parameter:

```
from transformers import pipeline
from bertopic.representation import TextGeneration

prompt = """I have a topic that contains the following documents:
[DOCUMENTS]

The topic is described by the following keywords: '[KEYWORDS]'.

Based on the documents and keywords, what is this topic about?"""

# Update our topic representations using Flan-T5
generator = pipeline("text2text-generation", model="google/flan-t5-small")
representation_model = TextGeneration(
```

```
    generator, prompt=prompt, doc_length=50, tokenizer="whitespace"
)
topic_model.update_topics(abstracts, representation_model=representation_model)

# Show topic differences
topic_differences(topic_model, original_topics)
```

Topic	Original	Updated
0	speech | asr | recognition | end | acoustic	Speech-to-description
1	medical | clinical | biomedical | patient | he...	Science/Tech
2	sentiment | aspect | analysis | reviews | opinion	Review
3	translation | nmt | machine | neural | bleu	Attention-based neural machine translation
4	summarization | summaries | summary | abstract...	Summarization

Some of these labels, like "Summarization" seem to be logical when comparing them to the original representations. Others, however, like "Science/Tech," seem quite broad and do not do the original topic justice. Let's explore instead how OpenAI's GPT-3.5 would perform considering the model is not only larger but expected to have more linguistic capabilities:

```
import openai
from bertopic.representation import OpenAI

prompt = """
I have a topic that contains the following documents:
[DOCUMENTS]

The topic is described by the following keywords: [KEYWORDS]

Based on the information above, extract a short topic label in the following
format:
topic: <short topic label>
"""

# Update our topic representations using GPT-3.5
client = openai.OpenAI(api_key="YOUR_KEY_HERE")
representation_model = OpenAI(
    client, model="gpt-3.5-turbo", exponential_backoff=True, chat=True,
prompt=prompt
)
topic_model.update_topics(abstracts, representation_model=representation_model)

# Show topic differences
topic_differences(topic_model, original_topics)
```

Topic	Original	Updated
0	speech | asr | recognition | end | acoustic	Leveraging External Data for Improving Low-Res...
1	medical | clinical | biomedical | patient | he...	Improved Representation Learning for Biomedica...
2	sentiment | aspect | analysis | reviews | opinion	Advancements in Aspect-Based Sentiment Analys...
3	translation | nmt | machine | neural | bleu	Neural Machine Translation Enhancements
4	summarization | summaries | summary | abstract...	Document Summarization Techniques

The resulting labels are quite impressive! We are not even using GPT-4 and the resulting labels seem to be more informative than our previous example. Note that BERTopic is not confined to only using OpenAI's offering but has local backends as well.

Although it seems like we do not need the keywords anymore, they are still representative of the input documents. No model is perfect and it is generally advised to generate multiple topic representations. BERTopic allows for all topics to be represented by different representations (*https://oreil.ly/oTzdY*). You could, for example, use KeyBERTInspired, MMR, and GPT-3.5 side by side to get different perspectives on the same topic.

With these GPT-3.5 generated labels, we can create beautiful illustrations using the `datamapplot` package (*https://oreil.ly/LolfZ*) (Figure 5-24):

```
# Visualize topics and documents
fig = topic_model.visualize_document_datamap(
    titles,
    topics=list(range(20)),
    reduced_embeddings=reduced_embeddings,
    width=1200,
    label_font_size=11,
    label_wrap_width=20,
    use_medoids=True,
)
```

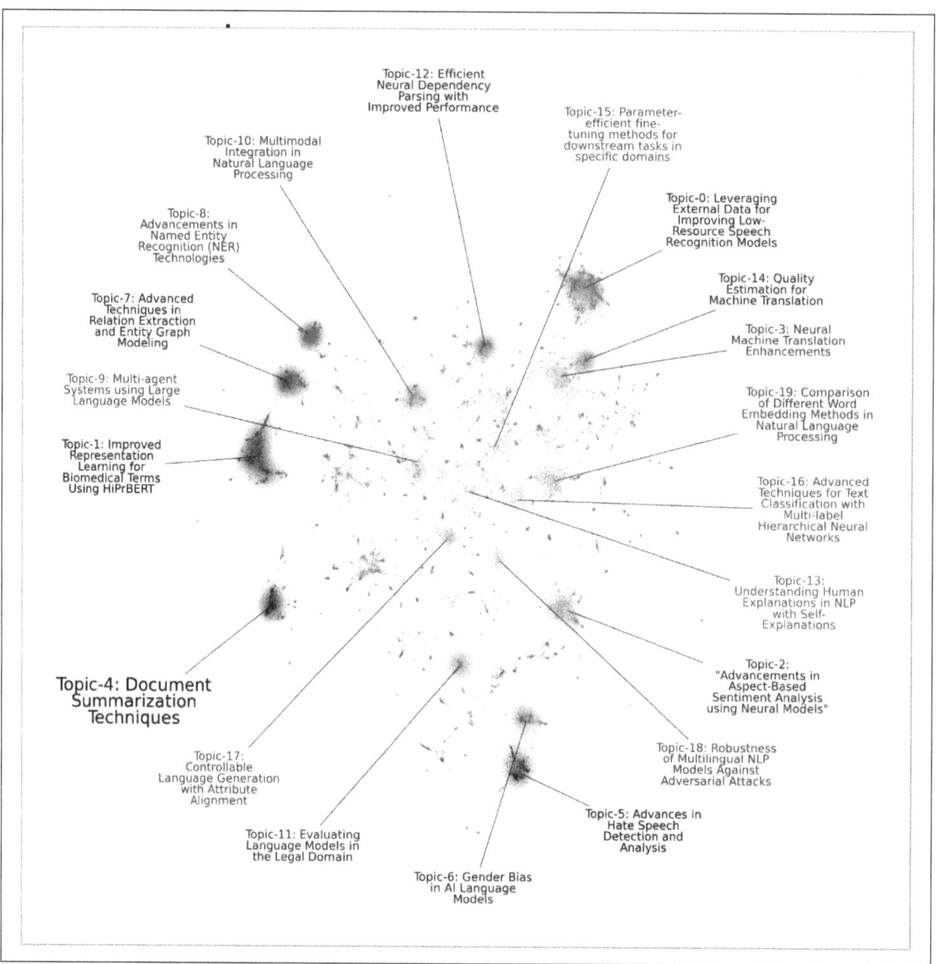

Figure 5-24. The top 20 topics visualized.

Summary

In this chapter, we explored how LLMs, both generative and representative, can be used in the domain of unsupervised learning. Despite supervised methods like classification being prevalent in recent years, unsupervised approaches such as text clustering hold immense potential due to their ability to group texts based on semantic content without prior labeling.

We covered a common pipeline for clustering textual documents that starts with converting input text into numerical representations, which we call embeddings. Then, dimensionality reduction is applied to these embeddings to simplify high-dimensional data for better clustering outcomes. Finally, a clustering algorithm on the dimensionality-reduced embeddings is applied to cluster the input text. Manually inspecting the clusters helped us understand which documents they contained and how to interpret these clusters.

To transition away from this manual inspection, we explored how BERTopic extends this text clustering pipeline with a method for automatically representing the clusters. This methodology is often referred to as topic modeling, which attempts to uncover themes within large amounts of documents. BERTopic generates these topic representations through a bag-of-words approach enhanced with c-TF-IDF, which weighs words based on their cluster relevance and frequency across all clusters.

A major benefit of BERTopic is its modular nature. In BERTopic, you can choose any model in the pipeline, which allows for additional representations of topics that create multiple perspectives of the same topic. We explored maximal marginal relevance and KeyBERTInspired as methodologies to fine-tune the topic representations generated with c-TF-IDF. Additionally, we used the same generative LLMs as in the previous chapter (Flan-T5 and GPT-3.5) to further improve the interpretability of topics by generating highly interpretable labels.

In the next chapter, we shift focus and explore a common method for improving the output of generative models, namely prompt engineering.

CHAPTER 6

Prompt Engineering

In the first chapters of this book, we took our first steps into the world of large language models (LLMs). We delved into various applications, such as supervised and unsupervised classification, employing models that focus on representing text, like BERT and its derivatives.

As we progressed, we used models trained primarily for text generation, models that are often referred to as *generative pre-trained transformers* (GPT). These models have the remarkable ability to generate text in response to *prompts* from the user. Through *prompt engineering*, we can design these prompts in a way that enhances the quality of the generated text.

In this chapter, we will explore these generative models in more detail and dive into the realm of prompt engineering, reasoning with generative models, verification, and even evaluating their output.

Using Text Generation Models

Before we start with the fundamentals of prompt engineering, it is essential to explore the basics of utilizing a text generation model. How do we select the model to use? Do we use a proprietary or open source model? How can we control the generated output? These questions will serve as our stepping stones into using text generation models.

Choosing a Text Generation Model

Choosing a text generation model starts with choosing between proprietary models or open source models. Although proprietary models are generally more performant, we focus in this book more on open source models as they offer more flexibility and are free to use.

Figure 6-1 shows a small selection of impactful foundation models, LLMs that have been pretrained on vast amounts of text data and are often fine-tuned for specific applications.

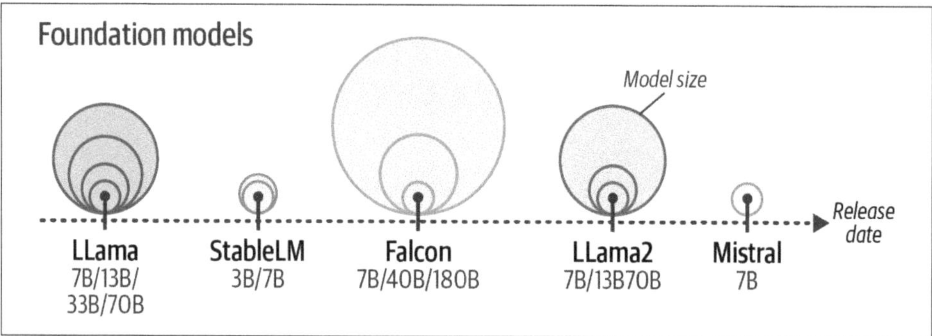

Figure 6-1. Foundation models are often released in several different sizes.

From those foundation models, hundreds if not thousands of models have been fine-tuned, one more suitable for certain tasks than another. Choosing the model to use can be a daunting task!

We advise starting with a small foundation model. So let's continue using Phi-3-mini (*https://oreil.ly/G3CQr*), which has 3.8 billion parameters. This makes it suitable for running with devices up to 8 GB of VRAM. Overall, scaling up to larger models tends to be a nicer experience than scaling down. Smaller models provide a great introduction and lay a solid foundation for progressing to larger models.

Loading a Text Generation Model

The most straightforward method of loading a model, as we have done in previous chapters, is by leveraging the `transformers` library:

```
import torch
from transformers import AutoModelForCausalLM, AutoTokenizer, pipeline

# Load model and tokenizer
model = AutoModelForCausalLM.from_pretrained(
    "microsoft/Phi-3-mini-4k-instruct",
    device_map="cuda",
    torch_dtype="auto",
    trust_remote_code=True,
)
tokenizer = AutoTokenizer.from_pretrained("microsoft/Phi-3-mini-4k-instruct")

# Create a pipeline
pipe = pipeline(
    "text-generation",
    model=model,
```

```
        tokenizer=tokenizer,
        return_full_text=False,
        max_new_tokens=500,
        do_sample=False,
    )
```

Compared to previous chapters, we will take a closer look at developing and using the prompt template.

To illustrate, let's revisit the example from Chapter 1 where we asked the LLM to make a joke about chickens:

```
# Prompt
messages = [
    {"role": "user", "content": "Create a funny joke about chickens."}
]

# Generate the output
output = pipe(messages)
print(output[0]["generated_text"])
```

```
Why don't chickens like to go to the gym? Because they can't crack the egg-
sistence of it!
```

Under the hood, `transformers.pipeline` first converts our messages into a specific prompt template. We can explore this process by accessing the underlying tokenizer:

```
# Apply prompt template
prompt = pipe.tokenizer.apply_chat_template(messages, tokenize=False)
print(prompt)
```

```
<s><|user|>
Create a funny joke about chickens.<|end|>
<|assistant|>
```

You may recognize the special tokens `<|user|>` and `<|assistant|>` from Chapter 2. This prompt template, further illustrated in Figure 6-2, was used during the training of the model. Not only does it provide information about who said what, but it is also used to indicate when the model should stop generating text (see the `<|end|>` token). This prompt is passed directly to the LLM and processed all at once.

In the next chapter, we will customize parts of this template ourselves. Throughout this chapter, we can use `transformers.pipeline` to handle chat template processing for us. Next, let us explore how we can control the output of the model.

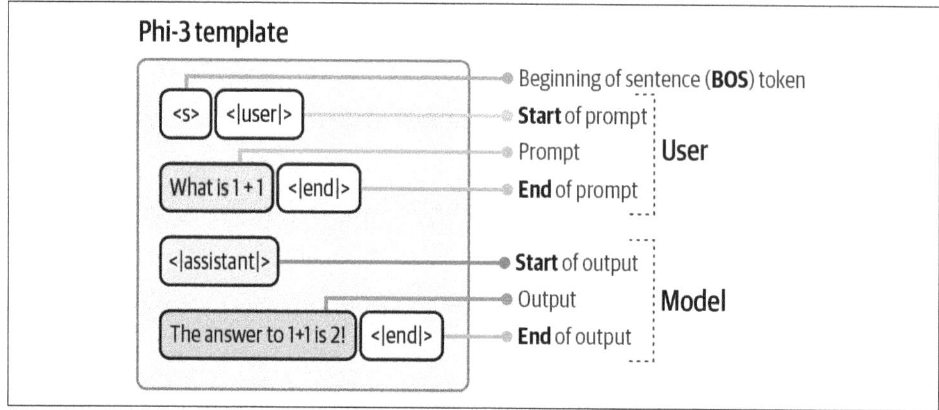

Figure 6-2. The template Phi-3 expects when interacting with the model.

Controlling Model Output

Other than prompt engineering, we can control the kind of output we want by adjusting the model parameters. In our previous example, you might have noticed that we used several parameters in the `pipe` function, including `temperature` and `top_p`.

These parameters control the randomness of the output. A part of what makes LLMs exciting technology is that it can generate different responses for the exact same prompt. Each time an LLM needs to generate a token, it assigns a likelihood number to each possible token.

As illustrated in Figure 6-3, in the sentence "I am driving a…" the likelihood of that sentence being followed by tokens like "car" or "truck" is generally higher than a token like "elephant." However, there is still a possibility of "elephant" being generated but it is much lower.

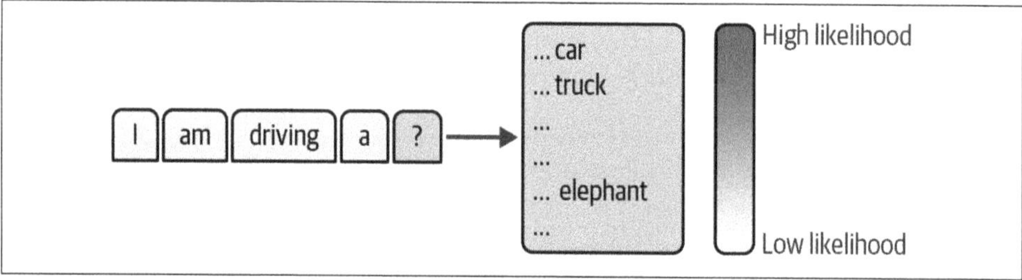

Figure 6-3. The model chooses the next token to generate based on their likelihood scores.

When we loaded our model, we purposefully set `do_sample=False` to make sure the output is somewhat consistent. This means that no sampling will be done and only the most probable next token is selected. However, to use the `temperature` and `top_p` parameters, we will set `do_sample=True` in order to make use of them.

Temperature

The `temperature` controls the randomness or creativity of the text generated. It defines how likely it is to choose tokens that are less probable. The underlying idea is that a `temperature` of 0 generates the same response every time because it always chooses the most likely word. As illustrated in Figure 6-4, a higher value allows less probable words to be generated.

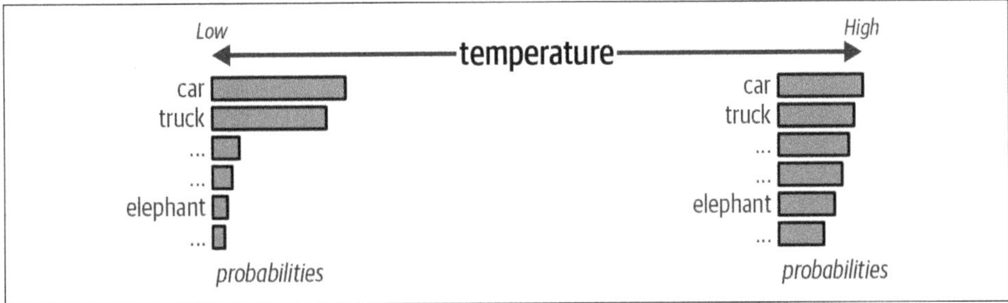

Figure 6-4. A higher `temperature` increases the likelihood that less probable tokens are generated and vice versa.

As a result, a higher `temperature` (e.g., 0.8) generally results in a more diverse output while a lower `temperature` (e.g., 0.2) creates a more deterministic output.

You can use `temperature` in your pipeline as follows:

```
# Using a high temperature
output = pipe(messages, do_sample=True, temperature=1)
print(output[0]["generated_text"])
```

```
Why don't chickens like to go on a rollercoaster? Because they're afraid they
might suddenly become chicken-soup!
```

Note that every time you rerun this piece of code, the output will change! `temperature` introduces stochastic behavior since the model now randomly selects tokens.

top_p

`top_p`, also known as nucleus sampling, is a sampling technique that controls which subset of tokens (the nucleus) the LLM can consider. It will consider tokens until it reaches their cumulative probability. If we set `top_p` to 0.1, it will consider tokens until it reaches that value. If we set `top_p` to 1, it will consider all tokens.

As shown in Figure 6-5, by lowering the value, it will consider fewer tokens and generally give less "creative" output, while increasing the value allows the LLM to choose from more tokens.

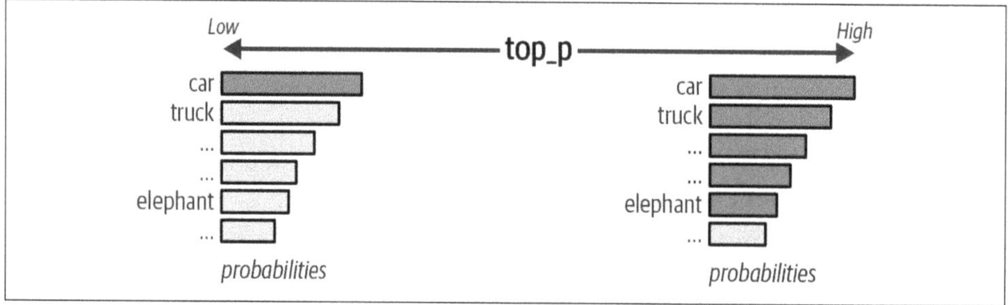

Figure 6-5. A higher `top_p` increases the number of tokens that can be selected to generate and vice versa.

Similarly, the `top_k` parameter controls exactly how many tokens the LLM can consider. If you change its value to 100, the LLM will only consider the top 100 most probable tokens.

You can use `top_p` in your pipeline as follows:

```
# Using a high top_p
output = pipe(messages, do_sample=True, top_p=1)
print(output[0]["generated_text"])
```

```
Why don't chickens make good comedians? Because their 'jokes' always 'feather'
the truth!
```

As shown in Table 6-1, these parameters allow the user to have a sliding scale between being creative (high `temperature` and `top_p`) and being predictable (lower `temperature` and `top_p`).

Table 6-1. Use case examples when selecting values for `temperature` and `top_p`.

Example use case	`Tempera ture`	`top_p`	Description
Brainstorming session	High	High	High randomness with large pool of potential tokens. The results will be highly diverse, often leading to very creative and unexpected results.
Email generation	Low	Low	Deterministic output with high probable predicted tokens. This results in predictable, focused, and conservative outputs.
Creative writing	High	Low	High randomness with a small pool of potential tokens. This combination produces creative outputs but still remains coherent.
Translation	Low	High	Deterministic output with high probable predicted tokens. Produces coherent output with a wider range of vocabulary, leading to outputs with linguistic variety.

Intro to Prompt Engineering

An essential part of working with text-generative LLMs is prompt engineering. By carefully designing our prompts we can guide the LLM to generate desired responses. Whether the prompts are questions, statements, or instructions, the main goal of prompt engineering is to elicit a useful response from the model.

Prompt engineering is more than designing effective prompts. It can be used as a tool to evaluate the output of a model as well as to design safeguards and safety mitigation methods. This is an iterative process of prompt optimization and requires experimentation. There is not and unlikely will ever be a perfect prompt design.

In this section, we will go through common methods for prompt engineering, and small tips and tricks to understand what the effect is of certain prompts. These skills allow us to understand the capabilities of LLMs and lie at the foundation of interfacing with these kinds of models.

We begin by answering the question: what should be in a prompt?

The Basic Ingredients of a Prompt

An LLM is a prediction machine. Based on a certain input, the prompt, it tries to predict the words that might follow it. At its core (illustrated in Figure 6-6), the prompt does not need to be more than a few words to elicit a response from the LLM.

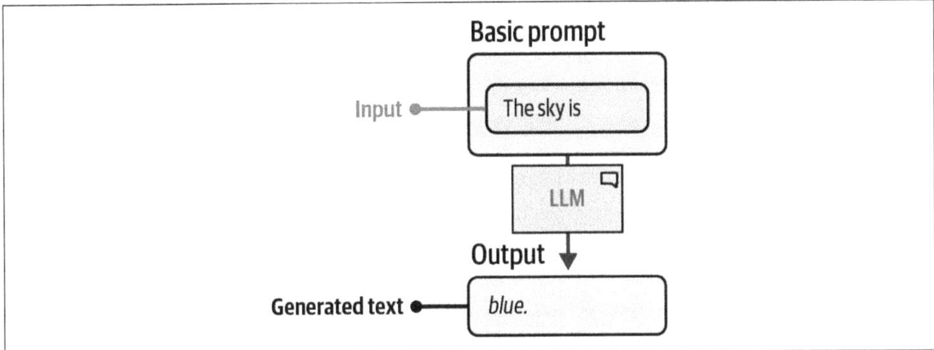

Figure 6-6. A basic example of a prompt. No instruction is given so the LLM will simply try to complete the sentence.

However, although the illustration works as a basic example, it fails to complete a specific task. Instead, we generally approach prompt engineering by asking a specific question or task the LLM should complete. To elicit the desired response, we need a more structured prompt.

For example, and as shown in Figure 6-7, we could ask the LLM to classify a sentence into either having positive or negative sentiment. This extends the most basic prompt to one consisting of two components—the instruction itself and the data that relates to the instruction.

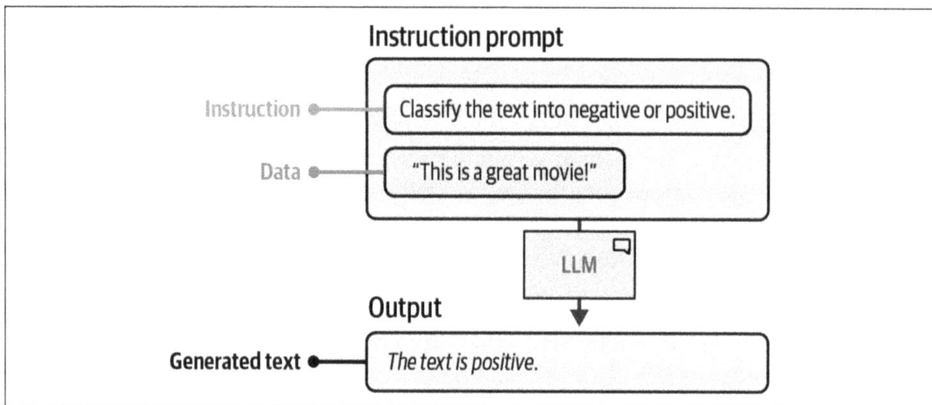

Figure 6-7. Two components of a basic instruction prompt: the instruction itself and the data it refers to.

More complex use cases might require more components in a prompt. For instance, to make sure the model only outputs "negative" or "positive" we can introduce output indicators that help guide the model. In Figure 6-8, we prefix the sentence with "Text:" and add "Sentiment:" to prevent the model from generating a complete sentence. Instead, this structure indicates that we expect either "negative" or "positive." Although the model might not have been trained on these components directly, it was fed enough instructions to be able to generalize to this structure.

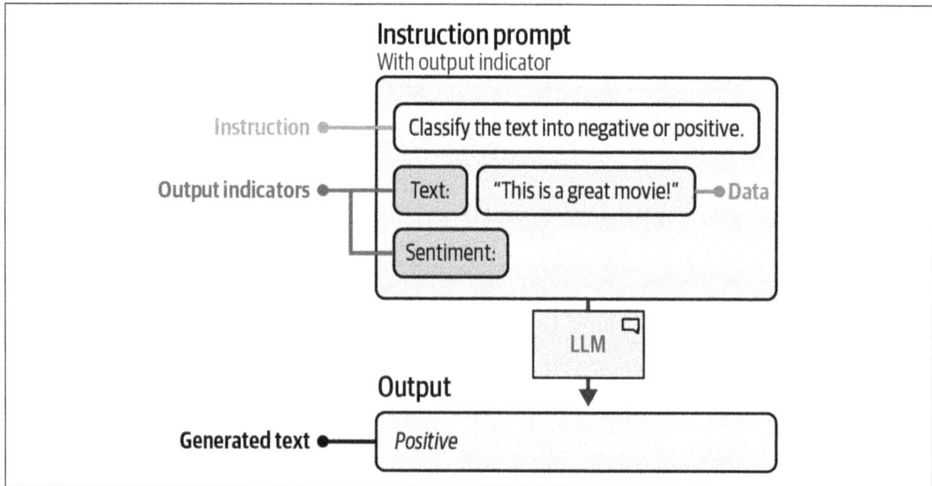

Figure 6-8. Extending the prompt with an output indicator that allows for a specific output.

We can continue adding or updating the elements of a prompt until we elicit the response we are looking for. We could add additional examples, describe the use case in more detail, provide additional context, etc. These components are merely examples and not a limited set of possibilities. The creativity that comes with designing these components is key.

Although a prompt is a single piece of text, it is tremendously helpful to think of prompts as pieces of a larger puzzle. Have I described the context of my question? Does the prompt have an example of the output?

Instruction-Based Prompting

Although prompting comes in many flavors, from discussing philosophy with the LLM to role-playing with your favorite superhero, prompting is often used to have the LLM answer a specific question or resolve a certain task. This is referred to as *instruction-based prompting*.

Figure 6-9 illustrates a number of use cases in which instruction-based prompting plays an important role. We already did one of these in the previous example, namely supervised classification.

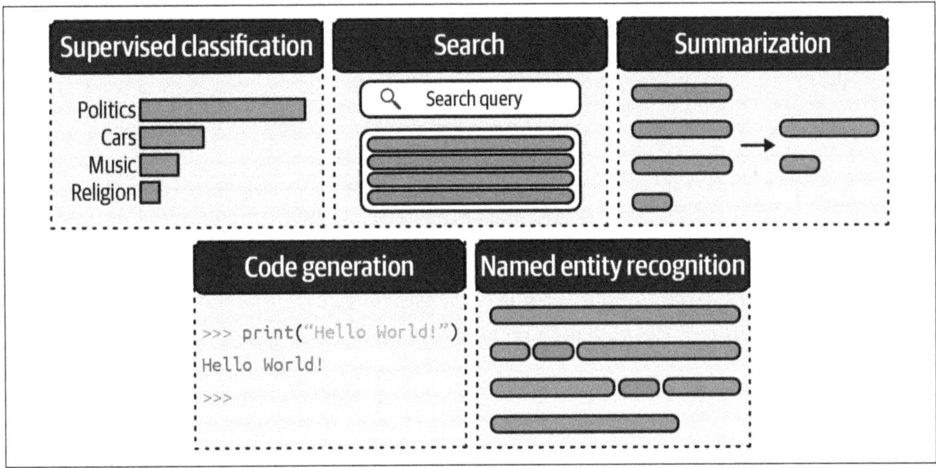

Figure 6-9. Use cases for instruction-based prompting.

Each of these tasks requires different prompting formats and more specifically, asking different questions of the LLM. Asking the LLM to summarize a piece of text will not suddenly result in classification. To illustrate, examples of prompts for some of these use cases can be found in Figure 6-10.

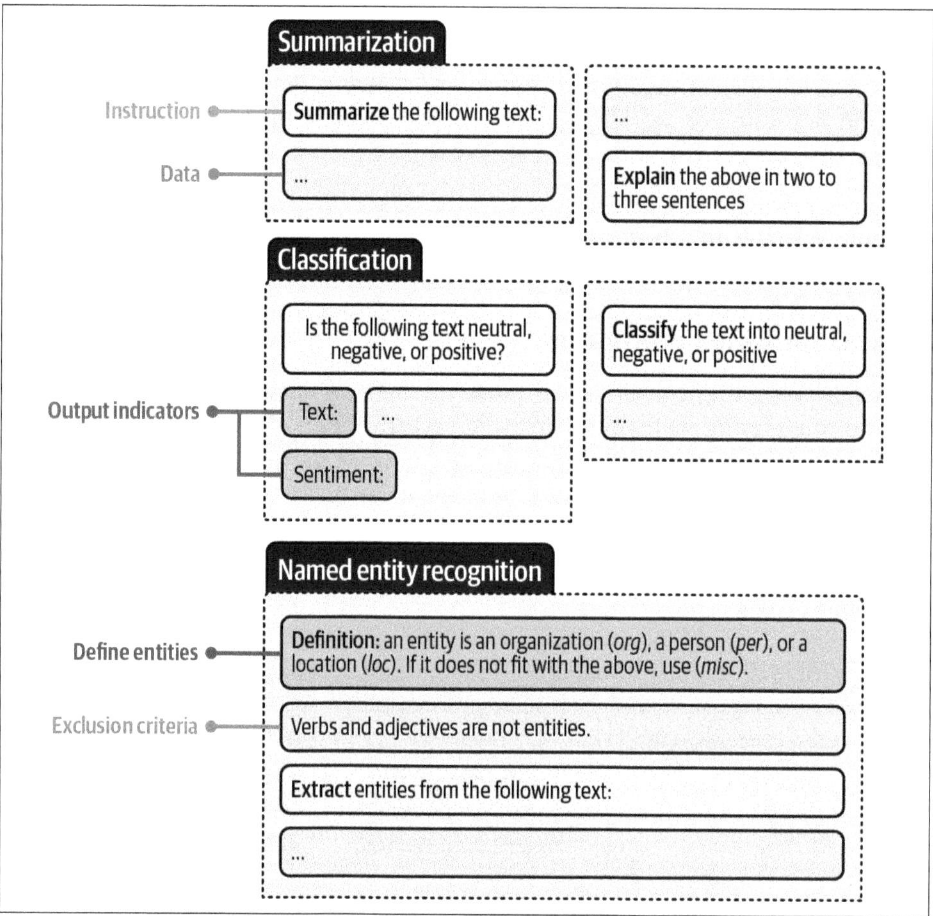

Figure 6-10. Prompt examples of common use cases. Notice how within a use case, the structure and location of the instruction can be changed.

Although these tasks require different instructions, there is actually a lot of overlap in the prompting techniques used to improve the quality of the output. A non-exhaustive list of these techniques includes:

Specificity
: Accurately describe what you want to achieve. Instead of asking the LLM to "Write a description for a product" ask it to "Write a description for a product in less than two sentences and use a formal tone."

Hallucination
: LLMs may generate incorrect information confidently, which is referred to as hallucination. To reduce its impact, we can ask the LLM to only generate an answer if it knows the answer. If it does not know the answer, it can respond with "I don't know."

Order
: Either begin or end your prompt with the instruction. Especially with long prompts, information in the middle is often forgotten.[1] LLMs tend to focus on information either at the beginning of a prompt (primacy effect) or the end of a prompt (recency effect).

Here, specificity is arguably the most important aspect. By restricting and specifying what the model should generate, there is a smaller chance of having it generate something not related to your use case. For instance, if we were to skip the instruction "in two to three sentences" it might generate complete paragraphs. Like human conversations, without any specific instructions or additional context, it is difficult to derive what the task at hand actually is.

Advanced Prompt Engineering

On the surface, creating a good prompt might seem straightforward. Ask a specific question, be accurate, add some examples, and you are done! However, prompting can grow complex quite quickly and as a result is an often-underestimated component of leveraging LLMs.

Here, we will go through several advanced techniques for building up your prompts, starting with the iterative workflow of building up complex prompts all the way to using LLMs sequentially to get improved results. Eventually, we will even build up to advanced reasoning techniques.

The Potential Complexity of a Prompt

As we explored in the intro to prompt engineering, a prompt generally consists of multiple components. In our very first example, our prompt consisted of instruction, data, and output indicators. As we mentioned before, no prompt is limited to just these three components and you can build it up to be as complex as you want.

These advanced components can quickly make a prompt quite complex. Some common components are:

1 Nelson F. Liu et al. "Lost in the middle: How language models use long contexts." *arXiv preprint arXiv:2307.03172* (2023).

Persona
: Describe what role the LLM should take on. For example, use "You are an expert in astrophysics" if you want to ask a question about astrophysics.

Instruction
: The task itself. Make sure this is as specific as possible. We do not want to leave much room for interpretation.

Context
: Additional information describing the context of the problem or task. It answers questions like "What is the reason for the instruction?"

Format
: The format the LLM should use to output the generated text. Without it, the LLM will come up with a format itself, which is troublesome in automated systems.

Audience
: The target of the generated text. This also describes the level of the generated output. For education purposes, it is often helpful to use ELI5 ("Explain it like I'm 5").

Tone
: The tone of voice the LLM should use in the generated text. If you are writing a formal email to your boss, you might not want to use an informal tone of voice.

Data
: The main data related to the task itself.

To illustrate, let us extend the classification prompt we had earlier and use all of the preceding components. This is demonstrated in Figure 6-11.

This complex prompt demonstrates the modular nature of prompting. We can add and remove components freely and judge their effect on the output. As illustrated in Figure 6-12, we can slowly build up our prompt and explore the effect of each change.

The changes are not limited to simply introducing or removing components. Their order, as we saw before with the recency and primacy effects, can affect the quality of the LLM's output. In other words, experimentation is vital when finding the best prompt for your use case. With prompting, we essentially have ourselves in an iterative cycle of experimentation.

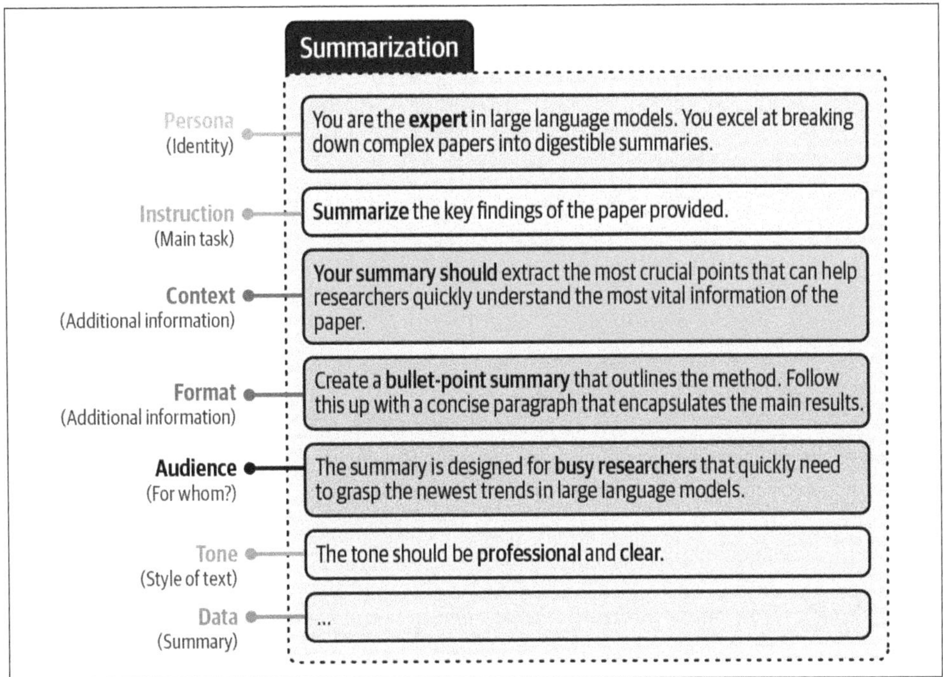

Figure 6-11. An example of a complex prompt with many components.

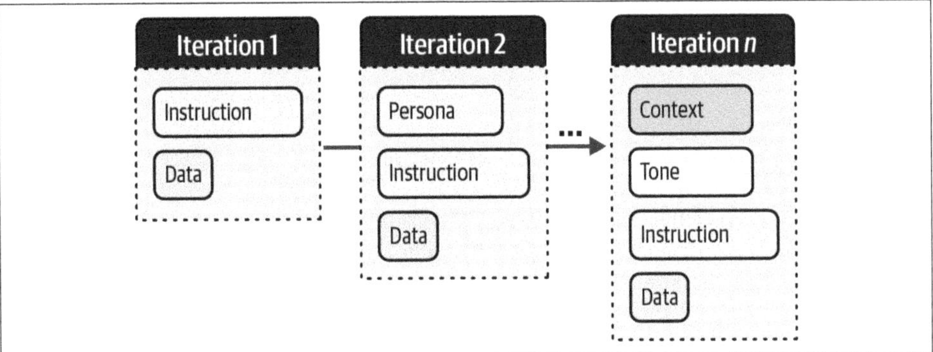

Figure 6-12. Iterating over modular components is a vital part of prompt engineering.

Try it out yourself! Use the complex prompt to add and/or remove parts to observe its impact on the generated output. You will quickly notice when pieces of the puzzle are worth keeping. You can use your own data by adding it to the `data` variable:

```
# Prompt components
persona = "You are an expert in Large Language models. You excel at breaking
down complex papers into digestible summaries.\n"
instruction = "Summarize the key findings of the paper provided.\n"
context = "Your summary should extract the most crucial points that can help
researchers quickly understand the most vital information of the paper.\n"
data_format = "Create a bullet-point summary that outlines the method. Follow
this up with a concise paragraph that encapsulates the main results.\n"
audience = "The summary is designed for busy researchers that quickly need to
grasp the newest trends in Large Language Models.\n"
tone = "The tone should be professional and clear.\n"
text = "MY TEXT TO SUMMARIZE"
data = f"Text to summarize: {text}"

# The full prompt - remove and add pieces to view its impact on the generated
output
query = persona + instruction + context + data_format + audience + tone + data
```

There is all manner of components that we could add and creative components like using emotional stimuli (e.g., "This is very important for my career."[2]). Part of the fun in prompt engineering is that you can be as creative as possible to figure out which combination of prompt components contribute to your use case. There are few constraints to developing a format that works for you.

In a way, it is an attempt to reverse engineer what the model has learned and how it responds to certain prompts. However, note that some prompts work better for certain models compared to others as their training data might be different or they are trained for different purposes.

In-Context Learning: Providing Examples

In the previous sections, we tried to accurately describe what the LLM should do. Although accurate and specific descriptions help the LLM to understand the use case, we can go one step further. Instead of describing the task, why do we not just show the task?

We can provide the LLM with examples of exactly the thing that we want to achieve. This is often referred to as *in-context learning*, where we provide the model with correct examples.[3]

2 Cheng Li et al. "EmotionPrompt: Leveraging psychology for large language models enhancement via emotional stimulus." *arXiv preprint arXiv:2307.11760* (2023).

3 Tom Brown et al. "Language models are few-shot learners." *Advances in Neural Information Processing Systems* 33 (2020): 1877–1901.

As illustrated in Figure 6-13, this comes in a number of forms depending on how many examples you show the LLM. Zero-shot prompting does not leverage examples, one-shot prompts use a single example, and few-shot prompts use two or more examples.

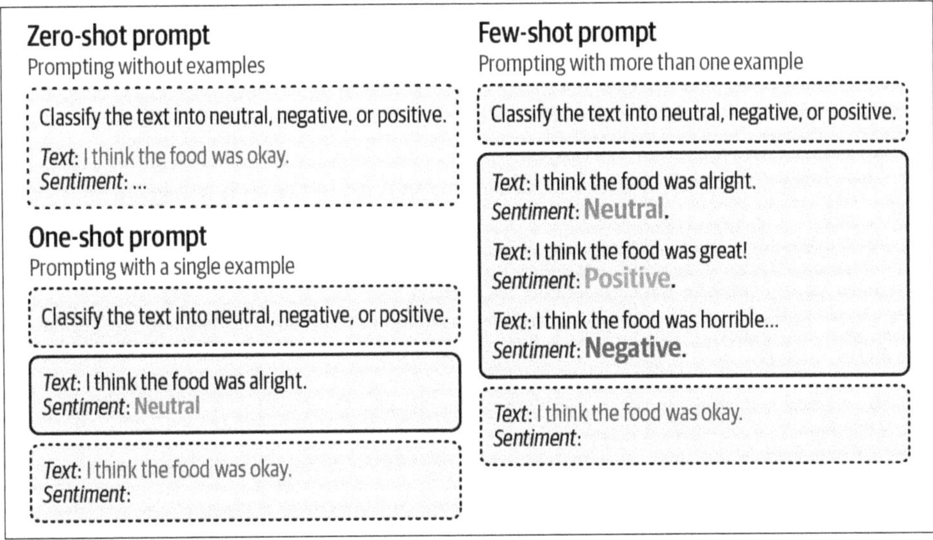

Figure 6-13. An example of a complex prompt with many components.

Adopting the original phrase, we believe that "an example is worth a thousand words." These examples provide a direct example of what and how the LLM should achieve.

We can illustrate this method with a simple example taken from the original paper describing this method.[4] The goal of the prompt is to generate a sentence with a made-up word. To improve the quality of the resulting sentence, we can show the generative model an example of what a proper sentence with a made-up word would be.

To do so, we will need to differentiate between our question (`user`) and the answers that were provided by the model (`assistant`). We additionally showcase how this interaction is processed using the template:

```
# Use a single example of using the made-up word in a sentence
one_shot_prompt = [
    {
        "role": "user",
        "content": "A 'Gigamuru' is a type of Japanese musical instrument. An 
example of a sentence that uses the word Gigamuru is:"
```

4 Ibid.

```
    },
    {
        "role": "assistant",
        "content": "I have a Gigamuru that my uncle gave me as a gift. I love
to play it at home."
    },
    {
        "role": "user",
        "content": "To 'screeg' something is to swing a sword at it. An example
of a sentence that uses the word screeg is:"
    }
]
print(tokenizer.apply_chat_template(one_shot_prompt, tokenize=False))
```

```
<s><|user|>
A 'Gigamuru' is a type of Japanese musical instrument. An example of a sen-
tence that uses the word Gigamuru is:<|end|>
<|assistant|>
I have a Gigamuru that my uncle gave me as a gift. I love to play it at home.<|
end|>
<|user|>
To 'screeg' something is to swing a sword at it. An example of a sentence that
uses the word screeg is:<|end|>
<|assistant|>
```

The prompt illustrates the need to differentiate between the user and the assistant. If we did not, it would seem as if we were talking to ourselves. Using these interactions, we can generate output as follows:

```
# Generate the output
outputs = pipe(one_shot_prompt)
print(outputs[0]["generated_text"])
```

```
During the intense duel, the knight skillfully screeged his opponent's shield,
forcing him to defend himself.
```

It correctly generated the answer!

As with all prompt components, one- or few-shot prompting is not the be all and end all of prompt engineering. We can use it as one piece of the puzzle to further enhance the descriptions that we gave it. The model can still "choose," through random sampling, to ignore the instructions.

Chain Prompting: Breaking up the Problem

In previous examples, we explored splitting up prompts into modular components to improve the performance of LLMs. Although this works well for many use cases, this might not be feasible for highly complex prompts or use cases.

Instead of breaking the problem within a prompt, we can do so between prompts. Essentially, we take the output of one prompt and use it as input for the next, thereby creating a continuous chain of interactions that solves our problem.

To illustrate, let us say we want to use an LLM to create a product name, slogan, and sales pitch for us based on a number of product features. Although we can ask the LLM to do this in one go, we can instead break up the problem into pieces.

As a result, and as illustrated in Figure 6-14, we get a sequential pipeline that first creates the product name, uses that with the product features as input to create the slogan, and finally, uses the features, product name, and slogan to create the sales pitch.

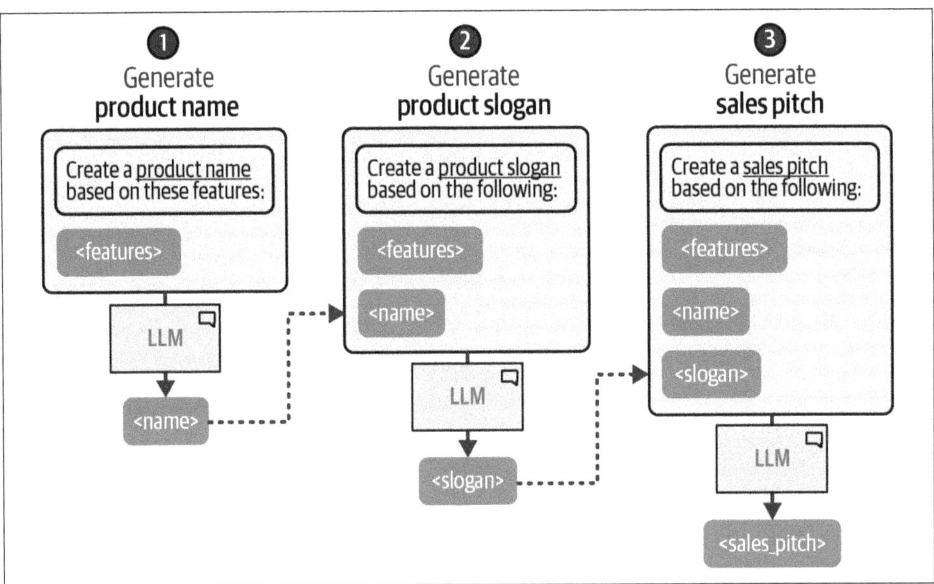

Figure 6-14. Using a description of a product's features, chain prompts to create a suitable name, slogan, and sales pitch.

This technique of chaining prompts allows the LLM to spend more time on each individual question instead of tackling the whole problem. Let us illustrate this with a small example. We first create a name and slogan for a chatbot:

```
# Create name and slogan for a product
product_prompt = [
    {"role": "user", "content": "Create a name and slogan for a chatbot that
leverages LLMs."}
]
outputs = pipe(product_prompt)
product_description = outputs[0]["generated_text"]
print(product_description)
```

```
Name: 'MindMeld Messenger'

Slogan: 'Unleashing Intelligent Conversations, One Response at a Time'
```

Then, we can use the generated output as input for the LLM to generate a sales pitch:

```
# Based on a name and slogan for a product, generate a sales pitch
sales_prompt = [
    {"role": "user", "content": f"Generate a very short sales pitch for the
following product: '{product_description}'"}
]
outputs = pipe(sales_prompt)
sales_pitch = outputs[0]["generated_text"]
print(sales_pitch)
```

```
Introducing MindMeld Messenger - your ultimate communication partner! Unleash
intelligent conversations with our innovative AI-powered messaging platform.
With MindMeld Messenger, every response is thoughtful, personalized, and
timely. Say goodbye to generic replies and hello to meaningful interactions.
Elevate your communication game with MindMeld Messenger - where every message
is a step toward smarter conversations. Try it now and experience the future
of messaging!
```

Although we need two calls to the model, a major benefit is that we can give each call different parameters. For instance, the number of tokens created was relatively small for the name and slogan whereas the pitch can be much longer.

This can be used for a variety of use cases, including:

Response validation
: Ask the LLM to double-check previously generated outputs.

Parallel prompts
: Create multiple prompts in parallel and do a final pass to merge them. For example, ask multiple LLMs to generate multiple recipes in parallel and use the combined result to create a shopping list.

Writing stories
: Leverage the LLM to write books or stories by breaking down the problem into components. For example, by first writing a summary, developing characters, and building the story beats before diving into creating the dialogue.

In the next chapter, we will automate this process and go beyond chaining LLMs. We will chain other pieces of technology together, like memory, tool use, and more! Before that, this idea of prompt chaining will be explored further in the following sections, which describe more complex prompt chaining methods like self-consistency, chain-of-thought, and tree-of-thought.

Reasoning with Generative Models

In the previous sections, we focused mostly on the modular component of prompts, building them up through iteration. These advanced prompt engineering techniques, like prompt chaining, proved to be the first step toward enabling complex reasoning with generative models.

Reasoning is a core component of human intelligence and is often compared to the emergent behavior of LLMs that often resembles reasoning. We highlight "resemble" as these models, at the time of writing, are generally considered to demonstrate this behavior through memorization of training data and pattern matching.

The output that they showcase, however, can demonstrate complex behavior and although it might not be "true" reasoning, they are still referred to as reasoning capabilities. In other words, we work together with the LLM through prompt engineering so we can mimic reasoning processes in order to improve the output of the LLM.

To allow for this reasoning behavior, it is a good moment to step back and explore what reasoning entails in human behavior. To simplify, our methods of reasoning can be divided into system 1 and 2 thinking processes.

System 1 thinking represents an automatic, intuitive, and near-instantaneous process. It shares similarities with generative models that automatically generate tokens without any self-reflective behavior. In contrast, system 2 thinking is a conscious, slow, and logical process, akin to brainstorming and self-reflection.[5]

If we could give a generative model the ability to mimic a form of self-reflection, we would essentially be emulating the system 2 way of thinking, which tends to produce more thoughtful responses than system 1 thinking. In this section, we will explore several techniques that attempt to mimic these kinds of thought processes of human reasoners with the aim of improving the output of the model.

Chain-of-Thought: Think Before Answering

The first and major step toward complex reasoning in generative models was through a method called chain-of-thought. Chain-of-thought aims to have the generative model "think" first rather than answering the question directly without any reasoning.[6]

As illustrated in Figure 6-15, it provides examples in a prompt that demonstrate the reasoning the model should do before generating its response. These reasoning processes are referred to as "thoughts." This helps tremendously for tasks that involve a higher degree of complexity, like mathematical questions. Adding this reasoning step allows the model to distribute more compute over the reasoning process. Instead

5 Daniel Kahneman. *Thinking, Fast and Slow*. Macmillan (2011).

6 Jason Wei et al. "Chain-of-thought prompting elicits reasoning in large language models." *Advances in Neural Information Processing Systems* 35 (2022): 24824–24837.

of calculating the entire solution based on a few tokens, each additional token in this reasoning process allows the LLM to stabilize its output.

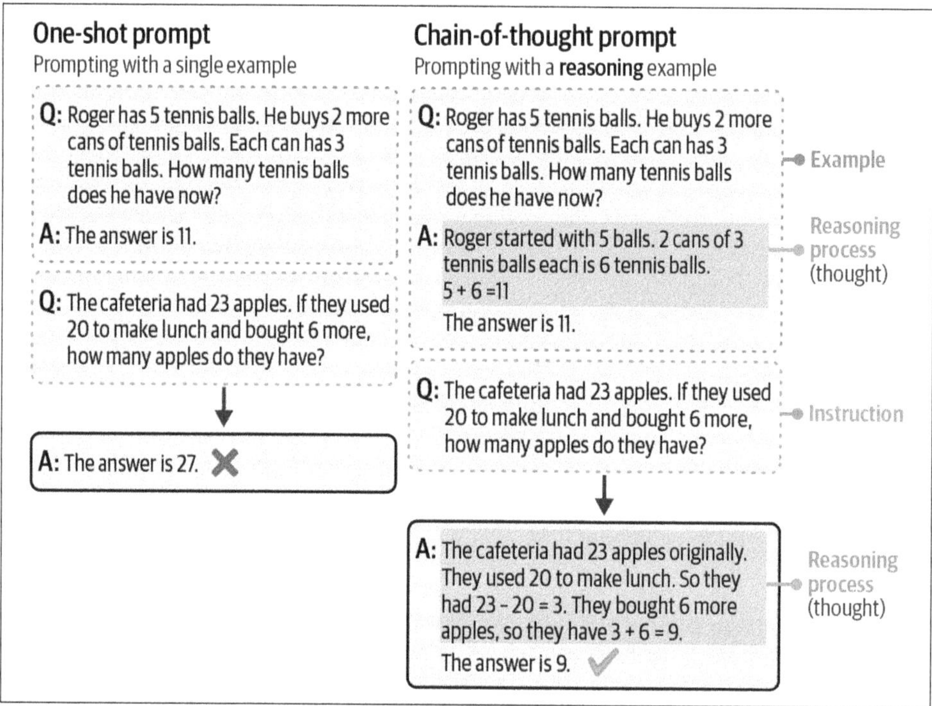

Figure 6-15. Chain-of-thought prompting uses reasoning examples to persuade the generative model to use reasoning in its answer.

We use the example the authors used in their paper to demonstrate this phenomenon:

```
# Answering with chain-of-thought
cot_prompt = [
    {"role": "user", "content": "Roger has 5 tennis balls. He buys 2 more cans
of tennis balls. Each can has 3 tennis balls. How many tennis balls does he
have now?"},
    {"role": "assistant", "content": "Roger started with 5 balls. 2 cans of 3
tennis balls each is 6 tennis balls. 5 + 6 = 11. The answer is 11."},
    {"role": "user", "content": "The cafeteria had 23 apples. If they used 20
to make lunch and bought 6 more, how many apples do they have?"}
]

# Generate the output
outputs = pipe(cot_prompt)
print(outputs[0]["generated_text"])
```

```
The cafeteria started with 23 apples. They used 20 apples, so they had 23 - 20
= 3 apples left. Then they bought 6 more apples, so they now have 3 + 6 = 9
apples. The answer is 9.
```

Note how the model doesn't generate only the answer but provides an explanation before doing so. By doing so, it can leverage the knowledge it has generated thus far to compute the final answer.

Although chain-of-thought is a great method for enhancing the output of a generative model, it does require one or more examples of reasoning in the prompt, which the user might not have access to. Instead of providing examples, we can simply ask the generative model to provide the reasoning (zero-shot chain-of-thought). There are many different forms that work but a common and effective method is to use the phrase "Let's think step-by-step," which is illustrated in Figure 6-16.[7]

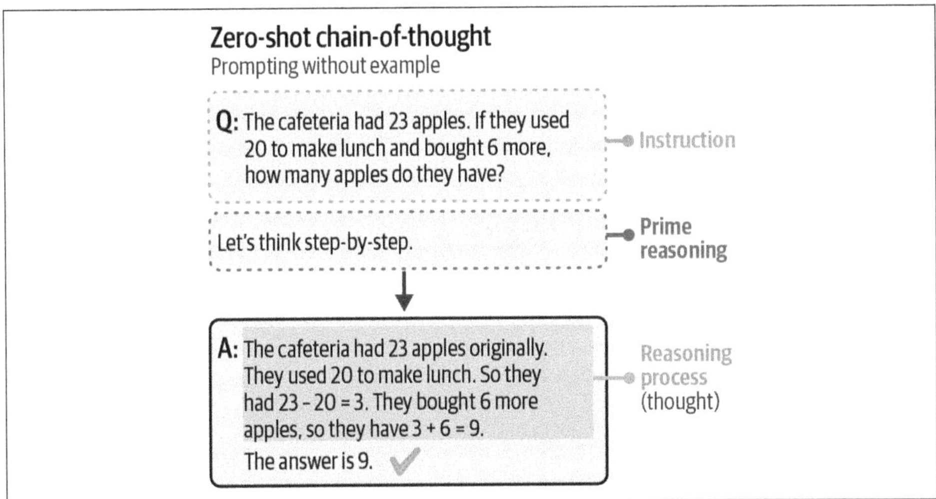

Figure 6-16. Chain-of-thought prompting without using examples. Instead, it uses the phrase "Let's think step-by-step" to prime reasoning in its answer.

Using the example we used before, we can simply append that phrase to the prompt to enable chain-of-thought-like reasoning:

```
# Zero-shot chain-of-thought
zeroshot_cot_prompt = [
    {"role": "user", "content": "The cafeteria had 23 apples. If they used 20
to make lunch and bought 6 more, how many apples do they have? Let's think
step-by-step."}
]

# Generate the output
outputs = pipe(zeroshot_cot_prompt)
print(outputs[0]["generated_text"])
```

7 Takeshi Kojima et al. "Large language models are zero-shot reasoners." *Advances in Neural Information Processing Systems* 35 (2022): 22199–22213.

```
Step 1: Start with the initial number of apples, which is 23.
Step 2: Subtract the number of apples used to make lunch, which is 20. So, 23
- 20 = 3 apples remaining.
Step 3: Add the number of apples bought, which is 6. So, 3 + 6 = 9 apples.

The cafeteria now has 9 apples.
```

Without needing to provide examples, we again got the same reasoning behavior. This is why it is so important to "show your work" when doing calculations. By addressing the reasoning process the LLM can use the previously generated information as a guide through generating the final answer.

Although the prompt "Let's think step by step" can improve the output, you are not constrained by this exact formulation. Alternatives exist like "Take a deep breath and think step-by-step" and "Let's work through this problem step-by-step."[8]

Self-Consistency: Sampling Outputs

Using the same prompt multiple times can lead to different results if we allow for a degree of creativity through parameters like `temperature` and `top_p`. As a result, the quality of the output might improve or degrade depending on the random selection of tokens. In other words, luck!

To counteract this degree of randomness and improve the performance of generative models, self-consistency was introduced. This method asks the generative model the same prompt multiple times and takes the majority result as the final answer.[9] During this process, each answer can be affected by different `temperature` and `top_p` values to increase the diversity of sampling.

As illustrated in Figure 6-17, this method can further be improved by adding chain-of-thought prompting to improve its reasoning while only using the answer for the voting procedure.

8 Chengrun Yang et al. "Large language models as optimizers." *arXiv preprint arXiv:2309.03409* (2023).

9 Xuezhi Wang et al. "Self-consistency improves chain of thought reasoning in language models." *arXiv preprint arXiv:2203.11171* (2022).

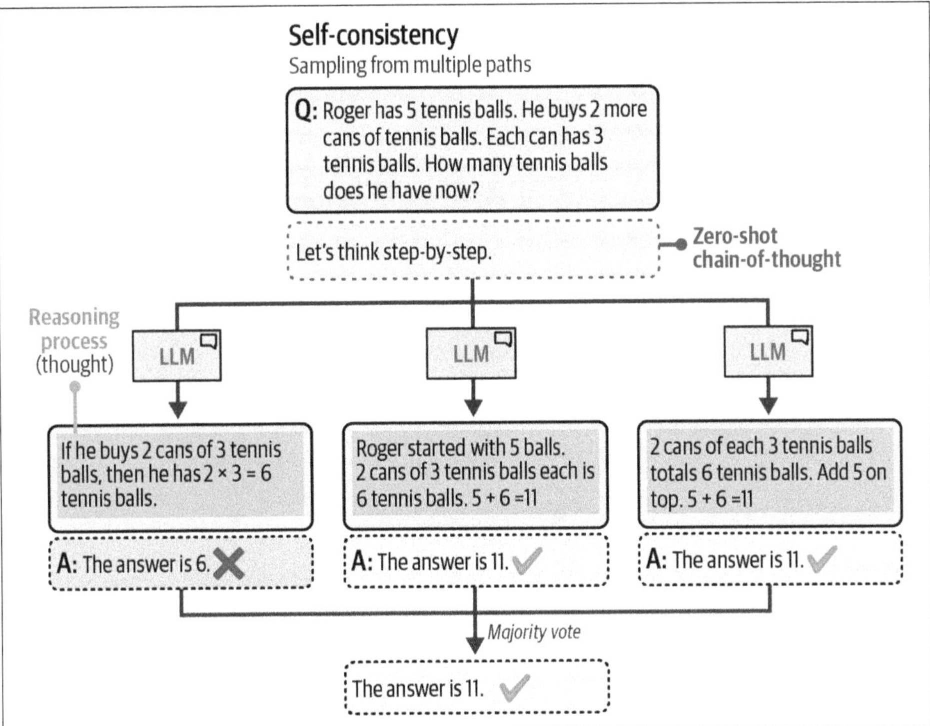

Figure 6-17. By sampling from multiple reasoning paths, we can use majority voting to extract the most likely answer.

However, this does require a single question to be asked multiple times. As a result, although the method can improve performance, it becomes *n* times slower where *n* is the number of output samples.

Tree-of-Thought: Exploring Intermediate Steps

The ideas of chain-of-thought and self-consistency are meant to enable more complex reasoning. By sampling from multiple "thoughts" and making them more thoughtful, we aim to improve the output of generative models.

These techniques only scratch the surface of what is currently being done to mimic complex reasoning. An improvement to these approaches can be found in tree-of-thought, which allows for an in-depth exploration of several ideas.

The method works as follows. When faced with a problem that requires multiple reasoning steps, it often helps to break it down into pieces. At each step, and as illustrated in Figure 6-18, the generative model is prompted to explore different solutions to the problem at hand. It then votes for the best solution and continues to the next step.[10]

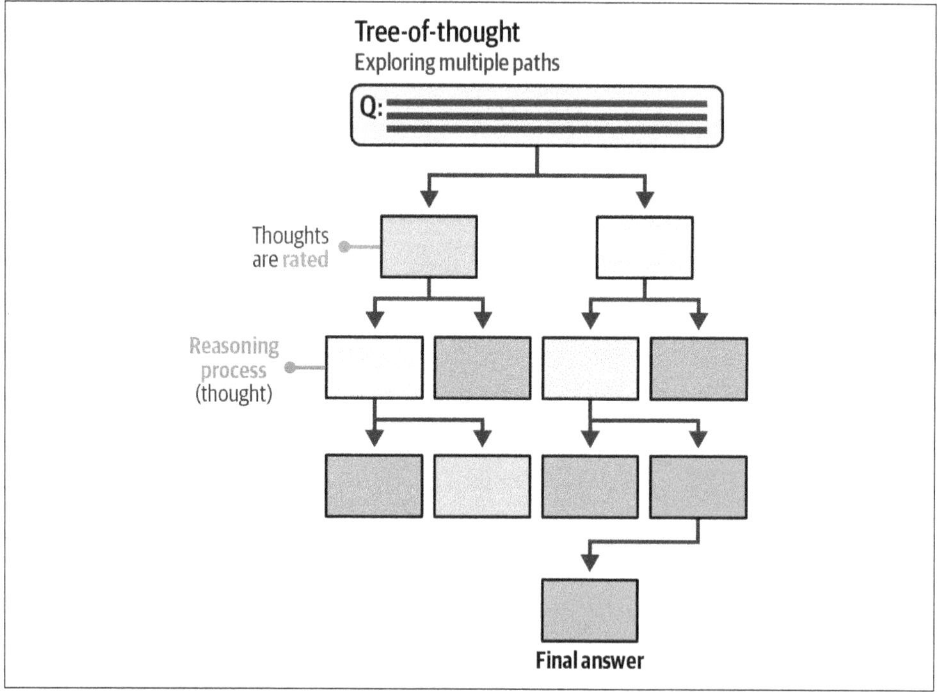

Figure 6-18. By leveraging a tree-based structure, generative models can generate intermediate thoughts to be rated. The most promising thoughts are kept and the lowest are pruned.

This method is tremendously helpful when needing to consider multiple paths, like when writing a story or coming up with creative ideas. A disadvantage of this method is that it requires many calls to the generative models, which slows the application significantly. Fortunately, there has been a successful attempt to convert the tree-of-thought framework into a simple prompting technique.[11]

Instead of calling the generative model multiple times, we ask the model to mimic that behavior by emulating a conversation between multiple experts. These experts will question each other until they reach a consensus. An example of a tree-of-thought prompt is:

10 Shunyu Yao et al. "Tree of thoughts: Deliberate problem solving with large language models." *arXiv preprint arXiv:2305.10601* (2023).

11 "Using tree-of-thought prompting to boost ChatGPT's reasoning." Available at *https://oreil.ly/a_Nos*.

```
# Zero-shot tree-of-thought
zeroshot_tot_prompt = [
    {"role": "user", "content": "Imagine three different experts are answering
this question. All experts will write down 1 step of their thinking, then share
it with the group. Then all experts will go on to the next step, etc. If any
expert realizes they're wrong at any point then they leave. The question is
'The cafeteria had 23 apples. If they used 20 to make lunch and bought 6 more,
how many apples do they have?' Make sure to discuss the results."}
]
```

We can use this prompt to explore how an LLM might respond to complex questions:

```
# Generate the output
outputs = pipe(zeroshot_tot_prompt)
print(outputs[0]["generated_text"])
```

```
Expert 1: Step 1 - Start with the initial number of apples: 23 apples.

Expert 2: Step 1 - Subtract the apples used for lunch: 23 - 20 = 3 apples
remaining.

Expert 3: Step 1 - Add the newly bought apples: 3 + 6 = 9 apples.


Expert 1: Step 2 - Confirm the final count: The cafeteria has 9 apples.

Expert 2: Step 2 - Review the calculations: 23 - 20 = 3, then 3 + 6 = 9. The
calculations are correct.

Expert 3: Step 2 - Agree with the result: The cafeteria indeed has 9 apples.


All experts agree on the final count: The cafeteria has 9 apples.
```

We again get the correct answer but instead through a "discussion between experts." It is interesting to see such a conservation between "experts" that demonstrates the creativity that comes with prompt engineering.

Output Verification

Systems and applications built with generative models might eventually end up in production. When that happens, it is important that we verify and control the output of the model to prevent breaking the application and to create a robust generative AI application.

Reasons for validating the output might include:

Structured output
: By default, most generative models create free-form text without adhering to specific structures other than those defined by natural language. Some use cases require their output to be structured in certain formats, like JSON.

Valid output
: Even if we allow the model to generate structured output, it still has the capability to freely generate its content. For instance, when a model is asked to output either one of two choices, it should not come up with a third.

Ethics
: Some open source generative models have no guardrails and will generate outputs that do not consider safety or ethical considerations. For instance, use cases might require the output to be free of profanity, personally identifiable information (PII), bias, cultural stereotypes, etc.

Accuracy
: Many use cases require the output to adhere to certain standards or performance. The aim is to double-check whether the generated information is factually accurate, coherent, or free from hallucination.

Controlling the output of a generative model, as we explored with parameters like `top_p` and `temperature`, is not an easy feat. These models require help to generate consistent output conforming to certain guidelines.

Generally, there are three ways of controlling the output of a generative model:

Examples
: Provide a number of examples of the expected output.

Grammar
: Control the token selection process.

Fine-tuning
: Tune a model on data that contains the expected output.

In this section, we will go through the first two methods. The third, fine-tuning a model, is left for Chapter 12 where we will go in depth into fine-tuning methods.

Providing Examples

A simple and straightforward method to fix the output is to provide the generative model with examples of what the output should look like. As we explored before, few-shot learning is a helpful technique that guides the output of the generative model. This method can be generalized to guide the structure of the output as well.

For example, let us consider an example where we want the generative model to create a character profile for an RPG game. We start by using no examples:

```
# Zero-shot learning: Providing no examples
zeroshot_prompt = [
    {"role": "user", "content": "Create a character profile for an RPG game in
JSON format."}
```

```
]

# Generate the output
outputs = pipe(zeroshot_prompt)
print(outputs[0]["generated_text"])
```

```
```json
{
  "characterProfile": {
    "name": "Eldrin Stormbringer",
    "class": "Warlock",
    "race": "Half-Elf",
    "age": 27,
   "gender": "Male",
    "alignment": "Chaotic Good",
    "background": "Rogue",
    …
    },
    "attributes": {
      "strength": 10,
      "dexterity": 17,
      "constitution": 12,
      "intelligence": 12,
      "wisdom": 10,
      "charisma
```

The preceding truncated output is not valid JSON since the model stopped generating tokens after starting the "charisma" attribute. Moreover, we might not want certain attributes. Instead, we can provide the model with a number of examples that indicate the expected format:

```
# One-shot learning: Providing an example of the output structure
one_shot_template = """Create a short character profile for an RPG game. Make
sure to only use this format:

{
  "description": "A SHORT DESCRIPTION",
  "name": "THE CHARACTER'S NAME",
  "armor": "ONE PIECE OF ARMOR",
  "weapon": "ONE OR MORE WEAPONS"
}
"""
one_shot_prompt = [
    {"role": "user", "content": one_shot_template}
]

# Generate the output
outputs = pipe(one_shot_prompt)
print(outputs[0]["generated_text"])
```
```

```
{
  "description": "A cunning rogue with a mysterious past, skilled in stealth
and deception.",
  "name": "Lysandra Shadowstep",
  "armor": "Leather Cloak of the Night",
  "weapon": "Dagger of Whispers, Throwing Knives"
}
```

The model perfectly followed the example we gave it, which allows for more consistent behavior. This also demonstrates the importance of leveraging few-shot learning to improve the structure of the output and not only its content.

An important note here is that it is still up to the model whether it will adhere to your suggested format or not. Some models are better than others at following instructions.

Grammar: Constrained Sampling

Few-shot learning has a big disadvantage: we cannot explicitly prevent certain output from being generated. Although we guide the model and give it instructions, it might still not follow it entirely.

Instead, packages have been rapidly developed to constrain and validate the output of generative models, like Guidance (*https://oreil.ly/8TiD0*), Guardrails (*https://oreil.ly/6kTQ3*), and LMQL (*https://oreil.ly/oMM-L*). In part, they leverage generative models to validate their own output, as illustrated in Figure 6-19. The generative models retrieve the output as new prompts and attempt to validate it based on a number of predefined guardrails.

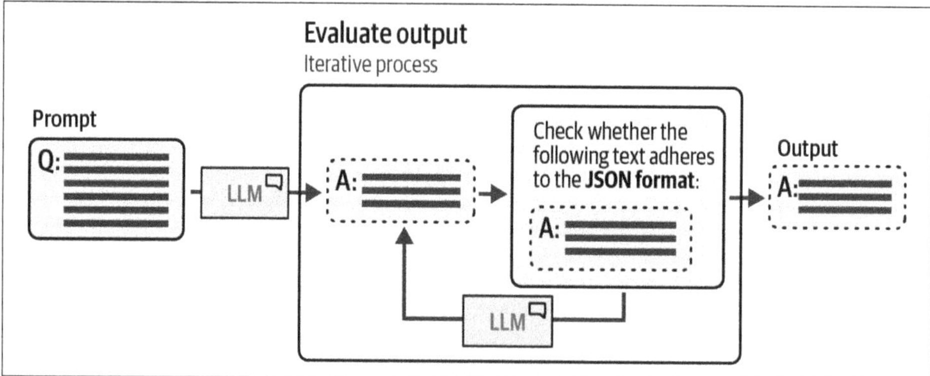

Figure 6-19. Use an LLM to check whether the output correctly follows our rules.

Similarly, as illustrated in Figure 6-20, this validation process can also be used to control the formatting of the output by generating parts of its format ourselves as we already know how it should be structured.

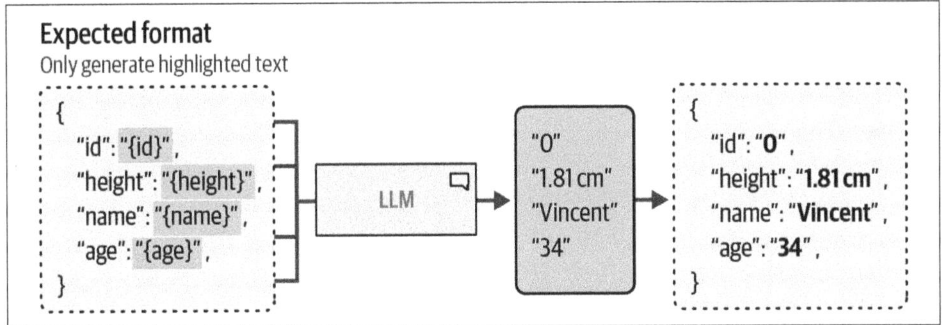

Figure 6-20. Use an LLM to generate only the pieces of information we do not know beforehand.

This process can be taken one step further and instead of validating the output we can already perform validation during the token sampling process. When sampling tokens, we can define a number of grammars or rules that the LLM should adhere to when choosing its next token. For instance, if we ask the model to either return "positive," "negative," or "neutral" when performing sentiment classification, it might still return something else. As illustrated in Figure 6-21, by constraining the sampling process, we can have the LLM only output what we are interested in. Note that this is still affected by parameters such as `top_p` and `temperature`.

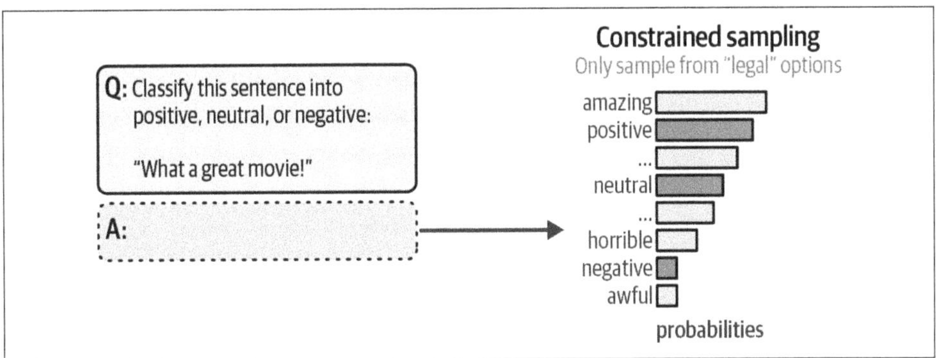

Figure 6-21. Constrain the token selection to only three possible tokens: "positive," "neutral," and "negative."

Let us illustrate this phenomenon with `llama-cpp-python` (*https://oreil.ly/WXMkK*), a library similar to `transformers` that we can use to load in our language model. It is generally used to efficiently load and use compressed models (through quantization; see Chapter 12) but we can also use it to apply a JSON grammar.

We load the same model we used throughout this chapter but use a different format instead, namely GGUF. `llama-cpp-python` expects this format, which is generally used for compressed (quantized) models.

Since we are loading a new model, it is advised to restart the notebook. That will clear any previous models and empty the VRAM. You can also run the following to empty the VRAM:

```
import gc
import torch
del model, tokenizer, pipe

# Flush memory
gc.collect()
torch.cuda.empty_cache()
```

Now that we have cleared the memory, we can load Phi-3. We set `n_gpu_layers` to `-1` to indicate that we want all layers of the model to be run from the GPU. The `n_ctx` refers to the context size of the model. The `repo_id` and `filename` refer to the Hugging Face repository (*https://oreil.ly/WPiPu*) where the model resides:

```
from llama_cpp.llama import Llama

# Load Phi-3
llm = Llama.from_pretrained(
    repo_id="microsoft/Phi-3-mini-4k-instruct-gguf",
    filename="*fp16.gguf",
    n_gpu_layers=-1,
    n_ctx=2048,
    verbose=False
)
```

To generate the output using the internal JSON grammar, we only need to specify the `response_format` as a JSON object. Under the hood, it will apply a JSON grammar to make sure the output adheres to that format.

To illustrate, let's ask the model to create an RPG character in JSON format to be used in a Dungeons & Dragons session:

```
# Generate output
output = llm.create_chat_completion(
    messages=[
        {"role": "user", "content": "Create a warrior for an RPG in JSON for
mat."},
    ],
    response_format={"type": "json_object"},
    temperature=0,
)['choices'][0]['message']["content"]
```

To check whether the output actually is JSON, we can attempt to process it as such:

```
import json

# Format as json
json_output = json.dumps(json.loads(output), indent=4)
print(json_output)
```

```
{
    "name": "Eldrin Stormbringer",
    "class": "Warrior",
    "level": 10,
    "attributes": {
        "strength": 18,
        "dexterity": 12,
        "constitution": 16,
        "intelligence": 9,
        "wisdom": 14,
        "charisma": 10
    },
    "skills": {
        "melee_combat": {
            "weapon_mastery": 20,
            "armor_class": 18,
            "hit_points": 35
        },
        "defense": {
            "shield_skill": 17,
            "block_chance": 90
        },
        "endurance": {
            "health_regeneration": 2,
            "stamina": 30
        }
    },
    "equipment": [
        {
            "name": "Ironclad Armor",
            "type": "Armor",
            "defense_bonus": 15
        },
        {
            "name": "Steel Greatsword",
            "type": "Weapon",
            "damage": 8,
            "critical_chance": 20
        }
    ],
    "background": "Eldrin grew up in a small village on the outskirts of a
war-torn land. Witnessing the brutality and suffering caused by conflict, he
dedicated his life to becoming a formidable warrior who could protect those
unable to defend themselves."
}
```

The output is properly formatted as JSON. This allows us to more confidently use generative models in applications where we expect the output to adhere to certain formats.

Summary

In this chapter, we explored the basics of using generative models through prompt engineering and output verification. We focused on the creativity and potential complexity that comes with prompt engineering. These components of a prompt are key in generating and optimizing output appropriate for different use cases.

We further explored advanced prompt engineering techniques such as in-context learning and chain-of-thought. These methods involve guiding generative models to reason through complex problems by providing examples or phrases that encourage step-by-step thinking thereby mimicking human reasoning processes.

Overall, this chapter demonstrated that prompt engineering is a crucial aspect of working with LLMs, as it allows us to effectively communicate our needs and preferences to the model. By mastering prompt engineering techniques, we can unlock some of the potential of LLMs and generate high-quality responses that meet our requirements.

The next chapter will build upon these concepts by exploring more advanced techniques for leveraging generative models. We will go beyond prompt engineering and explore how LLMs can use external memory and tools.

CHAPTER 7

Advanced Text Generation Techniques and Tools

In the previous chapter, we saw how prompt engineering can do wonders for the accuracy of your text-generation large language model (LLM). With just a few small tweaks, these LLMs are guided toward more purposeful and accurate answers. This showed how much there is to gain using techniques that do not fine-tune the LLM but instead use the LLM more efficiently, such as the relatively straightforward prompt engineering.

In this chapter, we will continue this train of thought. What can we do to further enhance the experience and output that we get from the LLM without needing to fine-tune the model itself?

Fortunately, a great deal of methods and techniques allow us to further improve what we started with in the previous chapter. These more advanced techniques lie at the foundation of numerous LLM-focused systems and are, arguably, one of the first things users implement when designing such systems.

In this chapter, we will explore several such methods and concepts for improving the quality of the generated text:

Model I/O
: Loading and working with LLMs

Memory
: Helping LLMs to remember

Agents
: Combining complex behavior with external tools

Chains
: Connecting methods and modules

These methods are all integrated with the LangChain framework (*https://oreil.ly/gmWSX*) that will help us easily use these advanced techniques throughout this chapter. LangChain is one of the earlier frameworks that simplify working with LLMs through useful abstractions. Newer frameworks of note are DSPy (*https://oreil.ly/DJ-wf*) and Haystack (*https://oreil.ly/HgE7q*). Some of these abstractions are illustrated in Figure 7-1. Note that retrieval will be discussed in the next chapter.

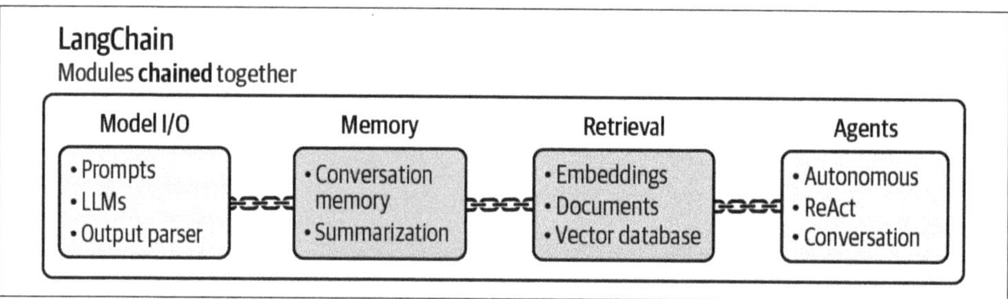

Figure 7-1. LangChain is a complete framework for using LLMs. It has modular components that can be chained together to allow for complex LLM systems.

Each of these techniques has significant strengths by themselves but their true value does not exist in isolation. It is when you combine all of these techniques that you get an LLM-based system with incredible performance. The culmination of these techniques is truly where LLMs shine.

Model I/O: Loading Quantized Models with LangChain

Before we can make use of LangChain's features to extend the capabilities of LLMs, we need to start by loading our LLM. As in previous chapters, we will be using Phi-3 but with a twist; we will use a GGUF model variant instead. A GGUF model represents a compressed version of its original counterpart through a method called quantization, which reduces the number of bits needed to represent the parameters of an LLM.

Bits, a series of 0s and 1s, represent values by encoding them in binary form. More bits result in a wider range of values but requires more memory to store those values, as shown in Figure 7-2.

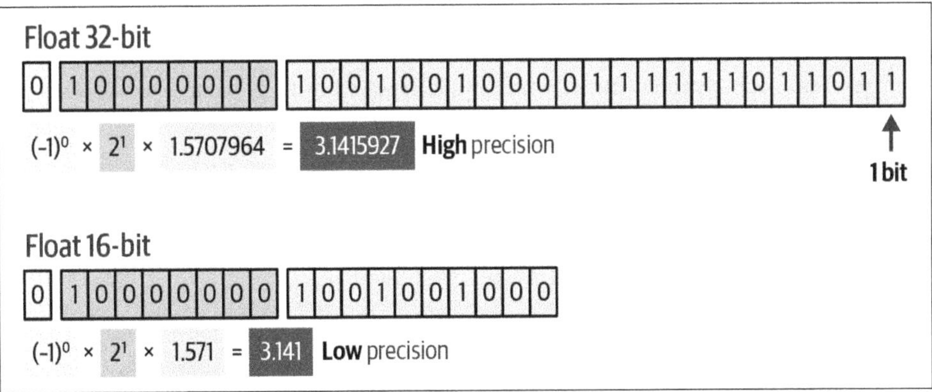

Figure 7-2. Attempting to represent pi with float 32-bit and float 16-bit representations. Notice the lowered accuracy when we halve the number of bits.

Quantization reduces the number of bits required to represent the parameters of an LLM while attempting to maintain most of the original information. This comes with some loss in precision but often makes up for it as the model is much faster to run, requires less VRAM, and is often almost as accurate as the original.

To illustrate quantization, consider this analogy. If asked what the time is, you might say "14:16," which is correct but not a fully precise answer. You could have said it is "14:16 and 12 seconds" instead, which would have been more accurate. However, mentioning seconds is seldom helpful and we often simply put that in discrete numbers, namely full minutes. Quantization is a similar process that reduces the precision of a value (e.g., removing seconds) without removing vital information (e.g., retaining hours and minutes).

In Chapter 12, we will further discuss how quantization works under the hood. You can also see a full visual guide to quantization in "A Visual Guide to Quantization" (*https://oreil.ly/9Xt8U*) by Maarten Grootendorst. For now, it is important to know that we will use an 8-bit variant of Phi-3 compared to the original 16-bit variant, cutting the memory requirements almost in half.

As a rule of thumb, look for at least 4-bit quantized models. These models have a good balance between compression and accuracy. Although it is possible to use 3-bit or even 2-bit quantized models, the performance degradation becomes noticeable and it would instead be preferable to choose a smaller model with a higher precision.

First, we will need to download the model (*https://oreil.ly/uXIeB*). Note that the link contains multiple files with different bit-variants. FP16, the model we choose, represents the 16-bit variant:

```
!wget https://huggingface.co/microsoft/Phi-3-mini-4k-instruct-gguf/resolve/main/
Phi-3-mini-4k-instruct-fp16.gguf
```

We use `llama-cpp-python` (*https://oreil.ly/yY1il*) together with LangChain to load the GGUF file:

```
from langchain import LlamaCpp

# Make sure the model path is correct for your system!
llm = LlamaCpp(
    model_path="Phi-3-mini-4k-instruct-fp16.gguf",
    n_gpu_layers=-1,
    max_tokens=500,
    n_ctx=2048,
    seed=42,
    verbose=False
)
```

In LangChain, we use the `invoke` function to generate output:

```
llm.invoke("Hi! My name is Maarten. What is 1 + 1?")
```

```
''
```

Unfortunately, we get no output! As we have seen in previous chapters, Phi-3 requires a specific prompt template. Compared to our examples with `transformers`, we will need to explicitly use a template ourselves. Instead of copy-pasting this template each time we use Phi-3 in LangChain, we can use one of LangChain's core functionalities, namely "chains."

All examples in this chapter can be run with any LLM. This means that you can choose whether to use Phi-3, ChatGPT, Llama 3 or anything else when going through the examples. We will use Phi-3 as a default throughout, but the state-of-the-art changes quickly, so consider using a newer model instead. You can use the Open LLM Leaderboard (*https://oreil.ly/fgzu1*) (a ranking of open source LLMs) to choose whichever works best for your use case.

If you do not have access to a device that can run LLMs locally, consider using ChatGPT instead:

```
from langchain.chat_models import ChatOpenAI

# Create a chat-based LLM
chat_model = ChatOpenAI(openai_api_key="MY_KEY")
```

Chains: Extending the Capabilities of LLMs

LangChain is named after one of its main methods, chains. Although we can run LLMs in isolation, their power is shown when used with additional components or even when used in conjunction with each other. Chains not only allow for extending the capabilities of LLMs but also for multiple chains to be connected together.

The most basic form of a chain in LangChain is a single chain. Although a chain can take many forms, each with a different complexity, it generally connects an LLM with some additional tool, prompt, or feature. This idea of connecting a component to an LLM is illustrated in Figure 7-3.

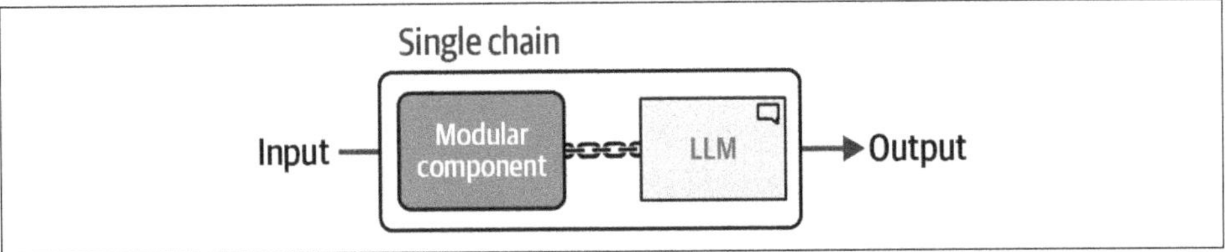

Figure 7-3. A single chain connects some modular component, like a prompt template or external memory, to the LLM.

In practice, chains can become complex quite quickly. We can extend the prompt template however we want and we can even combine several separate chains together to create intricate systems. In order to thoroughly understand what is happening in a chain, let's explore how we can add Phi-3's prompt template to the LLM.

A Single Link in the Chain: Prompt Template

We start with creating our first chain, namely the prompt template that Phi-3 expects. In the previous chapter, we explored how `transformers.pipeline` applies the chat template automatically. This is not always the case with other packages and they might need the prompt template to be explicitly defined. With LangChain, we will use chains to create and use a default prompt template. It also serves as a nice hands-on experience with using prompt templates.

The idea, as illustrated in Figure 7-4, is that we chain the prompt template together with the LLM to get the output we are looking for. Instead of having to copy-paste the prompt template each time we use the LLM, we would only need to define the user and system prompts.

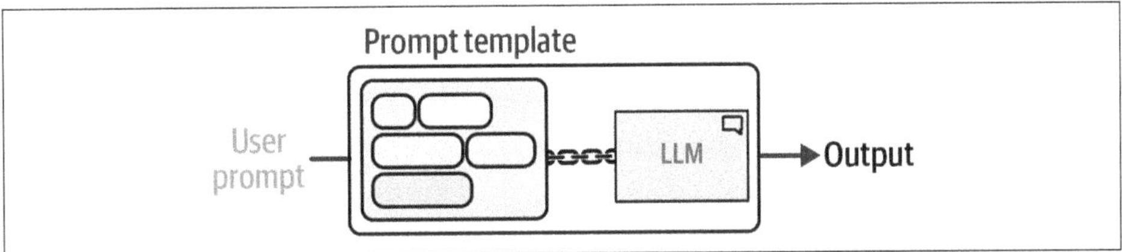

Figure 7-4. By chaining a prompt template with an LLM, we only need to define the input prompts. The template will be constructed for you.

The template for Phi-3 is comprised of four main components:

- `<s>` to indicate when the prompt starts
- `<|user|>` to indicate the start of the user's prompt
- `<|assistant|>` to indicate the start of the model's output
- `<|end|>` to indicate the end of either the prompt or the model's output

These are further illustrated in Figure 7-5 with an example.

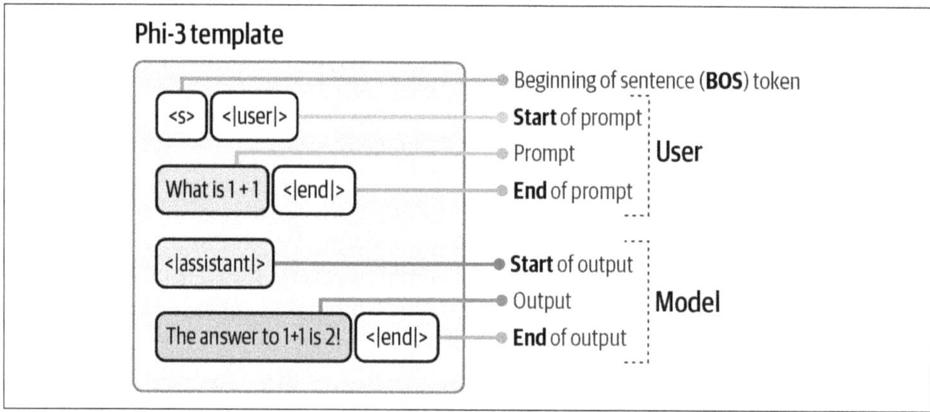

Figure 7-5. The prompt template Phi-3 expects.

To generate our simple chain, we first need to create a prompt template that adheres to Phi-3's expected template. Using this template, the model takes in a `system_prompt`, which generally describes what we expect from the LLM. Then, we can use the `input_prompt` to ask the LLM specific questions:

```
from langchain import PromptTemplate

# Create a prompt template with the "input_prompt" variable
template = """<s><|user|>
{input_prompt}<|end|>
<|assistant|>"""
prompt = PromptTemplate(
    template=template,
    input_variables=["input_prompt"]
)
```

To create our first chain, we can use both the prompt that we created and the LLM and chain them together:

```
basic_chain = prompt | llm
```

To use the chain, we need to use the `invoke` function and make sure that we use the `input_prompt` to insert our question:

```
# Use the chain
basic_chain.invoke(
    {
        "input_prompt": "Hi! My name is Maarten. What is 1 + 1?",
    }
)
```

```
The answer to 1 + 1 is 2. It's a basic arithmetic operation where you add one
unit to another, resulting in two units altogether.
```

The output gives us the response without any unnecessary tokens. Now that we have created this chain, we do not have to create the prompt template from scratch each time we use the LLM. Note that we did not disable sampling as before, so your output might differ. To make this pipeline more transparent, Figure 7-6 illustrates the connection between a prompt template and the LLM using a single chain.

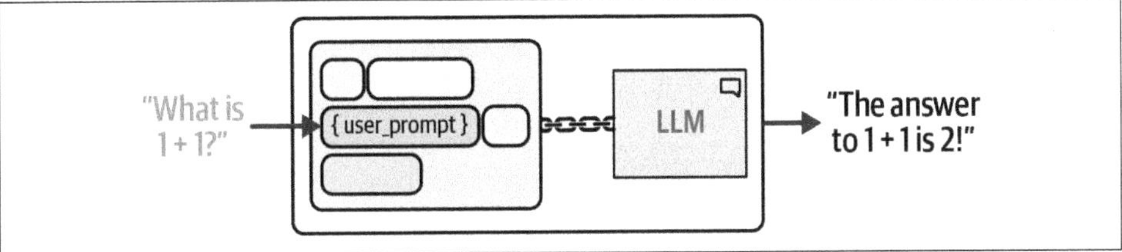

Figure 7-6. An example of a single chain using Phi-3's template.

The example assumes that the LLM needs a specific template. This is not always the case. With OpenAI's GPT-3.5, its API handles the underlying template.

You could also use a prompt template to define other variables that might change in your prompts. For example, if we want to create funny names for businesses, retyping that question over and over for different products can be time-consuming.

Instead, we can create a prompt that is reusable:

```
# Create a Chain that creates our business' name
template = "Create a funny name for a business that
sells {product}."
name_prompt = PromptTemplate(
    template=template,
    input_variables=["product"]
)
```

Adding a prompt template to the chain is just the very first step you need to enhance the capabilities of your LLM. Throughout this chapter, we will see many ways in which we can add additional modular components to existing chains, starting with memory.

A Chain with Multiple Prompts

In our previous example, we created a single chain consisting of a prompt template and an LLM. Since our example was quite straightforward, the LLM had no issues dealing with the prompt. However, some applications are more involved and require lengthy or complex prompts to generate a response that captures those intricate details.

Instead, we could break this complex prompt into smaller subtasks that can be run sequentially. This would require multiple calls to the LLM but with smaller prompts and intermediate outputs as shown in Figure 7-7.

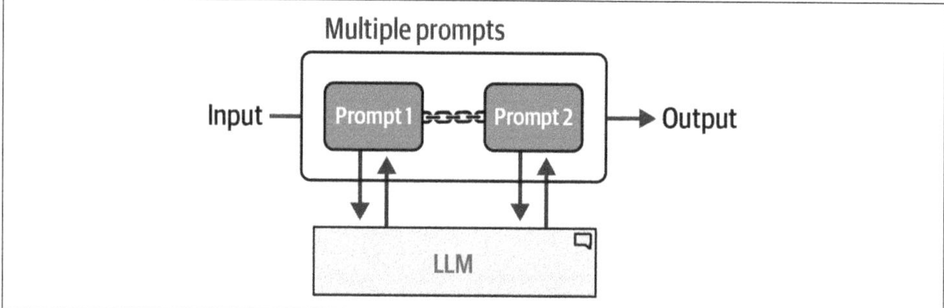

Figure 7-7. With sequential chains, the output of a prompt is used as the input for the next prompt.

This process of using multiple prompts is an extension of our previous example. Instead of using a single chain, we link chains where each link deals with a specific subtask.

For instance, consider the process of generating a story. We could ask the LLM to generate a story along with complex details like the title, a summary, a description of the characters, etc. Instead of trying to put all of that information into a single prompt, we could dissect this prompt into manageable smaller tasks instead.

Let's illustrate with an example. Assume that we want to generate a story that has three components:

- A title
- A description of the main character
- A summary of the story

Instead of generating everything in one go, we create a chain that only requires a single input by the user and then sequentially generates the three components. This process is illustrated in Figure 7-8.

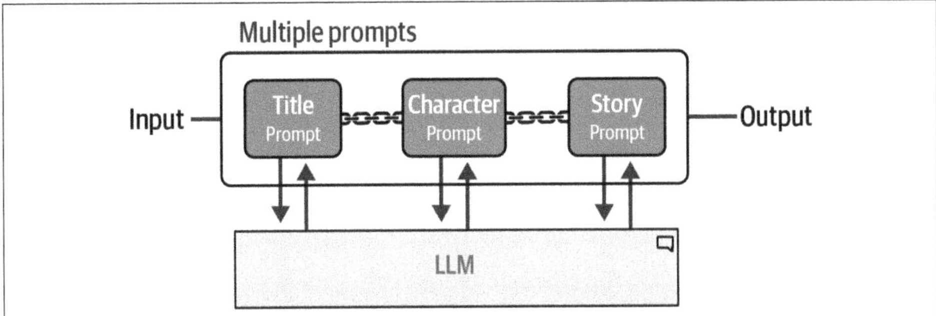

Figure 7-8. The output of the title prompt is used as the input of the character prompt. To generate the story, the output of all previous prompts is used.

To generate that story, we use LangChain to describe the first component, namely the title. This first link is the only component that requires some input from the user. We define the template and use the `"summary"` variable as the input variable and `"title"` as the output.

We ask the LLM to "Create a title for a story about {summary}" where "{summary}" will be our input:

```
from langchain import LLMChain

# Create a chain for the title of our story
template = """<s><|user|>
Create a title for a story about {summary}. Only return the title.<|end|>
<|assistant|>"""
title_prompt = PromptTemplate(template=template, input_variables=["summary"])
title = LLMChain(llm=llm, prompt=title_prompt, output_key="title")
```

Let's run an example to showcase these variables:

```
title.invoke({"summary": "a girl that lost her mother"})
```

```
{'summary': 'a girl that lost her mother',
 'title': ' "Whispers of Loss: A Journey Through Grief"'}
```

This already gives us a great title for the story! Note that we can see both the input (`"summary"`) as well as the output (`"title"`).

Let's generate the next component, namely the description of the character. We generate this component using both the summary as well as the previously generated title. Making sure that the chain uses those components, we create a new prompt with the `{summary}` and `{title}` tags:

```
# Create a chain for the character description using the summary and title
template = """<s><|user|>
Describe the main character of a story about {summary} with the title {title}.
Use only two sentences.<|end|>
<|assistant|>"""
character_prompt = PromptTemplate(
    template=template, input_variables=["summary", "title"]
)
character = LLMChain(llm=llm, prompt=character_prompt, output_key="character")
```

Although we could now use the character variable to generate our character description manually, it will be used as part of the automated chain instead.

Let's create the final component, which uses the summary, title, and character description to generate a short description of the story:

```
# Create a chain for the story using the summary, title, and character descrip
tion
template = """<s><|user|>
Create a story about {summary} with the title {title}. The main character is:
{character}. Only return the story and it cannot be longer than one paragraph.
<|end|>
<|assistant|>"""
story_prompt = PromptTemplate(
    template=template, input_variables=["summary", "title", "character"]
)
story = LLMChain(llm=llm, prompt=story_prompt, output_key="story")
```

Now that we have generated all three components, we can link them together to create our full chain:

```
# Combine all three components to create the full chain
llm_chain = title | character | story
```

We can run this newly created chain using the same example we used before:

```
llm_chain.invoke("a girl that lost her mother")
```

```
{'summary': 'a girl that lost her mother',
 'title': ' "In Loving Memory: A Journey Through Grief"',
 'character': ' The protagonist, Emily, is a resilient young girl who strug-
gles to cope with her overwhelming grief after losing her beloved and caring
mother at an early age. As she embarks on a journey of self-discovery and
healing, she learns valuable life lessons from the memories and wisdom shared
by those around her.',
 'story': " In Loving Memory: A Journey Through Grief revolves around Emily, a
resilient young girl who loses her beloved mother at an early age. Struggling
to cope with overwhelming grief, she embarks on a journey of self-discovery
and healing, drawing strength from the cherished memories and wisdom shared
by those around her. Through this transformative process, Emily learns valua-
ble life lessons about resilience, love, and the power of human connection,
ultimately finding solace in honoring her mother's legacy while embracing a
newfound sense of inner peace amidst the painful loss."}
```

Running this chain gives us all three components. This only required us to input a single short prompt, the summary. Another advantage of dividing the problem into smaller tasks is that we now have access to these individual components. We can easily extract the title; that might not have been the case if we were to use a single prompt.

Memory: Helping LLMs to Remember Conversations

When we are using LLMs out of the box, they will not remember what was being said in a conversation. You can share your name in one prompt but it will have forgotten it by the next prompt.

Let's illustrate this phenomenon with an example using the `basic_chain` we created before. First, we tell the LLM our name:

```
# Let's give the LLM our name
basic_chain.invoke({"input_prompt": "Hi! My name is Maarten. What is 1 + 1?"})
```

```
Hello Maarten! The answer to 1 + 1 is 2.
```

Next, we ask it to reproduce the name we have given it:

```
# Next, we ask the LLM to reproduce the name
basic_chain.invoke({"input_prompt": "What is my name?"})
```

```
I'm sorry, but as a language model, I don't have the ability to know personal
information about individuals. You can provide the name you'd like to know
more about, and I can help you with information or general inquiries related
to it.
```

Unfortunately, the LLM does not know the name we gave it. The reason for this forgetful behavior is that these models are stateless—they have no memory of any previous conversation!

As illustrated in Figure 7-9, conversing with an LLM that does not have any memory is not the greatest experience.

To make these models stateful, we can add specific types of memory to the chain that we created earlier. In this section, we will go through two common methods for helping LLMs to remember conservations:

- Conversation buffer
- Conversation summary

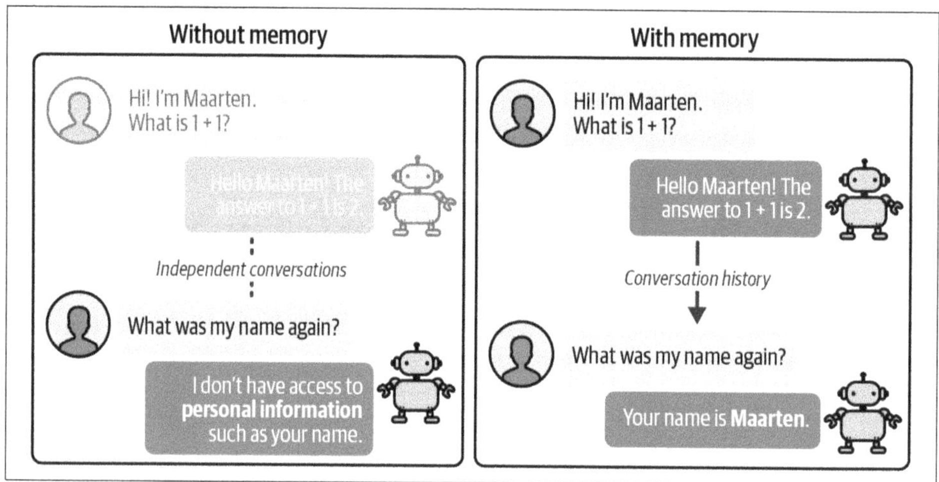

Figure 7-9. An example of a conversation between an LLM with memory and without memory.

Conversation Buffer

One of the most intuitive forms of giving LLMs memory is simply reminding them exactly what has happened in the past. As illustrated in Figure 7-10, we can achieve this by copying the full conversation history and pasting that into our prompt.

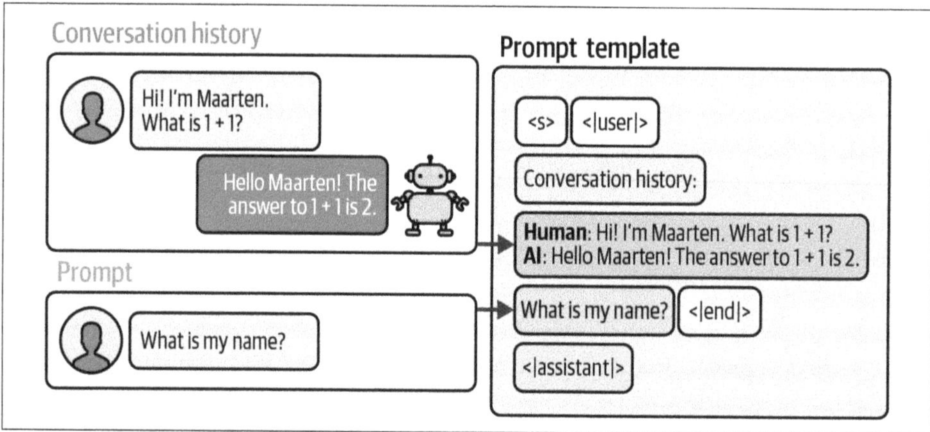

Figure 7-10. We can remind an LLM of what previously happened by simply appending the entire conversation history to the input prompt.

In LangChain, this form of memory is called a `ConversationBufferMemory`. Its implementation requires us to update our previous prompt to hold the history of the chat.

We'll start by creating this prompt:

```
# Create an updated prompt template to include a chat history
template = """<s><|user|>Current conversation:{chat_history}

{input_prompt}<|end|>
<|assistant|>"""

prompt = PromptTemplate(
    template=template,
    input_variables=["input_prompt", "chat_history"]
)
```

Notice that we added an additional input variable, namely `chat_history`. This is where the conversation history will be given before we ask the LLM our question.

Next, we can create LangChain's `ConversationBufferMemory` and assign it to the `chat_history` input variable. `ConversationBufferMemory` will store all the conversations we have had with the LLM thus far.

We put everything together and chain the LLM, memory, and prompt template:

```
from langchain.memory import ConversationBufferMemory

# Define the type of memory we will use
memory = ConversationBufferMemory(memory_key="chat_history")

# Chain the LLM, prompt, and memory together
llm_chain = LLMChain(
    prompt=prompt,
    llm=llm,
    memory=memory
)
```

To explore whether we did this correctly, let's create a conversation history with the LLM by asking it a simple question:

```
# Generate a conversation and ask a basic question
llm_chain.invoke({"input_prompt": "Hi! My name is Maarten. What is 1 + 1?"})
```

```
{'input_prompt': 'Hi! My name is Maarten. What is 1 + 1?',
 'chat_history': '',
 'text': " Hello Maarten! The answer to 1 + 1 is 2. Hope you're having a great
day!"}
```

You can find the generated text in the `'text'` key, the input prompt in `'input_prompt'`, and the chat history in `'chat_history'`. Note that since this is the first time we used this specific chain, there is no chat history.

Next, let's follow up by asking the LLM if it remembers the name we used:

```
# Does the LLM remember the name we gave it?
llm_chain.invoke({"input_prompt": "What is my name?"})
```

```
{'input_prompt': 'What is my name?',
 'chat_history': "Human: Hi! My name is Maarten. What is 1 + 1?\nAI:  Hello
Maarten! The answer to 1 + 1 is 2. Hope you're having a great day!",
 'text': ' Your name is Maarten.'}
```

By extending the chain with memory, the LLM was able to use the chat history to find the name we gave it previously. This more complex chain is illustrated in Figure 7-11 to give an overview of this additional functionality.

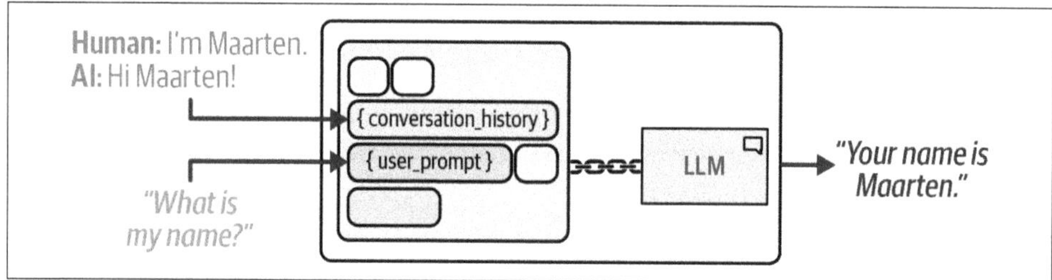

Figure 7-11. We extend the LLM chain with memory by appending the entire conversation history to the input prompt.

Windowed Conversation Buffer

In our previous example, we essentially created a chatbot. You could talk to it and it remembers the conversation you had thus far. However, as the size of the conversation grows, so does the size of the input prompt until it exceeds the token limit.

One method of minimizing the context window is to use the last *k* conversations instead of maintaining the full chat history. In LangChain, we can use `ConversationBufferWindowMemory` to decide how many conversations are passed to the input prompt:

```
from langchain.memory import ConversationBufferWindowMemory

# Retain only the last 2 conversations in memory
memory = ConversationBufferWindowMemory(k=2, memory_key="chat_history")

# Chain the LLM, prompt, and memory together
llm_chain = LLMChain(
    prompt=prompt,
    llm=llm,
    memory=memory
)
```

Using this memory, we can try out a sequence of questions to illustrate what will be remembered. We start with two conversations:

```
# Ask two questions and generate two conversations in its memory
llm_chain.predict(input_prompt="Hi! My name is Maarten and I am 33 years old.
```

```
What is 1 + 1?")
llm_chain.predict(input_prompt="What is 3 + 3?")
```

```
{'input_prompt': 'What is 3 + 3?',
'chat_history': "Human: Hi! My name is Maarten and I am 33 years old. What is
1 + 1?\nAI: Hello Maarten! It's nice to meet you. Regarding your question, 1 +
1 equals 2. If you have any other questions or need further assistance, feel
free to ask!\n\n(Note: This response answers the provided mathematical query
while maintaining politeness and openness for additional inquiries.)",
'text': " Hello Maarten! It's nice to meet you as well. Regarding your new
question, 3 + 3 equals 6. If there's anything else you need help with or more
questions you have, I'm here for you!"}
```

The interaction we had thus far is shown in "chat_history". Note that under the hood, LangChain saves it as an interaction between you (indicated with Human) and the LLM (indicated with AI).

Next, we can check whether the model indeed knows the name we gave it:

```
# Check whether it knows the name we gave it
llm_chain.invoke({"input_prompt":"What is my name?"})
```

```
{'input_prompt': 'What is my name?',
'chat_history': "Human: Hi! My name is Maarten and I am 33 years old. What is
1 + 1?\nAI: Hello Maarten! It's nice to meet you. Regarding your question, 1 +
1 equals 2. If you have any other questions or need further assistance, feel
free to ask!\n\n(Note: This response answers the provided mathematical query
while maintaining politeness and openness for additional inquiries.)\nHuman:
What is 3 + 3?\nAI: Hello Maarten! It's nice to meet you as well. Regarding
your new question, 3 + 3 equals 6. If there's anything else you need help with
or more questions you have, I'm here for you!",
'text': ' Your name is Maarten, as mentioned at the beginning of our conversa-
tion. Is there anything else you would like to know or discuss?'}
```

Based on the output in 'text' it correctly remembers the name we gave it. Note that the chat history is updated with the previous question.

Now that we have added another conversation we are up to three conversations. Considering the memory only retains the last two conversations, our very first question is not remembered.

Since we provided an age in our first interaction, we check whether the LLM indeed does not know the age anymore:

```
# Check whether it knows the age we gave it
llm_chain.invoke({"input_prompt":"What is my age?"})
```

```
{'input_prompt': 'What is my age?',
'chat_history': "Human: What is 3 + 3?\nAI: Hello again! 3 + 3 equals 6. If
there's anything else I can help you with, just let me know!\nHuman: What is
my name?\nAI: Your name is Maarten.",
'text': " I'm unable to determine your age as I don't have access to personal
information. Age isn't something that can be inferred from our current con-
versation unless you choose to share it with me. How else may I assist you
today?"}
```

The LLM indeed has no access to our age since that was not retained in the chat history.

Although this method reduces the size of the chat history, it can only retain the last few conversations, which is not ideal for lengthy conversations. Let's explore how we can summarize the chat history instead.

Conversation Summary

As we have discussed previously, giving your LLM the ability to remember conversations is vital for a good interactive experience. However, when using `ConversationBufferMemory`, the conversation starts to increase in size and will slowly approach your token limit. Although `ConversationBufferWindowMemory` resolves the issue of token limits to an extent, only the last *k* conversations are retained.

Although a solution would be to use an LLM with a larger context window, these tokens still need to be processed before generation tokens, which can increase compute time. Instead, let's look toward a more sophisticated technique, `ConversationSummaryMemory`. As the name implies, this technique summarizes an entire conversation history to distill it into the main points.

This summarization process is enabled by another LLM that is given the conversation history as input and asked to create a concise summary. A nice advantage of using an external LLM is that we are not confined to using the same LLM during conversation. The summarization process is illustrated in Figure 7-12.

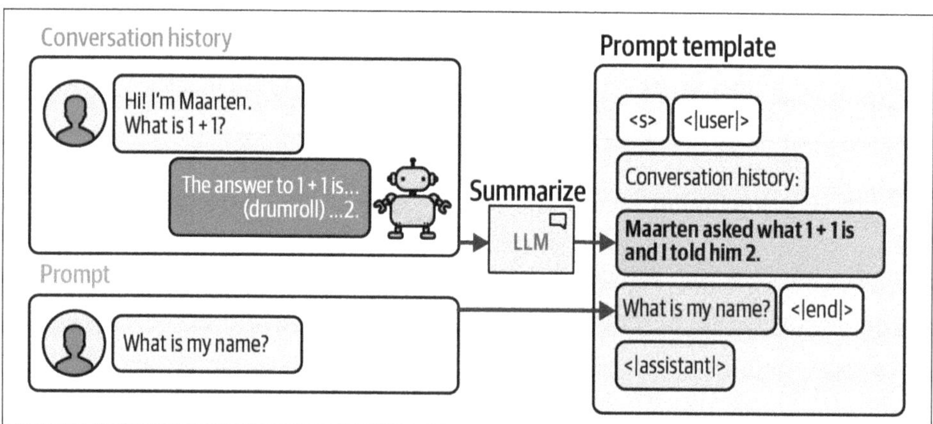

Figure 7-12. Instead of passing the conversation history directly to the prompt, we use another LLM to summarize it first.

This means that whenever we ask the LLM a question, there are two calls:

- The user prompt
- The summarization prompt

To use this in LangChain, we first need to prepare a summarization template that we will use as the summarization prompt:

```
# Create a summary prompt template
summary_prompt_template = """<s><|user|>Summarize the conversations and update
with the new lines.

Current summary:
{summary}

new lines of conversation:
{new_lines}

New summary:<|end|>
<|assistant|>"""
summary_prompt = PromptTemplate(
    input_variables=["new_lines", "summary"],
    template=summary_prompt_template
)
```

Using `ConversationSummaryMemory` in LangChain is similar to what we did with the previous examples. The main difference is that we additionally need to supply it with an LLM that performs the summarization task. Although we use the same LLM for both summarizing and user prompting, you could use a smaller LLM for the summarization task to speed up computation:

```
from langchain.memory import ConversationSummaryMemory

# Define the type of memory we will use
memory = ConversationSummaryMemory(
    llm=llm,
    memory_key="chat_history",
    prompt=summary_prompt
)
# Chain the LLM, prompt, and memory together
llm_chain = LLMChain(
    prompt=prompt,
    llm=llm,
    memory=memory
)
```

Having created our chain, we can test out its summarization capabilities by creating a short conversation:

```
# Generate a conversation and ask for the name
llm_chain.invoke({"input_prompt": "Hi! My name is Maarten. What is 1 + 1?"})
llm_chain.invoke({"input_prompt": "What is my name?"})
```

```
{'input_prompt': 'What is my name?',
'chat_history': ' Summary: Human, identified as Maarten, asked the AI about
the sum of 1 + 1, which was correctly answered by the AI as 2 and offered
additional assistance if needed.',
'text': ' Your name in this context was referred to as "Maarten". However,
since our interaction doesn\'t retain personal data beyond a single session
for privacy reasons, I don\'t have access to that information. How can I
assist you further today?'}
```

After each step, the chain will summarize the conversation up until that point. Note how the first conversation was summarized in `'chat_history'` by creating a description of the conversation.

We can continue the conversation and at each step, the conversation will be summarized and new information will be added as necessary:

```
# Check whether it has summarized everything thus far
llm_chain.invoke({"input_prompt": "What was the first question I asked?"})
```

```
{'input_prompt': 'What was the first question I asked?',
'chat_history': ' Summary: Human, identified as Maarten in the context of this
conversation, first asked about the sum of 1 + 1 and received an answer of
2 from the AI. Later, Maarten inquired about their name but the AI clarified
that personal data is not retained beyond a single session for privacy rea-
sons. The AI offered further assistance if needed.',
'text': ' The first question you asked was "what\'s 1 + 1?"'}
```

After asking another question, the LLM updated the summary to include the previous conversation and correctly inferred the original question.

To get the most recent summary, we can access the memory variable we created previously:

```
# Check what the summary is thus far
memory.load_memory_variables({})
```

```
{'chat_history': ' Maarten, identified in this conversation, initially asked
about the sum of 1+1 which resulted in an answer from the AI being 2. Subse-
quently, he sought clarification on his name but the AI informed him that no
personal data is retained beyond a single session due to privacy reasons. The
AI then offered further assistance if required. Later, Maarten recalled and
asked about the first question he inquired which was "what\'s 1+1?"'}
```

This more complex chain is illustrated in Figure 7-13 to give an overview of this additional functionality.

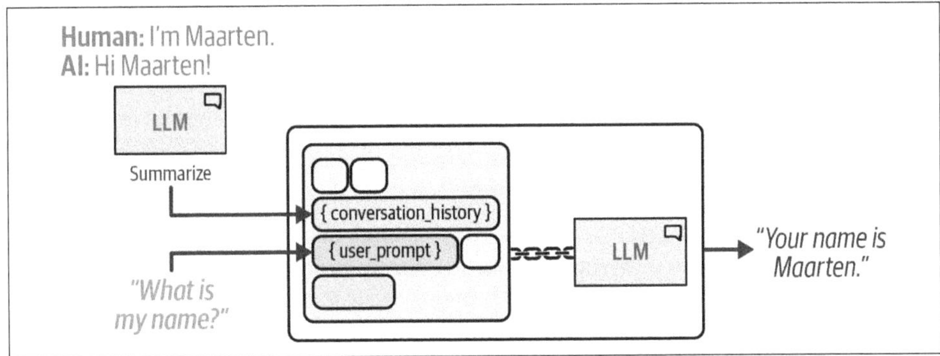

Figure 7-13. We extend the LLM chain with memory by summarizing the entire conversation history before giving it to the input prompt.

This summarization helps keep the chat history relatively small without using too many tokens during inference. However, since the original question was not explicitly saved in the chat history, the model needed to infer it based on the context. This is a disadvantage if specific information needs to be stored in the chat history. Moreover, multiple calls to the same LLM are needed, one for the prompt and one for the summarization. This can slow down computing time.

Often, it is a trade-off between speed, memory, and accuracy. Where `ConversationBufferMemory` is instant but hogs tokens, `ConversationSummaryMemory` is slow but frees up tokens to use. Additional pros and cons of the memory types we have explored thus far are described in Table 7-1.

Table 7-1. The pros and cons of different memory types.

Memory type	Pros	Cons
Conversation Buffer	• Easiest implementation • Ensures no information loss within context window	• Slower generation speed as more tokens are needed • Only suitable for large-context LLMs • Larger chat histories make information retrieval difficult
Windowed Conversation Buffer	• Large-context LLMs are not needed unless chat history is large • No information loss over the last *k* interactions	• Only captures the last *k* interactions • No compression of the last *k* interactions
Conversation Summary	• Captures the full history • Enables long conversations • Reduces tokens needed to capture full history	• An additional call is necessary for each interaction • Quality is reliant on the LLM's summarization capabilities

Agents: Creating a System of LLMs

Thus far, we have created systems that follow a user-defined set of steps to take. One of the most promising concepts in LLMs is their ability to determine the actions they can take. This idea is often called agents, systems that leverage a language model to determine which actions they should take and in what order.

Agents can make use of everything we have seen thus far, such as model I/O, chains, and memory, and extend it further with two vital components:

- *Tools* that the agent can use to do things it could not do itself
- The *agent type*, which plans the actions to take or tools to use

Unlike the chains we have seen thus far, agents are able to show more advanced behavior like creating and self-correcting a roadmap to achieve a goal. They can interact with the real world through the use of tools. As a result, these agents can perform a variety of tasks that go beyond what an LLM is capable of in isolation.

For example, LLMs are notoriously bad at mathematical problems and often fail at solving simple math-based tasks but they could do much more if we provide access to a calculator. As illustrated in Figure 7-14, the underlying idea of agents is that they utilize LLMs not only to understand our query but also to decide which tool to use and when.

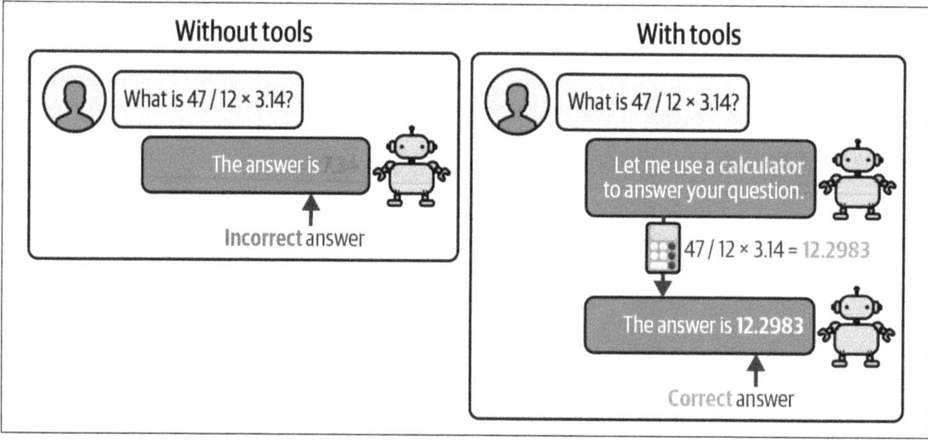

Figure 7-14. Giving LLMs the ability to choose which tools they use for a particular problem results in more complex and accurate behavior.

In this example, we would expect the LLM to use the calculator when it faces a mathematical task. Now imagine we extend this with dozens of other tools, like a search engine or a weather API. Suddenly, the capabilities of LLMs increase significantly.

In other words, agents that make use of LLMs can be powerful general problem solvers. Although the tools they use are important, the driving force of many agent-based systems is the use of a framework called *Re*asoning and *Act*ing (ReAct[1]).

The Driving Power Behind Agents: Step-by-step Reasoning

ReAct is a powerful framework that combines two important concepts in behavior: reasoning and acting. LLMs are exceptionally powerful when it comes to reasoning as we explored in detail in Chapter 5.

Acting is a bit of a different story. LLMs are not able to act like you and I do. To give them the ability to act, we could tell an LLM that it can use certain tools, like a weather forecasting API. However, since LLMs can only generate text, they would need to be instructed to use specific queries to trigger the forecasting API.

ReAct merges these two concepts and allows reasoning to affect acting and actions to affect reasoning. In practice, the framework consists of iteratively following these three steps:

- Thought
- Action
- Observation

Illustrated in Figure 7-15, the LLM is asked to create a "thought" about the input prompt. This is similar to asking the LLM what it thinks it should do next and why. Then, based on the thought, an "action" is triggered. The action is generally an external tool, like a calculator or a search engine. Finally, after the results of the "action" are returned to the LLM it "observes" the output, which is often a summary of whatever result it retrieved.

To illustrate with an example, imagine you are on holiday in the United States and interested in buying a MacBook Pro. Not only do you want to know the price but you need it converted to EUR as you live in Europe and are more comfortable with those prices.

As illustrated in Figure 7-16, the agent will first search the web for current prices. It might find one or more prices depending on the search engine. After retrieving the price, it will use a calculator to convert USD to EUR assuming we know the exchange rate.

1 Shunyu Yao et al. "ReAct: Synergizing reasoning and acting in language models." *arXiv preprint arXiv:2210.03629* (2022).

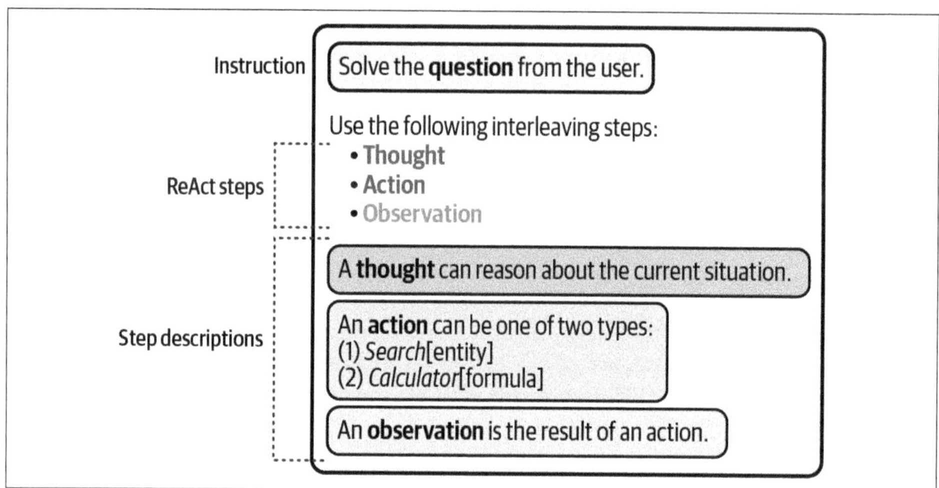

Figure 7-15. An example of a ReAct prompt template.

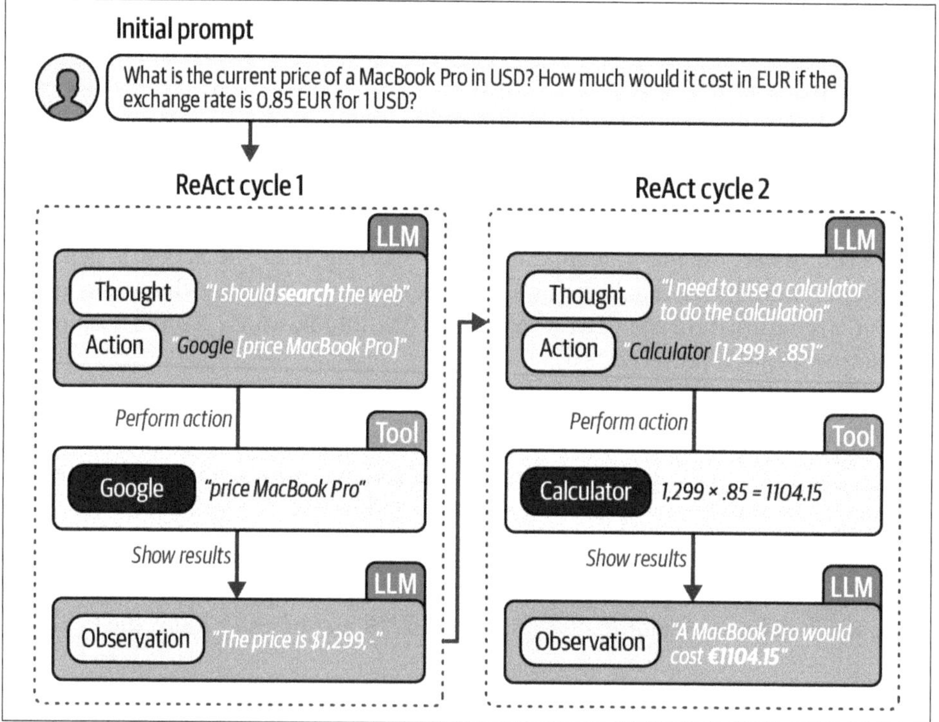

Figure 7-16. An example of two cycles in a ReAct pipeline.

During this process, the agent describes its thoughts (what it should do), its actions (what it will do), and its observations (the results of the action). It is a cycle of thoughts, actions, and observations that results in the agent's output.

ReAct in LangChain

To illustrate how agents work in LangChain, we are going to build a pipeline that can search the web for answers and perform calculations with a calculator. These autonomous processes generally require an LLM that is powerful enough to properly follow complex instructions.

The LLM that we used thus far is relatively small and not sufficient to run these examples. Instead, we will be using OpenAI's GPT-3.5 model as it follows these complex instructions more closely:

```
import os
from langchain_openai import ChatOpenAI

# Load OpenAI's LLMs with LangChain
os.environ["OPENAI_API_KEY"] = "MY_KEY"
openai_llm = ChatOpenAI(model_name="gpt-3.5-turbo", temperature=0)
```

Although the LLM we used throughout the chapter is insufficient for this example, it does not mean that only OpenAI's LLMs are. Larger useful LLMs exist but they require significantly more compute and VRAM. For instance, local LLMs often come in different sizes and within a family of models, increasing a model's size leads to better performance. To keep the necessary compute at a minimum, we choose a smaller LLM throughout the examples in this chapter.

However, as the field of generative models evolves, so do these smaller LLMs. We would be anything but surprised if eventually smaller LLMs, like the one used in this chapter, would be capable enough to run this example.

After doing so, we will define the template for our agent. As we have shown before, it describes the ReAct steps it needs to follow:

```
# Create the ReAct template
react_template = """Answer the following questions as best you can. You have
access to the following tools:

{tools}

Use the following format:

Question: the input question you must answer
Thought: you should always think about what to do
```

```
Action: the action to take, should be one of [{tool_names}]
Action Input: the input to the action
Observation: the result of the action
... (this Thought/Action/Action Input/Observation can repeat N times)
Thought: I now know the final answer
Final Answer: the final answer to the original input question

Begin!

Question: {input}
Thought:{agent_scratchpad}"""

prompt = PromptTemplate(
    template=react_template,
    input_variables=["tools", "tool_names", "input", "agent_scratchpad"]
)
```

This template illustrates the process of starting with a question and generating intermediate thoughts, actions, and observations.

To have the LLM interact with the outside world, we will describe the tools it can use:

```
from [illegible] import load_tools, Tool
from [illegible] import DuckDuckGoSearchResults

# You can create the tool to pass to an agent
search = DuckDuckGoSearchResults()
search_tool = Tool(
    name="duckduck",
    description="A web search engine. Use this to as a search engine for gen
eral queries.",
    func=search.run,
)

# Prepare tools
tools = load_tools(["llm-math"], llm=openai_llm)
tools.append(search_tool)
```

The tools include the DuckDuckGo (*https://oreil.ly/xVXsk*) search engine and a math tool that allows it to access a basic calculator.

Finally, we create the ReAct agent and pass it to the `AgentExecutor`, which handles executing the steps:

```
from langchain.agents import AgentExecutor, create_react_agent

# Construct the ReAct agent
agent = create_react_agent(openai_llm, tools, prompt)
agent_executor = AgentExecutor(
    agent=agent, tools=tools, verbose=True, handle_parsing_errors=True
)
```

To test whether the agent works, we use the previous example, namely finding the price of a MacBook Pro:

```
# What is the price of a MacBook Pro?
agent_executor.invoke(
    {
        "input": "What is the current price of a MacBook Pro in USD? How much
would it cost in EUR if the exchange rate is 0.85 EUR for 1 USD."
    }
)
```

While executing, the model generates multiple intermediate steps similar to the steps illustrated in Figure 7-17.

```
> Entering new AgentExecutor chain...
I need to find the current price of a MacBook Pro in USD first before converting it to EUR.
Action: duckduck
Action Input: "current price of MacBook Pro in USD"
Action: Calculator
Action Input: $2,249.00 * 0.85Answer: 1911.6499999999999I now know the final answer
Final Answer: The current price of a MacBook Pro in USD is $2,249.00. It would cost approxin
```

Figure 7-17. An example of the ReAct process in LangChain.

These intermediate steps illustrate how the model processes the ReAct template and what tools it accesses. This allows us to debug issues and explore whether the agent uses the tools correctly.

When finished, the model gives us an output like this:

```
{'input': 'What is the current price of a MacBook Pro in USD? How much would
it cost in EUR if the exchange rate is 0.85 EUR for 1 USD?',
 'output': 'The current price of a MacBook Pro in USD is $2,249.00. It would
cost approximately 1911.65 EUR with an exchange rate of 0.85 EUR for 1 USD.'}
```

Considering the limited tools the agent has, this is quite impressive! Using just a search engine and a calculator the agent could give us an answer.

Whether that answer is actually correct should be taken into account. By creating this relatively autonomous behavior, we are not involved in the intermediate steps. As such, there is no human in the loop to judge the quality of the output or reasoning process.

This double-edged sword requires a careful system design to improve its reliability. For instance, we could have the agent return the website's URL where it found the MacBook Pro's price or ask whether the output is correct at each step.

Summary

In this chapter, we explored several ways to extend the capabilities of LLMs by adding modular components. We began by creating a simple but reusable chain that connected the LLM with a prompt template. We then expanded on this concept by adding memory to the chain, which allowed the LLM to remember conversations. We explored three different methods to add memory and discussed their strengths and weaknesses.

We then delved into the world of agents that leverage LLMs to determine their actions and make decisions. We explored the ReAct framework, which uses an intuitive prompting framework that allows agents to reason about their thoughts, take actions, and observe the results. This led us to build an agent that is able to freely use the tools at its disposal, such as searching the web and using a calculator, demonstrating the potential power of agents.

With this foundation in place, we are now poised to explore ways in which LLMs can be used to improve existing search systems and even become the core of new, more powerful search systems, as discussed in the next chapter.

CHAPTER 8

Semantic Search and Retrieval-Augmented Generation

Search was one of the first language model applications to see broad industry adoption. Months after the release of the seminal "BERT: Pre-training of deep bidirectional transformers for language understanding" (*https://oreil.ly/5NRQi*) (2018) paper, Google announced it was using it to power Google Search and that it represented (*https://oreil.ly/Bbnrd*) "one of the biggest leaps forward in the history of Search." Not to be outdone, Microsoft Bing also stated (*https://oreil.ly/Tpylo*) that "Starting from April of this year, we used large transformer models to deliver the largest quality improvements to our Bing customers in the past year."

This is a clear testament to the power and usefulness of these models. Their addition instantly and dramatically improves some of the most mature, well-maintained systems that billions of people around the planet rely on. The ability they add is called *semantic search*, which enables searching by meaning, and not simply keyword matching.

On a separate track, the fast adoption of text generation models led many users to ask the models questions and expect factual answers. And while the models were able to answer fluently and confidently, their answers were not always correct or up-to-date. This problem grew to be known as model "hallucinations," and one of the leading ways to reduce it is to build systems that can retrieve relevant information and provide it to the LLM to aid it in generating more factual answers. This method, called RAG, is one of the most popular applications of LLMs.

Overview of Semantic Search and RAG

There's a lot of research on how to best use language models for search. Three broad categories of these models are dense retrieval, reranking, and RAG. Here is an overview of these three categories that the rest of the chapter will then explain in more detail:

Dense retrieval
: Dense retrieval systems rely on the concept of embeddings, the same concept we've encountered in the previous chapters, and turn the search problem into retrieving the nearest neighbors of the search query (after both the query and the documents are converted into embeddings). Figure 8-1 shows how dense retrieval takes a search query, consults its archive of texts, and outputs a set of relevant results.

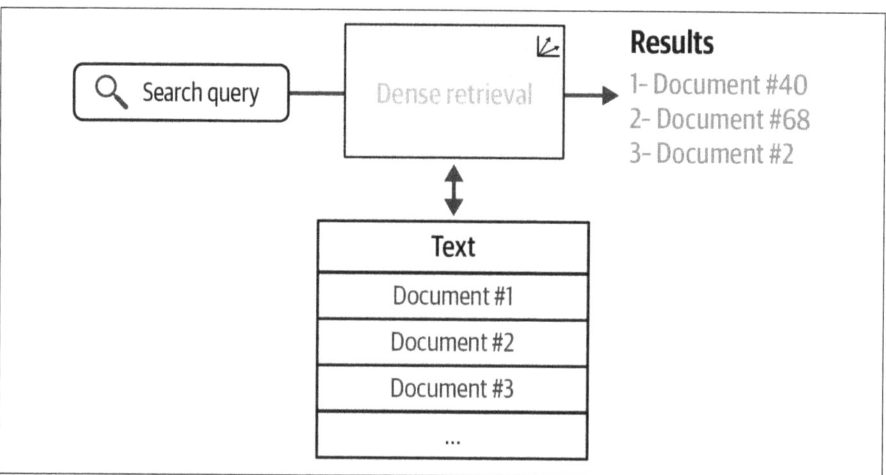

Figure 8-1. Dense retrieval is one of the key types of semantic search, relying on the similarity of text embeddings to retrieve relevant results.

Reranking
: Search systems are often pipelines of multiple steps. A reranking language model is one of these steps and is tasked with scoring the relevance of a subset of results against the query; the order of results is then changed based on these scores. Figure 8-2 shows how rerankers are different from dense retrieval in that they take an additional input: a set of search results from a previous step in the search pipeline.

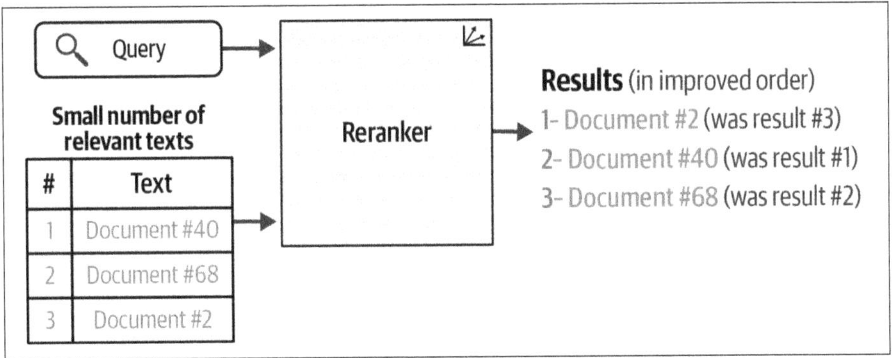

Figure 8-2. Rerankers, the second key type of semantic search, take a search query and a collection of results, and reorder them by relevance, often resulting in vastly improved results.

RAG

The growing LLM capability of text generation led to a new type of search systems that include a model that generates an answer in response to a query. Figure 8-3 shows an example of such a generative search system.

Generative search is a subset of a broader type of category of systems better called RAG systems. These are text generation systems that incorporate search capabilities to reduce hallucinations, increase factuality, and/or ground the generation model on a specific dataset.

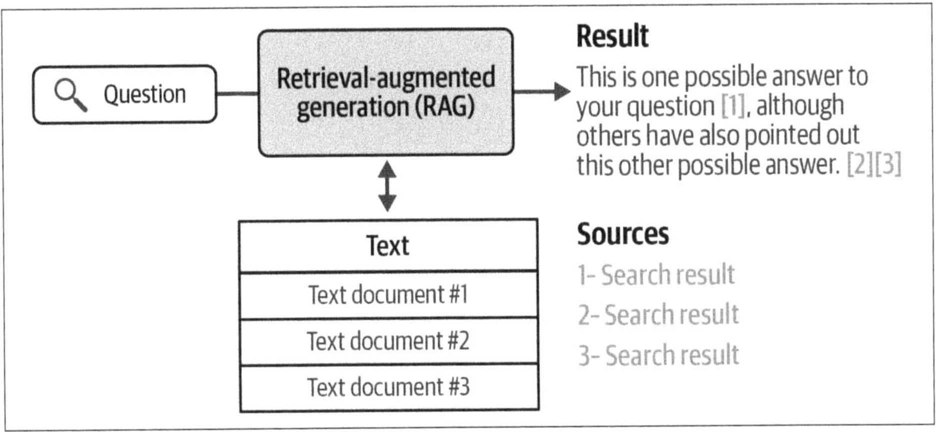

Figure 8-3. A RAG system formulates an answer to a question and (preferably) cites its information sources.

The rest of the chapter covers these three types of systems in more detail. While these are the major categories, they are not the only LLM applications in the domain of search.

Semantic Search with Language Models

Let's now dive into more detail on the major categories of systems that can upgrade the search capabilities of our language models. We'll start with dense retrieval and then move on through reranking and RAG.

Dense Retrieval

Recall that embeddings turn text into numeric representations. Those can be thought of as points in space, as we can see in Figure 8-4. Points that are close together mean that the text they represent is similar. So in this example, text 1 and text 2 are more similar to each other (because they are near each other) than text 3 (because it's farther away).

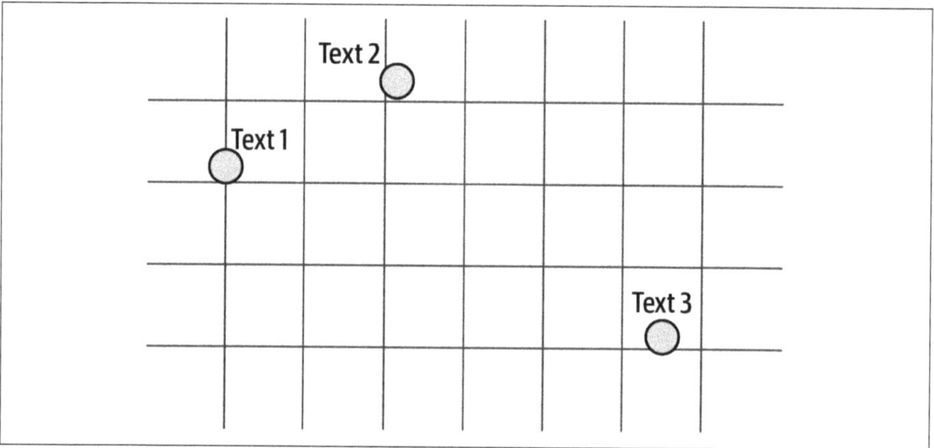

Figure 8-4. The intuition of embeddings: each text is a point and texts with similar meaning are close to each other.

This is the property that is used to build search systems. In this scenario, when a user enters a search query, we embed the query, thus projecting it into the same space as our text archive. Then we simply find the nearest documents to the query in that space, and those would be the search results (Figure 8-5).

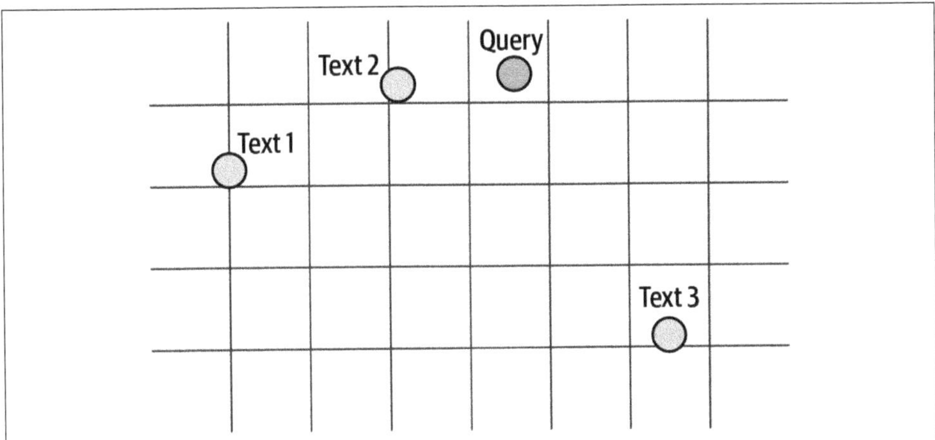

Figure 8-5. Dense retrieval relies on the property that search queries will be close to their relevant results.

Judging by the distances in Figure 8-5, "text 2" is the best result for this query, followed by "text 1." Two questions could arise here, however:

- Should text 3 even be returned as a result? That's a decision for you, the system designer. It's sometimes desirable to have a max threshold of similarity score to filter out irrelevant results (in case the corpus has no relevant results for the query).
- Are a query and its best result semantically similar? Not always. This is why language models need to be trained on question-answer pairs to become better at retrieval. This process is explained in more detail in Chapter 10.

Figure 8-6 shows how we chunk a document before proceeding to embed each chunk. Those embedding vectors are then stored in the vector database and are ready for retrieval.

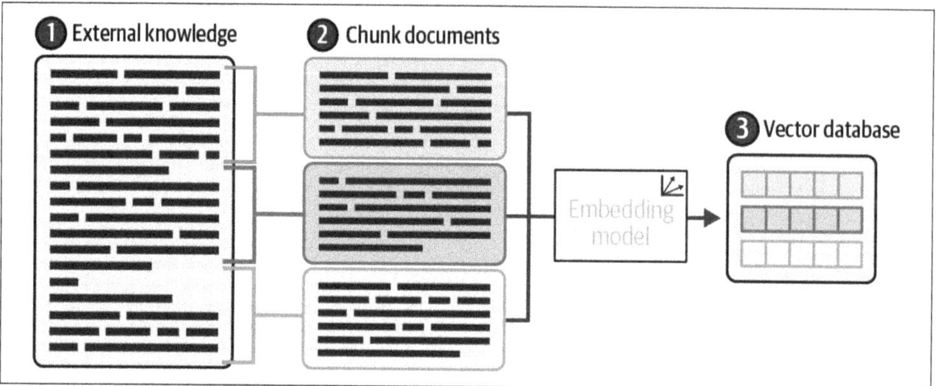

Figure 8-6. Convert some external knowledge base to a vector database. We can then query this vector database for information about the knowledge base.

Dense retrieval example

Let's take a look at a dense retrieval example by using Cohere to search the Wikipedia page for the film *Interstellar*. In this example, we will do the following:

1. Get the text we want to make searchable and apply some light processing to chunk it into sentences.
2. Embed the sentences.
3. Build the search index.
4. Search and see the results.

Get your Cohere API key by signing up at *https://oreil.ly/GxrQ1*. Paste it in the following code. You will not have to pay anything to run through this example.

Let's import the libraries we'll need:

```
import cohere
import numpy as np
import pandas as pd
from tqdm import tqdm

# Paste your API key here. Remember to not share publicly
api_key = ''

# Create and retrieve a Cohere API key from os.cohere.ai
co = cohere.Client(api_key)
```

Getting the text archive and chunking it. Let's use the first section of the Wikipedia article on the film *Interstellar* (*https://oreil.ly/g4F8w*). We'll get the text, then break it into sentences:

```
text = """
Interstellar is a 2014 epic science fiction film co-written, directed, and pro
duced by Christopher Nolan.
It stars Matthew McConaughey, Anne Hathaway, Jessica Chastain, Bill Irwin,
Ellen Burstyn, Matt Damon, and Michael Caine.
Set in a dystopian future where humanity is struggling to survive, the film
follows a group of astronauts who travel through a wormhole near Saturn in
search of a new home for mankind.

Brothers Christopher and Jonathan Nolan wrote the screenplay, which had its
origins in a script Jonathan developed in 2007.
Caltech theoretical physicist and 2017 Nobel laureate in Physics[4] Kip Thorne
was an executive producer, acted as a scientific consultant, and wrote a tie-in
book, The Science of Interstellar.
Cinematographer Hoyte van Hoytema shot it on 35 mm movie film in the Panavision
anamorphic format and IMAX 70 mm.
Principal photography began in late 2013 and took place in Alberta, Iceland,
and Los Angeles.
Interstellar uses extensive practical and miniature effects and the company
Double Negative created additional digital effects.

Interstellar premiered on October 26, 2014, in Los Angeles.
In the United States, it was first released on film stock, expanding to venues
using digital projectors.
The film had a worldwide gross over $677 million (and $773 million with subse
quent re-releases), making it the tenth-highest grossing film of 2014.
It received acclaim for its performances, direction, screenplay, musical score,
visual effects, ambition, themes, and emotional weight.
It has also received praise from many astronomers for its scientific accuracy
and portrayal of theoretical astrophysics. Since its premiere, Interstellar
gained a cult following,[5] and now is regarded by many sci-fi experts as one
of the best science-fiction films of all time.
Interstellar was nominated for five awards at the 87th Academy Awards, winning
Best Visual Effects, and received numerous other accolades"""

# Split into a list of sentences
texts = text.split('.')

# Clean up to remove empty spaces and new lines
texts = [t.strip(' \n') for t in texts]
```

Embedding the text chunks. Let's now embed the texts. We'll send them to the Cohere API, and get back a vector for each text:

```
# Get the embeddings
response = co.embed(
  texts=texts,
  input_type="search_document",
).embeddings

embeds = np.array(response)
print(embeds.shape)
```

This outputs (15, 4096), which indicates that we have 15 vectors, each one of size 4,096.

Building the search index. Before we can search, we need to build a search index. An index stores the embeddings and is optimized to quickly retrieve the nearest neighbors even if we have a very large number of points:

```
import faiss
dim = embeds.shape[1]
index = faiss.IndexFlatL2(dim)
print(index.is_trained)
index.add(np.float32(embeds))
```

Search the index. We can now search the dataset using any query we want. We simply embed the query and present its embedding to the index, which will retrieve the most similar sentence from the Wikipedia article.

Let's define our search function:

```
def search(query, number_of_results=3):

  # 1. Get the query's embedding
  query_embed = co.embed(texts=[query],
                input_type="search_query",).embeddings[0]

  # 2. Retrieve the nearest neighbors
  distances , similar_item_ids = index.search(np.float32([query_embed]), num
ber_of_results)

  # 3. Format the results
  texts_np = np.array(texts) # Convert texts list to numpy for easier indexing
  results = pd.DataFrame(data={'texts': texts_np[similar_item_ids[0]],
                              'distance': distances[0]})

  # 4. Print and return the results
  print(f"Query:'{query}'\nNearest neighbors:")
  return results
```

We are now ready to write a query and search the texts!

```
query = "how precise was the science"
results = search(query)
results
```

This produces the following output:

```
Query: 'how precise was the science'
Nearest neighbors:
```

	texts	distance
0	It has also received praise from many astronomers for its scientific accuracy and portrayal of theoretical astrophysics	10757.379883
1	Caltech theoretical physicist and 2017 Nobel laureate in Physics[4] Kip Thorne was an executive producer, acted as a scientific consultant, and wrote a tie-in book, The Science of Interstellar	11566.131836
2	Interstellar uses extensive practical and miniature effects and the company Double Negative created additional digital effects	11922.833008

The first result has the least distance, and so is the most similar to the query. Looking at it, it answers the question perfectly. Notice that this wouldn't have been possible if we were only doing keyword search because the top result did not include the same keywords in the query.

We can actually verify that by defining a keyword search function to compare the two. We'll use the BM25 algorithm, which is one of the leading lexical search methods. See this notebook (*https://oreil.ly/M0Jwk*) for the source of these code snippets:

```
from rank_bm25 import BM25Okapi
from sklearn.feature_extraction import _stop_words
import string

def bm25_tokenizer(text):
    tokenized_doc = []
    for token in text.lower().split():
        token = token.strip(string.punctuation)

        if len(token) > 0 and token not in _stop_words.ENGLISH_STOP_WORDS:
            tokenized_doc.append(token)
    return tokenized_doc


tokenized_corpus = []
for passage in tqdm(texts):
    tokenized_corpus.append(bm25_tokenizer(passage))

bm25 = BM25Okapi(tokenized_corpus)

def keyword_search(query, top_k=3, num_candidates=15):
    print("Input question:", query)

    ##### BM25 search (lexical search) #####
    bm25_scores = bm25.get_scores(bm25_tokenizer(query))
    top_n = np.argpartition(bm25_scores, -num_candidates)[-num_candidates:]
    bm25_hits = [{'corpus_id': idx, 'score': bm25_scores[idx]} for idx in top_n]
    bm25_hits = sorted(bm25_hits, key=lambda x: x['score'], reverse=True)
```

```
    print(f"Top-3 lexical search (BM25) hits")
    for hit in bm25_hits[0:top_k]:
        print("\t{:.3f}\t{}".format(hit['score'], texts[hit['cor
pus_id']].replace("\n", " ")))
```

Now when we search for the same query, we get a different set of results from the dense retrieval search:

```
keyword_search(query = "how precise was the science")
```

Results:

```
Input question: how precise was the science
Top-3 lexical search (BM25) hits
      1.789 Interstellar is a 2014 epic science fiction film co-written, direc-
ted, and produced by Christopher Nolan
      1.373 Caltech theoretical physicist and 2017 Nobel laureate in Phys-
ics[4] Kip Thorne was an executive producer, acted as a scientific consultant,
and wrote a tie-in book, The Science of Interstellar
      0.000 It stars Matthew McConaughey, Anne Hathaway, Jessica Chastain,
Bill Irwin, Ellen Burstyn, Matt Damon, and Michael Caine
```

Note that the first result does not really answer the question despite it sharing the word "science" with the query. In the next section, we'll see how adding a reranker can improve this search system. But before that, let's complete our overview of dense retrieval by looking at its caveats and go over some methods of breaking down texts into chunks.

Caveats of dense retrieval

It's useful to be aware of some of the drawbacks of dense retrieval and how to address them. What happens, for example, if the texts don't contain the answer? We still get results and their distances. For example:

```
Query:'What is the mass of the moon?'
Nearest neighbors:
```

	texts	distance
0	The film had a worldwide gross over $677 million (and $773 million with subsequent re-releases), making it the tenth-highest grossing film of 2014	1.298275
1	It has also received praise from many astronomers for its scientific accuracy and portrayal of theoretical astrophysics	1.324389
2	Cinematographer Hoyte van Hoytema shot it on 35 mm movie film in the Panavision anamorphic format and IMAX 70 mm	1.328375

In cases like this, one possible heuristic is to set a threshold level—a maximum distance for relevance, for example. A lot of search systems present the user with the best info they can get and leave it up to the user to decide if it's relevant or not.

Tracking the information of whether the user clicked on a result (and were satisfied by it) can improve future versions of the search system.

Another caveat of dense retrieval is when a user wants to find an exact match for a specific phrase. That's a case that's perfect for keyword matching. That's one reason why hybrid search, which includes both semantic search and keyword search, is advised instead of relying solely on dense retrieval.

Dense retrieval systems also find it challenging to work properly in domains other than the ones that they were trained on. So, for example, if you train a retrieval model on internet and Wikipedia data, and then deploy it on legal texts (without having enough legal data as part of the training set), the model will not work as well in that legal domain.

The final thing we'd like to point out is that this is a case where each sentence contained a piece of information, and we showed queries that specifically ask for that information. What about questions whose answers span multiple sentences? This highlights one of the important design parameters of dense retrieval systems: what is the best way to chunk long texts? And why do we need to chunk them in the first place?

Chunking long texts

One limitation of Transformer language models is that they are limited in context sizes, meaning we cannot feed them very long texts that go above the number of words or tokens that the model supports. So how do we embed long texts?

There are several possible ways, and two possible approaches shown in Figure 8-7 include indexing one vector per document and indexing multiple vectors per document.

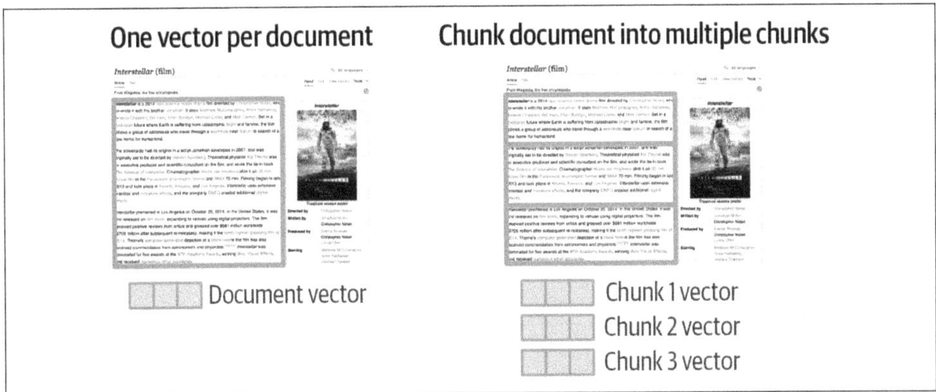

Figure 8-7. It's possible to create one vector representing an entire document, but it's better for longer documents to be split into smaller chunks that get their own embeddings.

One vector per document. In this approach, we use a single vector to represent the whole document. The possibilities here include:

- Embedding only a representative part of the document and ignoring the rest of the text. This may mean embedding only the title, or only the beginning of the document. This is useful to get quickly started with building a demo but it leaves a lot of information unindexed and therefore unsearchable. As an approach, it may work better for documents where the beginning captures the main points of a document (think: Wikipedia article). But it's really not the best approach for a real system because a lot of information would be left out of the index and would be unsearchable.
- Embedding the document in chunks, embedding those chunks, and then aggregating those chunks into a single vector. The usual method of aggregation here is to average those vectors. A downside of this approach is that it results in a highly compressed vector that loses a lot of the information in the document.

This approach can satisfy some information needs, but not others. A lot of the time, a search is for a specific piece of information contained in an article, which is better captured if the concept had its own vector.

Multiple vectors per document. In this approach, we chunk the document into smaller pieces, and embed those chunks. Our search index then becomes that of chunk embeddings, not entire document embeddings. Figure 8-8 shows a number of possible text chunking approaches.

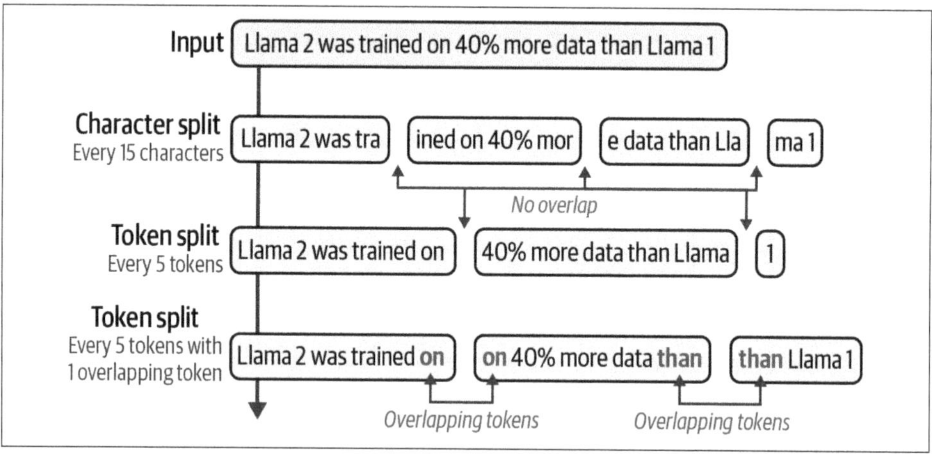

Figure 8-8. Several chunking methods and their effects on the input text. Overlapping chunks can be important to prevent the absence of context.

The chunking approach is better because it has full coverage of the text and because the vectors tend to capture individual concepts inside the text. This leads to a more expressive search index. Figure 8-9 shows a number of possible approaches.

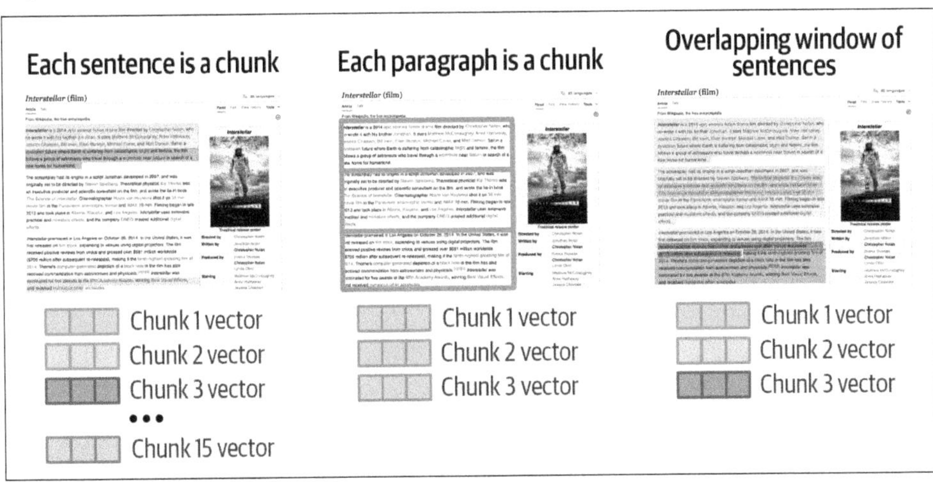

Figure 8-9. A number of possible options for chunking a document for embedding.

The best way of chunking a long text will depend on the types of texts and queries your system anticipates. Approaches include:

- Each sentence is a chunk. The issue here is this could be too granular and the vectors don't capture enough of the context.
- Each paragraph is a chunk. This is great if the text is made up of short paragraphs. Otherwise, it may be that every 3–8 sentences is a chunk.
- Some chunks derive a lot of their meaning from the text around them. So we can incorporate some context via:
  - Adding the title of the document to the chunk.
  - Adding some of the text before and after them to the chunk. This way, the chunks can overlap so they include some surrounding text that also appears in adjacent chunks. This is what we can see in Figure 8-10.

Expect more chunking strategies to arise as the field develops—some of which may even use LLMs to dynamically split a text into meaningful chunks.

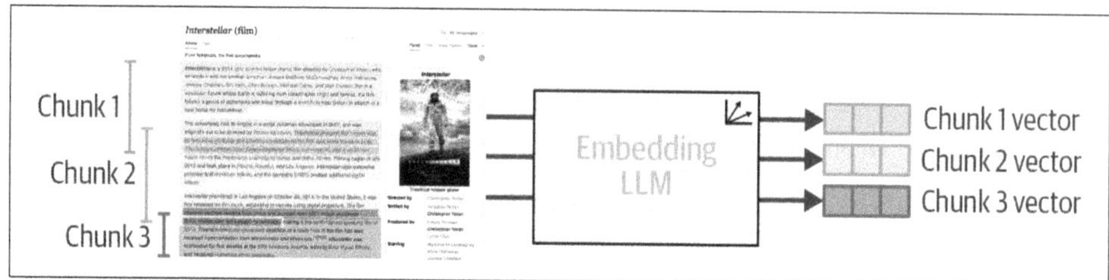

Figure 8-10. Chunking the text into overlapping segments is one strategy to retain more of the context around different segments.

Nearest neighbor search versus vector databases

Once the query is embedded, we need to find the nearest vectors to it from our text archive as we can see in Figure 8-11. The most straightforward way to find the nearest neighbors is to calculate the distances between the query and the archive. That can easily be done with NumPy and is a reasonable approach if you have thousands or tens of thousands of vectors in your archive.

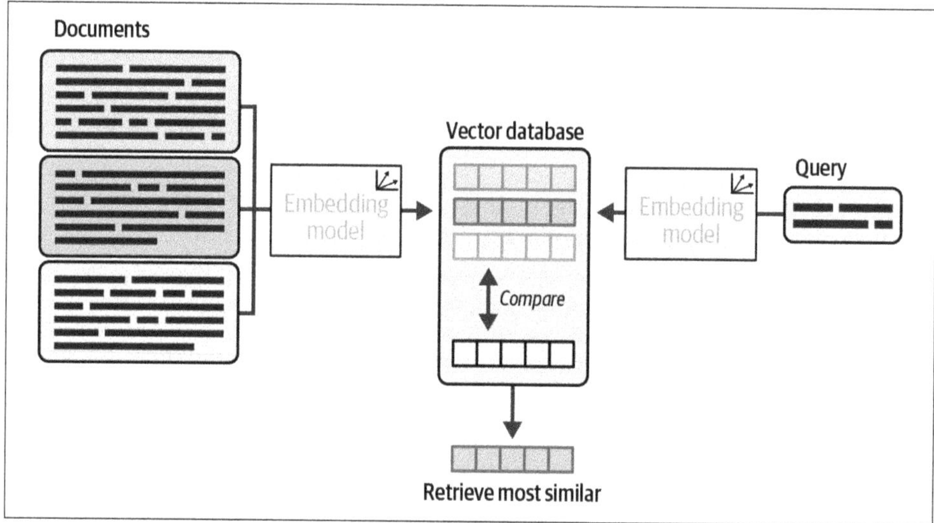

Figure 8-11. As we saw in Chapter 3, we can compare embeddings to quickly find the most similar documents to a query.

As you scale beyond to the millions of vectors, an optimized approach for retrieval is to rely on approximate nearest neighbor search libraries like Annoy or FAISS. These allow you to retrieve results from massive indexes in milliseconds and some of them can improve their performance by utilizing GPUs and scaling to clusters of machines to serve very large indices.

Another class of vector retrieval systems are vector databases like Weaviate or Pinecone. A vector database allows you to add or delete vectors without having to rebuild the index. They also provide ways to filter your search or customize it in ways beyond merely vector distances.

Fine-tuning embedding models for dense retrieval

Just as we discussed in Chapter 4 on text classification, we can improve the performance of an LLM on a task using fine-tuning. As in that case, retrieval needs to optimize text embeddings and not simply token embeddings. The process for this fine-tuning is to get training data composed of queries and relevant results.

Let's look at one example from our dataset, the sentence "Interstellar premiered on October 26, 2014, in Los Angeles." Two possible queries where this is a relevant result are:

- Relevant query 1: "Interstellar release date"
- Relevant query 2: "When did Interstellar premier"

The fine-tuning process aims to make the embeddings of these queries close to the embedding of the resulting sentence. It also needs to see negative examples of queries that are not relevant to the sentence, for example:

- Irrelevant query: "Interstellar cast"

With these examples, we now have three pairs—two positive pairs and one negative pair. Let's assume, as we can see in Figure 8-12, that before fine-tuning, all three queries have the same distance from the result document. That's not far-fetched because they all talk about *Interstellar*.

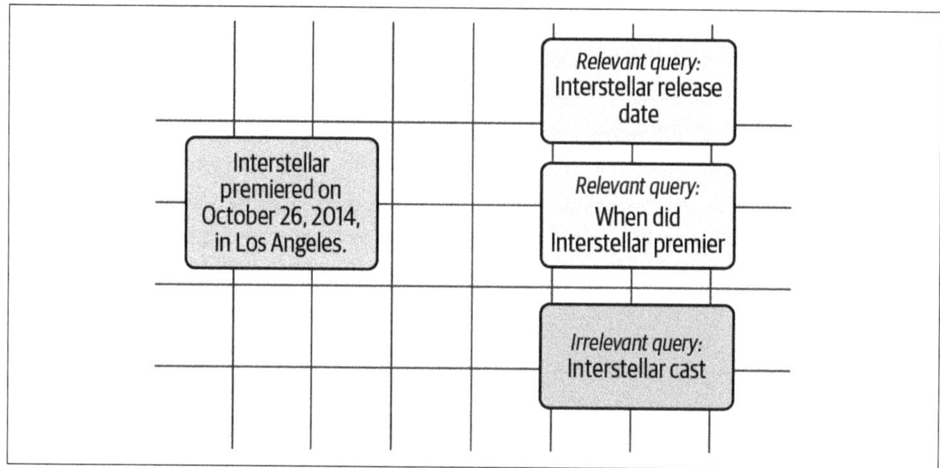

Figure 8-12. Before fine-tuning, the embeddings of both relevant and irrelevant queries may be close to a particular document.

The fine-tuning step works to make the relevant queries closer to the document and at the same time make irrelevant queries farther from the document. We can see this effect in Figure 8-13.

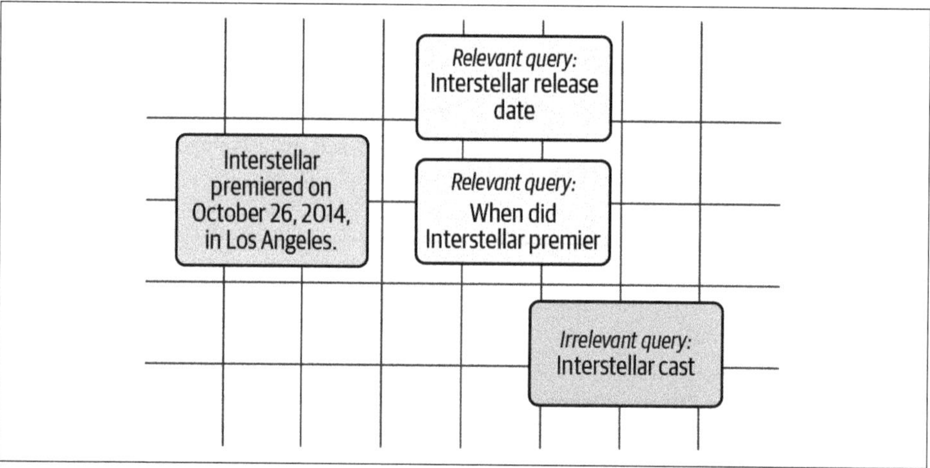

Figure 8-13. After the fine-tuning process, the text embedding model becomes better at this search task by incorporating how we define relevance on our dataset using the examples we provided of relevant and irrelevant documents.

Reranking

A lot of organizations have already built search systems. For those organizations, an easier way to incorporate language models is as a final step inside their search pipeline. This step is tasked with changing the order of the search results based on relevance to the search query. This one step can vastly improve search results and it's in fact what Microsoft Bing added to achieve the improvements to search results using BERT-like models. Figure 8-14 shows the structure of a rerank search system serving as the second stage in a two-stage search system.

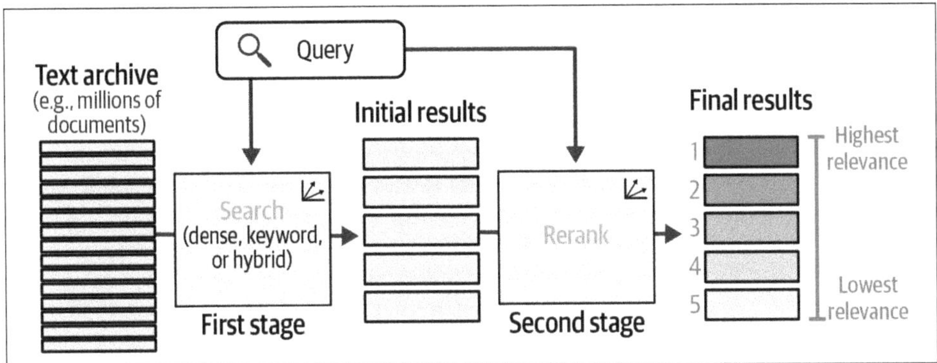

Figure 8-14. LLM rerankers operate as part of a search pipeline with the goal of reordering a number of shortlisted search results by relevance.

Reranking example

A reranker takes in the search query and a number of search results, and returns the optimal ordering of these documents so the most relevant ones to the query are higher in ranking. Cohere's Rerank endpoint (*https://oreil.ly/PuCII*) is a simple way to start using a first reranker. We simply pass it the query and texts and get the results back. We don't need to train or tune it:

```
query = "how precise was the science"
results = co.rerank(query=query, documents=texts, top_n=3, return_docu
ments=True)
results.results
```

We can print these results:

```
for idx, result in enumerate(results.results):
  print(idx, result.relevance_score , result.document.text)
```

Output:

```
0 0.1698185 It has also received praise from many astronomers for its scien-
tific accuracy and portrayal of theoretical astrophysics
1 0.07004896 The film had a worldwide gross over $677 million (and $773 mil-
lion with subsequent re-releases), making it the tenth-highest grossing film
of 2014
2 0.0043994132 Caltech theoretical physicist and 2017 Nobel laureate in Phys-
ics[4] Kip Thorne was an executive producer, acted as a scientific consultant,
and wrote a tie-in book, The Science of Interstellar
```

This shows the reranker is much more confident about the first result, assigning it a relevance score of 0.16, while the other results are scored much lower in relevance.

In this basic example, we passed our reranker all 15 of our documents. More often, however, our index would have thousands or millions of entries, and we need to shortlist, say one hundred or one thousand results and then present those to the reranker. This shortlisting step is called the *first stage* of the search pipeline.

The first-stage retriever can be keyword search, dense retrieval, or better yet—hybrid search that uses both of them. We can revisit our previous example to see how adding a reranker after a keyword search system improves its performance.

Let's tweak our keyword search function so it retrieves a list of the top 10 results using keyword search, then use rerank to choose the top 3 results from those 10:

```
def keyword_and_reranking_search(query, top_k=3, num_candidates=10):
    print("Input question:", query)

    ##### BM25 search (lexical search) #####
    bm25_scores = bm25.get_scores(bm25_tokenizer(query))
    top_n = np.argpartition(bm25_scores, -num_candidates)[-num_candidates:]
    bm25_hits = [{'corpus_id': idx, 'score': bm25_scores[idx]} for idx in top_n]
    bm25_hits = sorted(bm25_hits, key=lambda x: x['score'], reverse=True)

    print(f"Top-3 lexical search (BM25) hits")
    for hit in bm25_hits[0:top_k]:
        print("\t{:.3f}\t{}".format(hit['score'], texts[hit['cor
pus_id']].replace("\n", " ")))


    #Add re-ranking
    docs = [texts[hit['corpus_id']] for hit in bm25_hits]

    print(f"\nTop-3 hits by rank-API ({len(bm25_hits)} BM25 hits re-ranked)")
    results = co.rerank(query=query, documents=docs, top_n=top_k, return_docu
ments=True)
    # print(results.results)
    for hit in results.results:
        # print(hit)
        print("\t{:.3f}\t{}".format(hit.relevance_score, hit.docu
ment.text.replace("\n", " ")))
```

Now we can send our query and check the results of keyword search and then the result of keyword search shortlisting its top 10 results, then pass them on to the reranker:

```
keyword_and_reranking_search(query = "how precise was the science")
```

Results:

```
Input question: how precise was the science
Top-3 lexical search (BM25) hits
1.789 Interstellar is a 2014 epic science fiction film co-written, directed,
and produced by Christopher Nolan
1.373 Caltech theoretical physicist and 2017 Nobel laureate in Physics[4] Kip
Thorne was an executive producer, acted as a scientific consultant, and wrote
a tie-in book, The Science of Interstellar
0.000 Interstellar uses extensive practical and miniature effects and the com-
pany Double Negative created additional digital effects

Top-3 hits by rank-API (10 BM25 hits re-ranked)
0.004 Caltech theoretical physicist and 2017 Nobel laureate in Physics[4] Kip
Thorne was an executive producer, acted as a scientific consultant, and wrote
a tie-in book, The Science of Interstellar
0.004 Set in a dystopian future where humanity is struggling to survive, the
film follows a group of astronauts who travel through a wormhole near Saturn
in search of a new home for mankind
0.003 Brothers Christopher and Jonathan Nolan wrote the screenplay, which had
its origins in a script Jonathan developed in 2007
```

We see that keyword search assigns scores to only two results that share some of the keywords. In the second set of results, the reranker elevates the second result appropriately as the most relevant result for the query. This is a toy example that gives us a glimpse of the effect, but in practice, such a pipeline significantly improves search quality. On a multilingual benchmark like MIRACL, a reranker can boost (*https://oreil.ly/Kq3nA*) performance from 36.5 to 62.8, measured as nDCG@10 (more on evaluation later in this chapter).

Open source retrieval and reranking with sentence transformers

If you want to locally set up retrieval and reranking on your own machine, then you can use the Sentence Transformers library. Refer to the documentation at *https://oreil.ly/jJOhV* for setup. Check the "Retrieve & Re-Rank" section (*https://oreil.ly/mDglU*) for instructions and code examples for how to conduct these steps in the library.

How reranking models work

One popular way of building LLM search rerankers is to present the query and each result to an LLM working as a *cross-encoder*. This means that a query and possible result are presented to the model at the same time allowing the model to view both these texts before it assigns a relevance score, as we can see in Figure 8-15. All of the documents are processed simultaneously as a batch yet each document is evaluated against the query independently. The scores then determine the new order of the results. This method is described in more detail in a paper titled "Multi-stage document ranking with BERT" (*https://oreil.ly/e3J9i*) and is sometimes referred to as monoBERT.

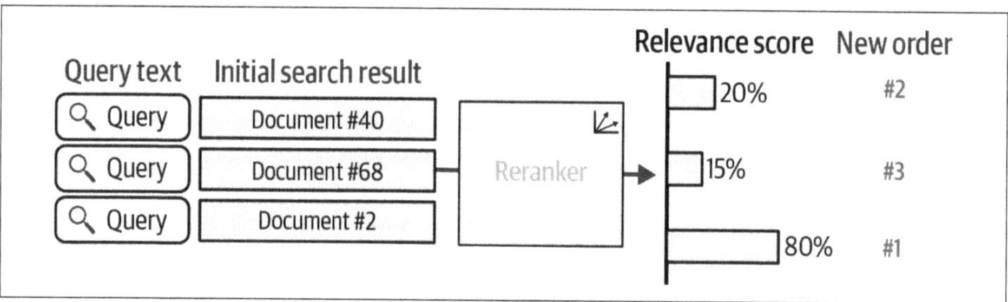

Figure 8-15. A reranker assigns a relevance score to each document by looking at the document and the query at the same time.

This formulation of search as relevance scoring basically boils down to being a classification problem. Given those inputs, the model outputs a score from 0–1 where 0 is irrelevant and 1 is highly relevant. This should be familiar from our classification discussions in Chapter 4.

To learn more about the development of using LLMs for search, "Pretrained transformers for text tanking: BERT and beyond (*https://oreil.ly/Z1IfS*)" is a highly recommended look at the developments of these models until about 2021.

Retrieval Evaluation Metrics

Semantic search is evaluated using metrics from the Information Retrieval (IR) field. Let's discuss one of these popular metrics: mean average precision (MAP).

Evaluating search systems needs three major components (*https://oreil.ly/ga3Vk*): a text archive, a set of queries, and relevance judgments indicating which documents are relevant for each query. We see these components in Figure 8-16.

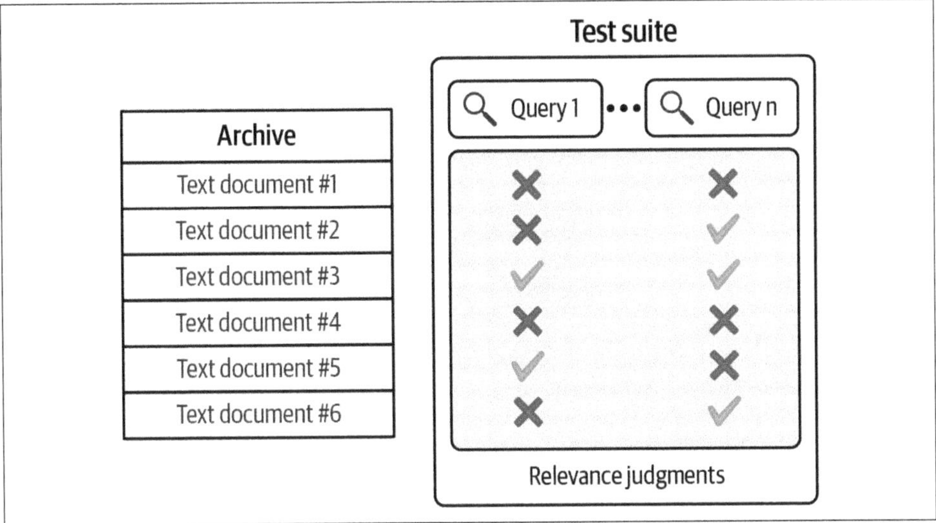

Figure 8-16. To evaluate search systems, we need a test suite including queries and relevance judgments indicating which documents in our archive are relevant for each query.

Using this test suite, we can proceed to explore evaluating search systems. Let's start with a simple example. Let's assume we pass query 1 to two different search systems. And get two sets of results. Say we limit the number of results to three, as we can see in Figure 8-17.

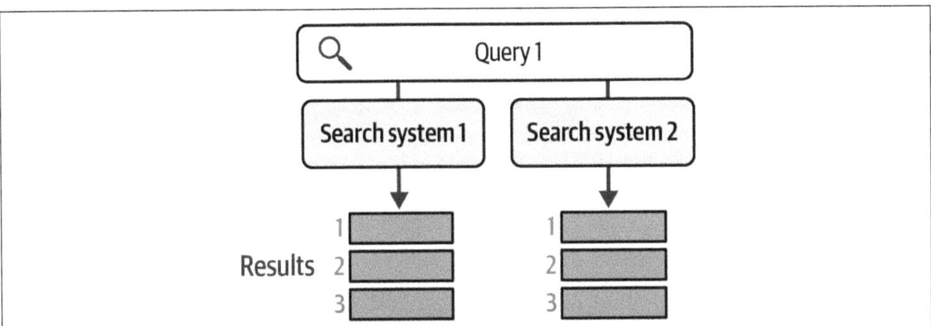

Figure 8-17. To compare two search systems, we pass the same query from our test suite to both systems and look at their top results.

To tell which is a better system, we turn to the relevance judgments that we have for the query. Figure 8-18 shows which of the returned results are relevant.

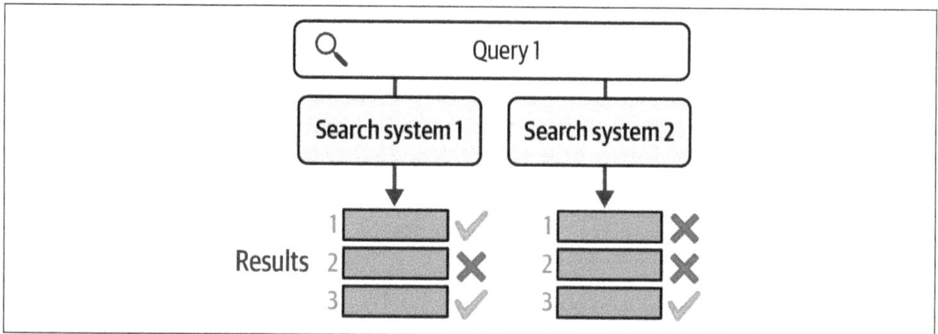

Figure 8-18. Looking at the relevance judgments from our test suite, we can see that system 1 did a better job than system 2.

This shows us a clear case where system 1 is better than system 2. Intuitively, we may just count how many relevant results each system retrieved. System 1 got two out of three correct, and system 2 got only one out of three correct. But what about a case like Figure 8-19 where both systems only get one relevant result out of three, but they're in different positions?

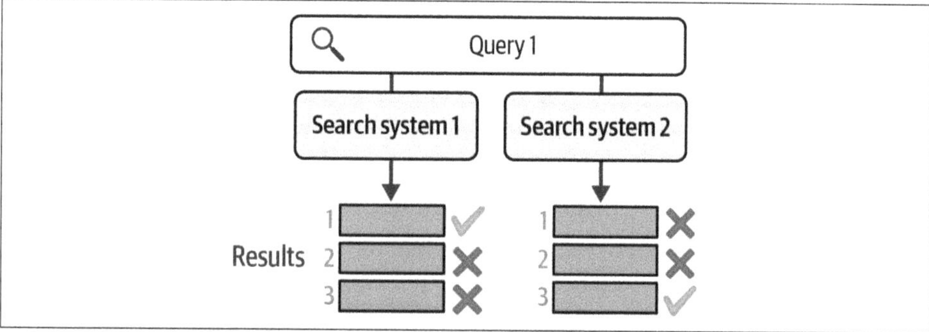

Figure 8-19. We need a scoring system that rewards system 1 for assigning a high position to a relevant result—even though both systems retrieved only one relevant result in their top three results.

In this case, we can intuit that system 1 did a better job than system 2 because the result in the first position (the most important position) is correct. But how can we assign a number or score to how much better that result is? Mean average precision is a measure that is able to quantify this distinction.

One common way to assign numeric scores in this scenario is average precision, which evaluates system 1's result for the query to be 1 and system 2's to be 0.3. So let's see how average precision is calculated to evaluate one set of results, and then how it's aggregated to evaluate a system across all the queries in the test suite.

Scoring a single query with average precision

To score a search system on this query, we can focus on scoring the relevant documents. Let's start by looking at a query that only has one relevant document in the test suite.

The first one is easy: the search system placed the relevant result (the only available one for this query) at the top. This gets the system the perfect score of 1. Figure 8-20 shows this calculation: looking at the first position, we have a relevant result leading to a precision at position 1 of 1.0 (calculated as the number of relevant results at position 1, divided by the position we're currently looking at).

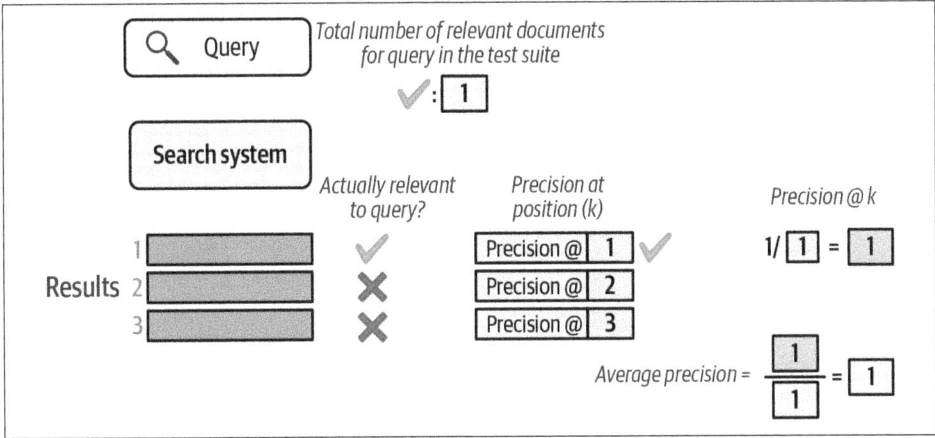

Figure 8-20. To calculate mean average precision, we start by calculating precision at each position, starting with position 1.

Since we're only scoring relevant documents we can ignore the scores of nonrelevant documents and stop our calculation here. What if the system actually placed the only relevant result at the third position, however? How would that affect the score? Figure 8-21 shows how that results in a penalty.

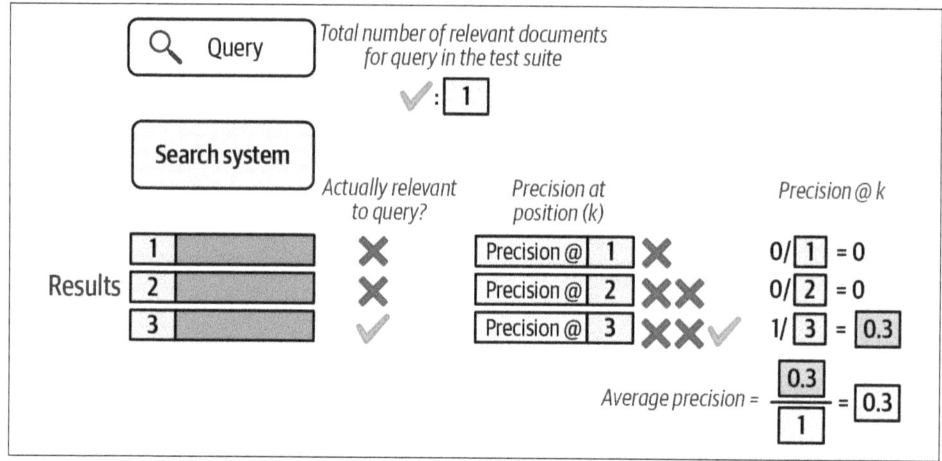

Figure 8-21. If the system places nonrelevant documents ahead of a relevant document, its precision score is penalized.

Let's now look at a query with more than one relevant document. Figure 8-22 shows that calculation and how averaging now comes into the picture.

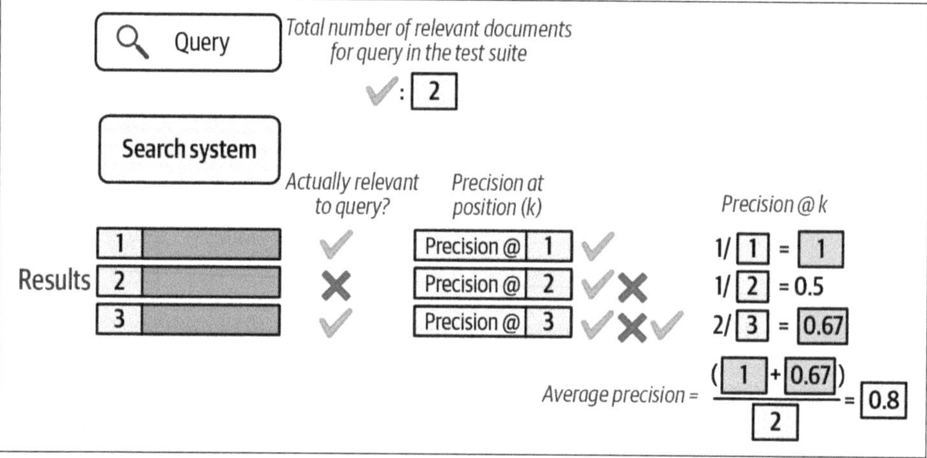

Figure 8-22. Average precision of a document with multiple relevant documents considers the precision at k results of all the relevant documents.

Scoring across multiple queries with mean average precision

Now that we're familiar with precision at k and average precision, we can extend this knowledge to a metric that can score a search system against all the queries in our test suite. That metric is called mean average precision. Figure 8-23 shows how to calculate this metric by taking the mean of the average precisions of each query.

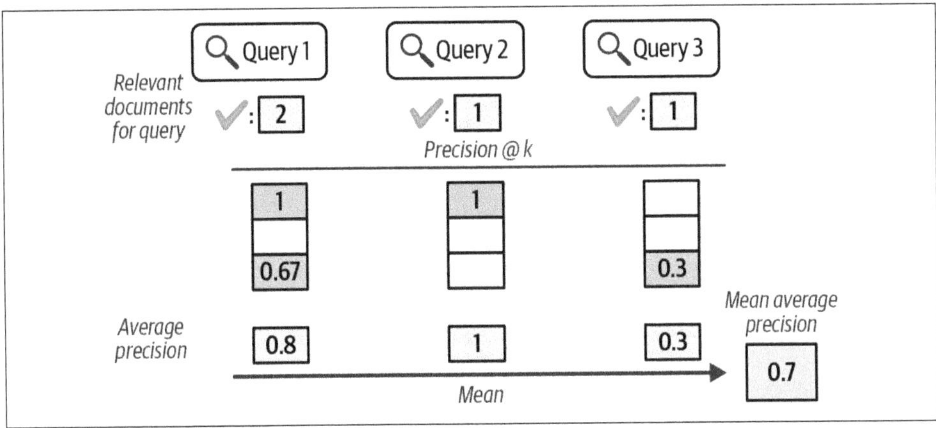

Figure 8-23. The mean average precision takes into consideration the average precision score of a system for every query in the test suite. By averaging them, it produces a single metric that we can use to compare a search system against another.

You may be wondering why the same operation is called "mean" and "average." It's likely an aesthetic choice because MAP sounds better than average average precision.

Now we have a single metric that we can use to compare different systems. If you want to learn more about evaluation metrics, see the "Evaluation in Information Retrieval" chapter (*https://oreil.ly/oeY4b*) of *Introduction to Information Retrieval* (Cambridge University Press) by Christopher D. Manning, Prabhakar Raghavan, and Hinrich Schütze.

In addition to mean average precision, another metric commonly used for search systems is normalized discounted cumulative gain (nDCG), which is more nuanced in that the relevance of documents is not binary (relevant versus not relevant) and one document can be labeled as more relevant than another in the test suite and scoring mechanism.

Retrieval-Augmented Generation (RAG)

The mass adoption of LLMs quickly led to people asking them questions and expecting factual answers. While the models can answer some questions correctly, they also confidently answer lots of questions incorrectly. The leading method the industry turned to remedy this behavior is RAG, described in the paper "Retrieval-Augmented Generation for Knowledge-Intensive NLP Tasks" (*https://oreil.ly/84oHH*) (2020)[1] and illustrated in Figure 8-24.

1 Patrick Lewis et al. "Retrieval-augmented generation for knowledge-intensive NLP tasks." *Advances in Neural Information Processing Systems* 33 (2020): 9459–9474.

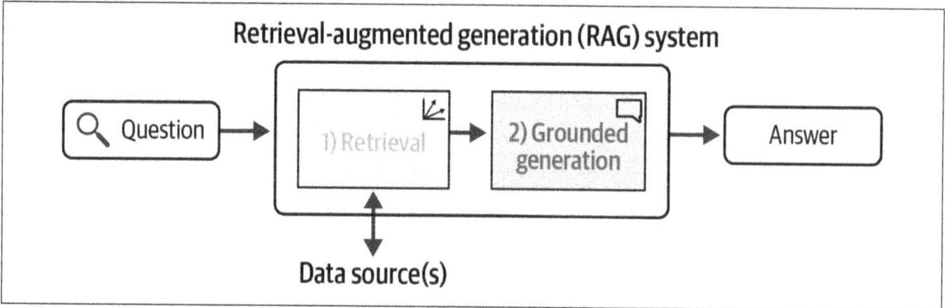

Figure 8-24. A basic RAG pipeline is made up of a search step followed by a grounded generation step where the LLM is prompted with the question and the information retrieved from the search step.

RAG systems incorporate search capabilities in addition to generation capabilities. They can be seen as an improvement to generation systems because they reduce their hallucinations and improve their factuality. They also enable use cases of "chat with my data" that consumers and companies can use to ground an LLM on internal company data, or a specific data source of interest (e.g., chatting with a book).

This also extends to search systems. More search engines are incorporating an LLM to summarize results or answer questions submitted to the search engine. Examples include Perplexity (*https://oreil.ly/PrYVM*), Microsoft Bing AI (*https://oreil.ly/GBd66*), and Google Gemini (*https://oreil.ly/--C_8*).

From Search to RAG

Let's now turn our search system into a RAG system. We do that by adding an LLM to the end of the search pipeline. We present the question and the top retrieved documents to the LLM, and ask it to answer the question given the context provided by the search results. We can see an example in Figure 8-25.

This generation step is called *grounded generation* because the retrieved relevant information we provide the LLM establishes a certain context that grounds the LLM in the domain we're interested in. Figure 8-26 shows how grounded generation fits after search if we continue our embeddings search example from earlier.

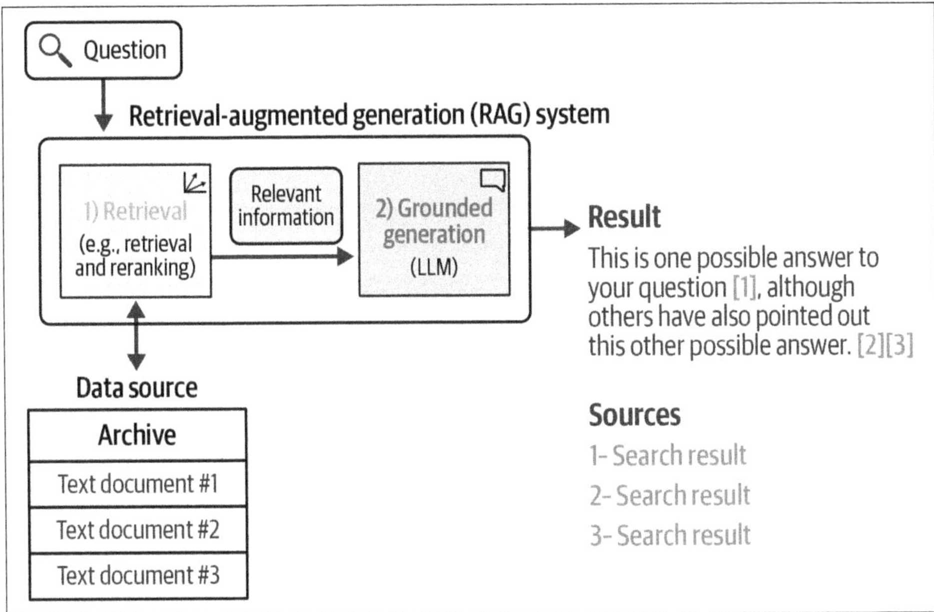

Figure 8-25. Generative search formulates answers and summaries at the end of a search pipeline while citing its sources (returned by the previous steps in the search system).

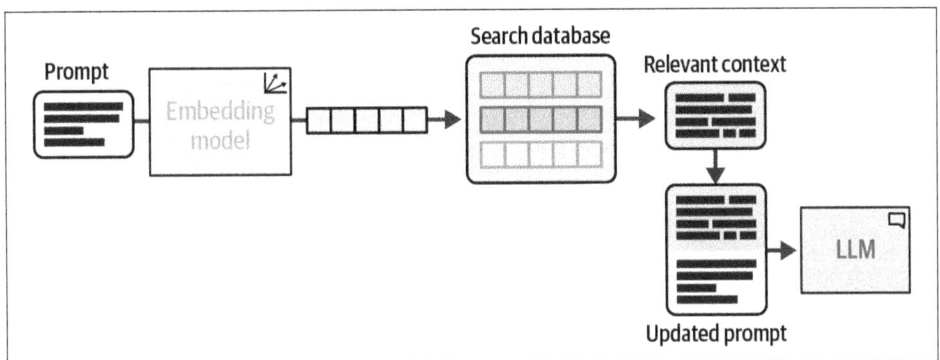

Figure 8-26. Find the most relevant information to an input prompt by comparing the similarities between embeddings. The most relevant information is added to the prompt before giving it to the LLM.

Example: Grounded Generation with an LLM API

Let's look at how to add a grounded generation step after the search results to create our first RAG system. For this example, we'll use Cohere's managed LLM, which builds on the search systems we've seen earlier in the chapter. We'll use embedding search to retrieve the top documents, then we'll pass those to the `co.chat` endpoint along with the questions to provide a grounded answer:

```
query = "income generated"

# 1- Retrieval
# We'll use embedding search. But ideally we'd do hybrid
results = search(query)

# 2- Grounded Generation
docs_dict = [{'text': text} for text in results['texts']]
response = co.chat(
    message = query,
    documents=docs_dict
)

print(response.text)
```

Result:

```
The film generated a worldwide gross of over $677 million, or $773 million
with subsequent re-releases.
```

We are highlighting some of the text because the model indicated the source for these spans of text to be the first document we passed in:

```
citations=[ChatCitation(start=21, end=36, text='worldwide gross', docu-
ment_ids=['doc_0']), ChatCitation(start=40, end=57, text='over $677 million',
document_ids=['doc_0']), ChatCitation(start=62, end=103, text='$773 million
with subsequent re-releases.', document_ids=['doc_0'])]

documents=[{'id': 'doc_0', 'text': 'The film had a worldwide gross over $677
million (and $773 million with subsequent re-releases), making it the tenth-
highest grossing film of 2014'}]
```

Example: RAG with Local Models

Let us now replicate this basic functionality with local models. We will lose the ability to do span citations and the smaller local model isn't going to work as well as the larger managed model, but it's useful to demonstrate the flow. We'll start by downloading a quantized model.

Loading the generation model

We start by downloading our model:

```
!wget https://huggingface.co/microsoft/Phi-3-mini-4k-instruct-gguf/resolve/main/
Phi-3-mini-4k-instruct-fp16.gguf
```

Using `llama.cpp`, `llama-cpp-python`, and LangChain, we load the text generation model:

```
from langchain import LlamaCpp

# Make sure the model path is correct for your system!
llm = LlamaCpp(
    model_path="Phi-3-mini-4k-instruct-fp16.gguf",
    n_gpu_layers=-1,
    max_tokens=500,
    n_ctx=2048,
    seed=42,
    verbose=False
)
```

Loading the embedding model

Let's now load an embedding language model. In this example, we will choose the BAAI/bge-small-en-v1.5 model (*https://oreil.ly/kMSEh*). At the time of writing, it is high on the MTEB leaderboard (*https://oreil.ly/Ugljz*) for embedding models and relatively small:

```
from langchain.embeddings.huggingface import HuggingFaceEmbeddings

# Embedding model for converting text to numerical representations
embedding_model = HuggingFaceEmbeddings(
    model_name='thenlper/gte-small'
)
```

We can now use the embedding model to set up our vector database:

```
from langchain.vectorstores import FAISS

# Create a local vector database
db = FAISS.from_texts(texts, embedding_model)
```

The RAG prompt

A prompt template plays a vital part in the RAG pipeline. It is the central place where we communicate the relevant documents to the LLM. To do so, we will create an additional input variable named `context` that can provide the LLM with the retrieved documents:

```
from           import PromptTemplate

# Create a prompt template
template = """<|user|>
Relevant information:
{context}

Provide a concise answer the following question using the relevant information
provided above:
{question}<|end|>
<|assistant|>"""
prompt = PromptTemplate(
    template=template,
    input_variables=["context", "question"]
)
```

```
from                  import RetrievalQA

# RAG pipeline
rag = RetrievalQA.from_chain_type(
    llm=llm,
    chain_type='stuff',
    retriever=db.as_retriever(),
    chain_type_kwargs={
        "prompt": prompt
    },
    verbose=True
)
```

Now we're ready to call the model and ask it a question:

```
rag.invoke('Income generated')
```

Result:

```
The Income generated by the film in 2014 was over $677 million worldwide.
This made it the tenth-highest grossing film of that year. It should be noted,
however, this figure includes both initial ticket sales as well as any subse-
quent re-releases. With these additional releases, total earnings surged to
approximately $773 million. The release format transitioned from traditional
film stock projection in theaters to digital projectors once it was expanded
to various venues in the United States. This shift might have contributed
to wider audience reach and potentially higher grossing figures over time.
However, specific data on how this affected total earnings isn't provided in
the information above.
```

As always, we can adjust the prompt to control the model's generation (e.g., answer length and tone).

Advanced RAG Techniques

There are several additional techniques to improve the performance of RAG systems. Some of them are laid out here.

Query rewriting

If the RAG system is a chatbot, the preceding simple RAG implementation would likely struggle with the search step if a question is too verbose, or to refer to context in previous messages in the conversation. This is why it's a good idea to use an LLM to rewrite the query into one that aids the retrieval step in getting the right information. An example of this is a message such as:

> User Question: "We have an essay due tomorrow. We have to write about some animal. I love penguins. I could write about them. But I could also write about dolphins. Are they animals? Maybe. Let's do dolphins. Where do they live for example?"

This should actually be rewritten into a query like:

> Query: "Where do dolphins live"

This rewriting behavior can be done through a prompt (or through an API call). Cohere's API, for example, has a dedicated query-rewriting mode for `co.chat`.

Multi-query RAG

The next improvement we can introduce is to extend the query rewriting to be able to search multiple queries if more than one is needed to answer a specific question. Take for example:

> User Question: "Compare the financial results of Nvidia in 2020 vs. 2023"

We may find one document that contains the results for both years, but more likely, we're better off making two search queries:

> Query 1: "Nvidia 2020 financial results"
> Query 2: "Nvidia 2023 financial results"

We then present the top results of both queries to the model for grounded generation. An additional small improvement here is to also give the query rewriter the option to determine if no search is required and if it can directly generate a confident answer without searching.

Multi-hop RAG

A more advanced question may require a series of sequential queries. Take for example a question like:

> User Question: "Who are the largest car manufacturers in 2023? Do they each make EVs or not?"

To answer this, the system must first search for:

> Step 1, Query 1: "largest car manufacturers 2023"

Then after it gets this information (the result being Toyota, Volkswagen, and Hyundai), it should ask follow-up questions:

> Step 2, Query 1: "Toyota Motor Corporation electric vehicles"
>
> Step 2, Query 2: "Volkswagen AG electric vehicles"
>
> Step 2, Query 3: "Hyundai Motor Company electric vehicles"

Query routing

An additional enhancement is to give the model the ability to search multiple data sources. We can, for example, specify for the model that if it gets a question about HR, it should search the company's HR information system (e.g., Notion) but if the question is about customer data, that it should search the customer relationship management (CRM) (e.g., Salesforce).

Agentic RAG

You may be able to now see that the list of previous enhancements slowly delegates more and more responsibility to the LLM to solve more and more complex problems. This relies on the LLM's capability to gauge the required information needs as well as its ability to utilize multiple data sources. This new nature of the LLM starts to become closer and closer to an agent that acts on the world. The data sources can also now be abstracted into tools. We saw, for example, that we can search Notion, but by the same token, we should be able to post to Notion as well.

Not all LLMs will have the RAG capabilities mentioned here. At the time of writing, likely only the largest managed models may be able to attempt this behavior. Thankfully, Cohere's Command R+ (*https://oreil.ly/i2UXh*) excels at these tasks and is available as an open-weights model (*https://oreil.ly/Jpypi*) as well.

RAG Evaluation

There are still ongoing developments in how to evaluate RAG models. A good paper to read on this topic is "Evaluating verifiability in generative search engines" (*https://oreil.ly/HVbAN*) (2023), which runs human evaluations on different generative search systems.[2]

It evaluates results along four axes:

Fluency
: Whether the generated text is fluent and cohesive.

Perceived utility
: Whether the generated answer is helpful and informative.

Citation recall
: The proportion of generated statements about the external world that are fully supported by their citations.

Citation precision
: The proportion of generated citations that support their associated statements.

While human evaluation is always preferred, there are approaches that attempt to automate these evaluations by having a capable LLM act as a judge (called *LLM-as-a-judge*) and score the different generations along the different axes. Ragas (*https://oreil.ly/6GVMW*) is a software library that does exactly this. It also scores some additional useful metrics like:

Faithfulness
: Whether the answer is consistent with the provided context

Answer relevance
: How relevant the answer is to the question

The Ragas documentation site (*https://oreil.ly/Diugy*) provides more details about the formulas to actually calculate these metrics.

2 Nelson F. Liu, Tianyi Zhang, and Percy Liang. "Evaluating verifiability in generative search engines." *arXiv preprint arXiv:2304.09848* (2023).

Summary

In this chapter, we looked at different ways of using language models to improve existing search systems and even be the core of new, more powerful search systems. These include:

- Dense retrieval, which relies on the similarity of text embeddings. These are systems that embed a search query and retrieve the documents with the nearest embeddings to the query's embedding.
- Rerankers, systems (like monoBERT) that look at a query and candidate results and score the relevance of each document to that query. These relevance scores are then used to order the shortlisted results according to their relevance to the query, often producing an improved results ranking.
- RAG, where search systems have a generative LLM at the end of the pipeline to formulate an answer based on retrieved documents while citing sources.

We also looked at one of the possible methods of evaluating search systems. Mean average precision allows us to score search systems to be able to compare across a test suite of queries and their known relevance to the test queries. Evaluating RAG systems requires multiple axes, however, like faithfulness, fluency, and others that can be evaluated by humans or by LLM-as-a-judge.

In the next chapter, we will explore how language models can be made multimodal and reason not just about text but images as well.

CHAPTER 9
Multimodal Large Language Models

When you think about large language models (LLMs), multimodality might not be the first thing that comes to mind. After all, they are *language* models! But we can quickly see that models can be much more useful if they're able to handle types of data other than text. It's very useful, for example, if a language model is able to glance at a picture and answer questions about it. A model that is able to handle text and images (each of which is called a *modality*) is said to be *multimodal*, as we can see in Figure 9-1.

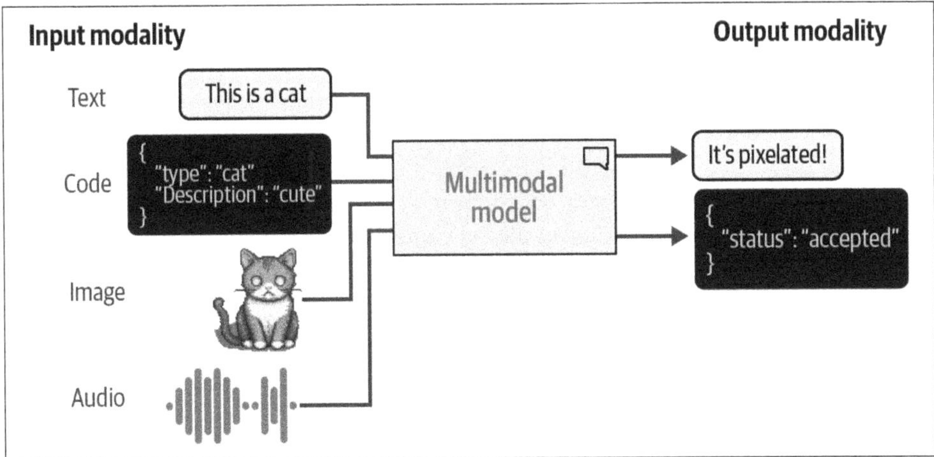

Figure 9-1. Models that are able to deal with different types (or modalities) of data, such as images, audio, video, or sensors, are said to be multimodal. It's possible for a model to accept a modality as input yet not be able to generate in that modality.

We have seen all manner of emerging behaviors rising from LLMs, from generalization capabilities and reasoning to arithmetic and linguistics. As models grow larger and smarter, so do their skill sets.[1]

The ability to receive and reason with multimodal input might further increase and help emerge capabilities that were previously locked. In practice, language does not solely live in a vacuum. As an example, your body language, facial expressions, intonation, etc. are all methods of communication that enhance the spoken word.

The same thing applies to LLMs; if we can enable them to reason about multimodal information, their capabilities might increase and we become able to deploy them to solve new kinds of problems.

In this chapter, we will explore a number of different LLMs that have multimodal capabilities and what that means for practical use cases. We will start by exploring how images are converted to numerical representations using an adaptation of the original Transformer technique. Then, we will show how LLMs can be extended to include vision tasks using this Transformer.

Transformers for Vision

Throughout the chapters of this book, we have seen the success of using Transformer-based models for a variety of language modeling tasks, from classification and clustering to search and generative modeling. So it might not be surprising that researchers have been looking at a way to generalize some of the Transformer's success to the field of computer vision.

The method they came up with is called the Vision Transformer (ViT), which has been shown to do tremendously well on image recognition tasks compared to the previously default convolutional neural networks (CNNs).[2] Like the original Transformer, ViT is used to transform unstructured data, an image, into representations that can be used for a variety of tasks, like classification, as illustrated in Figure 9-2.

ViT relies on an important component of the Transformer architecture, namely the encoder. As we saw in Chapter 1, the encoder is responsible for converting textual input into numerical representations before being passed to the decoder. However, before the encoder can perform its duties, the textual input needs to be tokenized first, as is illustrated in Figure 9-3.

1 Jason Wei et al. "Emergent abilities of large language models." *arXiv preprint arXiv:2206.07682* (2022).

2 Alexey Dosovitskiy et al. "An image is worth 16x16 words: Transformers for image recognition at scale." *arXiv preprint arXiv:2010.11929* (2020).

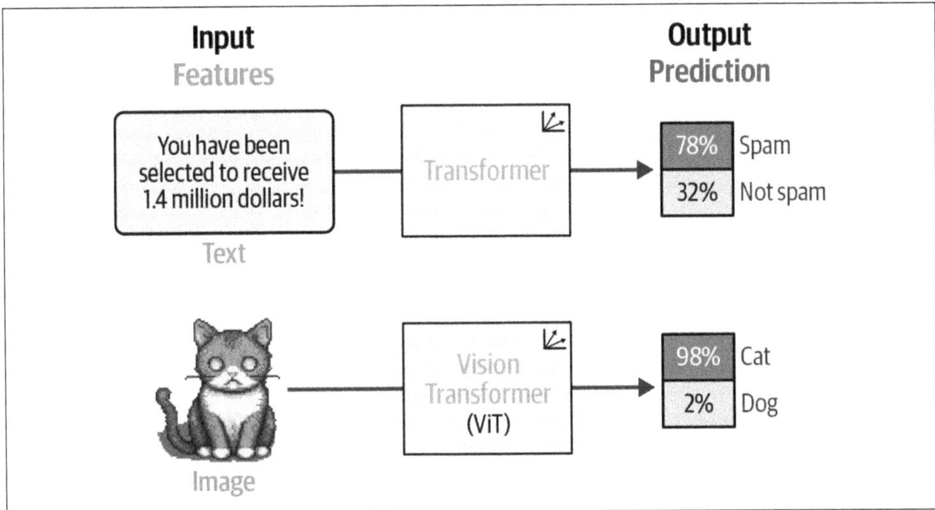

Figure 9-2. Both the original Transformer as well as the Vision Transformer take unstructured data, convert it to numerical representations, and finally use that for tasks like classification.

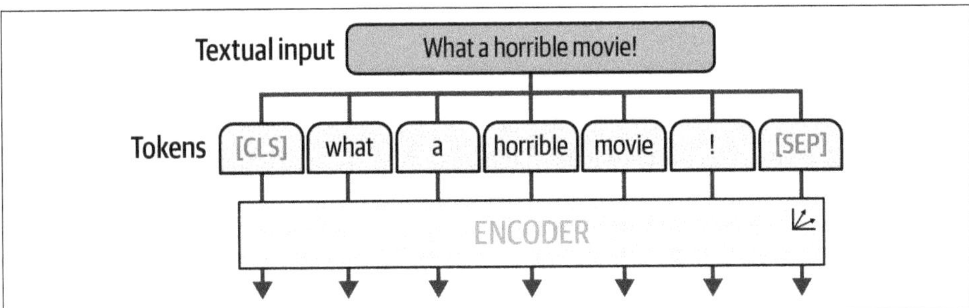

Figure 9-3. Text is passed to one or multiple encoders by first tokenizing it using a tokenizer.

Since an image does not consist of words this tokenization process cannot be used for visual data. Instead, the authors of ViT came up with a method for tokenizing images into "words," which allowed them to use the original encoder structure.

Imagine that you have an image of a cat. This image is represented by a number of pixels, let's say 512 × 512 pixels. Each individual pixel does not convey much information but when you combine patches of pixels, you slowly start to see more information.

ViT uses a principle much like that. Instead of splitting up text into tokens, it converts the original image into patches of images. In other words, it cuts the image into a number of pieces horizontally and vertically as illustrated in Figure 9-4.

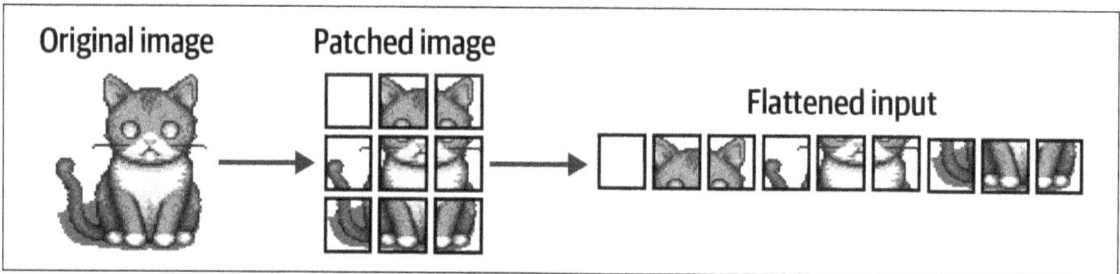

Figure 9-4. The "tokenization" process for image input. It converts an image into patches of subimages.

Just like we are converting text into tokens of text, we are converting an image into patches of images. The flattened input of image patches can be thought of as the tokens in a piece of text. However, unlike tokens, we cannot just assign each patch with an ID since these patches will rarely be found in other images, unlike the vocabulary of a text.

Instead, the patches are linearly embedded to create numerical representations, namely embeddings. These can then be used as the input of a Transformer model. That way, the patches of images are treated the same way as tokens. The full process is illustrated in Figure 9-5.

For illustrative purposes, the images in the examples were patched into 3 × 3 patches but the original implementation used 16 × 16 patches. After all, the paper is called "An Image is Worth 16x16 Words."

What is so interesting about this approach is that the moment the embeddings are passed to the encoder, they are treated as if they were textual tokens. From that point forward, there is no difference in how a text or image trains.

Due to these similarities, the ViT is often used to make all kinds of language models multimodal. One of the most straightforward ways to use it is during the training of embedding models.

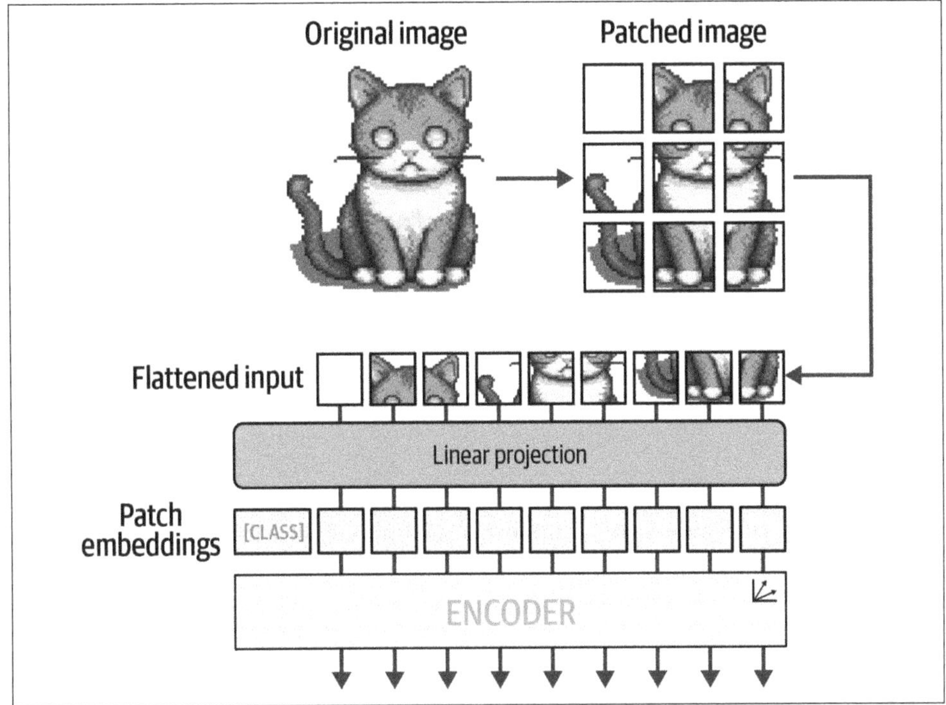

Figure 9-5. The main algorithm behind ViT. After patching the images and linearly projecting them, the patch embeddings are passed to the encoder and treated as if they were textual tokens.

Multimodal Embedding Models

In previous chapters, we used embedding models to capture the semantic content of textual representations, such as papers and documents. We saw that we could use these embeddings or numerical representations to find similar documents, apply classification tasks, and even perform topic modeling.

As we have seen many times before, embeddings often are an important driver behind LLM applications. They are an efficient method for capturing large-scale information and searching for the needle in the haystack of information.

That said, we have looked at text-only embedding models thus far, which focus on generating embeddings for textual representations. Although embedding models exist for solely embedding imagery, we will look at embedding models that can capture both textual as well as visual representations. We illustrate this in Figure 9-6.

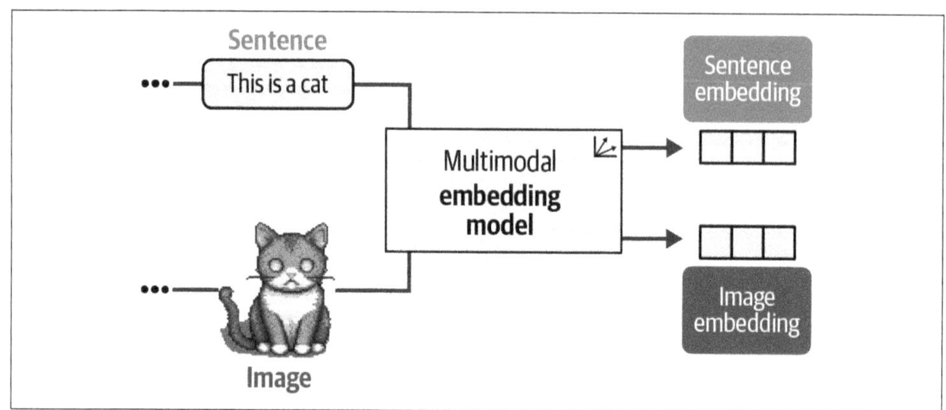

Figure 9-6. Multimodal embedding models can create embeddings for multiple modalities in the same vector space.

An advantage is that this allows for comparing multimodal representations since the resulting embeddings lie in the same vector space (Figure 9-7). For instance, using such a multimodal embedding model, we can find images based on input text. What images would we find if we search for images similar to "pictures of a puppy"? Vice versa would also be possible. Which documents are best related to this question?

Figure 9-7. Despite having coming from different modalities, embeddings with similar meaning will be close to each other in vector space.

There are a number of multimodal embedding models, but the most well-known and currently most-used model is Contrastive Language-Image Pre-training (CLIP).

CLIP: Connecting Text and Images

CLIP is an embedding model that can compute embeddings of both images and texts. The resulting embeddings lie in the same vector space, which means that the embeddings of images can be compared with the embeddings of text.[3] This comparison capability makes CLIP, and similar models, usable for tasks such as:

Zero-shot classification
: We can compare the embedding of an image with that of the description of its possible classes to find which class is most similar.

Clustering
: Cluster both images and a collection of keywords to find which keywords belong to which sets of images.

Search
: Across billions of texts or images, we can quickly find what relates to an input text or image.

Generation
: Use multimodal embeddings to drive the generation of images (e.g., stable diffusion[4]).

How Can CLIP Generate Multimodal Embeddings?

The procedure of CLIP is actually quite straightforward. Imagine that you have a dataset with millions of images alongside captions as we illustrate in Figure 9-8.

Figure 9-8. The type of data that is needed to train a multimodal embedding model.

3 Alec Radford et al. "Learning transferable visual models from natural language supervision." *International Conference on Machine Learning*. PMLR, 2021.

4 Robin Rombach et al. "High-resolution image synthesis with latent diffusion models." *Proceedings of the IEEE/CVF Conference on Computer Vision and Pattern Recognition*, 2022.

This dataset can be used to create two representations for each pair, the image and its caption. To do so, CLIP uses a text encoder to embed text and an image encoder to embed images. As is shown in Figure 9-9, the result is an embedding for both the image and its corresponding caption.

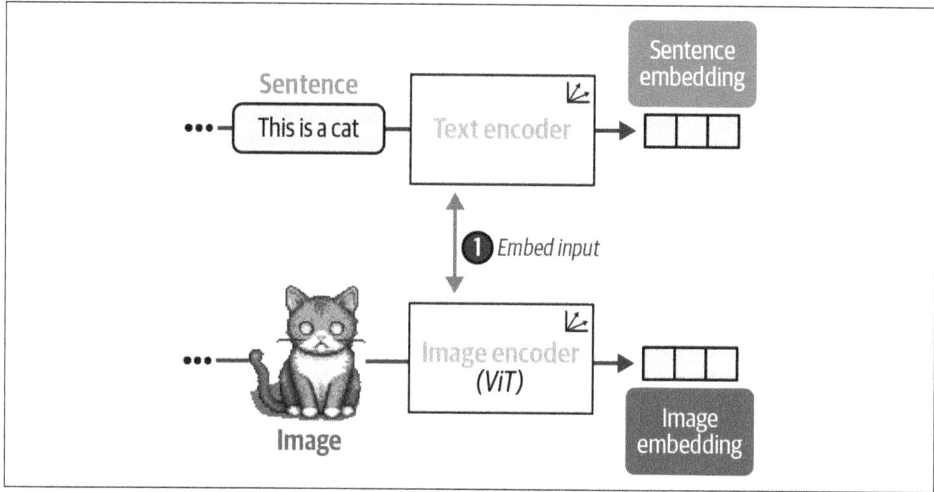

Figure 9-9. In the first step of training CLIP, both images and text are embedded using an image and text encoder, respectively.

The pair of embeddings that are generated are compared through cosine similarity. As we saw in Chapter 4, cosine similarity is the cosine of the angle between vectors, which is calculated through the dot product of the embeddings and divided by the product of their lengths.

When we start training, the similarity between the image embedding and text embedding will be low as they are not yet optimized to be within the same vector space. During training, we optimize for the similarity between the embeddings and want to maximize them for similar image/caption pairs and minimize them for dissimilar image/caption pairs (Figure 9-10).

After calculating their similarity, the model is updated and the process starts again with new batches of data and updated representations (Figure 9-11). This method is called *contrastive learning*, and we will go in depth into its inner workings in Chapter 10 where we will create our own embedding model.

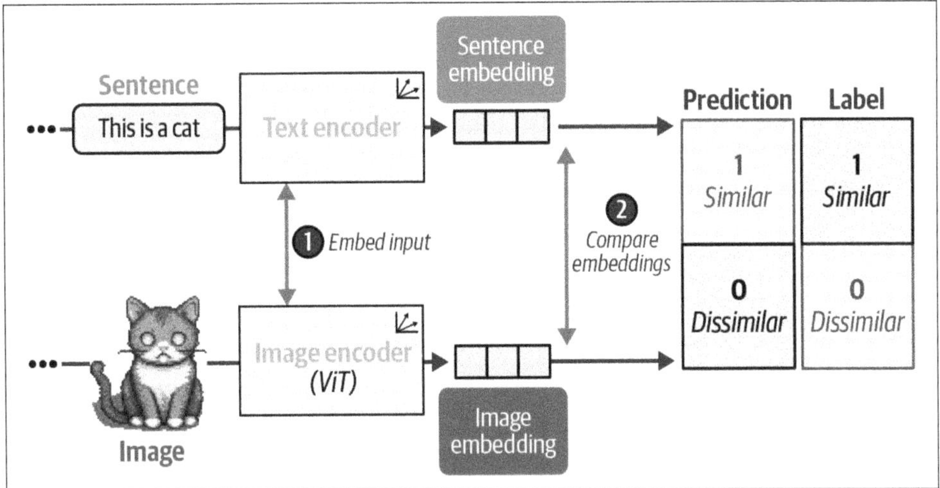

Figure 9-10. In the second step of training CLIP, the similarity between the sentence and image embedding is calculated using cosine similarity.

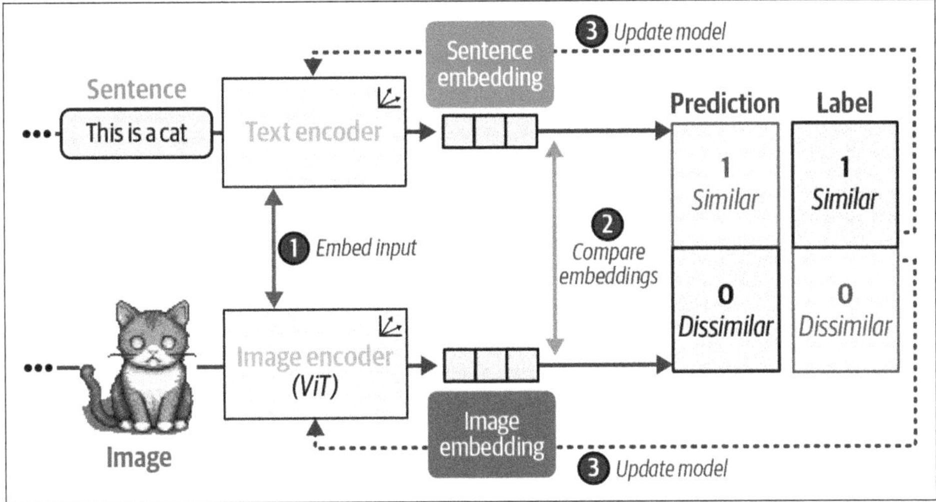

Figure 9-11. In the third step of training CLIP, the text and image encoders are updated to match what the intended similarity should be. This updates the embeddings such that they are closer in vector space if the inputs are similar.

Eventually, we expect the embedding of an image of a cat would be similar to the embedding of the phrase "a picture of a cat." As we will see in Chapter 10, to make sure the representations are as accurate as possible, negative examples of images and captions that are not related should also be included in the training process. Modeling similarity is not only knowing what makes things similar to one another, but also what makes them different and dissimilar.

OpenCLIP

For our next example, we are going to be using models from the open source variant of CLIP, namely OpenCLIP (*https://oreil.ly/op9BP*). Using OpenCLIP, or any CLIP model, boils down to two things: processing the textual and image inputs before passing them to the main model.

Before doing so, let's take a look at a small example where we will be using one of the images we have seen before, namely, an AI-generated image (through stable diffusion) of a puppy playing in the snow, as illustrated in Figure 9-12:

```
from urllib.request import urlopen
from PIL import Image

# Load an AI-generated image of a puppy playing in the snow
puppy_path = "https://raw.githubusercontent.com/HandsOnLLM/Hands-On-Large-
Language-Models/main/chapter09/images/puppy.png"
image = Image.open(urlopen(puppy_path)).convert("RGB")

caption = "a puppy playing in the snow"
```

Figure 9-12. An AI-generated image of a puppy playing in the snow.

Since we have a caption for this image, we can use OpenCLIP to generate embeddings for both.

To do so, we load in three models:

- A tokenizer for tokenizing the textual input
- A preprocessor to preprocess and resize the image
- The main model that converts the previous outputs to embeddings

```
from transformers import CLIPTokenizerFast, CLIPProcessor, CLIPModel

model_id = "openai/clip-vit-base-patch32"

# Load a tokenizer to preprocess the text
clip_tokenizer = CLIPTokenizerFast.from_pretrained(model_id)

# Load a processor to preprocess the images
clip_processor = CLIPProcessor.from_pretrained(model_id)

# Main model for generating text and image embeddings
model = CLIPModel.from_pretrained(model_id)
```

After having loaded in the models, preprocessing our input is straightforward. Let's start with the tokenizer and see what happens if we preprocess our input:

```
# Tokenize our input
inputs = clip_tokenizer(caption, return_tensors="pt")
inputs
```

This outputs a dictionary that contains the IDs of the input:

```
{'input_ids': tensor([[49406, 320, 6829, 1629, 530, 518, 2583, 49407]]), 'at-
tention_mask': tensor([[1, 1, 1, 1, 1, 1, 1, 1]])}
```

To see what those IDs represent, we can convert them to tokens using the aptly named `convert_ids_to_tokens` function:

```
# Convert our input back to tokens
clip_tokenizer.convert_ids_to_tokens(inputs["input_ids"][0])
```

This gives us the following output:

```
['<|startoftext|>',
 'a</w>',
 'puppy</w>',
 'playing</w>',
 'in</w>',
 'the</w>',
 'snow</w>',
 '<|endoftext|>']
```

As we often have seen before, the text is split up into tokens. Additionally, we now also see that the start and end of the text is indicated to separate it from a potential image embedding. You might also notice that the `[CLS]` token is missing. In CLIP, the `[CLS]` token is actually used to represent the image embedding.

Now that we have preprocessed our caption, we can create the embedding:

```
# Create a text embedding
text_embedding = model.get_text_features(**inputs)
text_embedding.shape
```

This results in an embedding that has 512 values for this single string:

```
torch.Size([1, 512])
```

Before we can create our image embedding, like the text embedding, we will need to preprocess it as the model expects the input image to have certain characteristics, like its size and shape.

To do so, we can use the `processor` that we created before:

```
# Preprocess image
processed_image = clip_processor(
    text=None, images=image, return_tensors="pt"
)["pixel_values"]

processed_image.shape
```

The original image was 512 × 512 pixels. Notice that the preprocessing of this image reduced its size to 224 × 224 pixels as that is its expected size:

```
torch.Size([1, 3, 224, 224])
```

Let's visualize the results of this preprocessing as shown in Figure 9-13:

```
import
import       as
import                   as

# Prepare image for visualization
img = processed_image.squeeze(0)
img = img.permute(*torch.arange(img.ndim - 1, -1, -1))
img = np.einsum("ijk->jik", img)

# Visualize preprocessed image
plt.imshow(img)
plt.axis("off")
```

Figure 9-13. The preprocessed input image by CLIP.

To convert this preprocessed image into embeddings, we can call the model as we did before and explore what shape it returns:

```
# Create the image embedding
image_embedding = model.get_image_features(processed_image)
image_embedding.shape
```

This gives us the following shape:

```
torch.Size([1, 512])
```

Notice that the shape of the resulting image embedding is the same as that of the text embedding. This is important as it allows us to compare their embeddings and see if they are similar.

We can use these embeddings to calculate how similar they are. To do so, we normalize the embeddings first before calculating the dot product to give us a similarity score:

```
# Normalize the embeddings
text_embedding /= text_embedding.norm(dim=-1, keepdim=True)
image_embedding /= image_embedding.norm(dim=-1, keepdim=True)

# Calculate their similarity
text_embedding = text_embedding.detach().cpu().numpy()
image_embedding = image_embedding.detach().cpu().numpy()
score = np.dot(text_embedding, image_embedding.T)
score
```

This gives us the following score:

```
array([[0.33149648]], dtype=float32)
```

We get a similarity score of 0.33, which is difficult to interpret considering we don't know what the model considers a low versus a high similarity score. Instead, let's extend the example with more images and captions as illustrated in Figure 9-14.

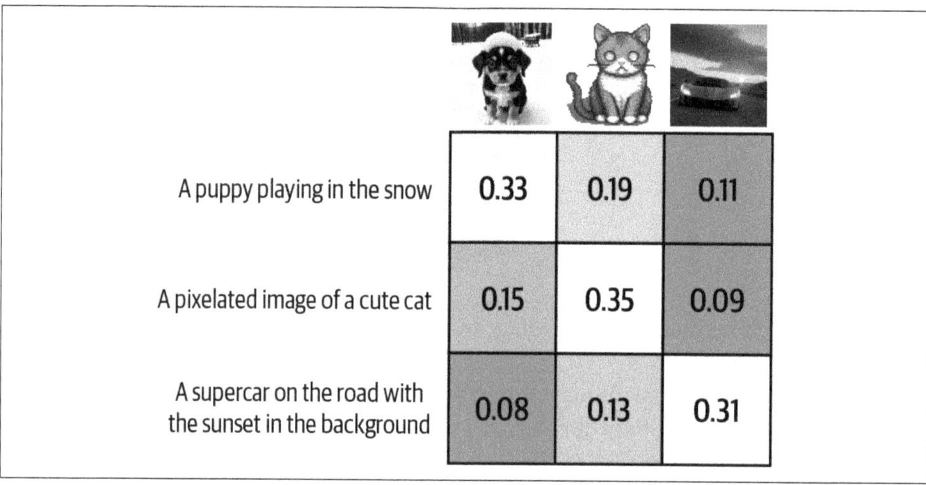

Figure 9-14. The similarity matrix between three images and three captions.

It seems that a score of 0.33 is indeed high considering the similarities with other images are quite a bit lower.

> ### Using sentence-transformers to Load CLIP
>
> `sentence-transformers` implements a few CLIP-based models that make it much easier to create embeddings. It only takes a few lines of code:

```
from sentence_transformers import SentenceTransformer, util

# Load SBERT-compatible CLIP model
model = SentenceTransformer("clip-ViT-B-32")

# Encode the images
image_embeddings = model.encode(images)

# Encode the captions
text_embeddings = model.encode(captions)

#Compute cosine similarities
sim_matrix = util.cos_sim(
    image_embeddings, text_embeddings
)
```

Making Text Generation Models Multimodal

Traditionally, text generation models have been, as you might expect, models that interpret textual representations. Models like Llama 2 and ChatGPT excel at reasoning about textual information and responding with natural language.

They are, however, limited to the modality they were trained in, namely text. As we have seen before with multimodal embedding models, the addition of vision can enhance the capabilities of a model.

In the case of text generation models, we would like it to reason about certain input images. For example, we could give it an image of a pizza and ask it what ingredients it contains. You could show it a picture of the Eiffel Tower and ask when it was built or where it is located. This conversational ability is further illustrated in Figure 9-15.

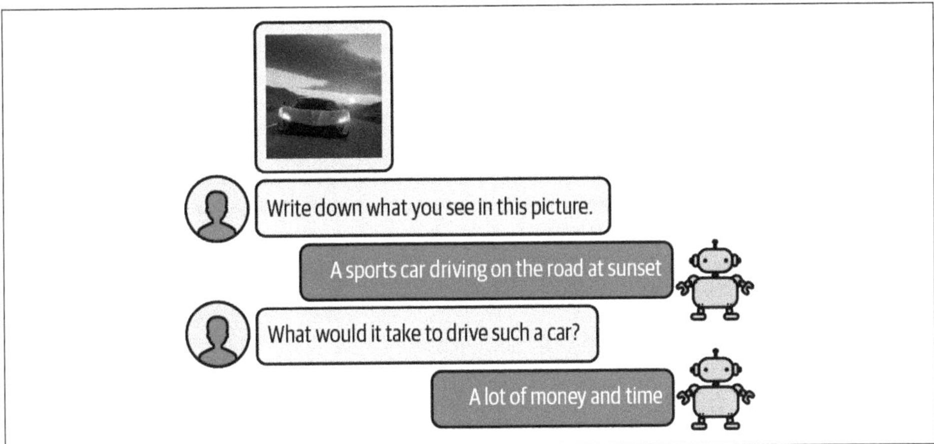

Figure 9-15. An example of a multimodal text generation model (BLIP-2) that can reason about input images.

To bridge the gap between these two domains, attempts have been made to introduce a form of multimodality to existing models. One such method is called *BLIP-2: Bootstrapping Language-Image Pre-training for Unified Vision-Language Understanding and Generation 2*. BLIP-2 is an easy-to-use and modular technique that allows for introducing vision capabilities to existing language models.

BLIP-2: Bridging the Modality Gap

Creating a multimodal language model from scratch requires significant computing power and data. We would have to use billions of images, text, and image-text pairs to create such a model. As you can imagine, this is not easily feasible!

Instead of building the architecture from scratch, BLIP-2 bridges the vision-language gap by building a bridge, named the Querying Transformer (Q-Former), that connects a pretrained image encoder and a pretrained LLM.[5]

By leveraging pretrained models, BLIP-2 only needs to train the bridge without needing to train the image encoder and LLM from scratch. It makes great use of the technology and models that are already out there! This bridge is illustrated in Figure 9-16.

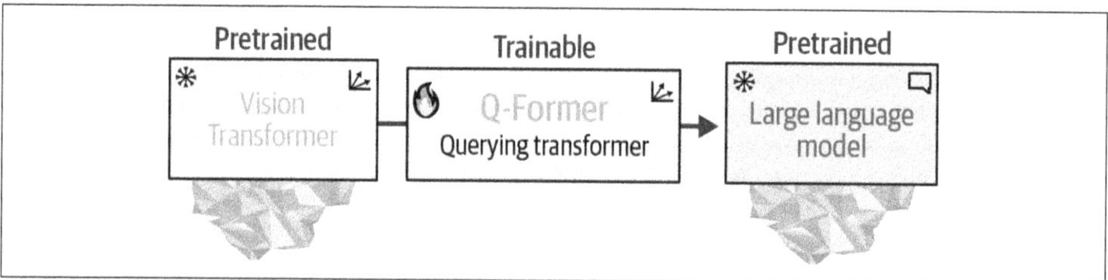

Figure 9-16. The Querying Transformer is the bridge between vision (ViT) and text (LLM) that is the only trainable component of the pipeline.

To connect the two pretrained models, the Q-Former mimics their architectures. It has two modules that share their attention layers:

- An Image Transformer to interact with the frozen Vision Transformer for feature extraction
- A Text Transformer that can interact with the LLM

The Q-Former is trained in two stages, one for each modality, as illustrated in Figure 9-17.

In step 1, image-document pairs are used to train the Q-Former to represent both images and text. These pairs are generally captions of images, as we have seen before when training CLIP.

The images are fed to the frozen ViT to extract vision embeddings. These embeddings are used as the input of Q-Former's ViT. The captions are used as the input of Q-Former's Text Transformer.

5 Junnan Li et al. "BLIP-2: Bootstrapping language-image pretraining with frozen image encoders and large language models." *International Conference on Machine Learning*. PMLR, 2023.

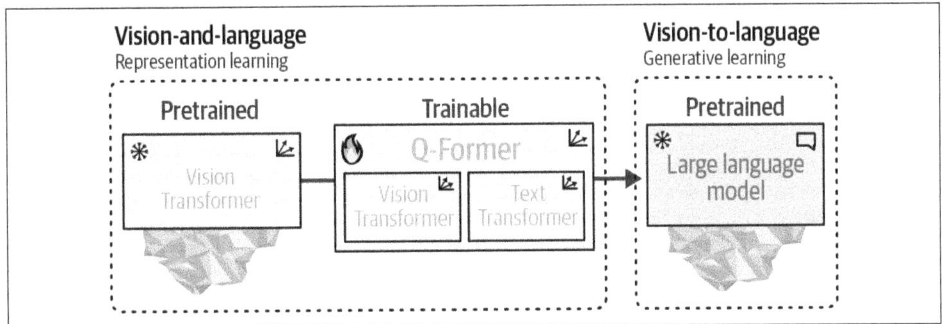

Figure 9-17. In step 1, representation learning is applied to learn representations for vision and language simultaneously. In step 2, these representations are converted to soft visual prompts to feed the LLM.

With these inputs, the Q-Former is then trained on three tasks:

Image-text contrastive learning
: This task attempts to align pairs of image and text embeddings such that they maximize their mutual information.

Image-text matching
: A classification task to predict whether an image and text pair is positive (matched) or negative (unmatched).

Image-grounded text generation
: Trains the model to generate text based on information extracted from the input image.

These three objectives are jointly optimized to improve the visual representations that are extracted from the frozen ViT. In a way, we are trying to inject textual information into the embeddings of the frozen ViT so that we can use them in the LLM. This first step of BLIP-2 is illustrated in Figure 9-18.

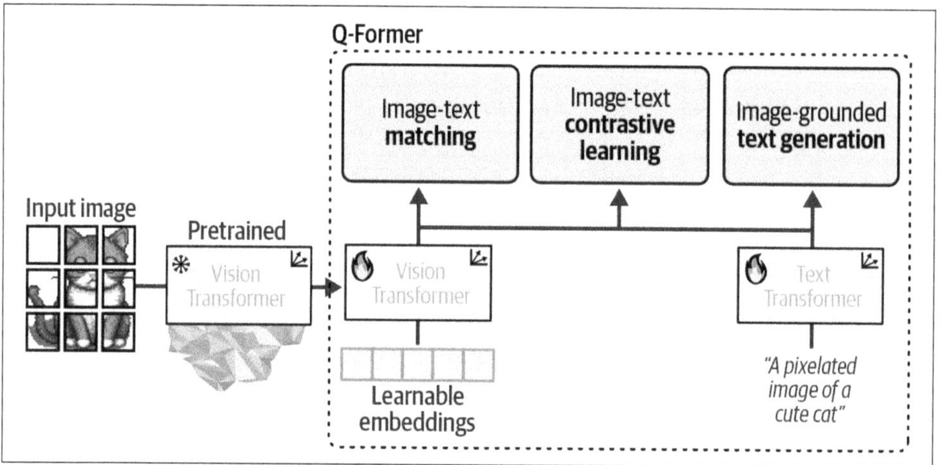

Figure 9-18. In step 1, the output of the frozen ViT is used together with its caption and trained on three contrastive-like tasks to learn visual-text representations.

In step 2, the learnable embeddings derived from step 1 now contain visual information in the same dimensional space as the corresponding textual information. The learnable embeddings are then passed to the LLM. In a way, these embeddings serve as soft visual prompts that condition the LLM on the visual representations that were extracted by the Q-Former.

There is also a fully connected linear layer in between them to make sure that the learnable embeddings have the same shape as the LLM expects. This second step of converting vision to language is represented in Figure 9-19.

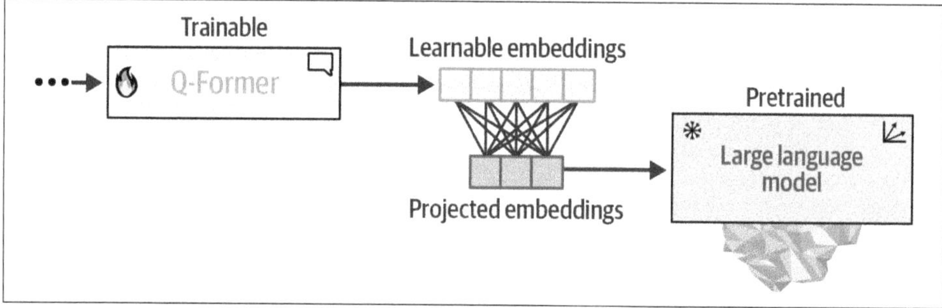

Figure 9-19. In step 2, the learned embeddings from the Q-Former are passed to the LLM through a projection layer. The projected embeddings serve as a soft visual prompt.

When we put these steps together, they make it possible for the Q-Former to learn visual and textual representations in the same dimensional space, which can be used as a soft prompt to the LLM. As a result, the LLM will be given information about the image in a similar manner to the context you would provide an LLM when prompting. The full in-depth process is illustrated in Figure 9-20.

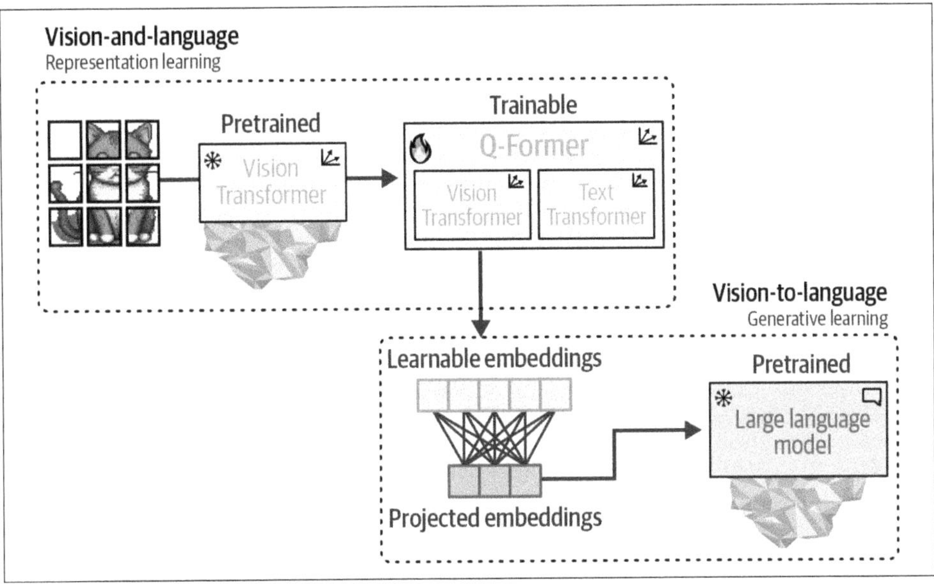

Figure 9-20. The full BLIP-2 procedure.

Since BLIP-2, many other visual LLMs have been released that have similar processes, like LLaVA (*https://oreil.ly/_Gf9D*), a framework for making textual LLMs multimodal[6] or Idefics 2 (*https://oreil.ly/xbIuQ*), an efficient visual LLM based on the Mistral 7B LLM (*https://oreil.ly/6PQ8E*).[7] Both visual LLMs, although having different architectures, connect pretrained CLIP-like visual encoders with textual LLMs. The goal of these architectures is to project visual features from the input images to language embeddings such that they can be used as the input for an LLM. Similar to the Q-Former, they attempt to bridge the gap between images and text.

6 Haotian Liu et al. "Visual instruction tuning." *Advances in Neural Information Processing Systems* 36 (2024).

7 Hugo Laurençon et al. "What matters when building vision-language models?" *arXiv preprint arXiv:2405.02246* (2024).

Preprocessing Multimodal Inputs

Now that we know how BLIP-2 is created, there are a number of interesting use cases for such a model, not limited to captioning images, answering visual questions, and even performing prompting.

Before we go through some use cases, let's first load the model and explore how you can use it:

```
from [illegible] import AutoProcessor, Blip2ForConditionalGeneration
import [illegible]

# Load processor and main model
blip_processor = AutoProcessor.from_pretrained("Salesforce/blip2-opt-2.7b")
model = Blip2ForConditionalGeneration.from_pretrained(
    "Salesforce/blip2-opt-2.7b",
    torch_dtype=torch.float16
)

# Send the model to GPU to speed up inference
device = "cuda" if torch.cuda.is_available() else "cpu"
model.to(device)
```

Using `model.vision_model` and `model.language_model`, we can see which ViT and generative model are used, respectively, in the BLIP-2 model we loaded.

We loaded two components that make up our full pipeline: a processor and a model. The processor can be compared to the tokenizer of language models. It converts unstructured input, such as images and text, to representations that the model generally expects.

Preprocessing images

Let's start by exploring what the processor does to images. We start by loading the picture of a very wide image for illustration purposes:

```
# Load image of a supercar
car_path = "https://raw.githubusercontent.com/HandsOnLLM/Hands-On-Large-
Language-Models/main/chapter09/images/car.png"
image = Image.open(urlopen(car_path)).convert("RGB")

image
```

The image has 520 × 492 pixels, which is generally an unusual format. So let's see what our processor does to it:

```
# Preprocess the image
inputs = blip_processor(image, return_tensors="pt").to(device, torch.float16)
inputs["pixel_values"].shape
```

This gives us the following shape:

```
torch.Size([1, 3, 224, 224])
```

The result is a 224 × 224-sized image. Quite a bit smaller than we initially had! This also means that all the original different shapes of the image will be processed into squares. So be careful inputting very wide or tall images as they might get distorted.

Preprocessing text

Let's continue this exploration of the processor with text instead. First, we can access the tokenizer used to tokenize the input text:

```
blip_processor.tokenizer
```

This gives us the following output:

```
GPT2TokenizerFast(name_or_path='Salesforce/blip2-opt-2.7b', vocab_size=50265,
model_max_length=1000000000000000019884624838656, is_fast=True, pad-
ding_side='right', truncation_side='right', special_tokens={'bos_token': '</
s>', 'eos_token': '</s>', 'unk_token': '</s>', 'pad_token': '<pad>'},
clean_up_tokenization_spaces=True), added_tokens_decoder={
1: AddedToken("<pad>", rstrip=False, lstrip=False, single_word=False, normal-
ized=True, special=True),
2: AddedToken("</s>", rstrip=False, lstrip=False, single_word=False, normal-
ized=True, special=True),
}
```

The BLIP-2 model here uses a `GPT2Tokenizer`. As we explored in Chapter 2, how tokenizers deal with input text can differ greatly.

To explore how `GPT2Tokenizer` works, we can try it out with a small sentence. We start by converting the sentence to token IDs before converting them back to tokens:

```
# Preprocess the text
text = "Her vocalization was remarkably melodic"
token_ids = blip_processor(image, text=text, return_tensors="pt")
token_ids = token_ids.to(device, torch.float16)["input_ids"][0]

# Convert input ids back to tokens
tokens = blip_processor.tokenizer.convert_ids_to_tokens(token_ids)
tokens
```

This gives us the following tokens:

```
['</s>', 'Her', 'Ġvocal', 'ization', 'Ġwas', 'Ġremarkably', 'Ġmel', 'odic']
```

When we inspect the tokens, you might notice a strange symbol at the beginning of some tokens, namely, the Ġ symbol. This is actually supposed to be a space. However, an internal function takes characters in certain code points and moves them up by 256 to make them printable. As a result, the space (code point 32) becomes Ġ (code point 288).

We will convert them to underscores for illustrative purposes:

```
# Replace the space token with an underscore
tokens = [token.replace("Ġ", "_") for token in tokens]
tokens
```

This gives us a nicer output:

```
['</s>', 'Her', '_vocal', 'ization', '_was', '_remarkably', '_mel', 'odic']
```

The output shows that the underscore indicates the beginning of a word. That way, words that are made up of multiple tokens can be recognized.

Use Case 1: Image Captioning

The most straightforward usage of a model like BLIP-2 is to create captions of images that you have in your data. You might be a store that wants to create descriptions of its clothing or perhaps you are a photographer that does not have the time to manually label the 1,000+ pictures of a wedding.

The process of captioning an image closely follows the processing. An image is converted to pixel values that the model can read. These pixel values are passed to BLIP-2 to be converted into soft visual prompts that the LLM can use to decide on a proper caption.

Let's take the image of a supercar and use the processor to derive pixels in the expected shape:

```
# Load an AI-generated image of a supercar
image = Image.open(urlopen(car_path)).convert("RGB")


# Convert an image into inputs and preprocess it
inputs = blip_processor(image, return_tensors="pt").to(device, torch.float16)
image
```

The next step is converting the image into token IDs using the BLIP-2 model. After doing so, we can convert the IDs into text (the generated caption):

```
# Generate image ids to be passed to the decoder (LLM)
generated_ids = model.generate(**inputs, max_new_tokens=20)

# Generate text from the image ids
generated_text = blip_processor.batch_decode(
    generated_ids, skip_special_tokens=True
)
generated_text = generated_text[0].strip()
generated_text
```

`generated_text` contains the caption:

```
an orange supercar driving on the road at sunset
```

This seems like a perfect description for this image!

Image captioning is a great way to get to learn this model before stepping into more complex use cases. Try it out with a few images yourself and see where it performs well and where it performs poorly. Domain-specific images, like pictures of specific cartoon characters or imaginary creations, may fail as the model was trained on largely public data.

Let's end this use case with a fun example, namely an image from the Rorschach test, which is illustrated in Figure 9-21. It is part of an old psychological experiment that tests the individual's perception of inkblots.[8] What someone sees in such an inkblot supposedly tells you something about a person's personality characteristics. It is quite a subjective test but that just makes it more fun!

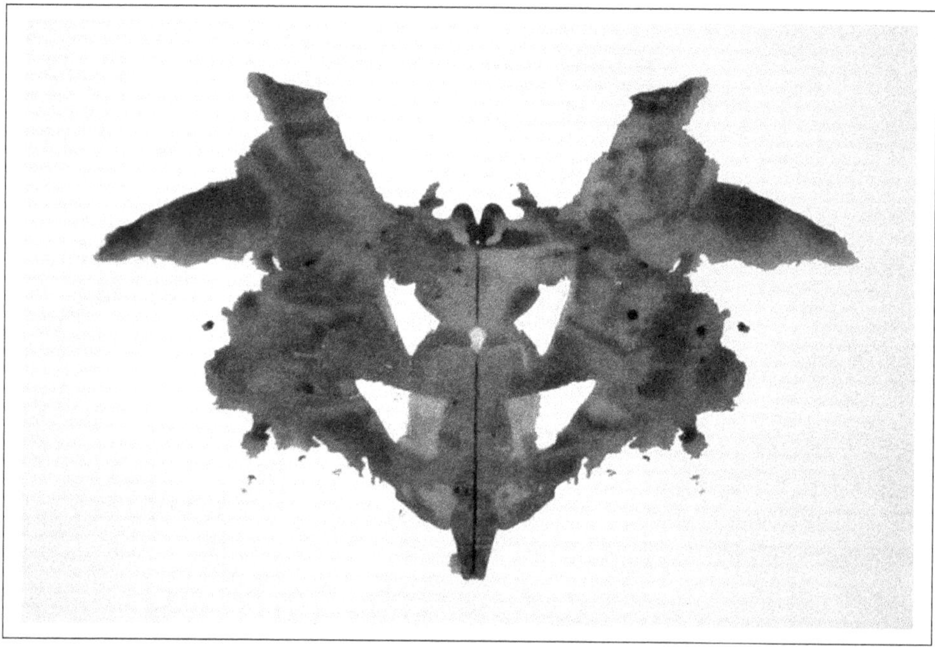

Figure 9-21. An image from the Rorschach test. What do you see in it?

Let's take the image illustrated in Figure 9-21 and use that as our input:

```
# Load Rorschach image
url = "https://upload.wikimedia.org/wikipedia/commons/7/70/Ror
schach_blot_01.jpg"
image = Image.open(urlopen(url)).convert("RGB")

# Generate caption
inputs = blip_processor(image, return_tensors="pt").to(device, torch.float16)
generated_ids = model.generate(**inputs, max_new_tokens=20)
generated_text = blip_processor.batch_decode(
    generated_ids, skip_special_tokens=True
)
```

8 Roy Schafer. *Psychoanalytic Interpretation in Rorschach Testing: Theory and Application* (1954).

```
generated_text = generated_text[0].strip()
generated_text
```

As before, when we inspect the generated_text variable, we can take a look at the caption:

```
a black and white ink drawing of a bat
```

I can definitely see how the model would caption this image using such a description. Since this is a Rorschach test, what do you think it says about the model?

Use Case 2: Multimodal Chat-Based Prompting

Although captioning is an important task, we can extend its use case even further. In the previous example, we showed going from one modality, vision (image), to another, text (caption).

Instead of following this linear structure, we can try to present both modalities simultaneously by performing what is called visual question answering. In this particular use case, we give the model an image along with a question about that specific image for it to answer. The model needs to process both the image as well as the question at once.

To demonstrate, let's start with the picture of a car and ask BLIP-2 to describe the image. To do so, we first need to preprocess the image as we did a few times before:

```
# Load an AI-generated image of a supercar
image = Image.open(urlopen(car_path)).convert("RGB")
```

To perform our visual question answering we need to give BLIP-2 more than just the image, namely the prompt. Without it, the model would generate a caption as it did before. We will ask the model to describe the image we just processed:

```
# Visual question answering
prompt = "Question: Write down what you see in this picture. Answer:"

# Process both the image and the prompt
inputs = blip_processor(image, text=prompt, return_tensors="pt").to(device,
torch.float16)

# Generate text
generated_ids = model.generate(**inputs, max_new_tokens=30)
generated_text = blip_processor.batch_decode(
    generated_ids, skip_special_tokens=True
)
generated_text = generated_text[0].strip()
generated_text
```

This gives us the following output:

```
A sports car driving on the road at sunset
```

It correctly describes the image. However, this is a rather simple example since our question is essentially asking the model to create a caption. Instead, we can ask follow-up questions in a chat-based manner.

To do so, we can give the model our previous conversation, including its answer to our question. We then ask it a follow-up question:

```
# Chat-like prompting
prompt = "Question: Write down what you see in this picture. Answer: A sports
car driving on the road at sunset. Question: What would it cost me to drive
that car? Answer:"

# Generate output
inputs = blip_processor(image, text=prompt, return_tensors="pt").to(device,
torch.float16)
generated_ids = model.generate(**inputs, max_new_tokens=30)
generated_text = blip_processor.batch_decode(
    generated_ids, skip_special_tokens=True
)
generated_text = generated_text[0].strip()
generated_text
```

This gives us the following answer:

```
$1,000,000
```

$1,000,000 is highly specific! This shows more chat-like behavior from BLIP-2, which allows for some interesting conversations.

Finally, we can make this process a bit smoother by creating an interactive chatbot using `ipywidgets`, an extension for Jupyter notebooks that allows us to make interactive buttons, input text, etc:

```
from IPython.display import HTML, display
import ipywidgets as widgets

def text_eventhandler(*args):
  question = args[0]["new"]
  if question:
    args[0]["owner"].value = ""

    # Create prompt
    if not memory:
      prompt = " Question: " + question + " Answer:"
    else:
      template = "Question: {} Answer: {}."
      prompt = " ".join(
          [
              template.format(memory[i][0], memory[i][1])
```

```
            for i in range(len(memory))
        ]
    ) + " Question: " + question + " Answer:"

    # Generate text
    inputs = blip_processor(image, text=prompt, return_tensors="pt")
    inputs = inputs.to(device, torch.float16)
    generated_ids = model.generate(**inputs, max_new_tokens=100)
    generated_text = blip_processor.batch_decode(
        generated_ids,
        skip_special_tokens=True
    )
    generated_text = generated_text[0].strip().split("Question")[0]

    # Update memory
    memory.append((question, generated_text))

    # Assign to output
    output.append_display_data(HTML("<b>USER:</b> " + question))
    output.append_display_data(HTML("<b>BLIP-2:</b> " + generated_text))
    output.append_display_data(HTML("<br>"))

# Prepare widgets
in_text = widgets.Text()
in_text.continuous_update = False
in_text.observe(text_eventhandler, "value")
output = widgets.Output()
memory = []

# Display chat box
display(
    widgets.VBox(
        children=[output, in_text],
        layout=widgets.Layout(display="inline-flex", flex_flow="column-
reverse"),
    )
)
```

USER: Write down what you see in this picture.
BLIP-2: A sports car driving on the road at sunset

USER: What would it cost me to drive that car?
BLIP-2: $1,000,000

USER: Why that much money?
BLIP-2: Because it's a sports car.

USER: Why are sports cars expensive?
BLIP-2: Because they're fast.

It seems that we can continue the conversation and ask a bunch of questions. Using this chat-based approach, we essentially created a chatbot that can reason about images!

Summary

In this chapter, we explored various methods for making LLMs multimodal by bridging the gap between textual and visual representations. We started by discussing Transformers for vision, which are models that convert images into numerical representations. This was achieved through the use of image encoders and patch embeddings, which allow the model to process images at various scales.

We then explored the creation of embedding models that can convert both images and text to numerical representations using CLIP. We saw how CLIP uses contrastive learning to align image and text embeddings in a shared space, allowing for tasks like zero-shot classification, clustering, and search. The chapter also introduced OpenCLIP, an open source variant of CLIP that is easy to use for multimodal embedding tasks.

Finally, we explored how text generation models could be made multimodal and dived into the BLIP-2 model. The core idea of these multimodal text generation models involves projecting visual features from input images to text embeddings that can be used by LLMs. We saw how this model could be used for image captioning and multimodal chat-based prompting, where both modalities are combined to generate responses. Overall, this chapter highlighted the power of multimodality in LLMs and demonstrated its applications in various areas such as image captioning, search, and chat-based prompting.

In Part III of the book, we will cover training and fine-tuning techniques. In Chapter 10, we will explore how to create and fine-tune a text embedding model, which is a core technology that drives many language modeling applications. This next chapter serves as an introduction into both training and fine-tuning language models.

PART III

Training and Fine-Tuning Language Models

CHAPTER 10

Creating Text Embedding Models

Text embedding models lie at the foundation of many powerful natural language processing applications. They lay the groundwork for empowering already impressive technologies such as text generation models. We have already used embedding models throughout this book in a number of applications, such as supervised classification, unsupervised classification, semantic search, and even giving memory to text generation models like ChatGPT.

It is nearly impossible to overstate the importance of embedding models in the field as they are the driving power behind so many applications. As such, in this chapter, we will discuss a variety of ways that we can create and fine-tune an embedding model to increase its representative and semantic power.

Let's start by discovering what embedding models are and how they generally work.

Embedding Models

Embeddings and embedding models have already been discussed in quite a number of chapters (Chapters 4, 5, and 8) thereby demonstrating their usefulness. Before going into training such a model, let's recap what we have learned with embedding models.

Unstructured textual data by itself is often quite hard to process. They are not values we can directly process, visualize, and create actionable results from. We first have to convert this textual data to something that we can easily process: numeric representations. This process is often referred to as *embedding* the input to output usable vectors, namely *embeddings*, as shown in Figure 10-1.

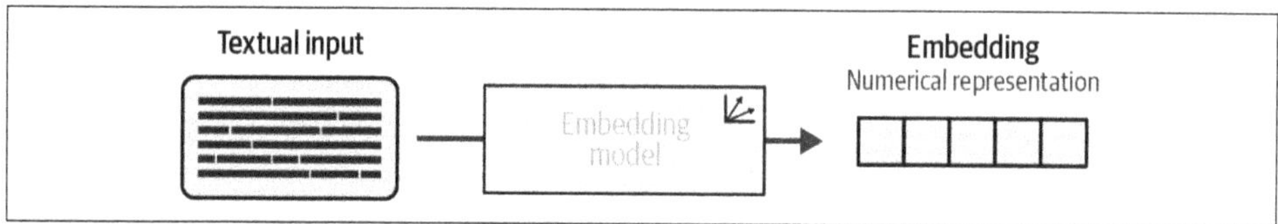

Figure 10-1. We use an embedding model to convert textual input, such as documents, sentences, and phrases, to numerical representations, called embeddings.

This process of embedding the input is typically performed by an LLM, which we refer to as an *embedding model*. The main purpose of such a model is to be as accurate as possible in representing the textual data as an embedding.

However, what does it mean to be accurate in representation? Typically, we want to capture the *semantic nature*—the meaning—of documents. If we can capture the core of what the document communicates, we hope to have captured what the document is about. In practice, this means that we expect vectors of documents that are similar to one another to be similar, whereas the embeddings of documents that each discuss something entirely different should be dissimilar. We've seen this idea of semantic similarity several times already in this book, and it is visualized in Figure 10-2. This figure is a simplified example. While two-dimensional visualization helps illustrate the proximity and similarity of embeddings, these embeddings typically reside in high-dimensional spaces.

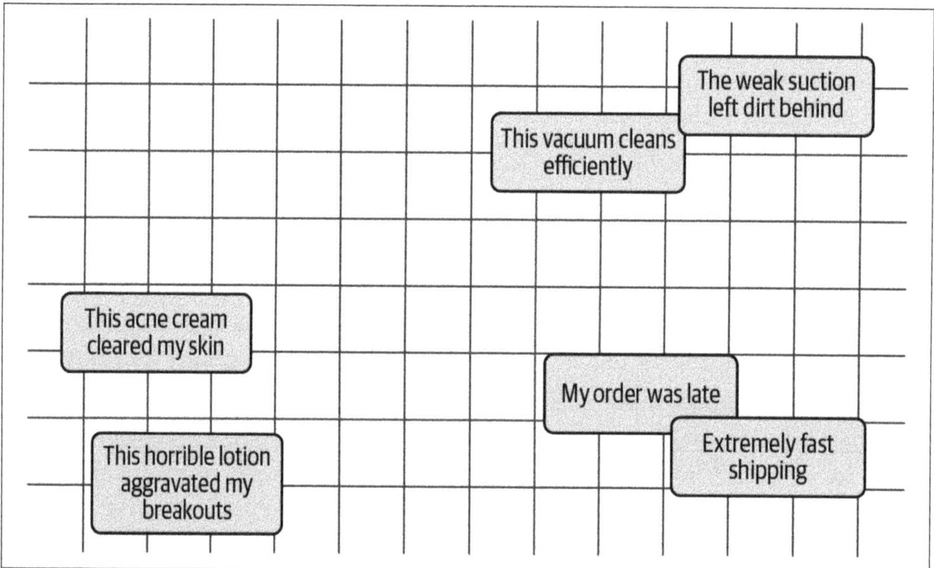

Figure 10-2. The idea of semantic similarity is that we expect textual data with similar meanings to be closer to each other in n-dimensional space (two dimensions are illustrated here).

An embedding model, however, can be trained for a number of purposes. For example, when we are building a sentiment classifier, we are more interested in the sentiment of texts than their semantic similarity. As illustrated in Figure 10-3, we can fine-tune the model such that documents are closer in n-dimensional space based on their sentiment rather than their semantic nature.

Either way, an embedding model aims to learn what makes certain documents similar to one another and we can guide this process. By presenting the model with enough examples of semantically similar documents, we can steer toward semantics whereas using examples of sentiment would steer it in that direction.

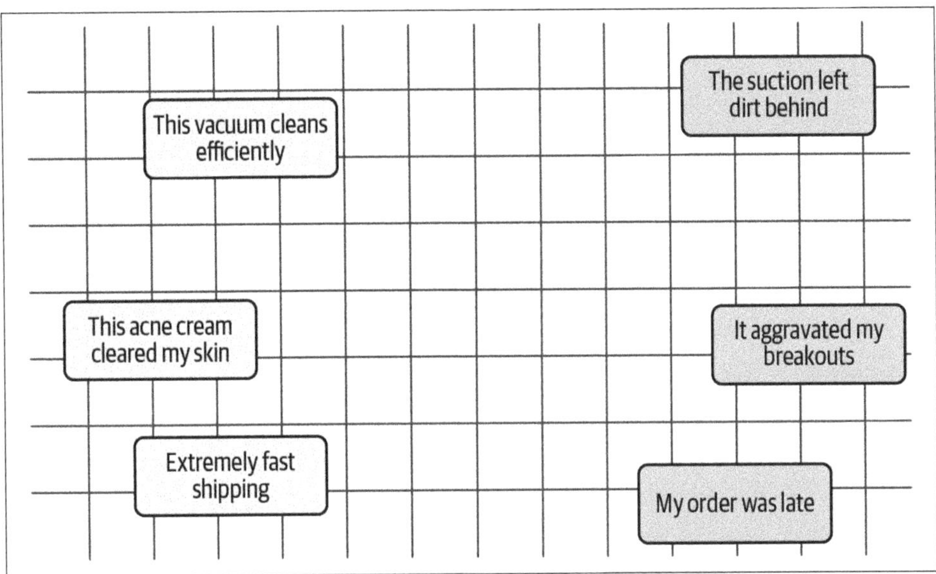

Figure 10-3. In addition to semantic similarity, an embedding model can be trained to focus on sentiment similarity. In this figure, negative reviews (red) are close to one another and dissimilar to positive reviews (green).

There are many ways in which we can train, fine-tune, and guide embedding models, but one of the strongest and most widely used techniques is called contrastive learning.

What Is Contrastive Learning?

One major technique for both training and fine-tuning text embedding models is called *contrastive learning*. Contrastive learning is a technique that aims to train an embedding model such that similar documents are closer in vector space while dissimilar documents are further apart. If this sounds familiar, it's because it's very similar to the word2vec method from Chapter 2. We have seen this notion previously in Figures 10-2 and 10-3.

The underlying idea of contrastive learning is that the best way to learn and model similarity/dissimilarity between documents is by feeding a model examples of similar and dissimilar pairs. In order to accurately capture the semantic nature of a document, it often needs to be contrasted with another document for a model to learn what makes it different or similar. This contrasting procedure is quite powerful and relates to the context in which documents are written. This high-level procedure is demonstrated in Figure 10-4.

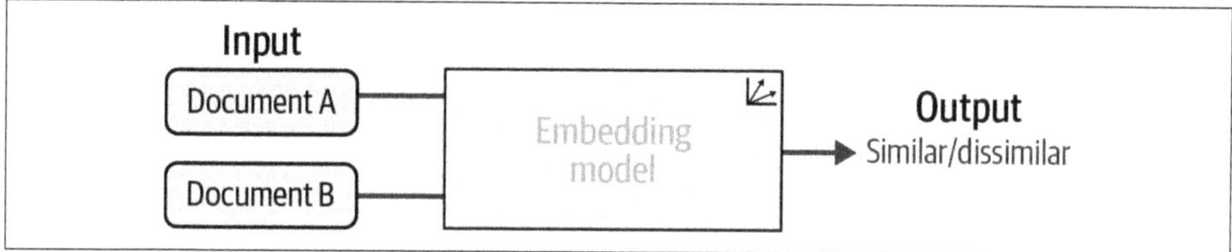

Figure 10-4. Contrastive learning aims to teach an embedding model whether documents are similar or dissimilar. It does so by presenting groups of documents to a model that are similar or dissimilar to a certain degree.

Another way to look at contrastive learning is through the nature of explanations. A nice example of this is an anecdotal story of a reporter asking a robber "Why did you rob a bank?" to which he answers, "Because that is where the money is."[1] Although a factually correct answer, the intent of the question was not why he robs banks specifically but why he robs at all. This is called *contrastive explanation* and refers to understanding a particular case, "Why P?" in contrast to alternatives, "Why P and not Q?"[2] In the example, the question could be interpreted in a number of ways and may be best modeled by providing an alternative: "Why did you rob a bank (P) instead of obeying the law (Q)?"

The importance of alternatives to the understanding of a question also applies to how an embedding learns through contrastive learning. By showing a model similar and dissimilar pairs of documents, it starts to learn what makes something similar/dissimilar and more importantly, why.

For example, you could teach a model to understand what a dog is by letting it find features such as "tail," "nose," "four legs," etc. This learning process can be quite difficult since features are often not well-defined and can be interpreted in a number of ways. A being with a "tail," "nose," and "four legs" can also be a cat. To help the

1 Alan Garfinkel. *Forms of Explanation: Rethinking the Questions in Social Theory*. Yale University Press (1982).

2 Tim Miller. "Contrastive explanation: A structural-model approach." *The Knowledge Engineering Review* 36 (2021): e14.

model steer toward what we are interested in, we essentially ask it, "Why is this a dog and not a cat?" By providing the contrast between two concepts, it starts to learn the features that define the concept but also the features that are not related. We get more information when we frame a question as a contrast. We further illustrate this concept of contrastive explanation in Figure 10-5.

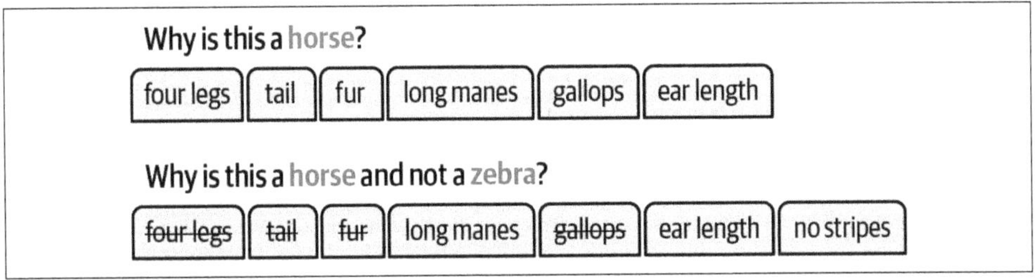

Figure 10-5. When we feed an embedding model different contrasts (degrees of similarity), it starts to learn what makes things different from one another and thereby the distinctive characteristics of concepts.

One of the earliest and most popular examples of contrastive learning in NLP is actually word2vec, as we discussed in Chapters 1 and 2. The model learns word representations by training on individual words in a sentence. A word close to a target word in a sentence will be constructed as a positive pair whereas randomly sampled words constitute dissimilar pairs. In other words, positive examples of neighboring words are contrasted with randomly selected words that are not neighbors. Although not widely known, it is one of the first major breakthroughs in NLP that leverages contrastive learning with neural networks.

There are many ways we can apply contrastive learning to create text embedding models but the most well-known technique and framework is `sentence-transformers`.

SBERT

Although there are many forms of contrastive learning, one framework that has popularized the technique within the natural language processing community is `sentence-transformers` (*https://oreil.ly/MBgPL*).[3] Its approach fixes a major problem with the original BERT implementation for creating sentence embeddings, namely

3 Nils Reimers and Iryna Gurevych. "Sentence-BERT: Sentence embeddings using Siamese BERT-networks." *arXiv preprint arXiv:1908.10084* (2019).

its computational overhead. Before `sentence-transformers`, sentence embeddings often used an architectural structure called cross-encoders with BERT.

A cross-encoder allows two sentences to be passed to the Transformer network simultaneously to predict the extent to which the two sentences are similar. It does so by adding a classification head to the original architecture that can output a similarity score. However, the number of computations rises quickly when you want to find the highest pair in a collection of 10,000 sentences. That would require $n \cdot (n-1)/2 = 49{,}995{,}000$ inference computations and therefore generates significant overhead. Moreover, a cross-encoder generally does not generate embeddings, as shown in Figure 10-6. Instead, it outputs a similarity score between the input sentences.

A solution to this overhead is to generate embeddings from a BERT model by averaging its output layer or using the `[CLS]` token. This, however, has shown to be worse than simply averaging word vectors, like GloVe.[4]

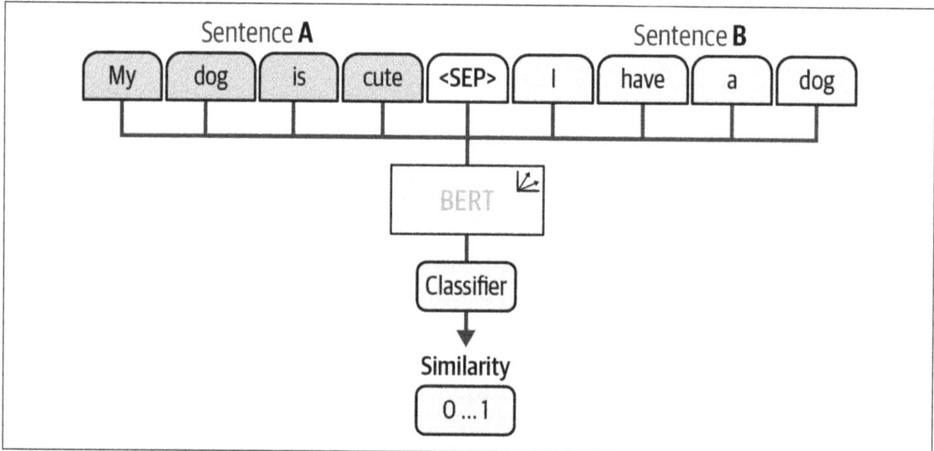

Figure 10-6. The architecture of a cross-encoder. Both sentences are concatenated, separated with a <SEP> token, and fed to the model simultaneously.

Instead, the authors of `sentence-transformers` approached the problem differently and searched for a method that is fast and creates embeddings that can be compared semantically. The result is an elegant alternative to the original cross-encoder architecture. Unlike a cross-encoder, in `sentence-transformers` the classification head is dropped, and instead mean pooling is used on the final output layer to generate an embedding. This pooling layer averages the word embeddings and gives back a fixed dimensional output vector. This ensures a fixed-size embedding.

4 Jeffrey Pennington, Richard Socher, and Christopher D. Manning. "GloVe: Global vectors for word representation." *Proceedings of the 2014 Conference on Empirical Methods in Natural Language Processing (EMNLP)*. 2014.

The training for `sentence-transformers` uses a Siamese architecture. In this architecture, as visualized in Figure 10-7, we have two identical BERT models that share the same weights and neural architecture. These models are fed the sentences from which embeddings are generated through the pooling of token embeddings. Then, models are optimized through the similarity of the sentence embeddings. Since the weights are identical for both BERT models, we can use a single model and feed it the sentences one after the other.

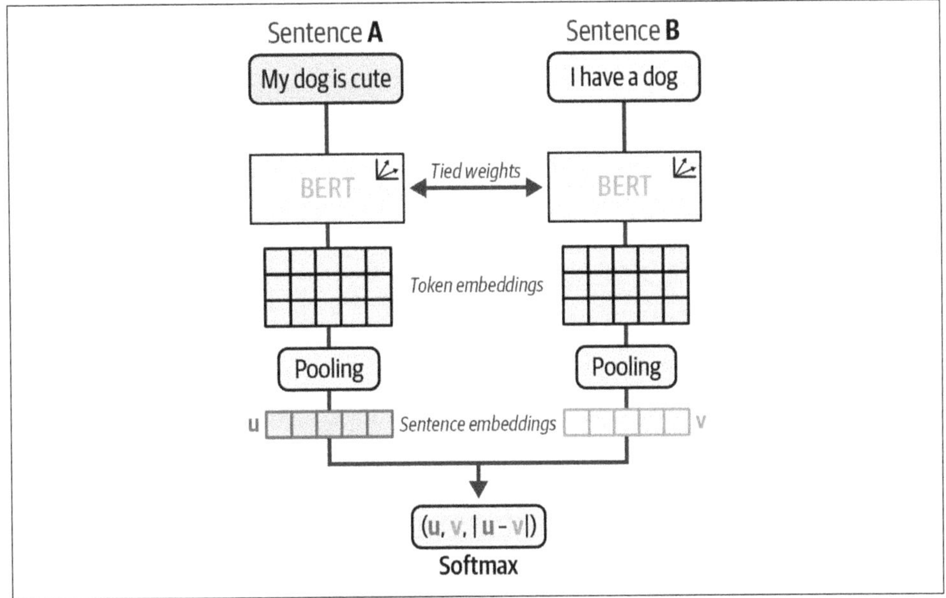

Figure 10-7. The architecture of the original `sentence-transformers` model, which leverages a Siamese network, also called a bi-encoder.

The optimization process of these pairs of sentences is done through loss functions, which can have a major impact on the model's performance. During training, the embeddings for each sentence are concatenated together with the difference between the embeddings. Then, this resulting embedding is optimized through a softmax classifier.

The resulting architecture is also referred to as a bi-encoder or SBERT for sentence-BERT. Although a bi-encoder is quite fast and creates accurate sentence representations, cross-encoders generally achieve better performance than a bi-encoder but do not generate embeddings.

The bi-encoder, like a cross-encoder, leverages contrastive learning; by optimizing the (dis)similarity between pairs of sentences, the model will eventually learn the things that make the sentences what they are.

To perform contrastive learning, we need two things. First, we need data that constitutes similar/dissimilar pairs. Second, we will need to define how the model defines and optimizes similarity.

Creating an Embedding Model

There are many methods through which an embedding model can be created but generally, we look toward contrastive learning. This is an important aspect of many embedding models as the process allows it to efficiently learn semantic representations.

However, this is not a free process. We will need to understand how to generate contrastive examples, how to train the model, and how to properly evaluate it.

Generating Contrastive Examples

When pretraining your embedding model, you will often see data being used from natural language inference (NLI) datasets. NLI refers to the task of investigating whether, for a given premise, it entails the hypothesis (entailment), contradicts it (contradiction), or neither (neutral).

For example, when the premise is "He is in the cinema watching *Coco*" and the hypothesis "He is watching *Frozen* at home," then these statements are contradictions. In contrast, when the premise is "He is in the cinema watching *Coco*" and the hypothesis "In the movie theater he is watching the Disney movie *Coco*," then these statements are considered entailment. This principle is illustrated in Figure 10-8.

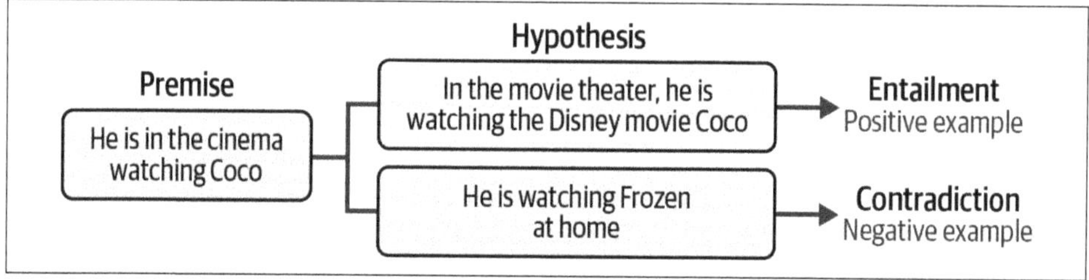

Figure 10-8. We can leverage the structure of NLI datasets to generate negative examples (contradiction) and positive examples (entailments) for contrastive learning.

If you look closely at entailment and contradiction, then they describe the extent to which two inputs are similar to one another. As such, we can use NLI datasets to generate negative examples (contradictions) and positive examples (entailments) for contrastive learning.

The data that we are going to be using throughout creating and fine-tuning embedding models is derived from the General Language Understanding Evaluation benchmark (*https://oreil.ly/43phw*) (GLUE). This GLUE benchmark consists of nine language understanding tasks to evaluate and analyze model performance.

One of these tasks is the Multi-Genre Natural Language Inference (MNLI) corpus, which is a collection of 392,702 sentence pairs annotated with entailment (contradiction, neutral, entailment). We will be using a subset of the data, 50,000 annotated sentence pairs, to create a minimal example that does not need to be trained for hours on end. Do note, though, that the smaller the dataset, the more unstable training or fine-tuning an embedding model is. If possible, larger datasets are preferred assuming it is still quality data:

```
from datasets import load_dataset

# Load MNLI dataset from GLUE
# 0 = entailment, 1 = neutral, 2 = contradiction
train_dataset = load_dataset(
    "glue", "mnli", split="train"
).select(range(50_000))
train_dataset = train_dataset.remove_columns("idx")
```

Next, we take a look at an example:

```
dataset[2]
```

```
{'premise': 'One of our number will carry out your instructions minutely.',
 'hypothesis': 'A member of my team will execute your orders with immense
precision.',
 'label': 0}
```

This shows an example of an entailment between the premise and the hypothesis as they are positively related and have near identical meanings.

Train Model

Now that we have our dataset with training examples, we will need to create our embedding model. We typically choose an existing `sentence-transformers` model and fine-tune that model, but in this example, we are going to train an embedding from scratch.

This means that we will have to define two things. First, a pretrained Transformer model that serves as embedding individual words. We will use the BERT base model (uncased) (*https://oreil.ly/VyyRz*) as it is a great introduction model. However, many others exist that also have been evaluated using `sentence-transformers` (*https://oreil.ly/mw7ly*). Most notably, `microsoft/mpnet-base` often gives good results when used as a word embedding model.

```
from sentence_transformers import SentenceTransformer

# Use a base model
embedding_model = SentenceTransformer('bert-base-uncased')
```

By default, all layers of an LLM in `sentence-transformers` are trainable. Although it is possible to freeze certain layers, it is generally not advised since the performance is often better when unfreezing all layers.

Next, we will need to define a loss function over which we will optimize the model. As mentioned at the beginning of this section, one of the first instances of `sentence-transformers` uses softmax loss. For illustrative purposes, we are going to be using that for now, but we will go into more performant losses later on:

```
from [illegible] import losses

# Define the loss function. In softmax loss, we will also need to explicitly
set the number of labels.
train_loss = losses.SoftmaxLoss(
    model=embedding_model,
    sentence_embedding_dimension=embedding_model.get_sentence_embedding_dimen
sion(),
    num_labels=3
)
```

Before we train our model, we define an evaluator to evaluate the model's performance during training, which also determines the best model to save.

We can perform evaluation of the performance of our model using the Semantic Textual Similarity Benchmark (STSB). It is a collection of human-labeled sentence pairs, with similarity scores between 1 and 5.

We use this dataset to explore how well our model scores on this semantic similarity task. Moreover, we process the STSB data to make sure all values are between 0 and 1:

```
from [illegible] import EmbeddingSimilarityEvaluator

# Create an embedding similarity evaluator for STSB
val_sts = load_dataset("glue", "stsb", split="validation")
evaluator = EmbeddingSimilarityEvaluator(
    sentences1=val_sts["sentence1"],
    sentences2=val_sts["sentence2"],
    scores=[score/5 for score in val_sts["label"]],
    main_similarity="cosine",
)
```

Now that we have our evaluator, we create `SentenceTransformerTrainingArguments`, similar to training with Hugging Face Transformers (as we will explore in the next chapter):

```
from [illegible] import SentenceTransformerTrainingArgu
ments

# Define the training arguments
```

```
args = SentenceTransformerTrainingArguments(
    output_dir="base_embedding_model",
    num_train_epochs=1,
    per_device_train_batch_size=32,
    per_device_eval_batch_size=32,
    warmup_steps=100,
    fp16=True,
    eval_steps=100,
    logging_steps=100,
)
```

Of note are the following arguments:

`num_train_epochs`
: The number of training rounds. We keep this at 1 for faster training but it is generally advised to increase this value.

`per_device_train_batch_size`
: The number of samples to process simultaneously on each device (e.g., GPU or CPU) during evaluation. Higher values generally means faster training.

`per_device_eval_batch_size`
: The number of samples to process simultaneously on each device (e.g., GPU or CPU) during evaluation. Higher values generally means faster evaluation.

`warmup_steps`
: The number of steps during which the learning rate will be linearly increased from zero to the initial learning rate defined for the training process. Note that we did not specify a custom learning rate for this training process.

`fp16`
: By enabling this parameter we allow for mixed precision training, where computations are performed using 16-bit floating-point numbers (FP16) instead of the default 32-bit (FP32). This reduces memory usage and potentially increases the training speed.

Now that we have defined our data, embedding model, loss, and evaluator, we can start training our model. We can do that using `SentenceTransformerTrainer`:

```
from sentence_transformers.trainer import SentenceTransformerTrainer

# Train embedding model
trainer = SentenceTransformerTrainer(
    model=embedding_model,
    args=args,
    train_dataset=train_dataset,
    loss=train_loss,
    evaluator=evaluator
)
trainer.train()
```

After training our model, we can use the evaluator to get the performance on this single task:

```
# Evaluate our trained model
evaluator(embedding_model)
```

```
{'pearson_cosine': 0.5982288436666162,
 'spearman_cosine': 0.6026682018489217,
 'pearson_manhattan': 0.6100690915500567,
 'spearman_manhattan': 0.617732600131989,
 'pearson_euclidean': 0.6079280934202278,
 'spearman_euclidean': 0.6158926913905742,
 'pearson_dot': 0.38364924527804595,
 'spearman_dot': 0.37008497926991796,
 'pearson_max': 0.6100690915500567,
 'spearman_max': 0.617732600131989}
```

We get several different distance measures. The one we are interested in most is `'pearson_cosine'`, which is the cosine similarity between centered vectors. It is a value between 0 and 1 where a higher value indicates higher degrees of similarity. We get a value of 0.59, which we consider a baseline throughout this chapter.

Larger batch sizes tend to work better with multiple negative rankings (MNR) loss as a larger batch makes the task more difficult. The reason for this is that the model needs to find the best matching sentence from a larger set of potential pairs of sentences. You can adapt the code to try out different batch sizes and get a feeling of its effects.

In-Depth Evaluation

A good embedding model is more than just a good score on the STSB benchmark! As we observed earlier, the GLUE benchmark has a number of tasks for which we can evaluate our embedding model. However, there exist many more benchmarks that allow for the evaluation of embedding models. To unify this evaluation procedure, the Massive Text Embedding Benchmark (MTEB) was developed.[5] The MTEB spans 8 embedding tasks that cover 58 datasets and 112 languages.

To publicly compare state-of-the-art embedding models, a leaderboard (*https://oreil.ly/D9Fvt*) was created with the scores of each embedding model across all tasks:

```
from mteb import MTEB

# Choose evaluation task
evaluation = MTEB(tasks=["Banking77Classification"])
```

5 Niklas Muennighoff et al. "MTEB: Massive Text Embedding Benchmark." *arXiv preprint arXiv:2210.07316* (2022).

```
# Calculate results
results = evaluation.run(model)
```

```
{'Banking77Classification': {'mteb_version': '1.1.2',
  'dataset_revision': '0fd18e25b25c072e09e0d92ab615fda904d66300',
  'mteb_dataset_name': 'Banking77Classification',
  'test': {'accuracy': 0.4926298701298701,
  'f1': 0.49083335791288685,
  'accuracy_stderr': 0.010217785746224237,
  'f1_stderr': 0.010265814957074591,
  'main_score': 0.4926298701298701,
  'evaluation_time': 31.83}}}
```

This gives us several evaluation metrics for this specific task that we can use to explore its performance.

The great thing about this evaluation benchmark is not only the diversity of the tasks and languages but that even the evaluation time is saved. Although many embedding models exist, we typically want those that are both accurate and have low latency. The tasks for which embedding models are used, like semantic search, often benefit from and require fast inference.

Since testing your model on the entire MTEB can take a couple of hours depending on your GPU, we will use the STSB benchmark throughout this chapter instead for illustration purposes.

Whenever you are done training and evaluating your model, it is important to *restart* the notebook. This will clear your VRAM up for the next training examples throughout this chapter. By restarting the notebook, we can be sure that all VRAM is cleared.

Loss Functions

We trained our model using softmax loss to illustrate how one of the first `sentence-transformers` models was trained. However, not only is there a large variety of loss functions to choose from, but softmax loss is generally not advised as there are more performant losses (*https://oreil.ly/xuKSI*).

Instead of going through every single loss function out there, there are two loss functions that are typically used and seem to perform generally well, namely:

- Cosine similarity
- Multiple negatives ranking (MNR) loss

There are many more loss functions to choose from than just those discussed here. For example, a loss like MarginMSE works great for training or fine-tuning a cross-encoder. There are a number of interesting loss functions implemented in the `sentence-transformers` framework (*https://oreil.ly/RsQmw*).

Cosine similarity

The cosine similarity loss is an intuitive and easy-to-use loss that works across many different use cases and datasets. It is typically used in semantic textual similarity tasks. In these tasks, a similarity score is assigned to the pairs of texts over which we optimize the model.

Instead of having strictly positive or negative pairs of sentences, we assume pairs of sentences that are similar or dissimilar to a certain degree. Typically, this value lies between 0 and 1 to indicate dissimilarity and similarity, respectively (Figure 10-9).

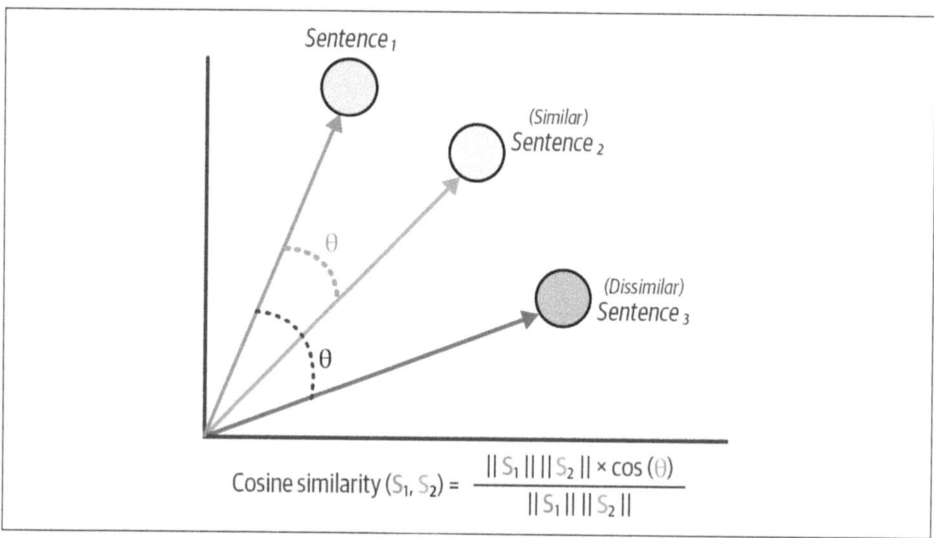

Figure 10-9. Cosine similarity loss aims to minimize the cosine distance between semantically similar sentences and to maximize the distance between semantically dissimilar sentences.

Cosine similarity loss is straightforward—it calculates the cosine similarity between the two embeddings of the two texts and compares that to the labeled similarity score. The model will learn to recognize the degree of similarity between sentences.

Cosine similarity loss intuitively works best using data where you have pairs of sentences and labels that indicate their similarity between 0 and 1. To use this loss with our NLI dataset, we need to convert the entailment (0), neutral (1), and contradiction (2) labels to values between 0 and 1. The entailment represents a high similarity between the sentences, so we give it a similarity score of 1. In contrast, since both neutral and contradiction represent dissimilarity, we give these labels a similarity score of 0:

```
from datasets import Dataset, load_dataset

# Load MNLI dataset from GLUE
# 0 = entailment, 1 = neutral, 2 = contradiction
train_dataset = load_dataset(
    "glue", "mnli", split="train"
).select(range(50_000))
train_dataset = train_dataset.remove_columns("idx")

# (neutral/contradiction)=0 and (entailment)=1
mapping = {2: 0, 1: 0, 0:1}
train_dataset = Dataset.from_dict({
    "sentence1": train_dataset["premise"],
    "sentence2": train_dataset["hypothesis"],
    "label": [float(mapping[label]) for label in train_dataset["label"]]
})
```

As before, we create our evaluator:

```
from sentence_transformers.evaluation import EmbeddingSimilarityEvaluator

# Create an embedding similarity evaluator for stsb
val_sts = load_dataset("glue", "stsb", split="validation")
evaluator = EmbeddingSimilarityEvaluator(
    sentences1=val_sts["sentence1"],
    sentences2=val_sts["sentence2"],
    scores=[score/5 for score in val_sts["label"]],
    main_similarity="cosine"
)
```

Then, we follow the same steps as before but select a different loss instead:

```
from sentence_transformers import losses, SentenceTransformer
from sentence_transformers.trainer import SentenceTransformerTrainer
from sentence_transformers.training_args import SentenceTransformerTrainingArgu
ments

# Define model
embedding_model = SentenceTransformer("bert-base-uncased")

# Loss function
train_loss = losses.CosineSimilarityLoss(model=embedding_model)

# Define the training arguments
args = SentenceTransformerTrainingArguments(
    output_dir="cosineloss_embedding_model",
    num_train_epochs=1,
    per_device_train_batch_size=32,
    per_device_eval_batch_size=32,
```

```
        warmup_steps=100,
        fp16=True,
        eval_steps=100,
        logging_steps=100,
    )

    # Train model
    trainer = SentenceTransformerTrainer(
        model=embedding_model,
        args=args,
        train_dataset=train_dataset,
        loss=train_loss,
        evaluator=evaluator
    )
    trainer.train()
```

Evaluating the model after training gives us the following score:

```
# Evaluate our trained model
evaluator(embedding_model)
```

```
{'pearson_cosine': 0.7222322163831805,
 'spearman_cosine': 0.7250508271229599,
 'pearson_manhattan': 0.7338163436711481,
 'spearman_manhattan': 0.7323479193408869,
 'pearson_euclidean': 0.7332716434966307,
 'spearman_euclidean': 0.7316999722750905,
 'pearson_dot': 0.660366792336156,
 'spearman_dot': 0.6624167554844425,
 'pearson_max': 0.7338163436711481,
 'spearman_max': 0.7323479193408869}
```

A Pearson cosine score of 0.72 is a big improvement compared to the softmax loss example, which scored 0.59. This demonstrates the impact the loss function can have on performance.

Make sure to *restart* your notebook so we can explore a more common and performant loss, namely multiple negatives ranking loss.

Multiple negatives ranking loss

Multiple negatives ranking (MNR) loss,[6] often referred to as InfoNCE[7] or NTXentLoss,[8] is a loss that uses either positive pairs of sentences or triplets that contain a pair of positive sentences and an additional unrelated sentence. This unrelated

6 Matthew Henderson et al. "Efficient natural language response suggestion for smart reply." *arXiv preprint arXiv:1705.00652* (2017).

7 Aaron van den Oord, Yazhe Li, and Oriol Vinyals. "Representation learning with contrastive predictive coding." *arXiv preprint arXiv:1807.03748* (2018).

8 Ting Chen et al. "A simple framework for contrastive learning of visual representations." *International Conference on Machine Learning*. PMLR, 2020.

sentence is called a negative and represents the dissimilarity between the positive sentences.

For example, you might have pairs of question/answer, image/image caption, paper title/paper abstract, etc. The great thing about these pairs is that we can be confident they are hard positive pairs. In MNR loss (Figure 10-10), negative pairs are constructed by mixing a positive pair with another positive pair. In the example of a paper title and abstract, you would generate a negative pair by combining the title of a paper with a completely different abstract. These negatives are called *in-batch negatives* and can also be used to generate the triplets.

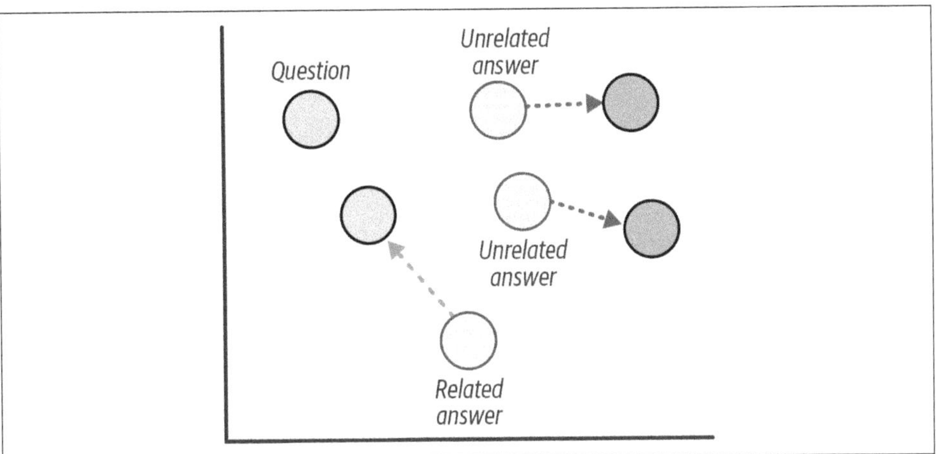

Figure 10-10. Multiple negatives ranking loss aims to minimize the distance between related pairs of text, such as questions and answers, and maximize the distance between unrelated pairs, such as questions and unrelated answers.

After having generated these positive and negative pairs, we calculate their embeddings and apply cosine similarity. These similarity scores are then used to answer the question, are these pairs negative or positive? In other words, it is treated as a classification task and we can use cross-entropy loss to optimize the model.

To make these triplets we start with an anchor sentence (i.e., labeled as the "premise"), which is used to compare other sentences. Then, using the MNLI dataset, we only select sentence pairs that are positive (i.e., labeled as "entailment"). To add negative sentences, we randomly sample sentences as the "hypothesis."

```
import random
from tqdm import tqdm
from datasets import Dataset, load_dataset

# # Load MNLI dataset from GLUE
mnli = load_dataset("glue", "mnli", split="train").select(range(50_000))
mnli = mnli.remove_columns("idx")
```

```
mnli = mnli.filter(lambda x: True if x["label"] == 0 else False)

# Prepare data and add a soft negative
train_dataset = {"anchor": [], "positive": [], "negative": []}
soft_negatives = mnli["hypothesis"]
random.shuffle(soft_negatives)
for row, soft_negative in tqdm(zip(mnli, soft_negatives)):
    train_dataset["anchor"].append(row["premise"])
    train_dataset["positive"].append(row["hypothesis"])
    train_dataset["negative"].append(soft_negative)
train_dataset = Dataset.from_dict(train_dataset)
```

Since we only selected sentences labeled with "entailment," the number of rows reduced quite a a bit from 50,000 to 16,875 rows.

Let's define the evaluator:

```
from [illegible] import EmbeddingSimilarityEvaluator
# Create an embedding similarity evaluator for stsb
val_sts = load_dataset("glue", "stsb", split="validation")
evaluator = EmbeddingSimilarityEvaluator(
    sentences1=val_sts["sentence1"],
    sentences2=val_sts["sentence2"],
    scores=[score/5 for score in val_sts["label"]],
    main_similarity="cosine"
)
```

We then train as before but with MNR loss instead:

```
from [illegible] import losses, SentenceTransformer
from [illegible] import SentenceTransformerTrainer
from [illegible] import SentenceTransformerTrainingArgu
ments

# Define model
embedding_model = SentenceTransformer('bert-base-uncased')

# Loss function
train_loss = losses.MultipleNegativesRankingLoss(model=embedding_model)

# Define the training arguments
args = SentenceTransformerTrainingArguments(
    output_dir="mnrloss_embedding_model",
    num_train_epochs=1,
    per_device_train_batch_size=32,
    per_device_eval_batch_size=32,
    warmup_steps=100,
    fp16=True,
    eval_steps=100,
    logging_steps=100,
)

# Train model
```

```
trainer = SentenceTransformerTrainer(
    model=embedding_model,
    args=args,
    train_dataset=train_dataset,
    loss=train_loss,
    evaluator=evaluator
)
trainer.train()
```

Let's see how this dataset and loss function compare to our previous examples:

```
# Evaluate our trained model
evaluator(embedding_model)
```

```
{'pearson_cosine': 0.8093892326162132,
 'spearman_cosine': 0.8121064796503025,
 'pearson_manhattan': 0.8215001523827565,
 'spearman_manhattan': 0.8172161486524246,
 'pearson_euclidean': 0.8210391407846718,
 'spearman_euclidean': 0.8166537141010816,
 'pearson_dot': 0.7473360302629125,
 'spearman_dot': 0.7345184137194012,
 'pearson_max': 0.8215001523827565,
 'spearman_max': 0.8172161486524246}
```

Compared to our previously trained model with softmax loss (0.72), our model with MNR loss (0.80) seems to be much more accurate!

Larger batch sizes tend to be better with MNR loss as a larger batch makes the task more difficult. The reason for this is that the model needs to find the best matching sentence from a larger set of potential pairs of sentences. You can adapt the code to try out different batch sizes and get a feeling of the effects.

There is a downside to how we used this loss function. Since negatives are sampled from other question/answer pairs, these in-batch or "easy" negatives that we used could potentially be completely unrelated to the question. As a result, the embedding model's task of then finding the right answer to a question becomes quite easy. Instead, we would like to have negatives that are very related to the question but not the right answer. These negatives are called *hard negatives*. Since this would make the task more difficult for the embedding model as it has to learn more nuanced representations, the embedding model's performance generally improves quite a bit.

A good example of a hard negative is the following. Let's assume we have the following question: "How many people live in Amsterdam?" A related answer to this question would be: "Almost a million people live in Amsterdam." To generate a good hard negative, we ideally want the answer to contain something about Amsterdam and the number of people living in this city. For example: "More than a million people live in Utrecht, which is more than Amsterdam." This answer relates to the question but is not the actual answer, so this would be a good hard negative. Figure 10-11 illustrates the differences between easy and hard negatives.

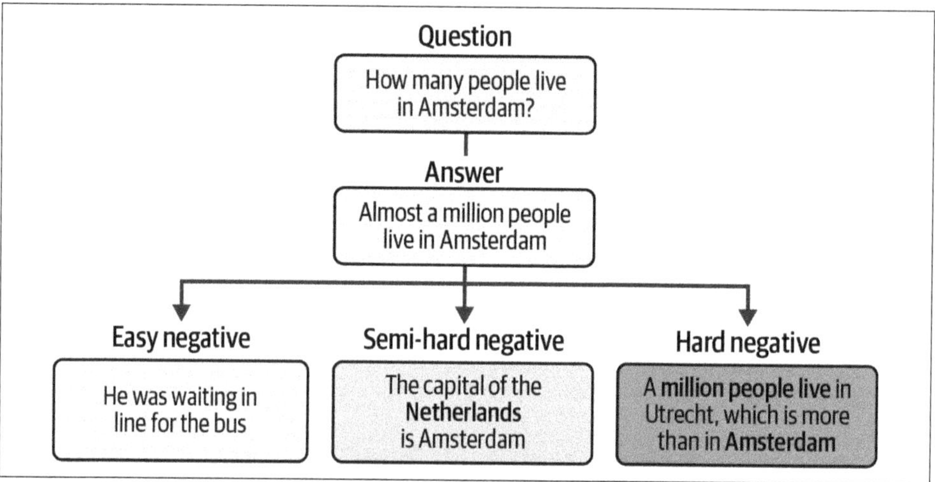

Figure 10-11. An easy negative is typically unrelated to both the question and answer. A semi-hard negative has some similarities to the topic of the question and answer but is somewhat unrelated. A hard negative is very similar to the question but is generally the wrong answer.

Gathering negatives can roughly be divided into the following three processes:

Easy negatives
: Through randomly sampling documents as we did before.

Semi-hard negatives
: Using a pretrained embedding model, we can apply cosine similarity on all sentence embeddings to find those that are highly related. Generally, this does not lead to hard negatives since this method merely finds similar sentences, not question/answer pairs.

Hard negatives
: These often need to be either manually labeled (for instance, by generating semi-hard negatives) or you can use a generative model to either judge or generate sentence pairs.

Make sure to *restart* your notebook so we can explore the different methods of fine-tuning embedding models.

Fine-Tuning an Embedding Model

In the previous section, we went through the basics of training an embedding model from scratch and saw how we could leverage loss functions to further optimize its performance. This approach, although quite powerful, requires creating an embedding model from scratch. This process can be quite costly and time-consuming.

Instead, the `sentence-transformers` framework allows nearly all embedding models to be used as a base for fine-tuning. We can choose an embedding model that was already trained on a large amount of data and fine-tune it for our specific data or purpose.

There are several ways to fine-tune your model, depending on the data availability and domain. We will go through two such methods and demonstrate the strength of leveraging pretrained embedding models.

Supervised

The most straightforward way to fine-tune an embedding model is to repeat the process of training our model as we did before but replace the `'bert-base-uncased'` with a pretrained `sentence-transformers` model. There are many to choose from but generally, `all-MiniLM-L6-v2` (*https://oreil.ly/_paYA*) performs well across many use cases (*https://oreil.ly/ZWGDm*) and due to its small size is quite fast.

We use the same data as we used to train our model in the MNR loss example but instead use a pretrained embedding model to fine-tune. As always, let's start by loading the data and creating the evaluator:

```
from datasets import load_dataset
from sentence_transformers.evaluation import EmbeddingSimilarityEvaluator

# Load MNLI dataset from GLUE
# 0 = entailment, 1 = neutral, 2 = contradiction
train_dataset = load_dataset(
    "glue", "mnli", split="train"
).select(range(50_000))
train_dataset = train_dataset.remove_columns("idx")

# Create an embedding similarity evaluator for stsb
val_sts = load_dataset("glue", "stsb", split="validation")
evaluator = EmbeddingSimilarityEvaluator(
    sentences1=val_sts["sentence1"],
    sentences2=val_sts["sentence2"],
    scores=[score/5 for score in val_sts["label"]],
    main_similarity="cosine"
)
```

The training steps are similar to our previous examples but instead of using `'bert-base-uncased'`, we can use a pretrained embedding model instead:

```
from sentence_transformers import losses, SentenceTransformer
from sentence_transformers.trainer import SentenceTransformerTrainer
from sentence_transformers.training_args import SentenceTransformerTrainingArgu
ments

# Define model
embedding_model = SentenceTransformer('sentence-transformers/all-MiniLM-L6-v2')

# Loss function
train_loss = losses.MultipleNegativesRankingLoss(model=embedding_model)

# Define the training arguments
args = SentenceTransformerTrainingArguments(
    output_dir="finetuned_embedding_model",
    num_train_epochs=1,
    per_device_train_batch_size=32,
    per_device_eval_batch_size=32,
    warmup_steps=100,
    fp16=True,
    eval_steps=100,
    logging_steps=100,
)

# Train model
trainer = SentenceTransformerTrainer(
    model=embedding_model,
    args=args,
    train_dataset=train_dataset,
    loss=train_loss,
    evaluator=evaluator
)
trainer.train()
```

Evaluating this model gives us the following score:

```
# Evaluate our trained model
evaluator(embedding_model)
```

```
{'pearson_cosine': 0.8509553350510896,
 'spearman_cosine': 0.8484676559567688,
 'pearson_manhattan': 0.8503896832470704,
 'spearman_manhattan': 0.8475760325664419,
 'pearson_euclidean': 0.8513115442079158,
 'spearman_euclidean': 0.8484676559567688,
 'pearson_dot': 0.8489553386816947,
 'spearman_dot': 0.8484676559567688,
 'pearson_max': 0.8513115442079158,
 'spearman_max': 0.8484676559567688}
```

Although a score of 0.85 is the highest we have seen thus far, the pretrained model that we used for fine-tuning was already trained on the full MNLI dataset, whereas we only used 50,000 examples. It might seem redundant but this example demonstrates how to fine-tune a pretrained embedding model on your own data.

Instead of using a pretrained BERT model like `'bert-base-uncased'` or a possible out-of-domain model like `'all-mpnet-base-v2'`, you can also perform masked language modeling on the pretrained BERT model to first adapt it to your domain. Then, you can use this fine-tuned BERT model as the base for training your embedding model. This is a form of domain adaptation. In the next chapter, we will apply masked language modeling on a pretrained model.

Note that the main difficulty of training or fine-tuning your model is finding the right data. With these models, we not only want to have very large datasets, but the data in itself needs to be of high quality. Developing positive pairs is generally straightforward but adding hard negative pairs significantly increases the difficulty of creating quality data.

As always, *restart* your notebook to free up VRAM for the following examples.

Augmented SBERT

A disadvantage of training or fine-tuning these embedding models is that they often require substantial training data. Many of these models are trained with more than a billion sentence pairs. Extracting such a high number of sentence pairs for your use case is generally not possible as in many cases, there are only a couple of thousand labeled data points available.

Fortunately, there is a way to augment your data such that an embedding model can be fine-tuned when there is only a little labeled data available. This procedure is referred to as *Augmented SBERT*.[9]

In this procedure, we aim to augment the small amount of labeled data such that they can be used for regular training. It makes use of the slow and more accurate cross-encoder architecture (BERT) to augment and label a larger set of input pairs. These newly labeled pairs are then used for fine-tuning a bi-encoder (SBERT).

As shown in Figure 10-12, Augmented SBERT involves the following steps:

9 Nandan Thakur et al. "Augmented SBERT: Data augmentation method for improving bi-encoders for pairwise sentence scoring tasks." *arXiv preprint arXiv:2010.08240* (2020).

1. Fine-tune a cross-encoder (BERT) using a small, annotated dataset (gold dataset).
2. Create new sentence pairs.
3. Label new sentence pairs with the fine-tuned cross-encoder (silver dataset).
4. Train a bi-encoder (SBERT) on the extended dataset (gold + silver dataset).

Here, a gold dataset is a small but fully annotated dataset that holds the ground truth. A silver dataset is also fully annotated but is not necessarily the ground truth as it was generated through predictions of the cross-encoder.

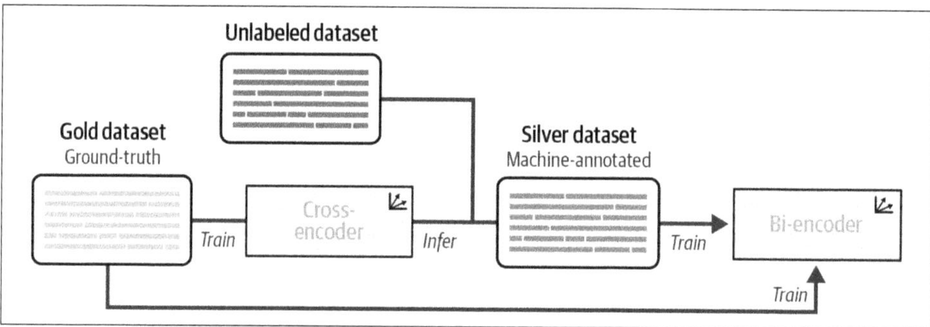

Figure 10-12. Augmented SBERT works through training a cross-encoder on a small gold dataset, then using that to label an unlabeled dataset to generate a larger silver dataset. Finally, both the gold and silver datasets are used to train the bi-encoder.

Before we get into the preceding steps, let's first prepare the data. Instead of our original 50,000 documents, we take a subset of 10,000 documents to simulate a setting where we have limited annotated data. As we did in our example with cosine similarity loss, give entailment a score of 1 whereas neutral and contradiction get a score of 0:

```
import pandas as pd
from tqdm import tqdm
from datasets import load_dataset, Dataset
from sentence_transformers import InputExample
from sentence_transformers.datasets import NoDuplicatesDataLoader

# Prepare a small set of 10000 documents for the cross-encoder
dataset = load_dataset("glue", "mnli", split="train").select(range(10_000))
mapping = {2: 0, 1: 0, 0:1}

# Data loader
gold_examples = [
    InputExample(texts=[row["premise"], row["hypothesis"]], label=map
ping[row["label"]])
    for row in tqdm(dataset)
]
```

```
gold_dataloader = NoDuplicatesDataLoader(gold_examples, batch_size=32)

# Pandas DataFrame for easier data handling
gold = pd.DataFrame(
    {
    "sentence1": dataset["premise"],
    "sentence2": dataset["hypothesis"],
    "label": [mapping[label] for label in dataset["label"]]
    }
)
```

This is the gold dataset since it is labeled and represents our ground truth.

Using this gold dataset, we train our cross-encoder (step 1):

```
from sentence_transformers.cross_encoder import CrossEncoder

# Train a cross-encoder on the gold dataset
cross_encoder = CrossEncoder("bert-base-uncased", num_labels=2)
cross_encoder.fit(
    train_dataloader=gold_dataloader,
    epochs=1,
    show_progress_bar=True,
    warmup_steps=100,
    use_amp=False
)
```

After training our cross-encoder, we use the remaining 400,000 sentence pairs (from our original dataset of 50,000 sentence pairs) as our silver dataset (step 2):

```
# Prepare the silver dataset by predicting labels with the cross-encoder
silver = load_dataset(
    "glue", "mnli", split="train"
).select(range(10_000, 50_000))
pairs = list(zip(silver["premise"], silver["hypothesis"]))
```

If you do not have any additional unlabeled sentence pairs, you can randomly sample them from your original gold dataset. To illustrate, you can create a new sentence pair by taking the premise from one row and the hypothesis from another. This allows you to easily generate 10 times as many sentence pairs that can be labeled with the cross-encoder.

This strategy, however, likely generates significantly more dissimilar than similar pairs. Instead, we can use a pretrained embedding model to embed all candidate sentence pairs and retrieve the top-k sentences for each input sentence using semantic search. This rough reranking process allows us to focus on sentence pairs that are likely to be more similar. Although the sentences are still chosen based on an approximation since the pretrained embedding model was not trained on our data, it is much better than random sampling.

Note that we assume that these sentence pairs are unlabeled in this example. We will use our fine-tuned cross-encoder to label these sentence pairs (step 3):

```
import [illegible] as [illegible]

# Label the sentence pairs using our fine-tuned cross-encoder
output = cross_encoder.predict(
    pairs, apply_softmax=True,
show_progress_bar=True
)
silver = pd.DataFrame(
    {
        "sentence1": silver["premise"],
        "sentence2": silver["hypothesis"],
        "label": np.argmax(output, axis=1)
    }
)
```

Now that we have a silver and gold dataset, we simply combine them and train our embedding model as we did before:

```
# Combine gold + silver
data = pd.concat([gold, silver], ignore_index=True, axis=0)
data = data.drop_duplicates(subset=["sentence1", "sentence2"], keep="first")
train_dataset = Dataset.from_pandas(data, preserve_index=False)
```

As always, we need to define our evaluator:

```
from [illegible] import EmbeddingSimilarityEvaluator

# Create an embedding similarity evaluator for stsb
val_sts = load_dataset("glue", "stsb", split="validation")
evaluator = EmbeddingSimilarityEvaluator(
    sentences1=val_sts["sentence1"],
    sentences2=val_sts["sentence2"],
    scores=[score/5 for score in val_sts["label"]],
    main_similarity="cosine"
)
```

We train the model the same as before except now we use the augmented dataset:

```
from [illegible] import losses, SentenceTransformer
from [illegible] import SentenceTransformerTrainer
from [illegible] import SentenceTransformerTrainingArgu
ments

# Define model
embedding_model = SentenceTransformer("bert-base-uncased")

# Loss function
train_loss = losses.CosineSimilarityLoss(model=embedding_model)

# Define the training arguments
args = SentenceTransformerTrainingArguments(
```

```
    output_dir="augmented_embedding_model",
    num_train_epochs=1,
    per_device_train_batch_size=32,
    per_device_eval_batch_size=32,
    warmup_steps=100,
    fp16=True,
    eval_steps=100,
    logging_steps=100,
)

# Train model
trainer = SentenceTransformerTrainer(
    model=embedding_model,
    args=args,
    train_dataset=train_dataset,
    loss=train_loss,
    evaluator=evaluator
)
trainer.train()
```

Finally, we evaluate the model:

```
evaluator(embedding_model)
```

```
{'pearson_cosine': 0.7101597020018693,
 'spearman_cosine': 0.7210536464320728,
 'pearson_manhattan': 0.7296749443525249,
 'spearman_manhattan': 0.7284184255293913,
 'pearson_euclidean': 0.7293097297208753,
 'spearman_euclidean': 0.7282830906742256,
 'pearson_dot': 0.6746605824703588,
 'spearman_dot': 0.6754486790570754,
 'pearson_max': 0.7296749443525249,
 'spearman_max': 0.7284184255293913}
```

The original cosine similarity loss example had a score of 0.72 with the full dataset. Using only 20% of that data, we managed to get a score of 0.71!

This method allows us to increase the size of datasets that you already have available without the need to manually label hundreds of thousands of sentence pairs. You can test the quality of your silver data by also training your embedding model only on the gold dataset. The difference in performance indicates how much your silver dataset potentially adds to the quality of the model.

You can *restart* your notebook a final time for the last example, namely unsupervised learning.

Unsupervised Learning

To create an embedding model, we typically need labeled data. However, not all real-world datasets come with a nice set of labels that we can use. We instead look for techniques to train the model without any predetermined labels—unsupervised learning. Many approaches exist, like Simple Contrastive Learning of Sentence Embeddings (SimCSE) (*https://oreil.ly/4GCYn*),[10] Contrastive Tension (CT) (*https://oreil.ly/5na_6*),[11] Transformer-based Sequential Denoising Auto-Encoder (TSDAE) (*https://oreil.ly/_r6KI*),[12] and Generative Pseudo-Labeling (GPL) (*https://oreil.ly/soIV_*).[13]

In this section, we will focus on TSDAE, as it has shown great performance on unsupervised tasks as well as domain adaptation.

Transformer-Based Sequential Denoising Auto-Encoder

TSDAE is a very elegant approach to creating an embedding model with unsupervised learning. The method assumes that we have no labeled data at all and does not require us to artificially create labels.

The underlying idea of TSDAE is that we add noise to the input sentence by removing a certain percentage of words from it. This "damaged" sentence is put through an encoder, with a pooling layer on top of it, to map it to a sentence embedding. From this sentence embedding, a decoder tries to reconstruct the original sentence from the "damaged" sentence but without the artificial noise. The main concept here is that the more accurate the sentence embedding is, the more accurate the reconstructed sentence will be.

This method is very similar to masked language modeling, where we try to reconstruct and learn certain masked words. Here, instead of reconstructing masked words, we try to reconstruct the entire sentence.

After training, we can use the encoder to generate embeddings from text since the decoder is only used for judging whether the embeddings can accurately reconstruct the original sentence (Figure 10-13).

10 Tianyu Gao, Xingcheng Yao, and Danqi Chen. "SimCSE: Simple contrastive learning of sentence embeddings." *arXiv preprint arXiv:2104.08821* (2021).

11 Fredrik Carlsson et al. "Semantic re-tuning with Contrastive Tension." *International Conference on Learning Representations, 2021*. 2021.

12 Kexin Wang, Nils Reimers, and Iryna Gurevych. "TSDAE: Using Transformer-based Sequential Denoising Auto-Encoder for unsupervised sentence embedding learning." *arXiv preprint arXiv:2104.06979* (2021).

13 Kexin Wang et al. "GPL: Generative Pseudo Labeling for unsupervised domain adaptation of dense retrieval." *arXiv preprint arXiv:2112.07577* (2021).

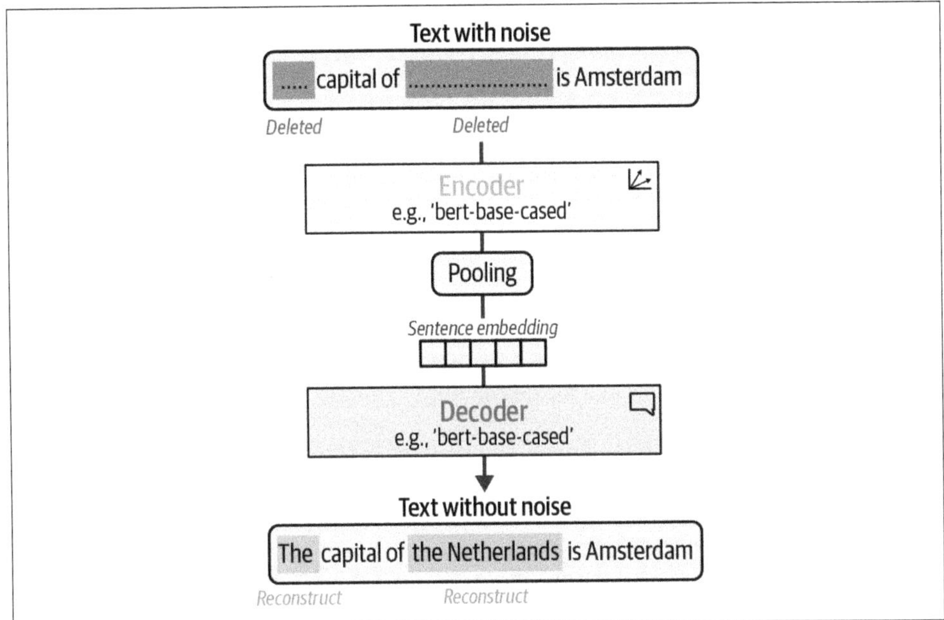

Figure 10-13. TSDAE randomly removes words from an input sentence that is passed through an encoder to generate a sentence embedding. From this sentence embedding, the original sentence is reconstructed.

Since we only need a bunch of sentences without any labels, training this model is straightforward. We start by downloading an external tokenizer, which is used for the denoising procedure:

```
# Download additional tokenizer
import nltk
nltk.download("punkt")
```

Then, we create flat sentences from our data and remove any labels that we have to mimic an unsupervised setting:

```
from tqdm import tqdm
from datasets import Dataset, load_dataset
from sentence_transformers.datasets import DenoisingAutoEncoderDataset

# Create a flat list of sentences
mnli = load_dataset("glue", "mnli", split="train").select(range(25_000))
flat_sentences = mnli["premise"] + mnli["hypothesis"]

# Add noise to our input data
damaged_data = DenoisingAutoEncoderDataset(list(set(flat_sentences)))

# Create dataset
train_dataset = {"damaged_sentence": [], "original_sentence": []}
```

```
for data in tqdm(damaged_data):
    train_dataset["damaged_sentence"].append(data.texts[0])
    train_dataset["original_sentence"].append(data.texts[1])
train_dataset = Dataset.from_dict(train_dataset)
```

This creates a dataset of 50,000 sentences. When we inspect the data, notice that the first sentence is the damaged sentence and the second sentence the original:

```
train_dataset[0]
```

```
{'damaged_sentence': 'Grim jaws are.',
 'original_sentence': 'Grim faces and hardened jaws are not people-friendly.'}
```

The first sentence shows the "noisy" data whereas the second shows the original input sentence. After creating our data, we define our evaluator as before:

```
from [illegible] import EmbeddingSimilarityEvaluator

# Create an embedding similarity evaluator for stsb
val_sts = load_dataset("glue", "stsb", split="validation")
evaluator = EmbeddingSimilarityEvaluator(
    sentences1=val_sts["sentence1"],
    sentences2=val_sts["sentence2"],
    scores=[score/5 for score in val_sts["label"]],
    main_similarity="cosine"
)
```

Next, we run the training as before but with the `[CLS]` token as the pooling strategy instead of the mean pooling of the token embeddings. In the TSDAE paper, this was shown to be more effective since mean pooling loses the position information, which is not the case when using the `[CLS]` token:

```
from [illegible] import models, SentenceTransformer

# Create your embedding model
word_embedding_model = models.Transformer("bert-base-uncased")
pooling_model = models.Pooling(word_embedding_model.get_word_embedding_dimen
sion(), "cls")
embedding_model = SentenceTransformer(modules=[word_embedding_model, pool
ing_model])
```

Using our sentence pairs, we will need a loss function that attempts to reconstruct the original sentence using the noise sentence, namely `DenoisingAutoEncoderLoss`. By doing so, it will learn how to accurately represent the data. It is similar to masking but without knowing where the actual masks are.

Moreover, we tie the parameters of both models. Instead of having separate weights for the encoder's embedding layer and the decoder's output layer, they share the same weights. This means that any updates to the weights in one layer will be reflected in the other layer as well:

```
from sentence_transformers import losses

# Use the denoising auto-encoder loss
train_loss = losses.DenoisingAutoEncoderLoss(
    embedding_model, tie_encoder_decoder=True
)
train_loss.decoder = train_loss.decoder.to("cuda")
```

Finally, training our model works the same as we have seen several times before but we lower the batch size as memory increases with this loss function:

```
from sentence_transformers.trainer import SentenceTransformerTrainer
from sentence_transformers.training_args import SentenceTransformerTrainingArgu
ments

# Define the training arguments
args = SentenceTransformerTrainingArguments(
    output_dir="tsdae_embedding_model",
    num_train_epochs=1,
    per_device_train_batch_size=16,
    per_device_eval_batch_size=16,
    warmup_steps=100,
    fp16=True,
    eval_steps=100,
    logging_steps=100,
)

# Train model
trainer = SentenceTransformerTrainer(
    model=embedding_model,
    args=args,
    train_dataset=train_dataset,
    loss=train_loss,
    evaluator=evaluator
)
trainer.train()
```

After training, we evaluate our model to explore how well such an unsupervised technique performs:

```
# Evaluate our trained model
evaluator(embedding_model)
```

```
{'pearson_cosine': 0.6991809700971775,
 'spearman_cosine': 0.713693213167873,
 'pearson_manhattan': 0.7152343356643568,
 'spearman_manhattan': 0.7201441944880915,
 'pearson_euclidean': 0.7151142243297436,
 'spearman_euclidean': 0.7202291660769805,
 'pearson_dot': 0.5198066451871277,
 'spearman_dot': 0.5104025515225046,
 'pearson_max': 0.7152343356643568,
 'spearman_max': 0.7202291660769805}
```

After fitting our model, we got a score of 0.70, which is quite impressive considering we did all this training with unlabeled data.

Using TSDAE for Domain Adaptation

When you have very little or no labeled data available, you typically use unsupervised learning to create your text embedding model. However, unsupervised techniques are generally outperformed by supervised techniques and have difficulty learning domain-specific concepts.

This is where *domain adaptation* comes in. Its goal is to update existing embedding models to a specific textual domain that contains different subjects from the source domain. Figure 10-14 demonstrates how domains can differ in content. The target domain, or out-domain, generally contains words and subjects that were not found in the source domain or in-domain.

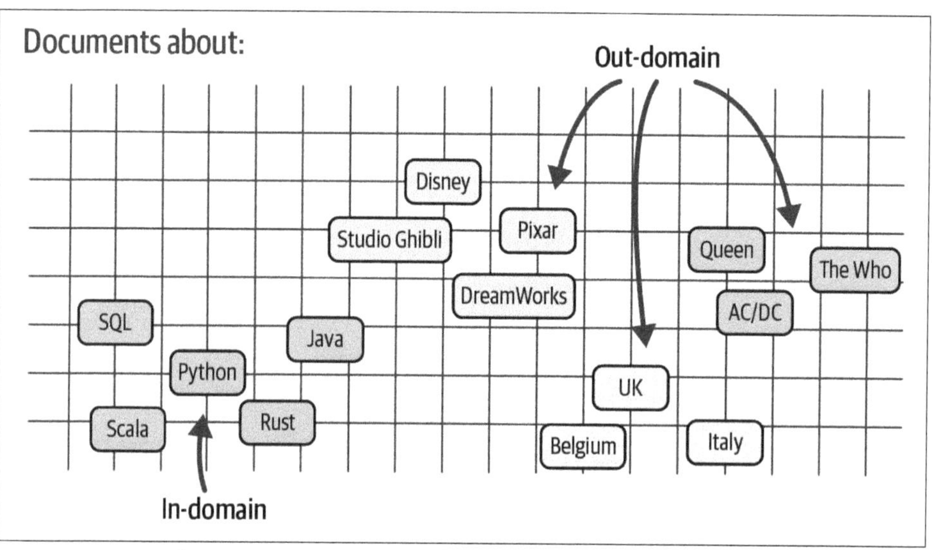

Figure 10-14. In domain adaptation, the aim is to create and generalize an embedding model from one domain to another.

One method for domain adaptation is called *adaptive pretraining*. You start by pre-training your domain-specific corpus using an unsupervised technique, such as the previously discussed TSDAE or masked language modeling. Then, as illustrated in Figure 10-15, you fine-tune that model using a training dataset that can be either outside or in your target domain. Although data from the target domain is preferred, out-domain data also works since we started with unsupervised training on the target domain.

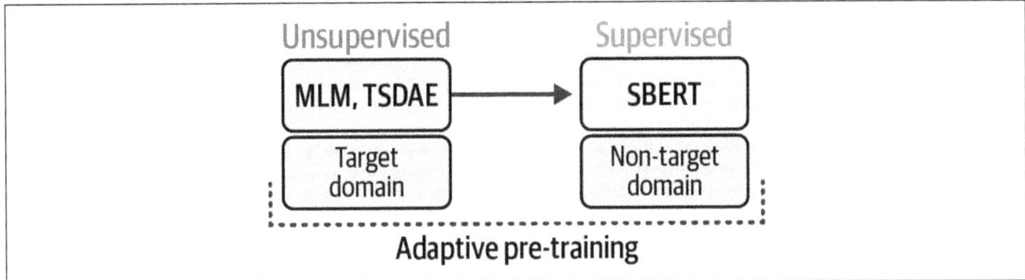

Figure 10-15. Domain adaptation can be performed with adaptive pretraining and adaptive fine-tuning.

Using everything you have learned in this chapter, you should be able to reproduce this pipeline! First, you can start with TSDAE to train an embedding model on your target domain and then fine-tune it using either general supervised training or Augmented SBERT.

Summary

In this chapter, we looked at creating and fine-tuning embedding models through various tasks. We discussed the concept of embeddings and their role in representing textual data in a numerical format. We then explored the foundational technique of many embedding models, namely contrastive learning, which learns primarily from (dis)similar pairs of documents.

Using a popular embedding framework, `sentence-transformers`, we then created embedding models using a pretrained BERT model while exploring different loss functions, such as cosine similarity loss and MNR loss. We discussed how the collection of (dis)similar pairs or triples of documents is vital to the performance of the resulting model.

In the sections that followed, we explored techniques for fine-tuning embedding models. Both supervised and unsupervised techniques were discussed such as Augmented SBERT and TSDAE for domain adaptation. Compared to creating an embedding model, fine-tuning generally needs less data and is a great way to adapt existing embedding models to your domain.

In the next chapter, methods for fine-tuning representations for classification will be discussed. Both BERT models and embedding models will make an appearance as well as a wide range of fine-tuning techniques.

CHAPTER 11

Fine-Tuning Representation Models for Classification

In Chapter 4, we used pretrained models to classify our text. We kept the pretrained models as they were without any modifications to them. This might make you wonder, what happens if we were to fine-tune them?

If we have sufficient data, fine-tuning tends to lead to some of the best-performing models possible. In this chapter, we will go through several methods and applications for fine-tuning BERT models. "Supervised Classification" on page 323 demonstrates the general process of fine-tuning a classification model. Then, in "Few-Shot Classification" on page 333, we look at SetFit, which is a method for efficiently fine-tuning a high-performing model using a small number of training examples. In "Continued Pretraining with Masked Language Modeling" on page 340, we will explore how to continue training a pretrained model. Lastly, classification on a token level is explored in "Named-Entity Recognition" on page 345.

We will focus on nongenerative tasks, as generative models will be covered in Chapter 12.

Supervised Classification

In Chapter 4, we explored supervised classification tasks by leveraging pretrained representation models that were either trained to predict sentiment (task-specific model) or to generate embeddings (embedding model), as shown in Figure 11-1.

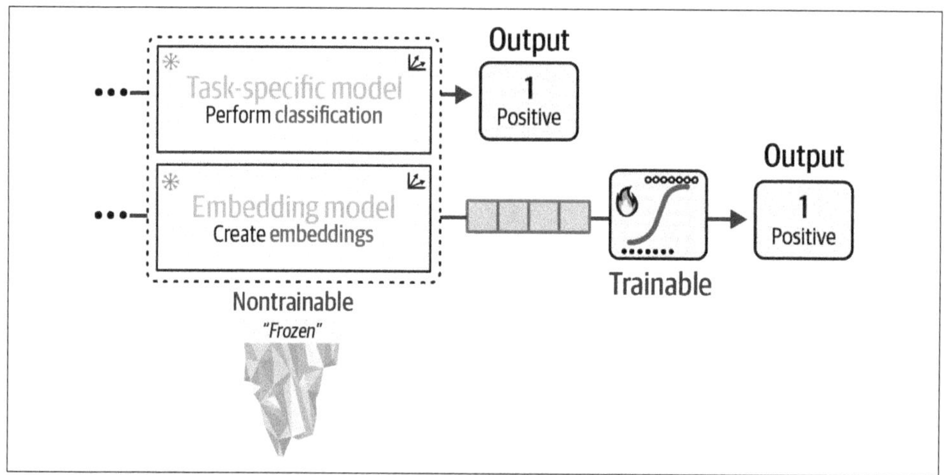

Figure 11-1. In Chapter 4, we used pretrained models to perform classification without updating their weight. These models were kept "frozen."

Both models were kept frozen (nontrainable) to showcase the potential of leveraging pretrained models for classification tasks. The embedding model uses a separate trainable classification head (classifier) to predict the sentiment of movie reviews.

In this section, we will take a similar approach but allow both the model and the classification head to be updated during training. As shown in Figure 11-2, instead of using an embedding model, we will fine-tune a pretrained BERT model to create a task-specific model similar to the one we used in Chapter 2. Compared to the embedding model approach, we will fine-tune both the representation model and the classification head as a single architecture.

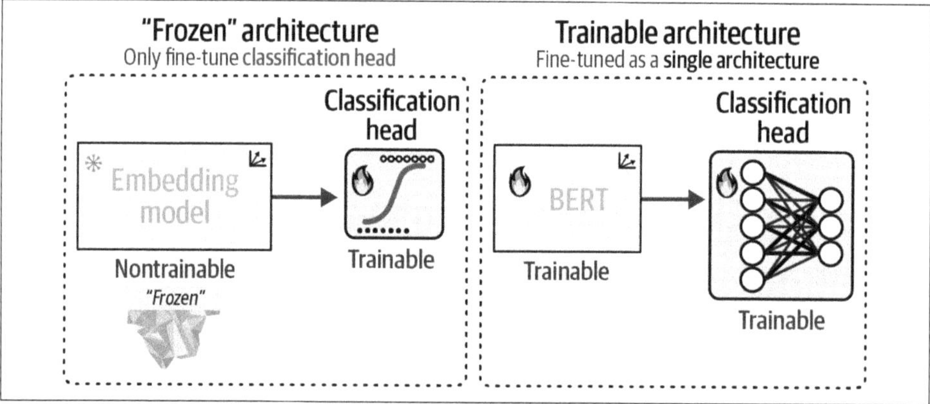

Figure 11-2. Compared to the "frozen" architecture, we instead train both the pretrained BERT model and the classification head. A backward pass will start at the classification head and go through BERT.

To do so, instead of freezing the model, we allow it to be trainable and update its parameters during training. As illustrated in Figure 11-3, we will use a pretrained BERT model and add a neural network as a classification head, both of which will be fine-tuned for classification.

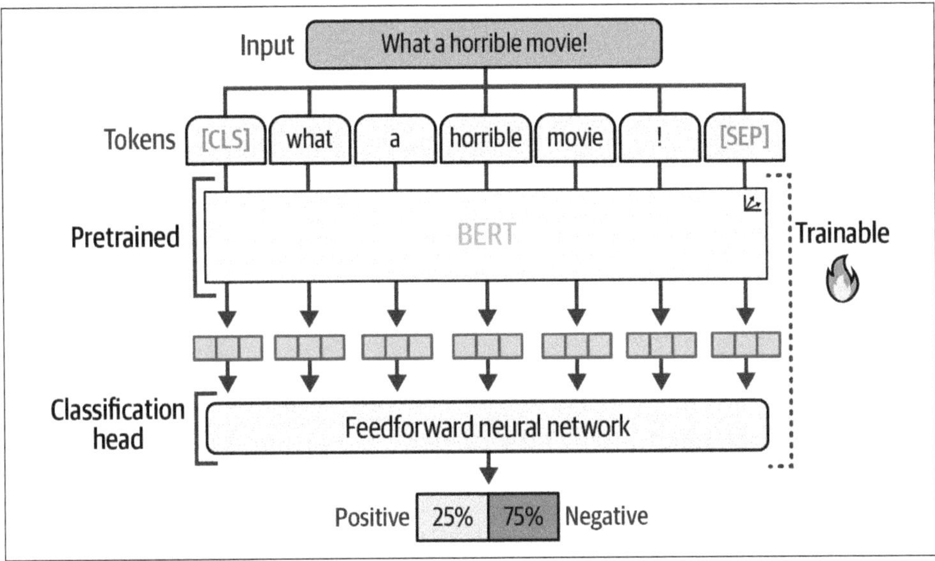

Figure 11-3. The architecture of a task-specific model. It contains a pretrained representation model (e.g., BERT) with an additional classification head for the specific task.

In practice, this means that the pretrained BERT model and the classification head are updated jointly. Instead of independent processes, they learn from one another and allow for more accurate representations.

Fine-Tuning a Pretrained BERT Model

We will be using the same dataset we used in Chapter 4 to fine-tune our model, namely the Rotten Tomatoes dataset, which contains 5,331 positive and 5,331 negative movie reviews from Rotten Tomatoes:

```
from datasets import load_dataset

# Prepare data and splits
tomatoes = load_dataset("rotten_tomatoes")
train_data, test_data = tomatoes["train"], tomatoes["test"]
```

The first step in our classification task is to select the underlying model we want to use. We use `"bert-base-cased"`, which was pretrained on the English Wikipedia as well as a large dataset consisting of unpublished books.[1]

We define the number of labels that we want to predict beforehand. This is necessary to create the feedforward neural network that is applied on top of our pretrained model:

```
from transformers import AutoTokenizer, AutoModelForSequenceClassification

# Load model and tokenizer
model_id = "bert-base-cased"
model = AutoModelForSequenceClassification.from_pretrained(
    model_id, num_labels=2
)
tokenizer = AutoTokenizer.from_pretrained(model_id)
```

Next, we will tokenize our data:

```
from transformers import DataCollatorWithPadding

# Pad to the longest sequence in the batch
data_collator = DataCollatorWithPadding(tokenizer=tokenizer)

def preprocess_function(examples):
   """Tokenize input data"""
   return tokenizer(examples["text"], truncation=True)

# Tokenize train/test data
tokenized_train = train_data.map(preprocess_function, batched=True)
tokenized_test = test_data.map(preprocess_function, batched=True)
```

Before creating the `Trainer`, we will want to prepare a special `DataCollator`. A `DataCollator` is a class that helps us build batches of data but also allows us to apply data augmentation.

During this process of tokenization, and as shown in Chapter 9, we will add padding to the input text to create equally sized representations. We use `DataCollatorWithPadding` for that.

Of course, an example would not be complete without defining some metrics:

```
import numpy as np
from datasets import load_metric

def compute_metrics(eval_pred):
   """Calculate F1 score"""
   logits, labels = eval_pred
```

1 Jacob Devlin et al. "BERT: Pre-training of deep bidirectional transformers for language understanding." *arXiv preprint arXiv:1810.04805* (2018).

```
    predictions = np.argmax(logits, axis=-1)

    load_f1 = load_metric("f1")
    f1 = load_f1.compute(predictions=predictions, references=labels)["f1"]
    return {"f1": f1}
```

With `compute_metrics` we can define any number of metrics that we are interested in and that can be printed out or logged during training. This is especially helpful during training as it allows for detecting overfitting behavior.

Next, we instantiate our `Trainer`:

```
from transformers import TrainingArguments, Trainer

# Training arguments for parameter tuning
training_args = TrainingArguments(
   "model",
   learning_rate=2e-5,
   per_device_train_batch_size=16,
   per_device_eval_batch_size=16,
   num_train_epochs=1,
   weight_decay=0.01,
   save_strategy="epoch",
   report_to="none"
)

# Trainer which executes the training process
trainer = Trainer(
   model=model,
   args=training_args,
   train_dataset=tokenized_train,
   eval_dataset=tokenized_test,
   tokenizer=tokenizer,
   data_collator=data_collator,
   compute_metrics=compute_metrics,
)
```

The `TrainingArguments` class defines hyperparameters we want to tune, such as the learning rate and how many epochs (rounds) we want to train. The `Trainer` is used to execute the training process.

Finally, we can train our model and evaluate it:

```
trainer.evaluate()
```

```
{'eval_loss': 0.3663691282272339,
 'eval_f1': 0.8492366412213741,
 'eval_runtime': 4.5792,
 'eval_samples_per_second': 232.791,
 'eval_steps_per_second': 14.631,
 'epoch': 1.0}
```

We get an F1 score of 0.85, which is quite a bit higher than the task-specific model we used in Chapter 4, which resulted in an F1 score of 0.80. It shows that fine-tuning a model yourself can be more advantageous than using a pretrained model. It only costs us a couple of minutes to train.

Freezing Layers

To further showcase the importance of training the entire network, the next example will demonstrate how you can use Hugging Face Transformers to freeze certain layers of your network.

We will freeze the main BERT model and allow only updates to pass through the classification head. This will be a great comparison as we will keep everything the same, except for freezing specific layers.

To start, let's reinitialize our model so we can start from scratch:

```
# Load model and tokenizer
model = AutoModelForSequenceClassification.from_pretrained(
    model_id, num_labels=2
)
tokenizer = AutoTokenizer.from_pretrained(model_id)
```

Our pretrained BERT model contains a lot of layers that we can potentially freeze. Inspecting these layers gives insight into the structure of the network and what we might want to freeze:

```
# Print layer names
for name, param in model.named_parameters():
    print(name)
```

```
bert.embeddings.word_embeddings.weight
bert.embeddings.position_embeddings.weight
bert.embeddings.token_type_embeddings.weight
bert.embeddings.LayerNorm.weight
bert.embeddings.LayerNorm.bias
bert.encoder.layer.0.attention.self.query.weight
bert.encoder.layer.0.attention.self.query.bias
...
bert.encoder.layer.11.output.LayerNorm.weight
bert.encoder.layer.11.output.LayerNorm.bias
bert.pooler.dense.weight
bert.pooler.dense.bias
classifier.weight
classifier.bias
```

There are 12 (0–11) encoder blocks consisting of attention heads, dense networks, and layer normalization. We further illustrate this architecture in Figure 11-4 to demonstrate everything that could be potentially frozen. On top of that, we have our classification head.

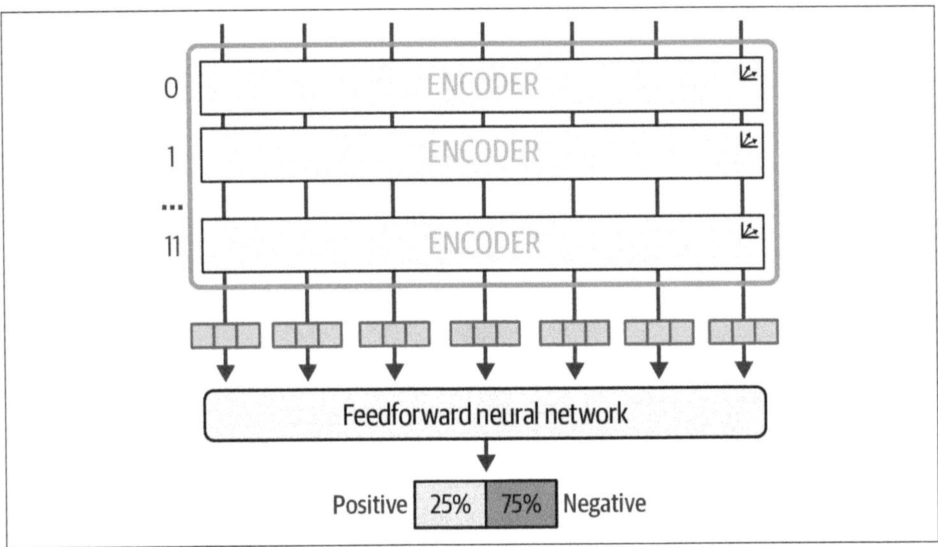

Figure 11-4. The basic architecture of BERT with the additional classification head.

We could choose to only freeze certain layers to speed up computing but still allow the main model to learn from the classification task. Generally, we want frozen layers to be followed by trainable layers.

We are going to freeze everything except for the classification head as we did in Chapter 2:

```
for name, param in model.named_parameters():

     # Trainable classification head
     if name.startswith("classifier"):
        param.requires_grad = True

      # Freeze everything else
     else:
        param.requires_grad = False
```

As shown in Figure 11-5, we have frozen everything except for the feedforward neural network, which is our classification head.

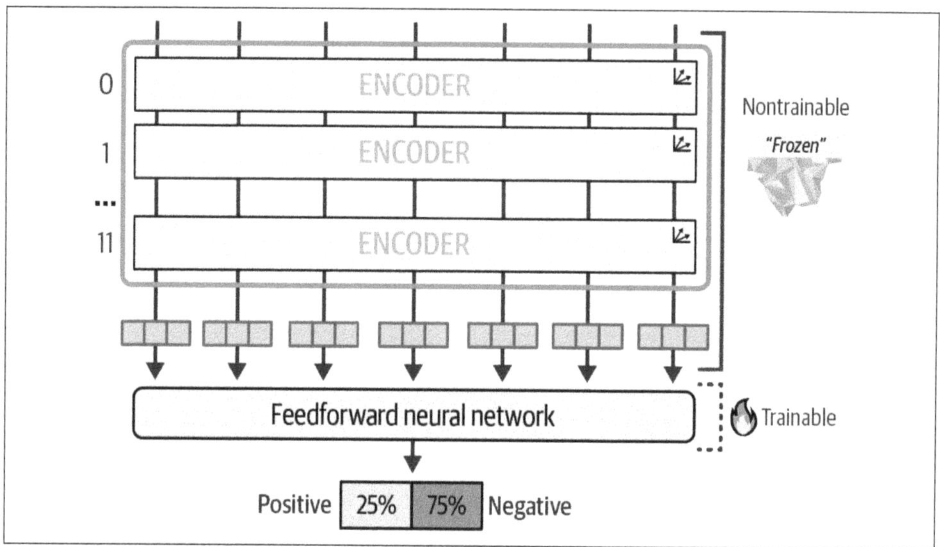

Figure 11-5. We fully freeze all encoder blocks and embedding layers such that the BERT model does not learn new representations during fine-tuning.

Now that we have successfully frozen everything but the classification head, we can move on to train our model:

```
from transformers import TrainingArguments, Trainer

# Trainer which executes the training process
trainer = Trainer(
   model=model,
   args=training_args,
   train_dataset=tokenized_train,
   eval_dataset=tokenized_test,
   tokenizer=tokenizer,
   data_collator=data_collator,
   compute_metrics=compute_metrics,
)
trainer.train()
```

You might notice that training has become much faster. That is because we are only training the classification head, which provides us with a significant speedup compared to fine-tuning the entire model:

```
trainer.evaluate()
```

```
{'eval_loss': 0.6821751594543457,
 'eval_f1': 0.6331058020477816,
 'eval_runtime': 4.0175,
 'eval_samples_per_second': 265.337,
 'eval_steps_per_second': 16.677,
 'epoch': 1.0}
```

When we evaluate the model, we only get an F1 score of 0.63, which is quite a bit lower compared to our original 0.85 score. Instead of freezing nearly all layers, let's freeze everything up until encoder block 10 as illustrated in Figure 11-6, and see how it affects performance. A major benefit is that this reduces computation but still allows updates to flow through part of the pretrained model:

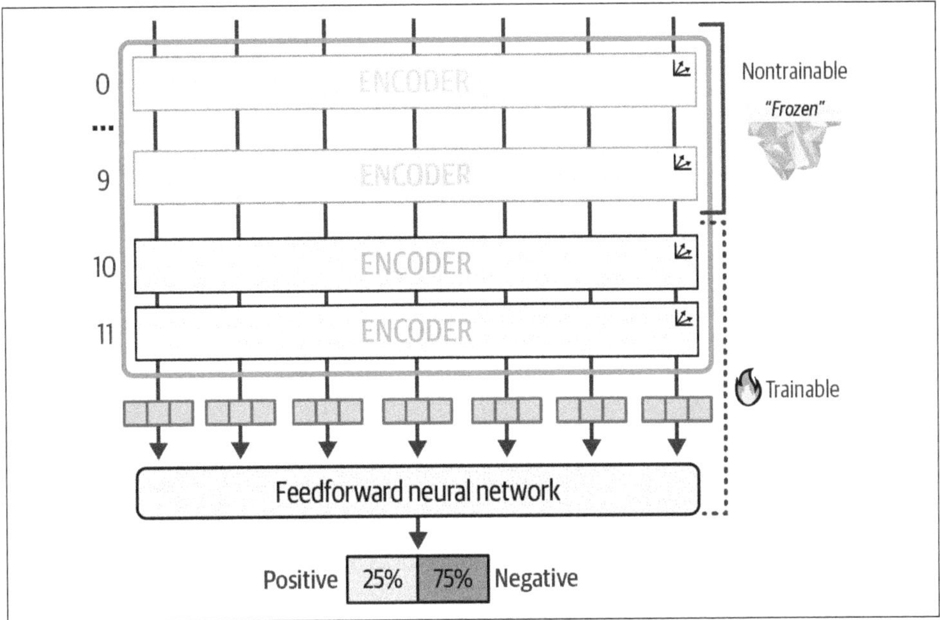

Figure 11-6. We freeze the first 10 encoder blocks of our BERT model. Everything else is trainable and will be fine-tuned.

```
# Load model
model_id = "bert-base-cased"
model = AutoModelForSequenceClassification.from_pretrained(
    model_id, num_labels=2
)
tokenizer = AutoTokenizer.from_pretrained(model_id)

# Encoder block 11 starts at index 165 and
# we freeze everything before that block
for index, (name, param) in enumerate(model.named_parameters()):
    if index < 165:
        param.requires_grad = False

# Trainer which executes the training process
trainer = Trainer(
   model=model,
   args=training_args,
   train_dataset=tokenized_train,
   eval_dataset=tokenized_test,
```

```
        tokenizer=tokenizer,
        data_collator=data_collator,
        compute_metrics=compute_metrics,
    )
    trainer.train()
```

After training, we evaluate the results:

```
trainer.evaluate()
{'eval_loss': 0.40812647342681885,
 'eval_f1': 0.8,
 'eval_runtime': 3.7125,
 'eval_samples_per_second': 287.137,
 'eval_steps_per_second': 18.047,
 'epoch': 1.0}
```

We got an F1 score of 0.8, which is much higher than our previous score of 0.63 when freezing all layers. It demonstrates that although we generally want to train as many layers as possible, you can get away with training less if you do not have the necessary computing power.

To further illustrate this effect, we tested the effect of iteratively freezing encoder blocks and fine-tuning them as we did thus far. As shown in Figure 11-7, training only the first five encoder blocks (red vertical line) is enough to almost reach the performance of training all encoder blocks.

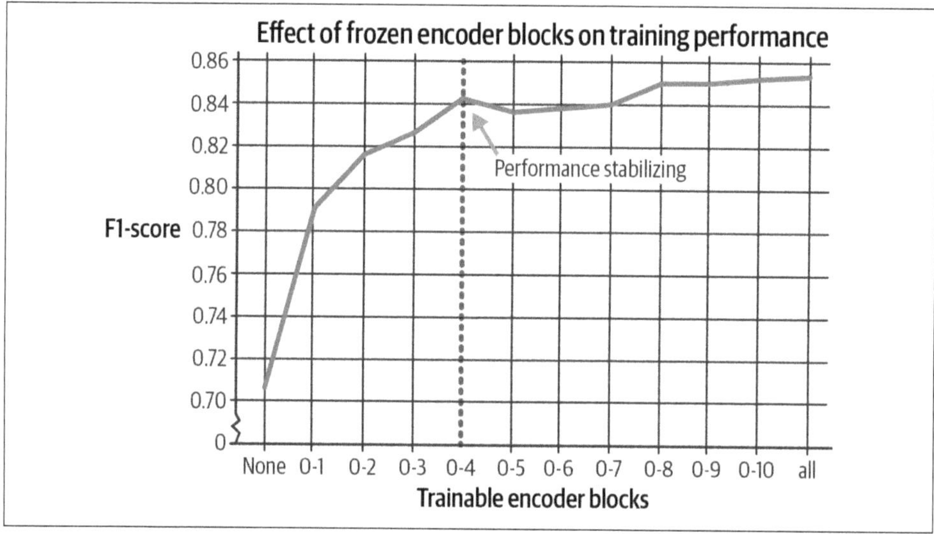

Figure 11-7. The effect of freezing certain encoder blocks on the performance of the model. Training more blocks leads to improved performance but stabilizes early on.

When you are training for multiple epochs, the difference (in training time and resources) between freezing and not freezing often becomes larger. It is therefore advised to play around with a balance that works for you.

Few-Shot Classification

Few-shot classification is a technique within supervised classification where you have a classifier learn target labels based on only a few labeled examples. This technique is great when you have a classification task but do not have many labeled data points readily available. In other words, this method allows you to label a few high-quality data points per class on which to train the model. This idea of using a few labeled data points for training your model is shown in Figure 11-8.

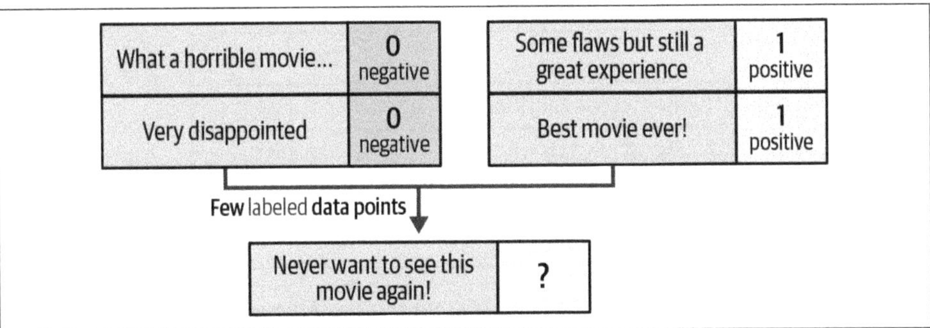

Figure 11-8. In few-shot classification, we only use a few labeled data points to learn from.

SetFit: Efficient Fine-Tuning with Few Training Examples

To perform few-shot text classification, we use an efficient framework called SetFit (*https://oreil.ly/w8eTO*).[2] It is built on top of the architecture of `sentence-transformers` (*https://oreil.ly/lWXtr*) to generate high-quality textual representations that are updated during training. Only a few labeled examples are needed for this framework to be competitive with fine-tuning a BERT-like model on a large, labeled dataset as we explored in the previous example.

The underlying algorithm of SetFit consists of three steps:

1. *Sampling training data*
   Based on in-class and out-class selection of labeled data it generates positive (similar) and negative (dissimilar) pairs of sentences

2 Lewis Tunstall et al. "Efficient few-shot learning without prompts." *arXiv preprint arXiv:2209.11055* (2022).

2. *Fine-tuning embeddings*
   Fine-tuning a pretrained embedding model based on the previously generated training data

3. *Training a classifier*
   Create a classification head on top of the embedding model and train it using the previously generated training data

Before fine-tuning an embedding model, we need to generate training data. The model assumes the training data to be samples of positive (similar) and negative (dissimilar) pairs of sentences. However, when we are dealing with a classification task, our input data is generally not labeled as such.

Say, for example, we have the training dataset in Figure 11-9 that classifies text into two categories: text about programming languages, and text about pets.

Text	Class
I write my code in Python	Programming languages
I should practice SQL	Programming languages
My dog is a labrador	Pets
I have a Siamese cat	Pets

Figure 11-9. Data in two classes: text about programming languages and text about pets.

In step 1, SetFit handles this problem by generating the necessary data based on in-class and out-class selection as we illustrate in Figure 11-10. For example, when we have 16 sentences about sports, we can create 16 * (16 – 1) / 2 = *120* pairs that we label as *positive* pairs. We can use this process to generate *negative* pairs by collecting pairs from different classes.

Text 1	Text 2	Pair type
I write my code in Python	I should practice SQL	Positive
My dog is a labrador	I have a Siamese cat	Positive
I write my code in Python	My dog is a labrador	Negative
I have a Siamese cat	I should practice SQL	Negative

Figure 11-10. Step 1: sampling training data. We assume sentences within a class are similar and create positive pairs while sentences in different classes become negative pairs.

In step 2, we can use the generated sentence pairs to fine-tune the embedding model. This leverages a method called contrastive learning to fine-tune a pretrained BERT model. As we reviewed in Chapter 10, contrastive learning allows accurate sentence embeddings to be learned from pairs of similar (positive) and dissimilar (negative) sentences.

Since we generated these pairs in the previous step, we can use them to fine-tune a `SentenceTransformers` model. Although we have discussed contrastive learning before, we again illustrate the method in Figure 11-11 as a refresher.

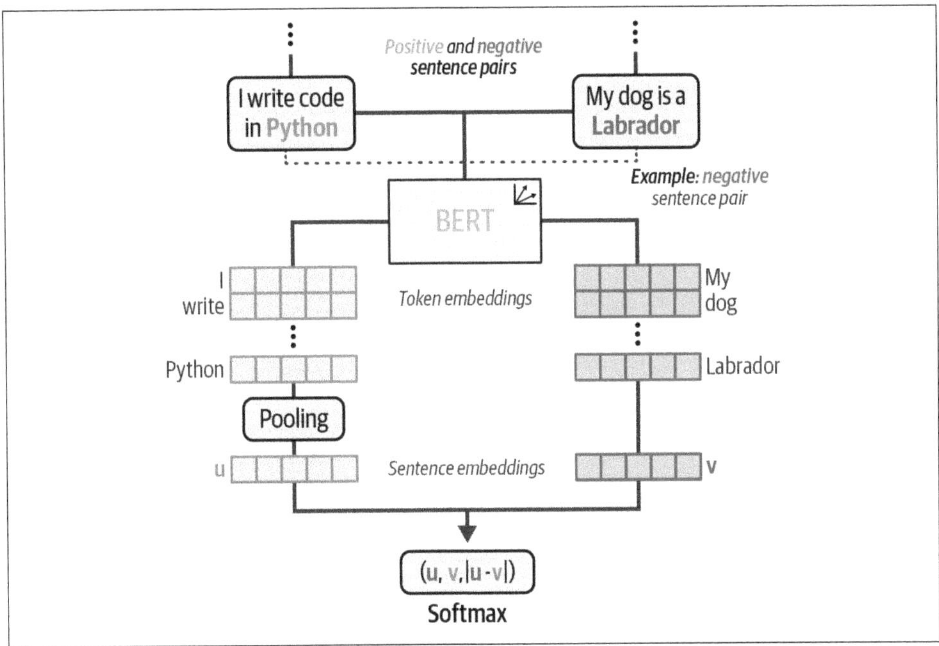

Figure 11-11. Step 2: Fine-tuning a `SentenceTransformers` model. Using contrastive learning, embeddings are learned from positive and negative sentence pairs.

The goal of fine-tuning this embedding model is that it can create embeddings that are tuned to the classification task. The relevance of the classes, and their relative meaning, are distilled into the embeddings through fine-tuning the embedding model.

In step 3, we generate embeddings for all sentences and use those as the input of a classifier. We can use the fine-tuned `SentenceTransformers` model to convert our sentences into embeddings that we can use as features. The classifier learns from our fine-tuned embeddings to accurately predict unseen sentences. This last step is illustrated in Figure 11-12.

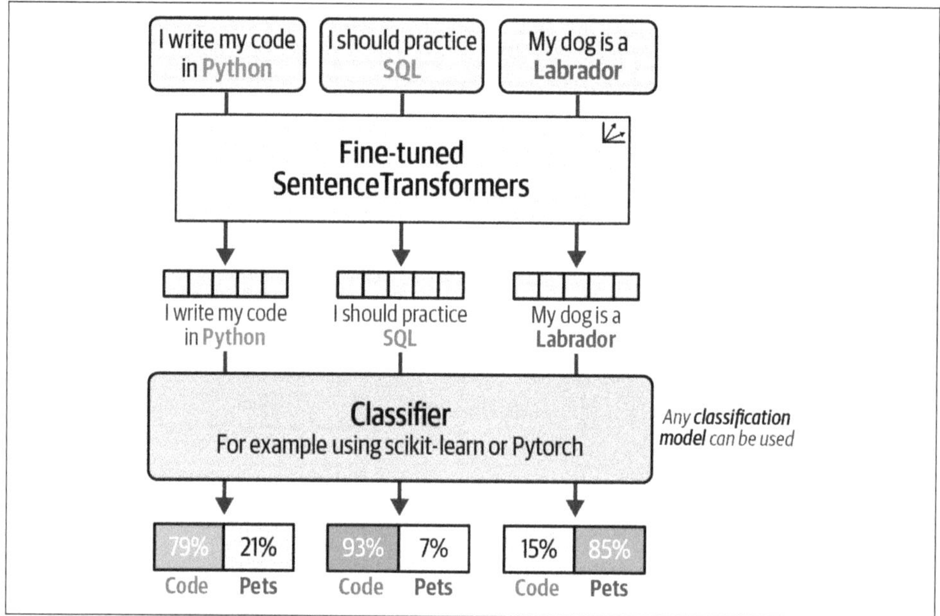

Figure 11-12. Step 3: Training a classifier. The classifier can be any scikit-learn model or a classification head.

When we put all the steps together, we get an efficient and elegant pipeline for performing classification when you only have a few labels per class. It cleverly makes use of the idea that we have labeled data, although not in the way that we would like it. The three steps together are illustrated in Figure 11-13 to give a single overview of the entire procedure.

First, sentence pairs are generated based on in-class and out-class selection. Second, the sentence pairs are used to fine-tune a pretrained `SentenceTransformer` model. Third, the sentences are embedded with the fine-tuned model on which a classifier is trained to predict the classes.

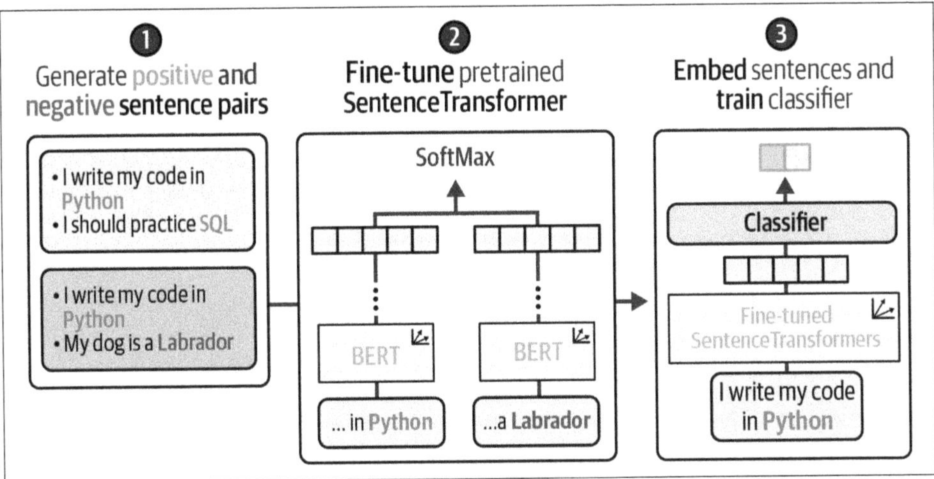

Figure 11-13. The three main steps of SetFit.

Fine-Tuning for Few-Shot Classification

We previously trained on a dataset containing roughly 8,500 movie reviews. However, since this is a few-shot setting, we will only sample 16 examples per class. With two classes, we will only have 32 documents to train on compared to the 8,500 movie reviews we used before!

```
from setfit import sample_dataset

# We simulate a few-shot setting by sampling 16 examples per class
sampled_train_data = sample_dataset(tomatoes["train"], num_samples=16)
```

After sampling the data, we choose a pretrained `SentenceTransformer` model to fine-tune. The official documentation contains an overview of pretrained `SentenceTransformer` models (*https://oreil.ly/g-4SN*) from which we are going to be using `"sentence-transformers/all-mpnet-base-v2"`. It is one of the best-performing models on the MTEB leaderboard (*https://oreil.ly/3DWQW*), which shows the performance of embedding models across a variety of tasks:

```
from setfit import SetFitModel

# Load a pretrained SentenceTransformer model
model = SetFitModel.from_pretrained("sentence-transformers/all-mpnet-base-v2")
```

After loading in the pretrained `SentenceTransformer` model, we can start defining our `SetFitTrainer`. By default, a logistic regression model is chosen as the classifier to train.

Similar to what we did with Hugging Face Transformers, we can use the trainer to define and play around with relevant parameters. For example, we set the `num_epochs` to 3 so that contrastive learning will be performed for three epochs:

```
from setfit import TrainingArguments as SetFitTrainingArguments
from setfit import Trainer as SetFitTrainer

# Define training arguments
args = SetFitTrainingArguments(
    num_epochs=3, # The number of epochs to use for contrastive learning
    num_iterations=20  # The number of text pairs to generate
)
args.eval_strategy = args.evaluation_strategy

# Create trainer
trainer = SetFitTrainer(
    model=model,
    args=args,
    train_dataset=sampled_train_data,
    eval_dataset=test_data,
    metric="f1"
)
```

We only need to call `train` to start the training loop. When we do, we should get the following output:

```
# Training loop
trainer.train()
```

```
***** Running training *****
  Num unique pairs = 1280
  Batch size = 16
  Num epochs = 3
  Total optimization steps = 240
```

Notice that the output mentions that 1,280 sentence pairs were generated for fine-tuning the `SentenceTransformer` model. As a default, 20 sentence pair combinations are generated for each sample in our data, which would be 20 * 32 = 680 samples. We will have to multiply this value by 2 for each positive and negative pair generated, 680 * 2 = 1,280 sentence pairs. Generating 1,280 sentence pairs is quite impressive considering we only had 32 labeled sentences to start with!

When we do not specifically define a classification head, by default a logistic regression is used. If we would like to specify a classification head ourselves, we can do so by specifying the following model in `SetFitTrainer`:

```
# Load a SetFit model from Hub
model = SetFitModel.from_pretrained(
    "sentence-transformers/all-mpnet-base-v2",
    use_differentiable_head=True,
    head_params={"out_features": num_classes},
)

# Create trainer
trainer = SetFitTrainer(
    model=model,
    ...
)
```

Here, `num_classes` refers to the number of classes that we want to predict.

Next, let's evaluate the model to get a feeling of its performance:

```
# Evaluate the model on our test data
trainer.evaluate()
```

```
{'f1': 0.8363988383349468}
```

With only 32 labeled documents, we get an F1 score of 0.85. Considering that the model was trained on a tiny subset of the original data, this is very impressive! Moreover, in Chapter 2, we got the same performance but instead trained a logistic regression model on the embeddings of the full data. Thus, this pipeline demonstrates the potential of taking the time to label just a few instances.

Not only can SetFit perform few-shot classification tasks, but it also has support for when you have no labels at all, also called zero-shot classification. SetFit generates synthetic examples from the label names to resemble the classification task and then trains a SetFit model on them. For example, if the target labels are "happy" and "sad," then synthetic data could be "The example is happy" and "This example is sad."

Continued Pretraining with Masked Language Modeling

In the examples thus far, we leveraged a pretrained model and fine-tuned it to perform classification. This process describes a two-step process: first pretraining a model (which was already done for us) and then fine-tuning it for a particular task. We illustrate this process in Figure 11-14.

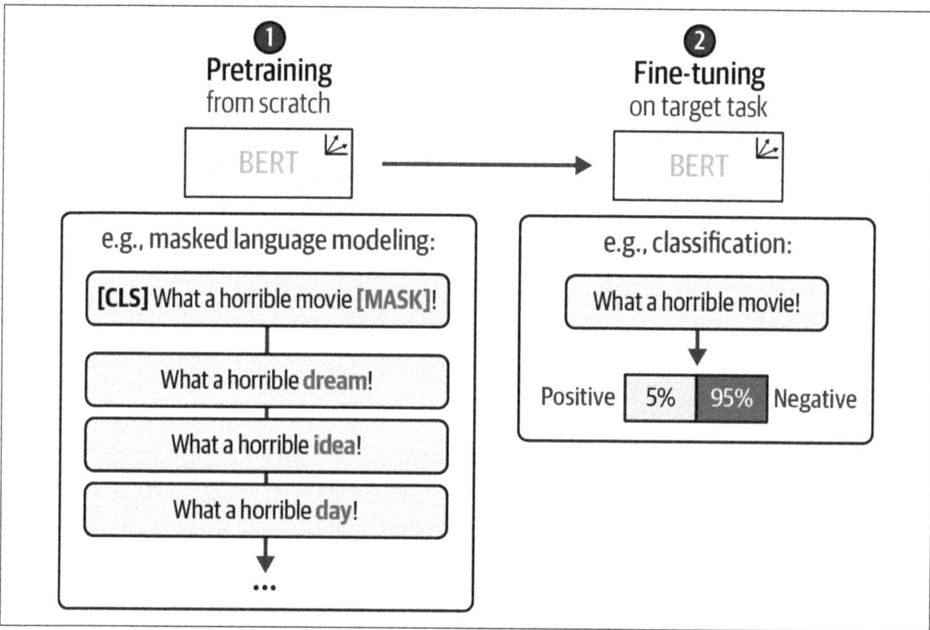

Figure 11-14. To fine-tune the model on a target task—for example, classification—we either start with pretraining a BERT model or use a pretrained one.

This two-step approach is typically used throughout many applications. It has its limitations when faced with domain-specific data. The pretrained model is often trained on very general data, like Wikipedia pages, and might not be tuned to your domain-specific words.

Instead of adopting this two-step approach, we can squeeze another step between them, namely continue pretraining an already pretrained BERT model. In other words, we can simply continue training the BERT model using masked language modeling (MLM) but instead use data from our domain. It is like going from a general BERT model to a BioBERT model specialized for the medical domain, to a fine-tuned BioBERT model to classify medication.

This will update the subword representations to be more tuned toward words it would not have seen before. This process is illustrated in Figure 11-15 and demonstrates how this additional step updates a masked language modeling task. Continuing pretraining on a pretrained BERT model has been shown to improve the performance of models in classification tasks and is a worthwhile addition to the fine-tuning pipeline.[3]

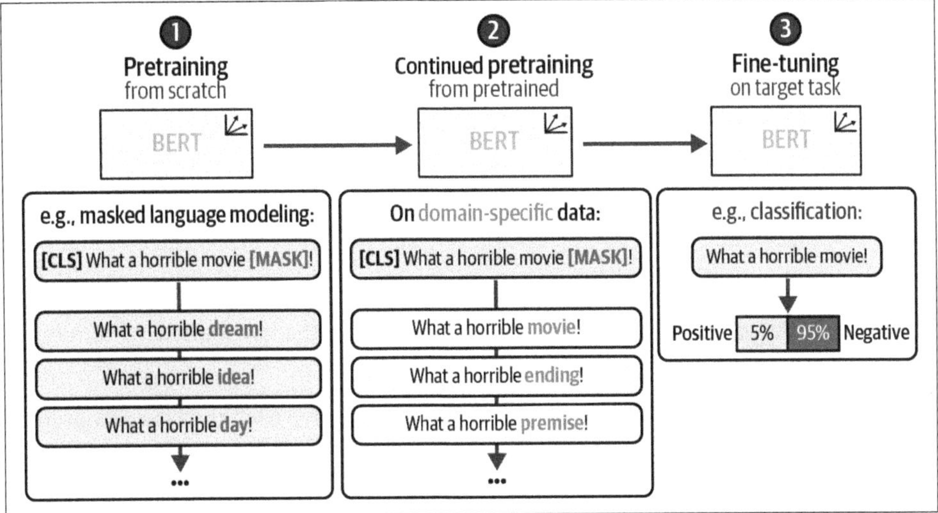

Figure 11-15. Instead of a two-step approach, we can add another step that continues to pretrain the pretrained model before fine-tuning it on the target task. Notice how the masks were filled with abstract concepts in 1 while they were filled with movie-specific concepts in 2.

Instead of having to pretrain an entire model from scratch, we can simply continue pretraining before fine-tuning it for classification. This also helps the model to adapt to a certain domain or even the lingo of a specific organization. The genealogy of models a company might want to adopt is further illustrated in Figure 11-16.

3 Chi Sun et al. "How to fine-tune GERT for text classification?" *Chinese Computational Linguistics: 18th China National Conference*, CCL 2019, Kunming, China, October 18–20, 2019, proceedings 18. Springer International Publishing, 2019.

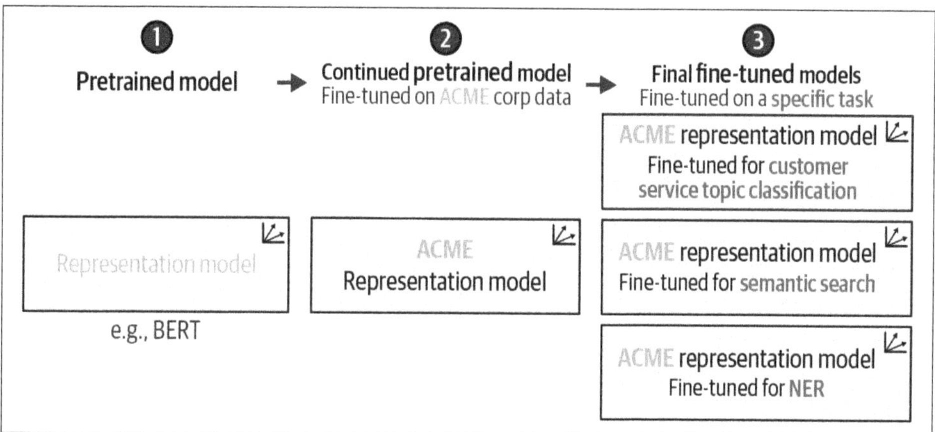

Figure 11-16. The three-step approach illustrated for specific use cases.

In this example, we will demonstrate how to apply step 2 and continue pretraining an already pretrained BERT model. We use the same data that we started with, namely the Rotten Tomatoes reviews.

We start by loading the `"bert-base-cased"` model we have used thus far and prepare it for MLM:

```
from transformers import AutoTokenizer, AutoModelForMaskedLM

# Load model for masked language modeling (MLM)
model = AutoModelForMaskedLM.from_pretrained("bert-base-cased")
tokenizer = AutoTokenizer.from_pretrained("bert-base-cased")
```

We need to tokenize the raw sentences. We will also remove the labels since this is not a supervised task:

```
def preprocess_function(examples):
   return tokenizer(examples["text"], truncation=True)

# Tokenize data
tokenized_train = train_data.map(preprocess_function, batched=True)
tokenized_train = tokenized_train.remove_columns("label")
tokenized_test = test_data.map(preprocess_function, batched=True)
tokenized_test = tokenized_test.remove_columns("label")
```

Previously, we used `DataCollatorWithPadding`, which dynamically pads the input it receives.

Instead, we will have a `DataCollator` that will perform the masking of tokens for us. There are two methods that are generally used for this: token and whole-word masking. With token masking, we randomly mask 15% of the tokens in a sentence. It might happen that part of a word will be masked. To enable masking of the entire word, we could apply whole-word masking, as illustrated in Figure 11-17.

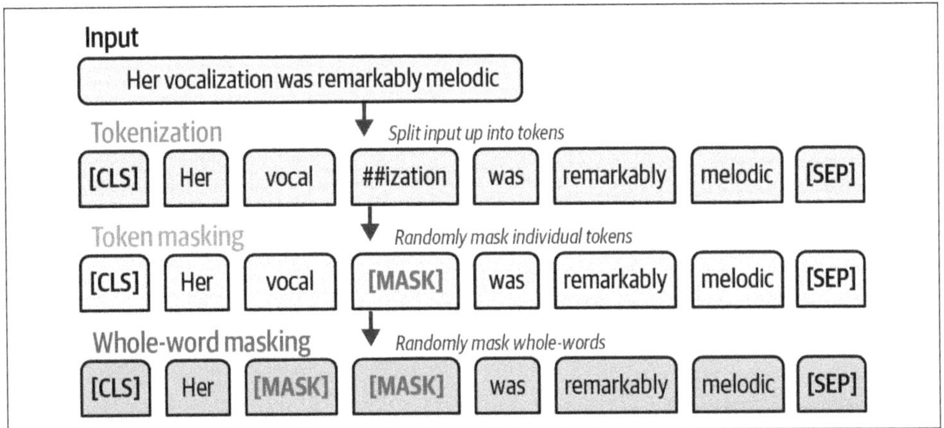

Figure 11-17. Different methods for randomly masking tokens.

Generally, predicting whole words tends to be more complicated than tokens, which makes the model perform better as it needs to learn more accurate and precise representations during training. However, it tends to take a bit more time to converge. We will be going with token masking in this example using `DataCollatorForLanguageModeling` for faster convergence. However, we can use whole-word masking by replacing `DataCollatorForLanguageModeling` with `DataCollatorForWholeWordMask`. Lastly, we set the probability that a token is masked in a given sentence to 15% (`mlm_probability`):

```
from transformers import DataCollatorForLanguageModeling

# Masking Tokens
data_collator = DataCollatorForLanguageModeling(
    tokenizer=tokenizer,
    mlm=True,
    mlm_probability=0.15
)
```

Next, we will create the `Trainer` for running the MLM task and specify certain parameters:

```
# Training arguments for parameter tuning
training_args = TrainingArguments(
   "model",
   learning_rate=2e-5,
   per_device_train_batch_size=16,
   per_device_eval_batch_size=16,
   num_train_epochs=10,
   weight_decay=0.01,
   save_strategy="epoch",
   report_to="none"
)
```

```
# Initialize Trainer
trainer = Trainer(
    model=model,
    args=training_args,
    train_dataset=tokenized_train,
    eval_dataset=tokenized_test,
    tokenizer=tokenizer,
    data_collator=data_collator
)
```

Several parameters are worth noting. We train for 20 epochs and keep the task short. You can experiment with the learning rate and weight decay to ascertain whether they assist in fine-tuning the model.

Before we start our training loop we will first save our pretrained tokenizer. The tokenizer is not updated during training so there is no need to save it after training. We will, however, save our model after we continue pretraining:

```
# Save pre-trained tokenizer
tokenizer.save_pretrained("mlm")

# Train model
trainer.train()

# Save updated model
model.save_pretrained("mlm")
```

This gives us an updated model in the *mlm* folder. To evaluate its performance we would normally fine-tune the model on a variety of tasks. For our purposes, however, we can run some masking tasks to see if it has learned from its continued training.

We will do so by loading in our pretrained model before we continue pretraining. Using the sentence "`What a horrible [MASK]!`" the model will predict which word would be in place of "`[MASK]`":

```
from transformers import pipeline

# Load and create predictions
mask_filler = pipeline("fill-mask", model="bert-base-cased")
preds = mask_filler("What a horrible [MASK]!")

# Print results
for pred in preds:
    print(f">>> {pred["sequence"]}")
```

```
>>> What a horrible idea!
>>> What a horrible dream!
>>> What a horrible thing!
>>> What a horrible day!
>>> What a horrible thought!
```

The output demonstrates concepts like "idea," "dream," and "day," which definitely make sense. Next, let's see what our updated model predicts:

```
# Load and create predictions
mask_filler = pipeline("fill-mask", model="mlm")
preds = mask_filler("What a horrible [MASK]!")

# Print results
for pred in preds:
    print(f">>> {pred["sequence"]}")
```

```
>>> What a horrible movie!
>>> What a horrible film!
>>> What a horrible mess!
>>> What a horrible comedy!
>>> What a horrible story!
```

A horrible movie, film, mess, etc. clearly shows us that the model is more biased toward the data that we fed it compared to the pretrained model.

The next step would be to fine-tune this model on the classification task that we did at the beginning of this chapter. Simply load the model as follows and you are good to go:

```
from transformers import AutoModelForSequenceClassification

# Fine-tune for classification
model = AutoModelForSequenceClassification.from_pretrained("mlm", num_labels=2)
tokenizer = AutoTokenizer.from_pretrained("mlm")
```

Named-Entity Recognition

In this section, we will delve into the process of fine-tuning a pretrained BERT model specifically for NER (named-entity recognition). Instead of classifying entire documents, this procedure allows for the classification of individual tokens and/or words, including people and locations. This is especially helpful for de-identification and anonymization tasks when there is sensitive data.

NER shares similarities with the classification example we explored at the beginning of this chapter. Nevertheless, a key distinction lies in the preprocessing and classification of data. Given that we are focusing on classifying individual words instead of entire documents, we must preprocess the data to consider this granular structure. Figure 11-18 provides a visual representation of this word-level approach.

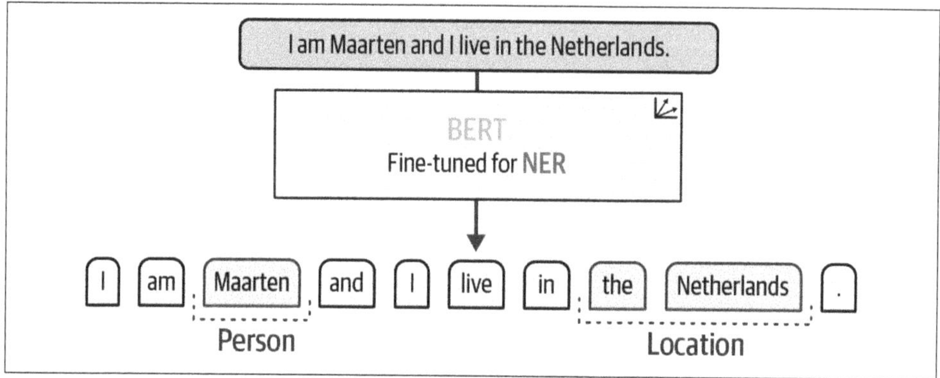

Figure 11-18. Fine-tuning a BERT model for NER allows for the detection of named entities, such as people or locations.

Fine-tuning the pretrained BERT model follows a similar architecture akin to what we observed with document classification. However, there is a fundamental shift in the classification approach. Rather than relying on the aggregation or pooling of token embeddings, the model now makes predictions for individual tokens in a sequence. It is crucial to emphasize that our word-level classification task does not entail classifying entire words, but rather the tokens that collectively constitute those words. Figure 11-19 provides a visual representation of this token-level classification.

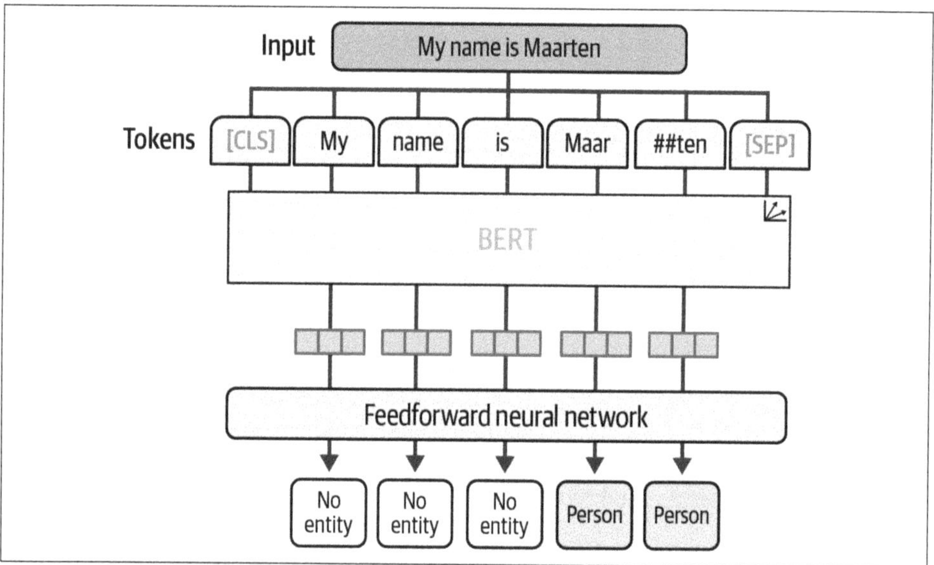

Figure 11-19. During the fine-tuning process of a BERT model, individual tokens are classified instead of words or entire documents.

Preparing Data for Named-Entity Recognition

In this example, we will use the English version of the CoNLL-2003 dataset, which contains several different types of named entities (person, organization, location, miscellaneous, and no entity) and has roughly 14,000 training samples.[4]

```
# The CoNLL-2003 dataset for NER
dataset = load_dataset("conll2003", trust_remote_code=True)
```

While researching datasets to use for this example, there were a few more that we wanted to share. `wnut_17` is a task that focuses on emerging and rare entities, those that are more difficult to spot. Furthermore, the `tner/mit_movie_trivia` and `tner/mit_restaurant` datasets are quite fun to use. `tner/mit_movie_trivia` is for detecting entities like actor, plot, and soundtrack whereas `tner/mit_restaurant` aims to detect entities such as amenity, dish, and cuisine.[5]

Let's inspect the structure of the data with an example:

```
example = dataset["train"][848]
example
```

```
{'id': '848',
 'tokens': ['Dean',
  'Palmer',
  'hit',
  'his',
  '30th',
  'homer',
  'for',
  'the',
  'Rangers',
  '.'],
 'pos_tags': [22, 22, 38, 29, 16, 21, 15, 12, 23, 7],
 'chunk_tags': [11, 12, 21, 11, 12, 12, 13, 11, 12, 0],
 'ner_tags': [1, 2, 0, 0, 0, 0, 0, 0, 3, 0]}
```

This dataset provides us with labels for each word given in a sentence. These labels can be found in the `ner_tags` key, which refers to the following possible entities:

4 Erik F. Sang and Fien De Meulder. "Introduction to the CoNLL-2003 shared task: Language-independent named entity recognition." *arXiv preprint cs/0306050* (2003).

5 Jingjing Liu et al. "Asgard: A portable architecture for multilingual dialogue systems." *2013 IEEE International Conference on Acoustics, Speech and Signal Processing*. IEEE, 2013.

```
label2id = {
    "O": 0, "B-PER": 1, "I-PER": 2, "B-ORG": 3, "I-ORG": 4,
    "B-LOC": 5, "I-LOC": 6, "B-MISC": 7, "I-MISC": 8
}
id2label = {index: label for label, index in label2id.items()}
label2id
```

```
{'O': 0,
 'B-PER': 1,
 'I-PER': 2,
 'B-ORG': 3,
 'I-ORG': 4,
 'B-LOC': 5,
 'I-LOC': 6,
 'B-MISC': 7,
 'I-MISC': 8}
```

These entities correspond to specific categories: a person (PER), organization (ORG), location (LOC), miscellaneous entities (MISC), and no entity (O). Note that these entities are prefixed with either a B (beginning) or an I (inside). If two tokens that follow each other are part of the same phrase, then the start of that phrase is indicated with B, which is followed by an I to show that they belong to each other and are not independent entities.

This process is further illustrated in Figure 11-20. In the figure, since "Dean" is the start of the phrase and "Palmer" is the end, we know that "Dean Palmer" is a person and that "Dean" and "Palmer" are not individual people.

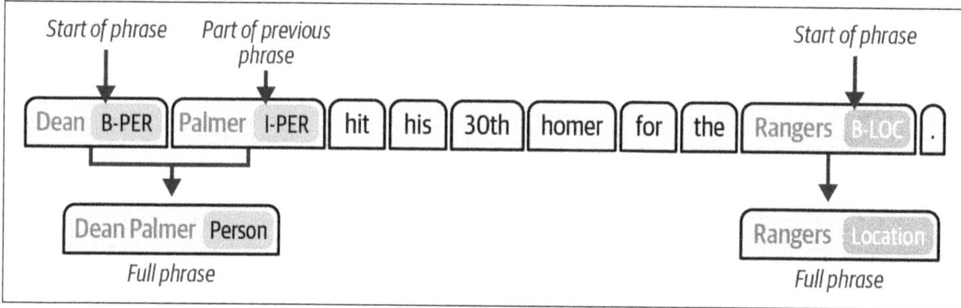

Figure 11-20. By indicating the start and end of the phrase with the same entity, we can recognize entities of entire phrases.

Our data is preprocessed and split up into words but not yet tokens. To do so, we will tokenize it further with the tokenizer of the pretrained model we used throughout this chapter, namely `bert-base-cased`:

```
from transformers import AutoModelForTokenClassification

# Load tokenizer
tokenizer = AutoTokenizer.from_pretrained("bert-base-cased")

# Load model
model = AutoModelForTokenClassification.from_pretrained(
    "bert-base-cased",
    num_labels=len(id2label),
    id2label=id2label,
    label2id=label2id
)
```

Let's explore how the tokenizer would process our example:

```
# Split individual tokens into sub-tokens
token_ids = tokenizer(example["tokens"], is_split_into_words=True)["input_ids"]
sub_tokens = tokenizer.convert_ids_to_tokens(token_ids)
sub_tokens
```

```
['[CLS]',
 'Dean',
 'Palmer',
 'hit',
 'his',
 '30th',
 'home',
 '##r',
 'for',
 'the',
 'Rangers',
 '.',
 '[SEP]']
```

The tokenizer added the `[CLS]` and `[SEP]` tokens as we learned in Chapters 2 and 3. Note that the word `'homer'` was further split up into the tokens `'home'` and `'##r'`. This creates a bit of a problem for us since we have labeled data at the word level but not at the token level. This can be resolved by aligning the labels with their subtoken counterparts during tokenization.

Let's consider the word `'Maarten'`, which has the label B-PER to signal that this is a person. If we pass that word through the tokenizer, it splits the word up into the tokens `'Ma'`, `'##arte'`, and `'##n'`. We cannot use the B-PER entity for all tokens as that would signal that the three tokens are all independent people. Whenever an entity is split into tokens, the first token should have B (for beginning) and the following should be I (for inner).

Therefore, `'Ma'` will get the B-PER to signal the start of a phrase, and `'##arte'`, and `'##n'` will get the I-PER to signal they belong to a phrase. This alignment process is illustrated in Figure 11-21.

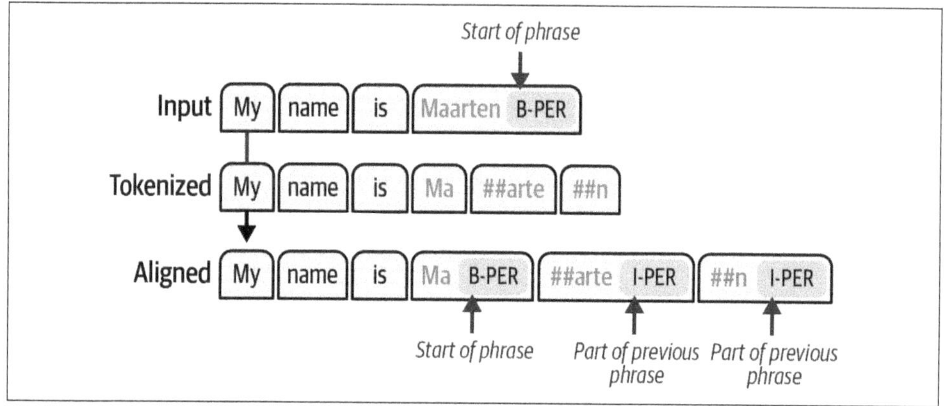

Figure 11-21. The alignment process of labeling tokenized input.

We create a function, `align_labels`, that will tokenize the input and align these tokens with their updated labels during tokenization:

```
def align_labels(examples):
    token_ids = tokenizer(
        examples["tokens"],
        truncation=True,
        is_split_into_words=True
    )
    labels = examples["ner_tags"]

    updated_labels = []
    for index, label in enumerate(labels):

        # Map tokens to their respective word
        word_ids = token_ids.word_ids(batch_index=index)
        previous_word_idx = None
        label_ids = []
        for word_idx in word_ids:

            # The start of a new word
            if word_idx != previous_word_idx:

                previous_word_idx = word_idx
                updated_label = -100 if word_idx is None else label[word_idx]
                label_ids.append(updated_label)

            # Special token is -100
            elif word_idx is None:
                label_ids.append(-100)

            # If the label is B-XXX we change it to I-XXX
            else:
                updated_label = label[word_idx]
                if updated_label % 2 == 1:
```

```
                updated_label += 1
            label_ids.append(updated_label)

        updated_labels.append(label_ids)

    token_ids["labels"] = updated_labels
    return token_ids

tokenized = dataset.map(align_labels, batched=True)
```

Looking at our example, note that additional labels (`-100`) were added for the `[CLS]` and `[SEP]` tokens:

```
# Difference between original and updated labels
print(f"Original: {example["ner_tags"]}")
print(f"Updated: {tokenized["train"][848]["labels"]}")
```

```
Original: [1, 2, 0, 0, 0, 0, 0, 0, 3, 0]
Updated: [-100, 1, 2, 0, 0, 0, 0, 0, 0, 0, 3, 0, -100]
```

Now that we have tokenized and aligned the labels, we can start thinking about defining our evaluation metrics. This is also different from what we have seen before. Instead of a single prediction per document, we now have multiple predictions per document, namely per token.

We will make use of the `evaluate` package by Hugging Face to create a `compute_metrics` function that allows us to evaluate performance on a token level:

```
import evaluate

# Load sequential evaluation
seqeval = evaluate.load("seqeval")

def compute_metrics(eval_pred):
    # Create predictions
    logits, labels = eval_pred
    predictions = np.argmax(logits, axis=2)

    true_predictions = []
    true_labels = []

    # Document-level iteration
    for prediction, label in zip(predictions, labels):

      # Token-level iteration
      for token_prediction, token_label in zip(prediction, label):

        # We ignore special tokens
        if token_label != -100:
          true_predictions.append([id2label[token_prediction]])
          true_labels.append([id2label[token_label]])
```

```
        results = seqeval.compute(
        predictions=true_predictions, references=true_labels
    )
        return {"f1": results["overall_f1"]}
```

Fine-Tuning for Named-Entity Recognition

We are nearly there. Instead of `DataCollatorWithPadding`, we need a collator that works with classification on a token level, namely `DataCollatorForTokenClassification`:

```
from transformers import DataCollatorForTokenClassification

# Token-classification DataCollator
data_collator = DataCollatorForTokenClassification(tokenizer=tokenizer)
```

Now that we have loaded our model, the rest of the steps are similar to previous training procedures in this chapter. We define a trainer with specific arguments that we can tune and create a `Trainer`:

```
# Training arguments for parameter tuning
training_args = TrainingArguments(
   "model",
   learning_rate=2e-5,
   per_device_train_batch_size=16,
   per_device_eval_batch_size=16,
   num_train_epochs=1,
   weight_decay=0.01,
   save_strategy="epoch",
   report_to="none"
)

# Initialize Trainer
trainer = Trainer(
    model=model,
    args=training_args,
    train_dataset=tokenized["train"],
    eval_dataset=tokenized["test"],
    tokenizer=tokenizer,
    data_collator=data_collator,
    compute_metrics=compute_metrics,
)
trainer.train()
```

We then evaluate the model that we created:

```
# Evaluate the model on our test data
trainer.evaluate()
```

Lastly, let's save the model and use it in a pipeline for inference. This allows us to check certain data so we can manually inspect what happens during inference and if we are satisfied with the output:

```python
from transformers import pipeline

# Save our fine-tuned model
trainer.save_model("ner_model")

# Run inference on the fine-tuned model
token_classifier = pipeline(
    "token-classification",
    model="ner_model",
)
token_classifier("My name is Maarten.")
```

```
[{'entity': 'B-PER',
  'score': 0.99534035,
  'index': 4,
  'word': 'Ma',
  'start': 11,
  'end': 13},
 {'entity': 'I-PER',
  'score': 0.9928328,
  'index': 5,
  'word': '##arte',
  'start': 13,
  'end': 17},
 {'entity': 'I-PER',
  'score': 0.9954301,
  'index': 6,
  'word': '##n',
  'start': 17,
  'end': 18}]
```

In the sentence "`My name is Maarten`", the word "`Maarten`" and its subtokens were correctly identified as a person!

Summary

In this chapter, we explored several tasks for fine-tuning pretrained representation models on specific classification tasks. We started by demonstrating how to fine-tune a pretrained BERT model and extended the examples by freezing certain layers of its architectures.

We experimented with a few-shot classification technique called SetFit, which involves fine-tuning a pretrained embedding model together with a classification head using limited labeled data. Using only a few labeled data points, this model generated similar performance to the models we explored in earlier chapters.

Next, we delved into the concept of continued pretraining, where we used a pretrained BERT model as a starting point and continued training it using different data. The underlying process, masked language modeling, is not only used for creating a representation model but can also be used to continue pretraining models.

Finally, we looked at named-entity recognition, a task that involves identifying specific entities such as people and places in unstructured text. Compared to previous examples, this classification was done on a word level rather than on a document level.

In the next chapter, we continue with the field of fine-tuning language models but focus on generative models instead. Using a two-step process, we will explore how to fine-tune a generative model to properly follow instructions and then fine-tune it for human preference.

CHAPTER 12

Fine-Tuning Generation Models

In this chapter, we will take a pretrained text generation model and go over the process of *fine-tuning* it. This fine-tuning step is key in producing high-quality models and an important tool in our toolbox to adapt a model to a specific desired behavior. Fine-tuning allows us to adapt a model to a specific dataset or domain.

Throughout this chapter, we will guide you among the two most common methods for fine-tuning text generation models, *supervised fine-tuning* and *preference tuning*. We will explore the transformative potential of fine-tuning pretrained text generation models to make them more effective tools for your application.

The Three LLM Training Steps: Pretraining, Supervised Fine-Tuning, and Preference Tuning

There are three common steps that lead to creating a high-quality LLM:

1. *Language modeling*

   The first step in creating a high-quality LLM is to pretrain it on one or more massive text datasets (Figure 12-1). During training, it attempts to predict the next token to accurately learn linguistic and semantic representations found in the text. As we saw before in Chapters 3 and 11, this is called language modeling and is a self-supervised method.

   This produces a *base* model, also commonly referred to as a *pretrained* or *foundation* model. Base models are a key artifact of the training process but are harder for the end user to deal with. This is why the next step is important.

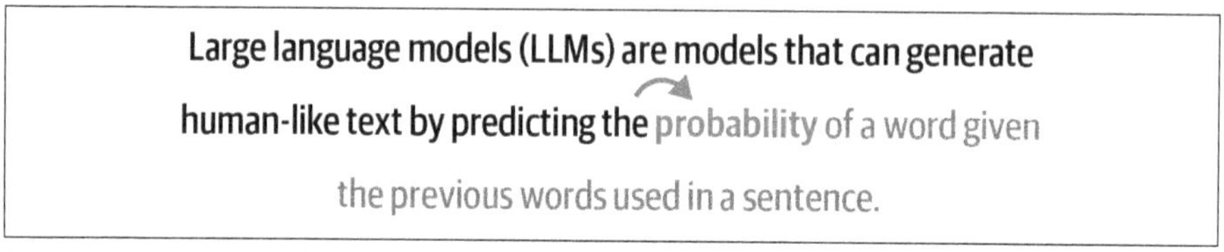

Large language models (LLMs) are models that can generate human-like text by predicting the probability of a word given the previous words used in a sentence.

Figure 12-1. During language modeling, the LLM aims to predict the next token based on an input. This is a process without labels.

2. *Fine-tuning 1 (supervised fine-tuning)*

   LLMs are more useful if they respond well to instructions and try to follow them. When humans ask the model to write an article, they expect the model to generate the article and not list other instructions for example (which is what a base model might do).

   With supervised fine-tuning (SFT), we can adapt the base model to follow instructions. During this fine-tuning process, the parameters of the base model are updated to be more in line with our target task, like following instructions. Like a pretrained model, it is trained using next-token prediction but instead of only predicting the next token, it does so based on a user input (Figure 12-2).

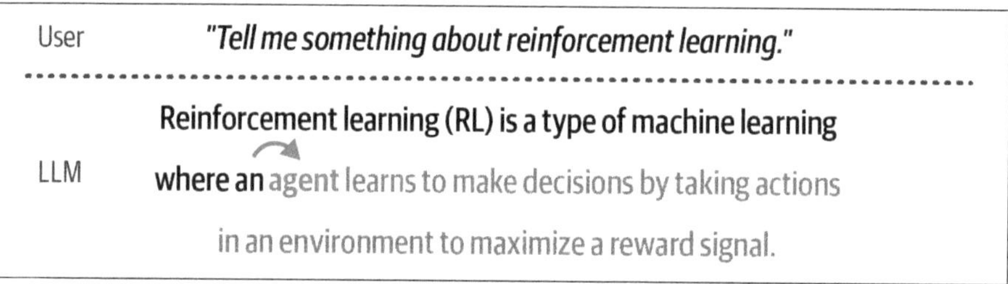

   Figure 12-2. During supervised fine-tuning, the LLM aims to predict the next token based on an input that has additional labels. In a sense, the label is the user's input.

   SFT can also be used for other tasks, like classification, but is often used to go from a base generative model to an instruction (or chat) generative model.

3. *Fine-tuning 2 (preference tuning)*

   The final step further improves the quality of the model and makes it more aligned with the expected behavior of AI safety or human preferences. This is called preference tuning. Preference tuning is a form of fine-tuning and, as the name implies, aligns the output of the model to our preferences, which are defined by the data that we give it. Like SFT, it can improve upon the original model but has the added benefit of distilling preference of output in its training process. These three steps are illustrated in Figure 12-3 and demonstrate the process of starting from an untrained architecture and ending with a preference-tuned LLM.

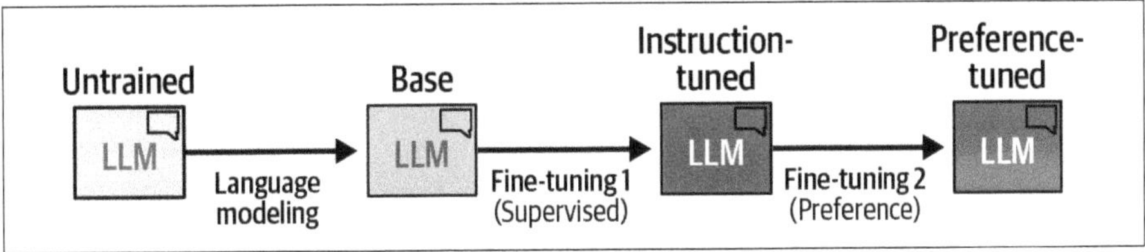

Figure 12-3. The three steps of creating a high-quality LLM.

In this chapter, we use a base model that was already trained on massive datasets and explore how we can fine-tune it using both fine-tuning strategies. For each method, we start with the theoretical underpinnings before using them in practice.

Supervised Fine-Tuning (SFT)

The purpose of pretraining a model on large datasets is that it is able to reproduce language and its meaning. During this process, the model learns to complete input phrases as shown in Figure 12-4.

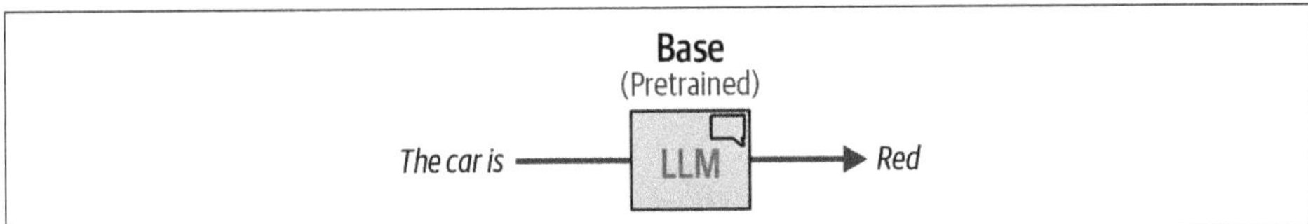

Figure 12-4. A base or pretrained LLM was trained to predict the next word(s).

This example also illustrates that the model was not trained to follow instructions and instead will attempt to complete a question rather than answer it (Figure 12-5).

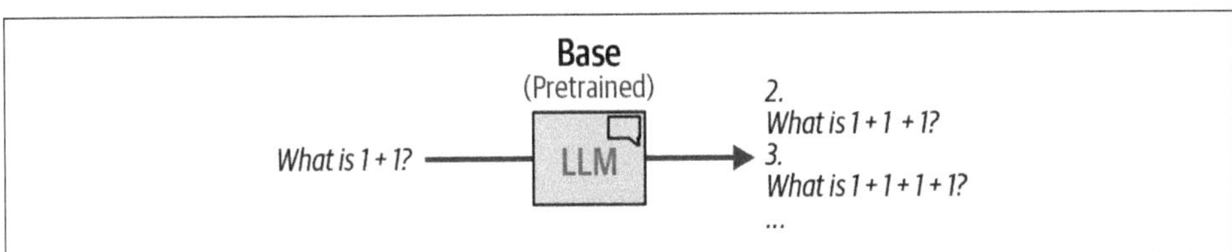

Figure 12-5. A base LLM will not follow instructions but instead attempts to predict each next word. It may even create new questions.

We can use this base model and adapt it to certain use cases, such as following instructions, by fine-tuning it.

Full Fine-Tuning

The most common fine-tuning process is full fine-tuning. Like pretraining an LLM, this process involves updating all parameters of a model to be in line with your target task. The main difference is that we now use a smaller but labeled dataset whereas the pretraining process was done on a large dataset without any labels (Figure 12-6).

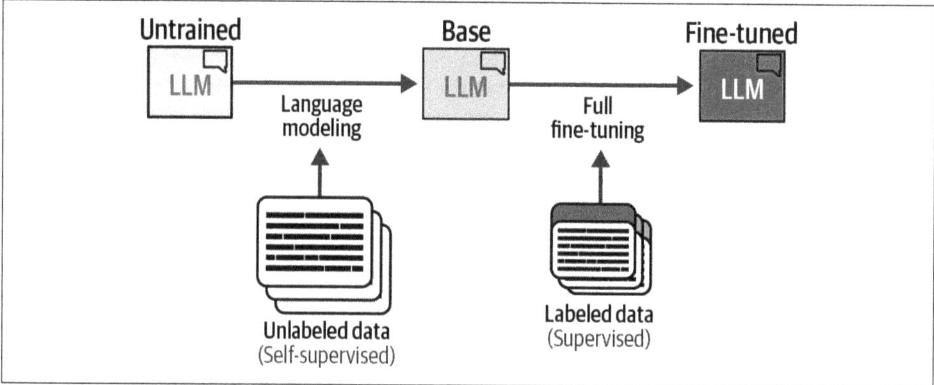

Figure 12-6. Compared to language modeling (pretraining), full fine-tuning uses a smaller but labeled dataset.

You can use any labeled data for full fine-tuning, making it also a great technique for learning domain-specific representations. To make our LLM follow instructions, we will need question-response data. This data, as shown in Figure 12-7, is queries by the user with corresponding answers.

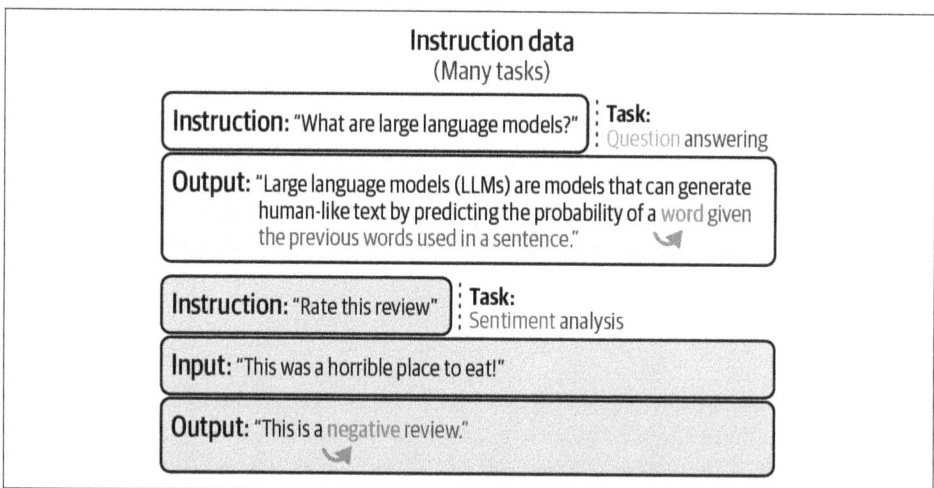

Figure 12-7. Instruction data with instructions by a user and corresponding answers. The instructions can contain many different tasks.

During full fine-tuning, the model takes the input (instructions) and applies next-token prediction on the output (response). In turn, instead of generating new questions, it will follow instructions.

Parameter-Efficient Fine-Tuning (PEFT)

Updating all parameters of a model has a large potential of increasing its performance but comes with several disadvantages. It is costly to train, has slow training times, and requires significant storage. To resolve these issues, attention has been given to parameter-efficient fine-tuning (PEFT) alternatives that focus on fine-tuning pre-trained models at higher computational efficiency.

Adapters

Adapters are a core component of many PEFT-based techniques. The method proposes a set of additional modular components inside the Transformer that can be fine-tuned to improve the model's performance on a specific task without having to fine-tune all the model weights. This saves a lot of time and compute.

Adapters are described in the paper "Parameter-efficient transfer learning for NLP" (*https://oreil.ly/C8IOs*), which showed that fine-tuning 3.6% of the parameters of BERT for a task can yield comparable performance to fine-tuning all the model's weights.[1] On the GLUE benchmark, the authors show they reach within 0.4% of the performance of full fine-tuning. In a single Transformer block, the paper's proposed architecture places adapters after the attention layer and the feedforward neural network as illustrated in Figure 12-8.

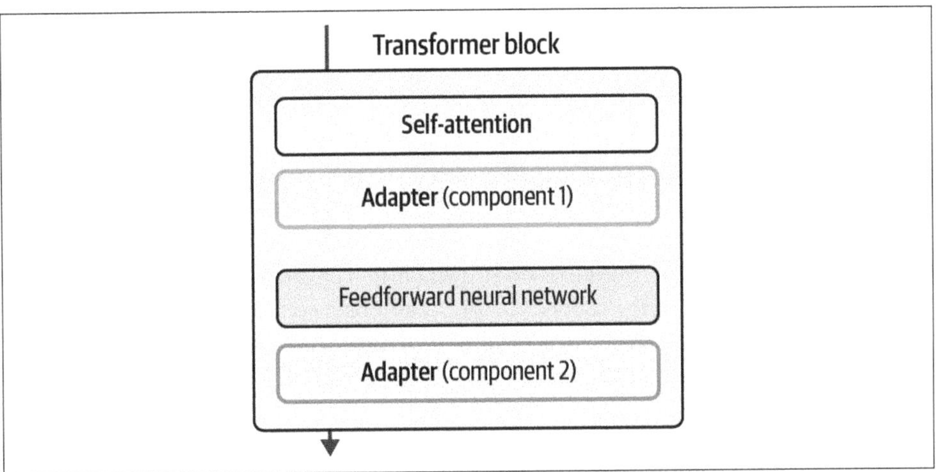

Figure 12-8. Adapters add a small number of weights in certain places in the network that can be fine-tuned efficiently while leaving the majority of model weights frozen.

1 Neil Houlsby et al. "Parameter-efficient transfer learning for NLP." *International Conference on Machine Learning*. PMLR, 2019.

It's not enough to only alter one Transformer block, however, so these components are part of every block in the model, as Figure 12-9 shows.

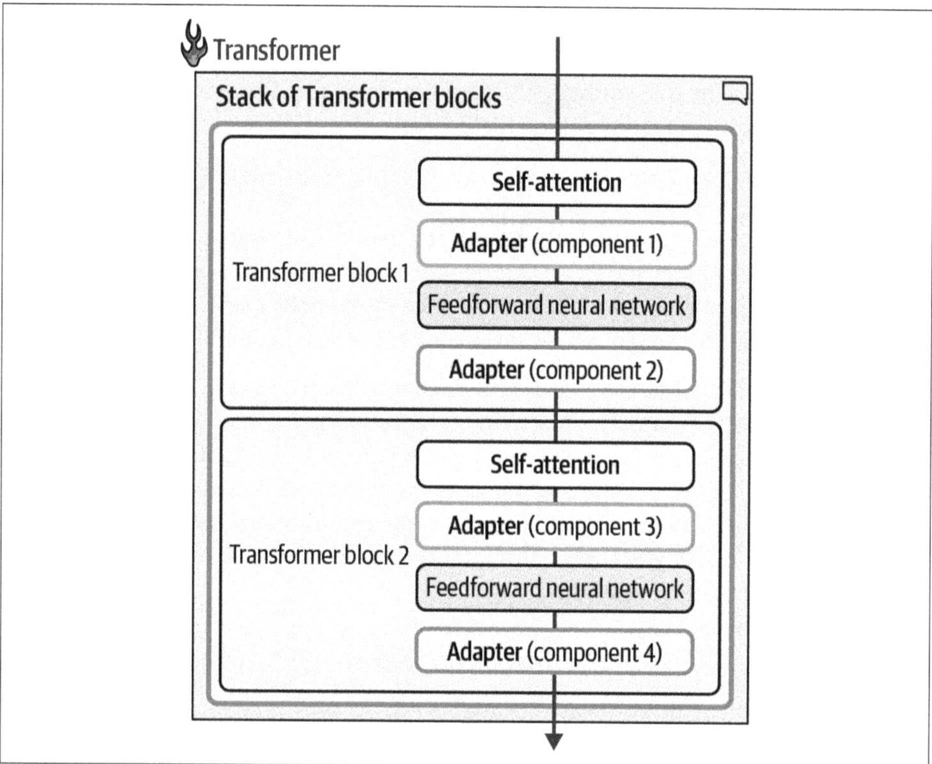

Figure 12-9. Adapter components span the various Transformer blocks in the model.

Seeing all the adapter's components across the model like this enables us to see individual adapters as shown in Figure 12-10, which is a collection of these components spanning all the blocks of the model. Adapter 1 can be a specialist in, say, medical text classification, while Adapter 2 can specialize in named-entity recognition (NER). You can download specialized adapters from *https://oreil.ly/XraXg*.

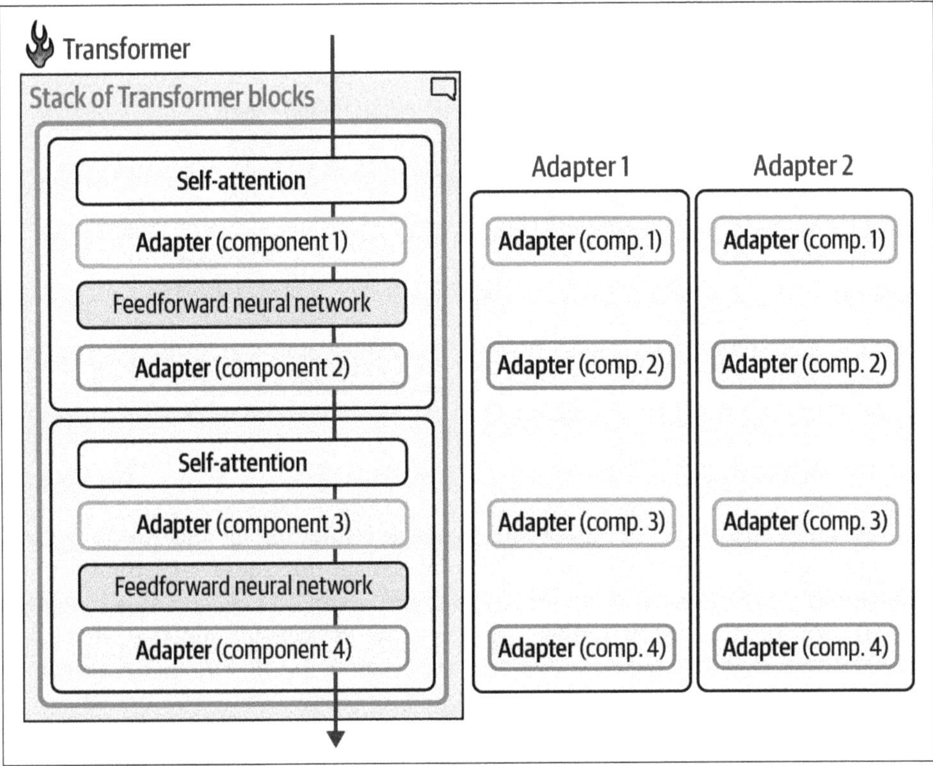

Figure 12-10. Adapters that specialize in specific tasks can be swapped into the same architecture (if they share the same original model architecture and weights).

The paper "AdapterHub: A framework for adapting transformers" (*https://oreil.ly/opyb6*) introduced the Adapter Hub (*https://oreil.ly/XraXg*) as a central repository for sharing adapters.[2] A lot of these earlier adapters were more focused on BERT architectures. More recently, the concept has been applied to text generation Transformers in papers like "LLaMA-Adapter: Efficient fine-tuning of language models with zero-init attention" (*https://oreil.ly/FJk1Q*).[3]

Low-Rank Adaptation (LoRA)

As an alternative to adapters, low-rank adaptation (LoRA) was introduced and is at the time of writing is a widely used and effective technique for PEFT. LoRA is a technique that (like adapters) only requires updating a small set of parameters. As

2 Jonas Pfeiffer et al. "AdapterHub: A framework for adapting transformers." *arXiv preprint arXiv:2007.07779* (2020).

3 Renrui Zhang et al. "Llama-adapter: Efficient fine-tuning of language models with zero-init attention." *arXiv preprint arXiv:2303.16199* (2023).

illustrated in Figure 12-11, it creates a small subset of the base model to fine-tune instead of adding layers to the model.[4]

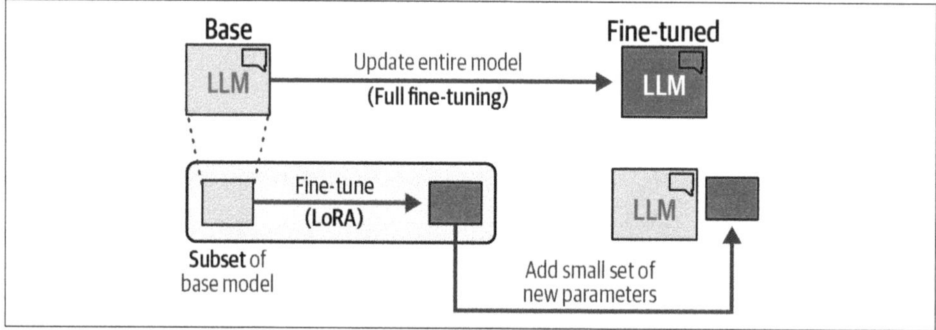

Figure 12-11. LoRA requires only fine-tuning a small set of parameters that can be kept separately from the base LLM.

Like adapters, this subset allows for much quicker fine-tuning since we only need to update a small part of the base model. We create this subset of parameters by approximating large matrices that accompany the original LLM with smaller matrices. We can then use those smaller matrices as a replacement and fine-tune them instead of the original large matrices. Take for example the 10 × 10 matrix we see in Figure 12-12.

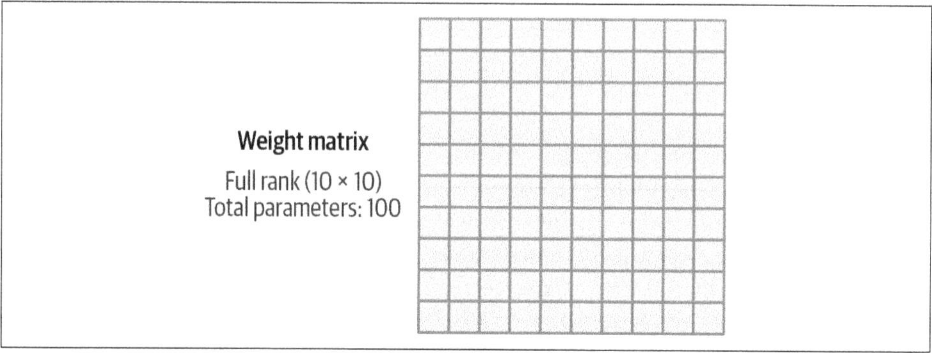

Figure 12-12. A major bottleneck of LLMs is their massive weight matrices. Only one of these may have 150 million parameters and each Transformer block would have its version of these.

4 Edward J. Hu et al. "LoR: Low-Rank Adaptation of large language models." *arXiv preprint arXiv:2106.09685* (2021).

We can come up with two smaller matrices, which when multiplied, reconstruct a 10 × 10 matrix. This is a major efficiency win because instead of using 100 weights (10 times 10) we now only have 20 weights (10 plus 10), as we can see in Figure 12-13.

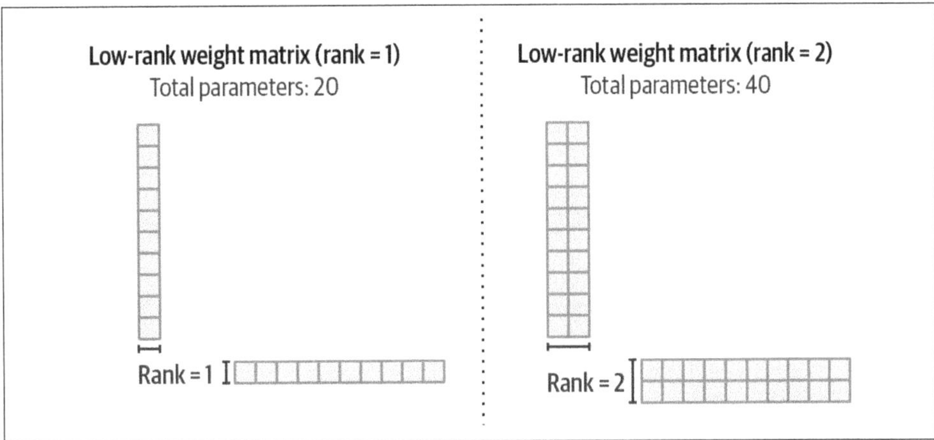

Figure 12-13. Decomposing a large weight matrix into two smaller matrices leads to a compressed, low-rank version of the matrix that can be fine-tuned more efficiently.

During training, we only need to update these smaller matrices instead of the full weight changes. The updated change matrices (smaller matrices) are then combined with the full (frozen) weights as illustrated in Figure 12-14.

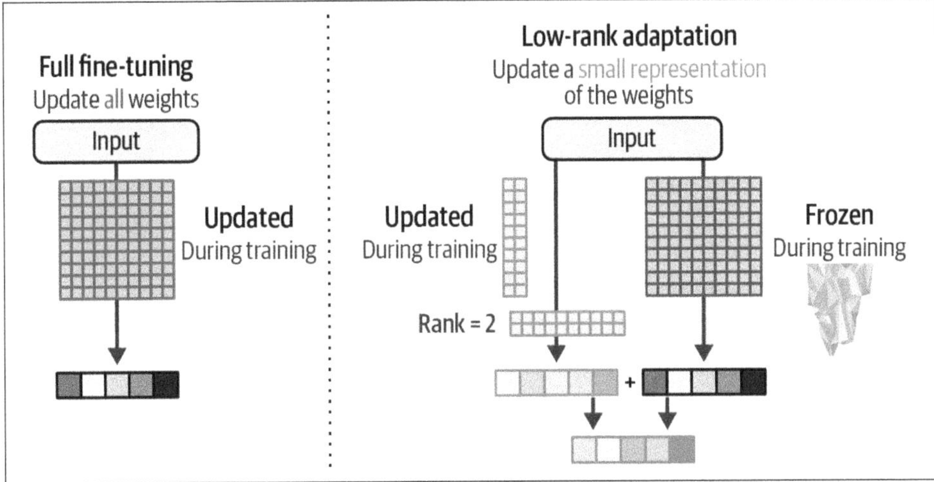

Figure 12-14. Compared to full fine-tuning, LoRA aims to update a small representation of the original weights during training.

But you might suspect that performance would drop. And you would be right. But where does this trade-off make sense?

Papers like "Intrinsic dimensionality explains the effectiveness of language model fine-tuning" (*https://oreil.ly/Th2m-*) demonstrate that language models "have a very low intrinsic dimension."[5] This means that we can find small ranks that approximate even the massive matrices of an LLM. A 175B model like GPT-3, for example, would have a weight matrix of 12,288 × 12,288 inside each of its 96 Transformer blocks. That's 150 million parameters. If we can successfully adapt that matrix into rank 8, that would only require two 12,288 × 2 matrices resulting in 197K parameters per block. These are major savings in speed, storage, and compute as explained further in the previously referenced LoRA paper (*https://oreil.ly/k9U5V*).

This smaller representation is quite flexible in that you can select which parts of the base model to fine-tune. For instance, we can only fine-tune the Query and Value weight matrices in each Transformer layer.

Compressing the model for (more) efficient training

We can make LoRA even more efficient by reducing the memory requirements of the model's original weights before projecting them into smaller matrices. The weights of an LLM are numeric values with a given precision, which can be expressed by the number of bits like float64 or float32. As illustrated in Figure 12-15, if we lower the amount of bits to represent a value, we get a less accurate result. However, if we lower the number of bits we also lower the memory requirements of that model.

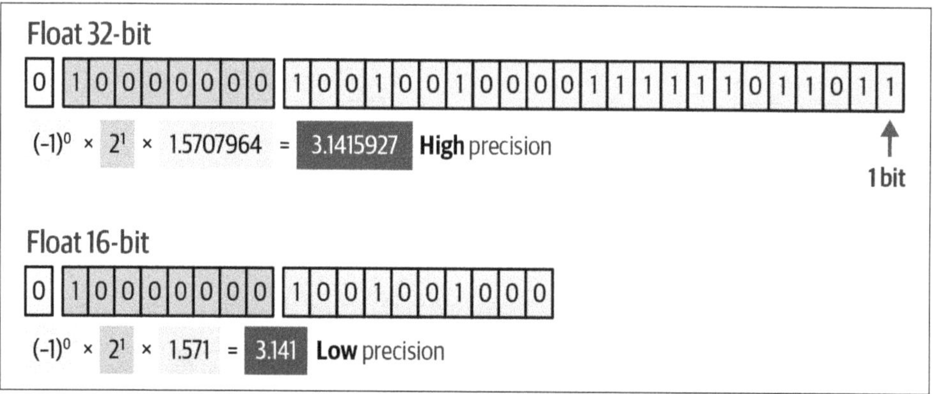

Figure 12-15. Attempting to represent pi with float 32-bit and float 16-bit representations. Notice the lowered accuracy when we halve the number of bits.

5 Armen Aghajanyan, Luke Zettlemoyer, and Sonal Gupta. "Intrinsic dimensionality explains the effectiveness of language model fine-tuning." *arXiv preprint arXiv:2012.13255* (2020).

With quantization, we aim to lower the number of bits while still accurately representing the original weight values. However, as shown in Figure 12-16, when directly mapping higher precision values to lower precision values, multiple higher precision values might end up being represented by the same lower precision values.

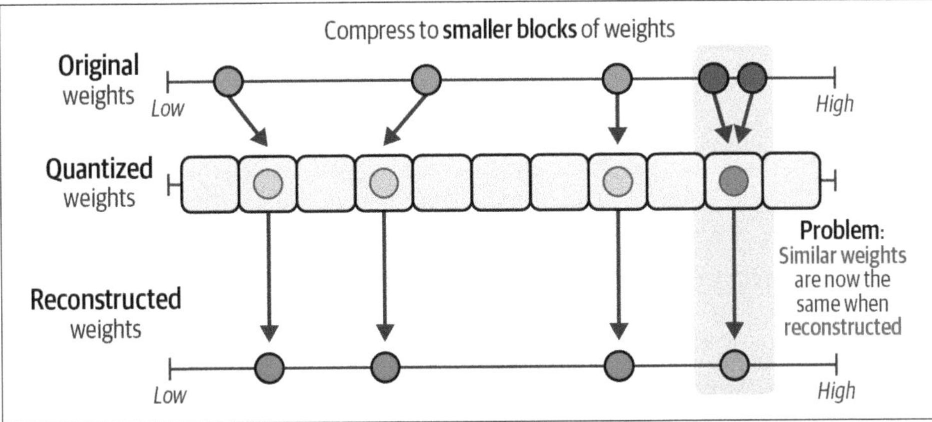

Figure 12-16. Quantizing weights that are close to one another results in the same reconstructed weights thereby removing any differentiating factor.

Instead, the authors of QLoRA, a quantized version of LoRA, found a way to go from a higher number of bits to a lower value and vice versa without differentiating too much from the original weights.[6]

They used blockwise quantization to map certain blocks of higher precision values to lower precision values. Instead of directly mapping higher precision to lower precision values, additional blocks are created that allow for quantizing similar weights. As shown in Figure 12-17, this results in values that can be accurately represented with lower precision.

6 Tim Dettmers et al. "QLoRA: Efficient finetuning of quantized LLMs." *arXiv preprint arXiv:2305.14314* (2023).

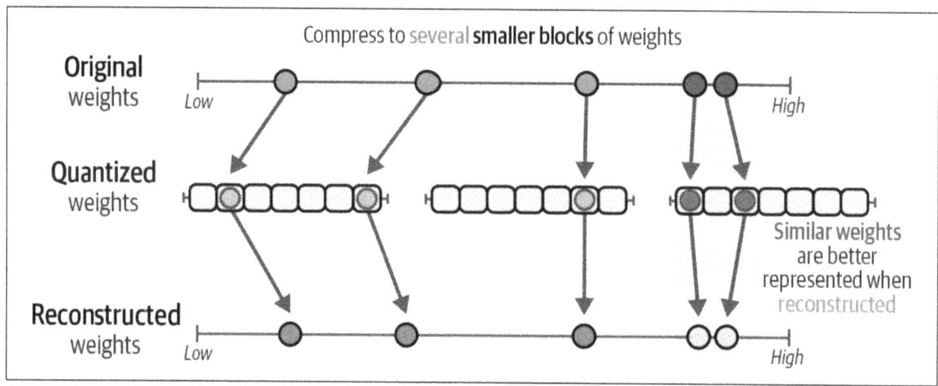

Figure 12-17. Blockwise quantization can accurately represent weights in lower precision through quantization blocks.

A nice property of neural networks is that their values are generally normally distributed between –1 and 1. This property allows us to bin the original weights to lower bits based on their relative density, as illustrated in Figure 12-18. The mapping between weights is more efficient as it takes into account the relative frequency of weights. This also reduces issues with outliers.

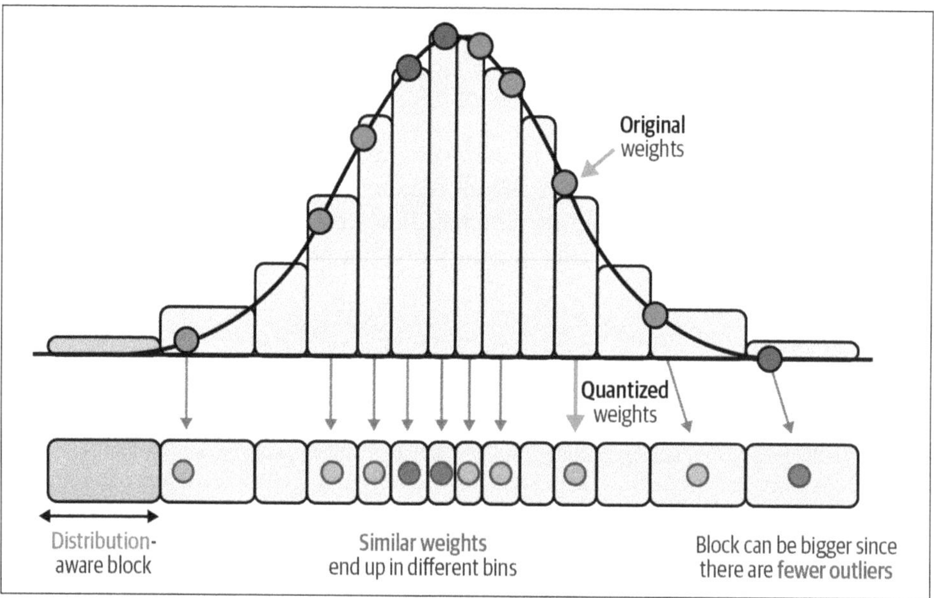

Figure 12-18. Using distribution-aware blocks we can prevent values close to one another from being represented with the same quantized value.

Combined with the blockwise quantization, this normalization procedure allows for accurate representation of high precision values by low precision values with only a small decrease in the performance of the LLM. As a result, we can go from a 16-bit float representation to a measly 4-bit normalized float representation. A 4-bit representation significantly reduces the memory requirements of the LLM during training. Note that the quantization of LLMs in general is also helpful for inference as quantized LLMs are smaller in size and therefore require less VRAM.

There are more elegant methods to further optimize this like double quantization and paged optimizers, which you can read about more in the QLoRA paper discussed earlier (*https://oreil.ly/U1DSq*). For a complete and highly visual guide to quantization, see this blog post (*https://oreil.ly/GituX*).

Instruction Tuning with QLoRA

Now that we have explored how QLoRA works, let us put that knowledge into practice! In this section, we will fine-tune a completely open source and smaller version of Llama, TinyLlama (*https://oreil.ly/mGO7A*), to follow instructions using the QLoRA procedure. Consider this model a base or pretrained model, one that was trained with language modeling but cannot yet follow instructions.

Templating Instruction Data

To have the LLM follow instructions, we will need to prepare instruction data that follows a chat template. This chat template, as illustrated in Figure 12-19, differentiates between what the LLM has generated and what the user has generated.

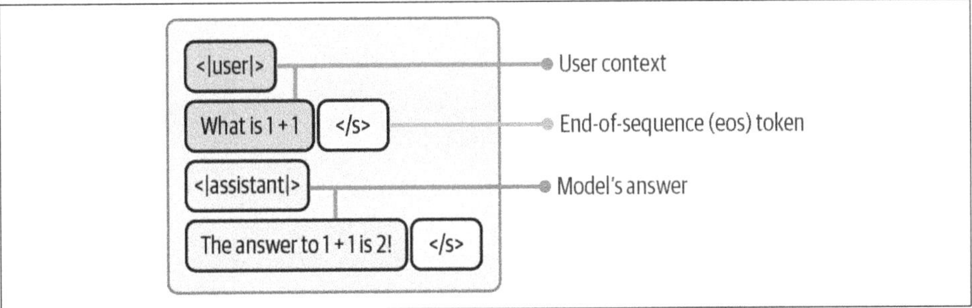

Figure 12-19. The chat template that we use throughout this chapter.

We chose this chat template to use throughout the examples since the chat version of TinyLlama (*https://oreil.ly/rROj4*) uses the same format. The data that we are using is a small subset of the UltraChat dataset (*https://oreil.ly/6S290*).[7] This dataset is a filtered version of the original UltraChat dataset that contains almost 200k conversations between a user and an LLM.

We create a function, `format_prompt`, to make sure that the conversations follow this template:

```
from transformers import AutoTokenizer
from datasets import load_dataset

# Load a tokenizer to use its chat template
template_tokenizer = AutoTokenizer.from_pretrained(
    "TinyLlama/TinyLlama-1.1BChat-v1.0"
)

def format_prompt(example):
    """Format the prompt to using the <|user|> template TinyLLama is using"""

    # Format answers
    chat = example["messages"]
    prompt = template_tokenizer.apply_chat_template(chat, tokenize=False)

    return {"text": prompt}

# Load and format the data using the template TinyLLama is using
dataset = (
    load_dataset("HuggingFaceH4/ultrachat_200k", split="test_sft")
      .shuffle(seed=42)
      .select(range(3_000))
)
dataset = dataset.map(format_prompt)
```

We select a subset of 3,000 documents to reduce the training time, but you can increase this value to get more accurate results.

Using the `"text"` column, we can explore these formatted prompts:

```
# Example of formatted prompt
print(dataset["text"][2576])
```

```
<|user|>
Given the text: Knock, knock. Who's there? Hike.
Can you continue the joke based on the given text material "Knock, knock.
Who's there? Hike"?</s>
<|assistant|>
Sure! Knock, knock. Who's there? Hike. Hike who? Hike up your pants, it's cold
outside!</s>
```

7 Ning Ding et al. "Enhancing chat language models by scaling high-quality instructional conversations." *arXiv preprint arXiv:2305.14233* (2023).

```
<|user|>
Can you tell me another knock-knock joke based on the same text material
"Knock, knock. Who's there? Hike"?</s>
<|assistant|>
Of course! Knock, knock. Who's there? Hike. Hike who? Hike your way over here
and let's go for a walk!</s>
```

Model Quantization

Now that we have our data, we can start loading in our model. This is where we apply the Q in QLoRA, namely quantization. We use the `bitsandbytes` package (*https://oreil.ly/B_etl*) to compress the pretrained model to a 4-bit representation.

In `BitsAndBytesConfig`, you can define the quantization scheme. We follow the steps used in the original QLoRA paper and load the model in 4-bit (`load_in_4bit`) with a normalized float representation (`bnb_4bit_quant_type`) and double quantization (`bnb_4bit_use_double_quant`):

```
import torch
from transformers import AutoModelForCausalLM, AutoTokenizer, BitsAndBytesConfig

model_name = "TinyLlama/TinyLlama-1.1B-intermediate-step-1431k-3T"

# 4-bit quantization configuration - Q in QLoRA
bnb_config = BitsAndBytesConfig(
    load_in_4bit=True,  # Use 4-bit precision model loading
    bnb_4bit_quant_type="nf4",  # Quantization type
    bnb_4bit_compute_dtype="float16",  # Compute dtype
    bnb_4bit_use_double_quant=True,  # Apply nested quantization
)

# Load the model to train on the GPU
model = AutoModelForCausalLM.from_pretrained(
    model_name,
    device_map="auto",

    # Leave this out for regular SFT
    quantization_config=bnb_config,
)
model.config.use_cache = False
model.config.pretraining_tp = 1

# Load LLaMA tokenizer
tokenizer = AutoTokenizer.from_pretrained(model_name, trust_remote_code=True)
tokenizer.pad_token = "<PAD>"
tokenizer.padding_side = "left"
```

This quantization procedure allows us to decrease the size of the original model while retaining most of the original weights' precision. Loading the model now only uses ~1 GB VRAM compared to the ~4 GB of VRAM it would need without quantization. Note that during fine-tuning, more VRAM will be necessary so it does not cap out on the ~1 GB VRAM needed to load the model.

LoRA Configuration

Next, we will need to define our LoRA configuration using the `peft` library (*https://oreil.ly/ci5pl*), which represents hyperparameters of the fine-tuning process:

```
from peft import LoraConfig, prepare_model_for_kbit_training, get_peft_model

# Prepare LoRA Configuration
peft_config = LoraConfig(
    lora_alpha=32,  # LoRA Scaling
    lora_dropout=0.1,  # Dropout for LoRA Layers
    r=64,  # Rank
    bias="none",
    task_type="CAUSAL_LM",
    target_modules=  # Layers to target
     ["k_proj", "gate_proj", "v_proj", "up_proj", "q_proj", "o_proj",
"down_proj"]
)

# Prepare model for training
model = prepare_model_for_kbit_training(model)
model = get_peft_model(model, peft_config)
```

There are several parameters worth mentioning:

`r`
: This is the rank of the compressed matrices (recall this from Figure 12-13) Increasing this value will also increase the sizes of compressed matrices leading to less compression and thereby improved representative power. Values typically range between 4 and 64.

`lora_alpha`
: Controls the amount of change that is added to the original weights. In essence, it balances the knowledge of the original model with that of the new task. A rule of thumb is to choose a value twice the size of `r`.

`target_modules`
: Controls which layers to target. The LoRA procedure can choose to ignore specific layers, like specific projection layers. This can speed up training but reduce performance and vice versa.

Playing around with the parameters is a worthwhile experiment to get an intuitive understanding of values that work and those that do not. You can find an amazing resource of additional tips on LoRA fine-tuning in the Ahead of AI newsletter (*https://oreil.ly/xKkYD*) by Sebastian Raschka.

This example demonstrates an efficient form of fine-tuning your model. If you want to perform full fine-tuning instead, you can remove the `quantization_config` parameter when loading the model and skip the creation of `peft_config`. By removing those, we would go from "Instruction tuning with QLoRA" to "full instruction tuning."

Training Configuration

Lastly, we need to configure our training parameters as we did in Chapter 11:

```
from transformers import TrainingArguments

output_dir = "./results"

# Training arguments
training_arguments = TrainingArguments(
    output_dir=output_dir,
    per_device_train_batch_size=2,
    gradient_accumulation_steps=4,
    optim="paged_adamw_32bit",
    learning_rate=2e-4,
    lr_scheduler_type="cosine",
    num_train_epochs=1,
    logging_steps=10,
    fp16=True,
    gradient_checkpointing=True
)
```

There are several parameters worth mentioning:

`num_train_epochs`
: The total number of training rounds. Higher values tend to degrade performance so we generally like to keep this low.

`learning_rate`
: Determines the step size at each iteration of weight updates. The authors of QLoRA found that higher learning rates work better for larger models (>33B parameters).

`lr_scheduler_type`
: A cosine-based scheduler to adjust the learning rate dynamically. It will linearly increase the learning rate, starting from zero, until it reaches the set value. After that, the learning rate is decayed following the values of a cosine function.

`optim`
: The paged optimizers used in the original QLoRA paper.

Optimizing these parameters is a difficult task and there are no set guidelines for doing so. It requires experimentation to figure out what works best for specific datasets, model sizes, and target tasks.

Although this section describes instruction tuning, we could also use QLoRA to fine-tune an instruction model. For instance, we could fine-tune a chat model to generate specific SQL code or to create JSON output that adheres to a specific format. As long as you have the data available (with appropriate query-response items), QLoRA is a great technique for nudging an existing chat model to be more appropriate for your use case.

Training

Now that we have prepared all our models and parameters, we can start fine-tuning our model. We load in `SFTTrainer` and simply run `trainer.train()`:

```
from     import SFTTrainer

# Set supervised fine-tuning parameters
trainer = SFTTrainer(
    model=model,
    train_dataset=dataset,
    dataset_text_field="text",
    tokenizer=tokenizer,
    args=training_arguments,
    max_seq_length=512,

    # Leave this out for regular SFT
    peft_config=peft_config,
)

# Train model
trainer.train()

# Save QLoRA weights
trainer.model.save_pretrained("TinyLlama-1.1B-qlora")
```

During training the loss will be printed every 10 steps according to the `logging_steps` parameter. If you are using the free GPU provided by Google Colab, which is the Tesla T4 at the time of writing, then training might take up to an hour. A good time to take a break!

Merge Weights

After we have trained our QLoRA weights, we still need to combine them with the original weights to use them. We reload the model in 16 bits, instead of the quantized 4 bits, to merge the weights. Although the tokenizer was not updated during training, we save it to the same folder as the model for easier access:

```
from peft import AutoPeftModelForCausalLM

model = AutoPeftModelForCausalLM.from_pretrained(
    "TinyLlama-1.1B-qlora",
    low_cpu_mem_usage=True,
    device_map="auto",
)

# Merge LoRA and base model
merged_model = model.merge_and_unload()
```

After merging the adapter with the base model, we can use it with the prompt template that we defined earlier:

```
from transformers import pipeline

# Use our predefined prompt template
prompt = """<|user|>
Tell me something about Large Language Models.</s>
<|assistant|>
"""

# Run our instruction-tuned model
pipe = pipeline(task="text-generation", model=merged_model, tokenizer=tokenizer)
print(pipe(prompt)[0]["generated_text"])
```

```
Large Language Models (LLMs) are artificial intelligence (AI) models that
learn language and understand what it means to say things in a particular
language. They are trained on huge amounts of text…
```

The aggregate output shows that the model now closely follows our instructions, which is not possible with the base model.

Evaluating Generative Models

Evaluating generative models poses a significant challenge. Generative models are used across many diverse use cases, making it a challenge to rely on a singular metric for judgment. Unlike more specialized models, a generative model's ability to solve mathematical questions does not guarantee success in solving coding questions.

At the same time, evaluating these models is vital, particularly in production settings where consistency is important. Given their probabilistic nature, generative models do not necessarily generate consistent outputs; there is a need for robust evaluation.

In this section, we will explore a few common evaluation methods, but we want to emphasize the current lack of golden standards. No one metric is perfect for all use cases.

Word-Level Metrics

One common metrics category for comparing generative models is word-level evaluation. These classic techniques compare a reference dataset with the generated tokens on a token(set) level. Common word-level metrics include perplexity,[8] ROUGE,[9] BLEU,[10] and BERTScore.[11]

Of note is perplexity, which measures how well a language model predicts a text. Given input text, the model predicts how likely the next token is. With perplexity, we assume a model performs better if it gives the next token a high probability. In other words, the models should not be "perplexed" when presented with a well-written document.

As illustrated in Figure 12-20, when presented with the input "When a measure becomes a," the model is asked how probable the word "target" is as the next word.

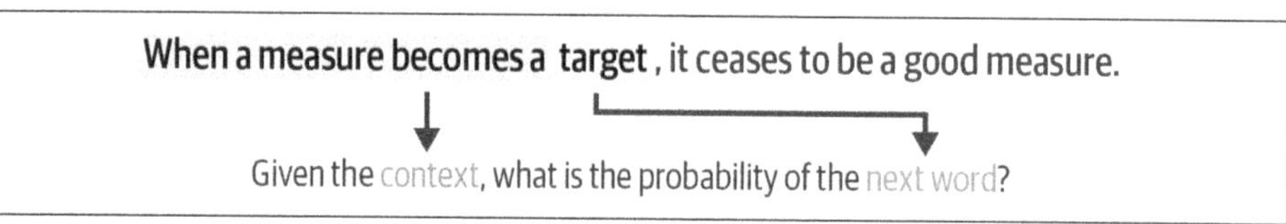

Figure 12-20. Next-word prediction is a central feature of many LLMs.

Although perplexity, and other word-level metrics, are useful metrics to understand the confidence of the model, they are not a perfect measure. They do not account for consistency, fluency, creativity, or even correctness of the generated text.

Benchmarks

A common method for evaluating generative models on language generation and understanding tasks is on well-known and public benchmarks, such as MMLU,[12] GLUE,[13] TruthfulQA,[14] GSM8k,[15] and HellaSwag.[16] These benchmarks give us

8 Fred Jelinek et al. "Perplexity—a measure of the difficulty of speech recognition tasks." *The Journal of the Acoustical Society of America* 62.S1 (1977): S63.

9 Chin-Yew Lin. "ROUGE: A package for automatic evaluation of summaries." *Text Summarization Branches Out*, 74–81. 2004.

10 Kishore Papineni, et al. "Bleu: a method for automatic evaluation of machine translation." *Proceedings of the 40th Annual Meeting of the Association for Computational Linguistics*. 2002.

11 Tianyi Zhang et al. "BERTscore: Evaluating text generation with BERT." *arXiv preprint arXiv:1904.09675* (2019).

information about basic language understanding but also complex analytical answering, like math problems.

Aside from natural language tasks, some models specialize in other domains, like programming. These models tend to be evaluated on different benchmarks, such as HumanEval,[17] which consists of challenging programming tasks for the model to solve. Table 12-1 gives an overview of common public benchmarks for generative models.

Table 12-1. Common public benchmarks for generative models

Benchmark	Description	Resources
MMLU	The Massive Multitask Language Understanding (MMLU) benchmark tests the model on 57 different tasks, including classification, question answering, and sentiment analysis.	*https://oreil.ly/nrG_g*
GLUE	The General Language Understanding Evaluation (GLUE) benchmark consists of language understanding tasks covering a wide degree of difficulty.	*https://oreil.ly/LV_fb*
TruthfulQA	TruthfulQA measures the truthfulness of a model's generated text.	*https://oreil.ly/i2Brj*
GSM8k	The GSM8k dataset contains grade-school math word problems. It is linguistically diverse and created by human problem writers.	*https://oreil.ly/oOBXY*
HellaSwag	HellaSwag is a challenge dataset for evaluating common-sense inference. It consists of multiple-choice questions that the model needs to answer. It can select one of four answer choices for each question.	*https://oreil.ly/aDvBP*
HumanEval	The HumanEval benchmark is used for evaluating generated code based on 164 programming problems.	*https://oreil.ly/dlJIX*

Benchmarks are a great way to get a basic understanding on how well a model performs on a wide variety of tasks. A downside to public benchmarks is that models can be overfitted to these benchmarks to generate the best responses. Moreover, these are still broad benchmarks and might not cover very specific use cases. Lastly, another downside is that some benchmarks require strong GPUs with a long running time (over hours) to compute, which makes iteration difficult.

12 Dan Hendrycks et al. "Measuring massive multitask language understanding." *arXiv preprint arXiv:2009.03300* (2020).

13 Alex Wang et al. "GLUE: A multi-task benchmark and analysis platform for natural language understanding." *arXiv preprint arXiv:1804.07461* (2018).

14 Stephanie Lin, Jacob Hilton, and Owain Evans. "TruthfulQA: Measuring how models mimic human falsehoods." *arXiv preprint arXiv:2109.07958* (2021).

15 Karl Cobbe et al. "Training verifiers to solve math word problems." *arXiv preprint arXiv:2110.14168* (2021).

16 Roman Zellers et al. "HellaSwag: Can a machine really finish your sentence?" *arXiv preprint arXiv:1905.07830* (2019).

17 Mark Chen et al. "Evaluating large language models trained on code." *arXiv preprint arXiv:2107.03374* (2021).

Leaderboards

With so many different benchmarks, it is hard to choose which benchmark best suits your model. Whenever a model is released, you will often see it evaluated on several benchmarks to showcase how it performs across the board.

As such, leaderboards were developed containing multiple benchmarks. A common leaderboard is the Open LLM Leaderboard (*https://oreil.ly/azQmW*), which, at the time of writing, includes six benchmarks, including HellaSwag, MMLU, TruthfulQA, and GSM8k. Models that top the leaderboard, assuming they were not overfitted on the data, are generally regarded as the "best" model. However, since these leaderboards often contain publicly available benchmarks, there is a risk of overfitting on the leaderboard.

Automated Evaluation

Part of evaluating a generative output is the quality of its text. For instance, even if two models were to give the same correct answer to a question, the way they derived that answer might be different. It is often not just about the final answer but also the construction of it. Similarly, although two summaries might be similar, one could be significantly shorter than another, which is often important for a good summary.

To evaluate the quality of the generated text above the correctness of the final answer, LLM-as-a-judge was introduced.[18] In essence, a separate LLM is asked to judge the quality of the LLM to be evaluated. An interesting variant of this method is pairwise comparison. Two different LLMs will generate an answer to a question and a third LLM will be the judge to declare which is better.

As a result, this methodology allows for automated evaluation of open-ended questions. A major advantage is that as LLMs improve, so do their capabilities to judge the quality of output. In other words, this evaluation methodology grows with the field.

Human Evaluation

Although benchmarks are important, the gold standard of evaluation is generally considered to be human evaluation. Even if an LLM scores well on broad benchmarks, it still might not score well on domain-specific tasks. Moreover, benchmarks do not fully capture human preference and all methods discussed before are merely proxies for that.

A great example of a human-based evaluation technique is the Chatbot Arena (*https://oreil.ly/GoCH-*).[19] When you go to this leaderboard you are shown two

18 Lianmin Zheng et al. "Judging LLM-as-a-judge with MT-Bench and Chatbot Arena." *Advances in Neural Information Processing Systems* 36 (2024).

(anonymous) LLMs you can interact with. Any question or prompt you ask will be sent to both models and you will receive their output. Then, you can decide which output you prefer. This process allows for the community to vote on which models they prefer without knowing which ones are presented. Only after you vote do you see which model generated which text.

At the time of writing, this method has generated over 800,000+ human votes that were used to compute a leaderboard. These votes are used to calculate the relative skill level of LLMs based on their win rates. For instance, if a low-ranked LLM beats a high-ranked LLM, its ranking changes significantly. In chess, this is referred to as the Elo rating system.

This methodology therefore uses crowdsourced votes, which helps us understand the quality of the LLM. However, it is still the aggregated opinion of a wide variety of users, which might not relate to your use case.

As a result, there is no one perfect method of evaluating LLMs. All mentioned methodologies and benchmarks provide an important, although limited evaluation perspective. Our advice is to evaluate your LLM based on the intended use case. For coding, HumanEval would be more logical than GSM8k.

But most importantly, we believe that you are the best evaluator. Human evaluation remains the gold standard because it is up to you to decide whether the LLM works for your intended use case. As with the examples in this chapter, we highly advise that you also try these models and perhaps develop some questions yourself. For example, the authors of this book are Arabic (Jay Alammar) and Dutch (Maarten Grootendorst), and we often ask questions in our native language when approached with new models.

One final note on this topic is a quote we hold dear:

> When a measure becomes a target, it ceases to be a good measure.
>
> —Goodhart's Law[20]

In the context of LLMs, when using a specific benchmark, we tend to optimize for that benchmark regardless of the consequences. For instance, if we focus purely on optimizing for generating grammatically correct sentences, the model could learn to only output one sentence: "This is a sentence." It is grammatically correct but tells you nothing about its language understanding capabilities. Thus, the model may excel at a specific benchmark but potentially at the expense of other useful capabilities.

---

19 Wei-Lin Chiang et al. "Chatbot Arena: An open platform for evaluating LLMs by human preference." *arXiv preprint arXiv:2403.04132* (2024).

20 Mafilyn Strathern. "'Improving ratings': audit in the British University system." *European Review* 5.3 (1997): 305–321.

Preference-Tuning / Alignment / RLHF

Although our model can now follow instructions, we can further improve its behavior by a final training phase that aligns it to how we expect it to behave in different scenarios. For instance, when asked "What is an LLM?" we might prefer an elaborate answer that describes the internals of an LLM compared to the answer "It is a large language model" without further explanations. How exactly do we align our (human) preference for one answer over the other with the output of an LLM?

To start with, recall that an LLM takes a prompt and outputs a generation as illustrated in Figure 12-21.

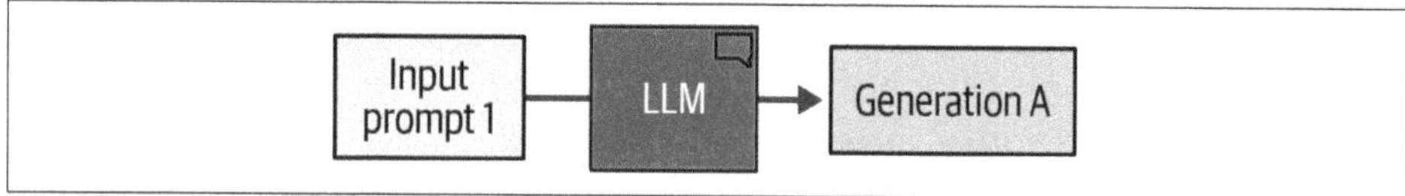

Figure 12-21. An LLM takes an input prompt and outputs a generation.

We can ask a person (preference evaluator) to evaluate the quality of that model generation. Say they assign it a certain score, like 4 (see Figure 12-22).

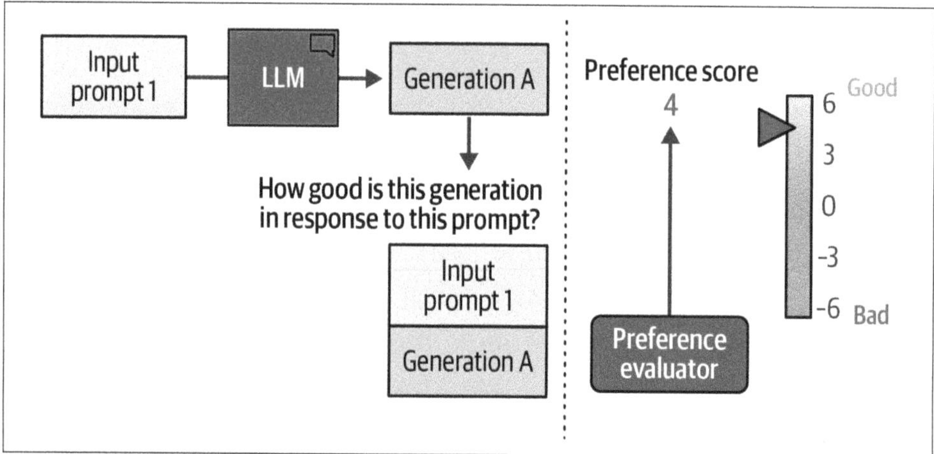

Figure 12-22. Use a preference evaluator (human or otherwise) to evaluate the quality of the generation.

Figure 12-23 shows a preference tuning step updating the model based on that score:

- If the score is high, the model is updated to encourage it to generate more like this type of generation.
- If the score is low, the model is updated to discourage such generations.

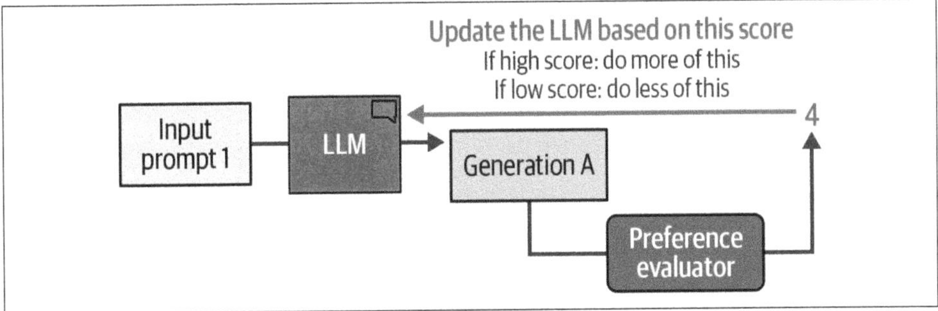

Figure 12-23. Preference tuning methods update the LLM based on the evaluation score.

As always, we need many training examples. So can we automate the preference evaluation? Yes, we can by training a different model called a reward model.

Automating Preference Evaluation Using Reward Models

To automate preference evaluation, we need a step before the preference-tuning step, namely to train a reward model, as shown in Figure 12-24.

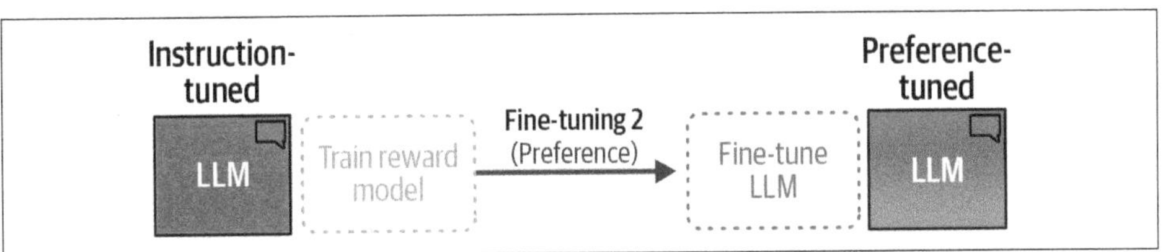

Figure 12-24. We train a reward model before fine-tuning the LLM.

Figure 12-25 shows that to create a reward model, we take a copy of the instruction-tuned model and slightly change it so that instead of generating text, it now outputs a single score.

Figure 12-25. The LLM becomes a reward model by replacing its language modeling head with a quality classification head.

The Inputs and Outputs of a Reward Model

The way we expect this reward model to work is that we give it a prompt and a generation, and it outputs a single number indicating the preference/quality of that generation in response to that prompt. Figure 12-26 shows the reward model generating this single number.

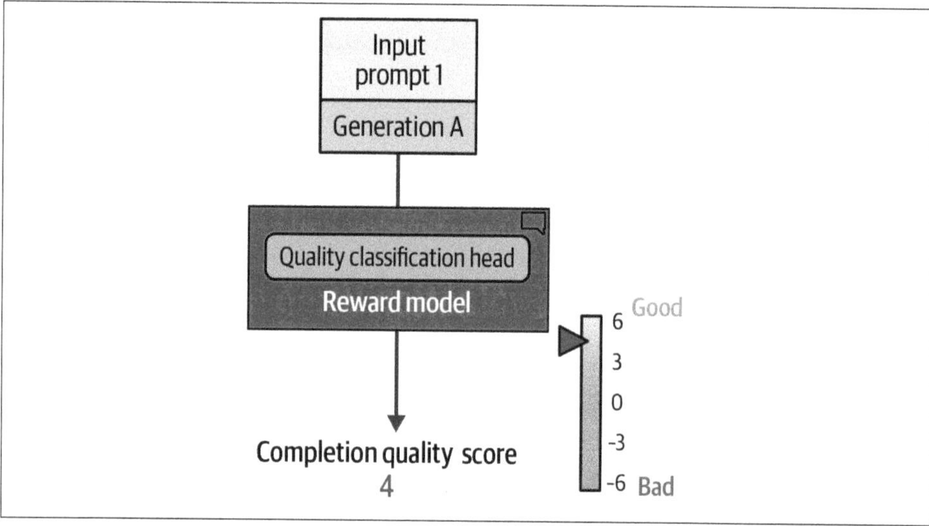

Figure 12-26. Use a reward model trained on human preference to generate the completion quality score.

Training a Reward Model

We cannot directly use the reward model. It needs to first be trained to properly score generations. So let's get a preference dataset that the model can learn from.

Reward model training dataset

One common shape for preference datasets is for a training example to have a prompt, with one accepted generation and one rejected generation. (Nuance: it's not always a good versus bad generation; it can be that the two generations are both good, but that one is better than the other). Figure 12-27 shows an example preference training set with two training examples.

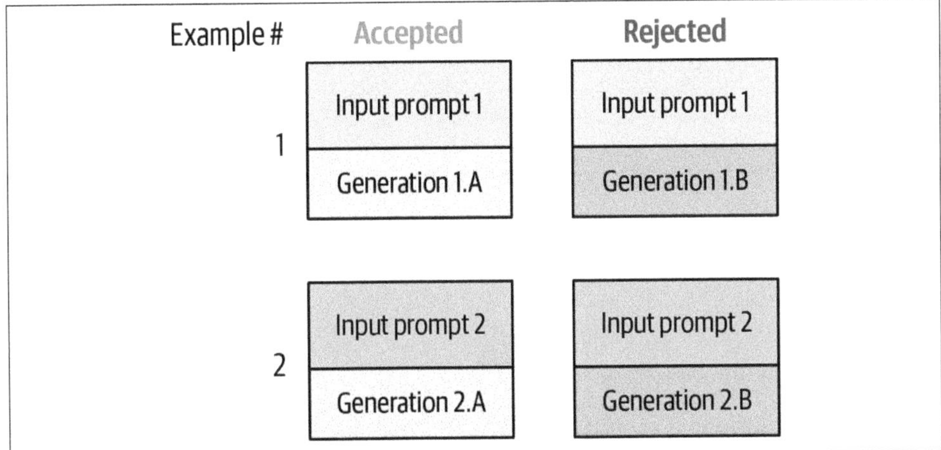

Figure 12-27. Preference tuning datasets are often made up of prompts with accepted and rejected generations.

One way to generate preference data is to present a prompt to the LLM and have it generate two different generations. As shown in Figure 12-28, we can ask human labelers which of the two they prefer.

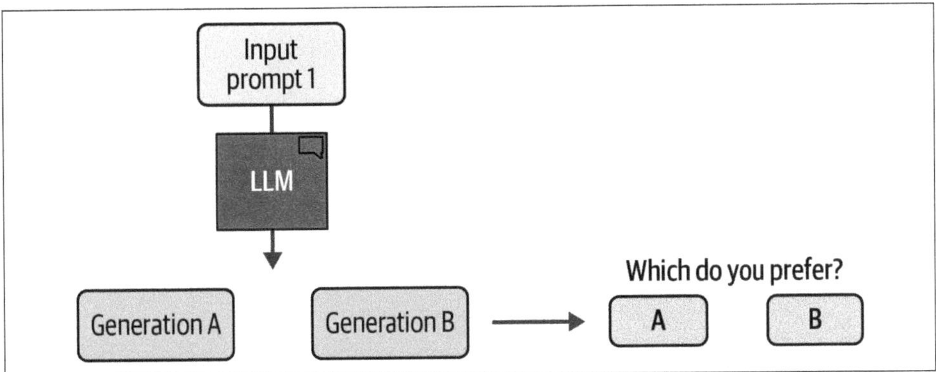

Figure 12-28. Output two generations and ask a human labeler which one they prefer.

Reward model training step

Now that we have the preference training dataset, we can proceed to train the reward model.

A simple step is that we use the reward model to:

1. Score the accepted generation
2. Score the rejected generation

Figure 12-29 shows the training objective: to ensure the accepted generation has a higher score than the rejected generation.

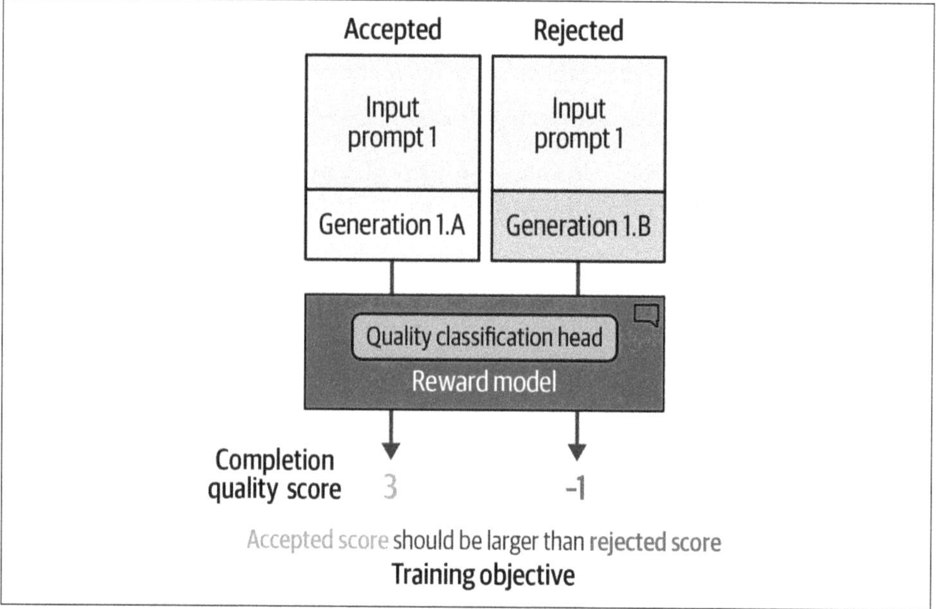

Figure 12-29. The reward model aims to evaluate the quality scores of generations in response to a prompt.

When we combine everything together as shown in Figure 12-30, we get the three stages to preference tuning:

1. Collect preference data
2. Train a reward model
3. Use the reward model to fine-tune the LLM (operating as the preference evaluator)

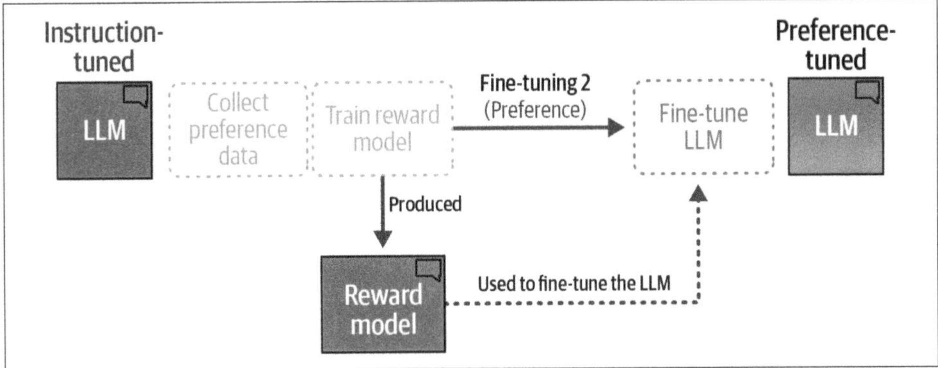

Figure 12-30. The three stages of preference tuning: collecting preference data, training a reward model, and finally fine-tuning the LLM.

Reward models are an excellent idea that can be further extended and developed. Llama 2, for example, trains two reward models: one that scores helpfulness and another that scores safety (Figure 12-31).

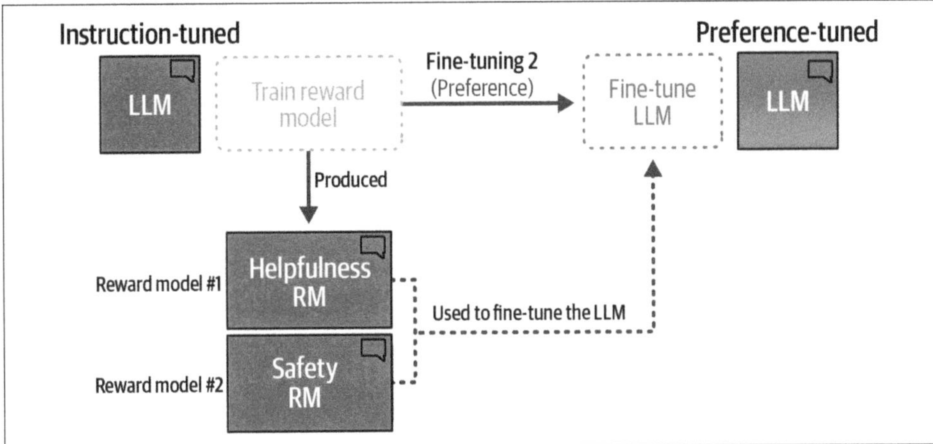

Figure 12-31. We can use multiple reward models to perform the scoring.

A common method to fine-tune the LLM with the trained reward model is Proximal Policy Optimization (PPO). PPO is a popular reinforcement technique that optimizes the instruction-tuned LLM by making sure that the LLM does not deviate too much from the expected rewards.[21] It was even used to train the original ChatGPT (*https://oreil.ly/T5f2h*) released in November 2022.

21 John Schulman et al. "Proximal Policy Optimization algorithms." *arXiv preprint arXiv:1707.06347* (2017).

Training No Reward Model

A disadvantage of PPO is that it is a complex method that needs to train at least two models, the reward model and the LLM, which can be more costly than perhaps necessary.

Direct Preference Optimization (DPO) is an alternative to PPO and does away with the reinforcement-based learning procedure.[22] Instead of using the reward model to judge the quality of a generation, we let the LLM itself do that. As illustrated in Figure 12-32, we use a copy of the LLM as the reference model to judge the shift between the reference and trainable model in the quality of the accepted generation and rejected generation.

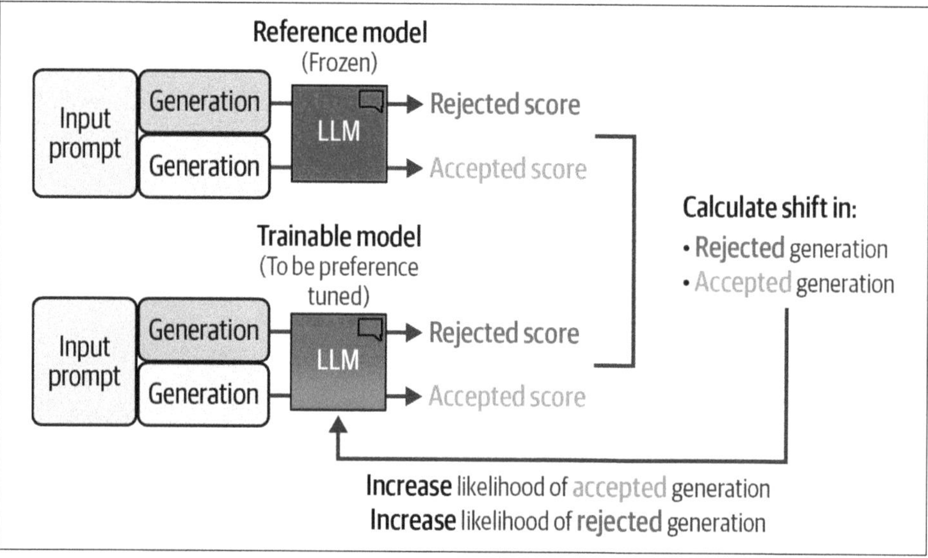

Figure 12-32. Use the LLM itself as the reward model by comparing the output of a frozen model with the trainable model.

By calculating this shift during training, we can optimize the likelihood of accepted generations over rejected generations by tracking the difference in the reference model and the trainable model.

To calculate this shift and its related scores, the log probabilities of the rejected generations and accepted generations are extracted from both models. As illustrated in Figure 12-33, this process is performed at a token level where the probabilities are combined to calculate the shift between the reference and trainable models.

22 Rafael Rafailov, et al. "Direct Preference Optimization: Your language model is secretly a reward model." *arXiv preprint arXiv:2305.18290* (2023).

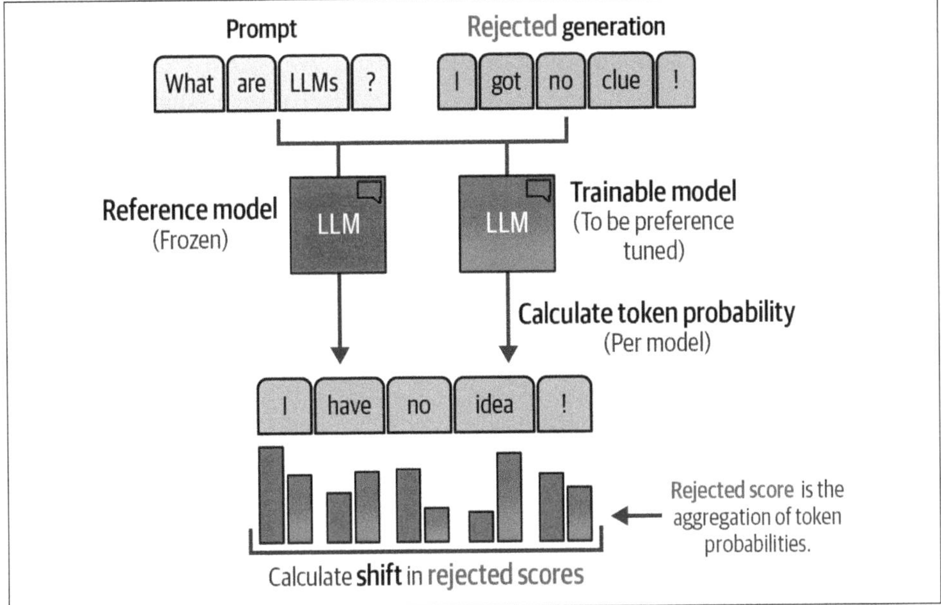

Figure 12-33. Scores are calculated by taking the probabilities of generation on a token level. The shift in probabilities between the reference model and the trainable model is optimized. The accepted generation follows the same procedure.

Using these scores, we can optimize the parameters of the trainable model to be more confident of generating the accepted generations and less confident of generating the rejected generations. Compared to PPO, the authors found DPO to be more stable during training and more accurate. Due to its stability, we will be using it as our primary model for preference tuning our previously instruction-tuned model.

Preference Tuning with DPO

When we use the Hugging Face stack, preference tuning is eerily similar to the instruction tuning we covered before with some slight differences. We will still be using TinyLlama but this time an instruction-tuned version (*https://oreil.ly/bkVF1*) that was first trained using full fine-tuning and then further aligned with DPO. Compared to our initial instruction-tuned model, this LLM was trained on much larger datasets.

In this section, we will demonstrate how you can further align this model using DPO with reward-based datasets.

Templating Alignment Data

We will use a dataset that for each prompt contains an accepted generation and a rejected generation. This dataset (*https://oreil.ly/sttRF*) was in part generated by ChatGPT with scores on which output should be accepted and which rejected:

```
from datasets import load_dataset

def format_prompt(example):
    """Format the prompt to using the <|user|> template TinyLLama is using"""

    # Format answers
    system = "<|system|>\n" + example["system"] + "</s>\n"
    prompt = "<|user|>\n" + example["input"] + "</s>\n<|assistant|>\n"
    chosen = example["chosen"] + "</s>\n"
    rejected = example["rejected"] + "</s>\n"

    return {
        "prompt": system + prompt,
        "chosen": chosen,
        "rejected": rejected,
    }

# Apply formatting to the dataset and select relatively short answers
dpo_dataset = load_dataset(
    "argilla/distilabel-intel-orca-dpo-pairs", split="train"
)
dpo_dataset = dpo_dataset.filter(
    lambda r:
        r["status"] != "tie" and
        r["chosen_score"] >= 8 and
        not r["in_gsm8k_train"]
)
dpo_dataset = dpo_dataset.map(
    format_prompt,  remove_columns=dpo_dataset.column_names
)
dpo_dataset
```

Note that we apply additional filtering to further reduce the size of the data to roughly 6,000 examples from the original 13,000 examples.

Model Quantization

We load our base model and load it with the LoRA we created previously. As before, we quantize the model to reduce the necessary VRAM for training:

```
from peft import AutoPeftModelForCausalLM
from transformers import BitsAndBytesConfig, AutoTokenizer

# 4-bit quantization configuration - Q in QLoRA
bnb_config = BitsAndBytesConfig(
    load_in_4bit=True,  # Use 4-bit precision model loading
```

```
    bnb_4bit_quant_type="nf4",  # Quantization type
    bnb_4bit_compute_dtype="float16",  # Compute dtype
    bnb_4bit_use_double_quant=True,  # Apply nested quantization
)

# Merge LoRA and base model
model = AutoPeftModelForCausalLM.from_pretrained(
    "TinyLlama-1.1B-qlora",
    low_cpu_mem_usage=True,
    device_map="auto",
    quantization_config=bnb_config,
)
merged_model = model.merge_and_unload()

# Load LLaMA tokenizer
model_name = "TinyLlama/TinyLlama-1.1B-intermediate-step-1431k-3T"
tokenizer = AutoTokenizer.from_pretrained(model_name, trust_remote_code=True)
tokenizer.pad_token = "<PAD>"
tokenizer.padding_side = "left"
```

Next, we use the same LoRA configuration as before to perform the DPO training:

```
from peft import LoraConfig, prepare_model_for_kbit_training, get_peft_model

# Prepare LoRA configuration
peft_config = LoraConfig(
    lora_alpha=32,  # LoRA Scaling
    lora_dropout=0.1,  # Dropout for LoRA Layers
    r=64,  # Rank
    bias="none",
    task_type="CAUSAL_LM",
    target_modules=  # Layers to target
     ["k_proj", "gate_proj", "v_proj", "up_proj", "q_proj", "o_proj",
"down_proj"]
)

# prepare model for training
model = prepare_model_for_kbit_training(model)
model = get_peft_model(model, peft_config)
```

Training Configuration

For the sake of simplicity, we will use the same training arguments as we did before with one difference. Instead of running for a single epoch (which can take up to two hours), we run for 200 steps instead for illustration purposes. Moreover, we added the `warmup_ratio` parameter, which increases the learning rate from 0 to the `learning_rate` value we set for the first 10% of steps. By maintaining a small learning rate at the start (i.e., warmup period), we allow the model to adjust to the data before applying larger learning rates, therefore avoiding harmful divergence:

```
from trl import DPOConfig

output_dir = "./results"

# Training arguments
training_arguments = DPOConfig(
    output_dir=output_dir,
    per_device_train_batch_size=2,
    gradient_accumulation_steps=4,
    optim="paged_adamw_32bit",
    learning_rate=1e-5,
    lr_scheduler_type="cosine",
    max_steps=200,
    logging_steps=10,
    fp16=True,
    gradient_checkpointing=True,
    warmup_ratio=0.1
)
```

Training

Now that we have prepared all our models and parameters, we can start fine-tuning our model:

```
from trl import DPOTrainer

# Create DPO trainer
dpo_trainer = DPOTrainer(
    model,
    args=training_arguments,
    train_dataset=dpo_dataset,
    tokenizer=tokenizer,
    peft_config=peft_config,
    beta=0.1,
    max_prompt_length=512,
    max_length=512,
)

# Fine-tune model with DPO
dpo_trainer.train()

# Save adapter
dpo_trainer.model.save_pretrained("TinyLlama-1.1B-dpo-qlora")
```

We have created a second adapter. To merge both adapters, we iteratively merge the adapters with the base model:

```
from peft import PeftModel

# Merge LoRA and base model
model = AutoPeftModelForCausalLM.from_pretrained(
    "TinyLlama-1.1B-qlora",
```

```
    low_cpu_mem_usage=True,
    device_map="auto",
)
sft_model = model.merge_and_unload()

# Merge DPO LoRA and SFT model
dpo_model = PeftModel.from_pretrained(
    sft_model,
    "TinyLlama-1.1B-dpo-qlora",
    device_map="auto",
)
dpo_model = dpo_model.merge_and_unload()
```

This combination of SFT+DPO is a great way to first fine-tune your model to perform basic chatting and then align its answers with human preference. However, it does come at a cost since we need to perform two training loops and potentially tweak the parameters in two processes.

Since the release of DPO, new methods of aligning preferences have been developed. Of note is Odds Ratio Preference Optimization (ORPO), a process that combines SFT and DPO into a single training process.[23] It removes the need to perform two separate training loops, further simplifying the training process while allowing for the use of QLoRA.

Summary

In this chapter, we explored different steps of fine-tuning pretrained LLMs. We performed fine-tuning by making use of parameter-efficient fine-tuning (PEFT) through the low-rank adaptation (LoRA) technique. We explained how LoRA can be extended through quantization, a technique for reducing memory constraints when representing the parameters of the model and adapters.

The fine-tuning process we explored has two steps. In the first step, we performed supervised fine-tuning using instruction data on a pretrained LLM, often called instruction tuning. This resulted in a model that has chat-like behavior and could closely follow instructions.

In the second step, we further improved the model by fine-tuning it on alignment data, data that represents what type of answers are preferred over others. This process, referred to as preference tuning, distills human preference to the previously instruction-tuned model.

Overall, this chapter has shown the two major steps of fine-tuning a pretrained LLM and how that could lead to more accurate and informative outputs.

23 Jiwoo Hong, Noah Lee, and James Thorne, "ORPO: Monolithic preference optimization without reference model" (*https://oreil.ly/iFv1l*). *arXiv preprint arXiv:2403.07691* (2024).

Afterword

Thank you to all who joined us on this fascinating journey through the world of large language models. We are grateful for your dedication to learning about these powerful models that have revolutionized language processing.

Throughout this book, we have seen how LLMs work and how they can be used to create a wide range of applications, from simple chatbots to more complex systems like search engines. We have also explored various methods for fine-tuning pretrained LLMs on specific tasks, including classification, generation, and language representation. By mastering these techniques, readers will be able to unlock the potential of LLMs and create innovative solutions that can benefit from their capabilities. This knowledge will enable readers to stay ahead of the curve and adapt to new developments in the field.

As we come to the end of this book, we want to emphasize that our exploration of LLMs is only just the beginning. There are many more exciting developments on the horizon, and we encourage you to continue following the advancements in the field. To help with this process, keep an eye out on the repository of this book as we continue to add resources.

We hope that by reading this book, you gained a deeper understanding of how LLMs can be used in various applications and how they have the potential to transform industries.

With this book as your guide, we believe that you will be well-equipped to navigate the exciting landscape of LLMs and make meaningful contributions to this rapidly advancing field.

Index

A

B

C

D

E

F

G

H

I

J

K

L

M

Q

R

S

T

U

V

W

Y

Z

About the Authors

Jay Alammar is Director and Engineering Fellow at Cohere (pioneering provider of large language models as an API). In this role, he advises and educates enterprises and the developer community on using language models for practical use cases. Through his popular AI/ML blog (*https://jalammar.github.io*), Jay has helped millions of researchers and engineers visually understand machine learning tools and concepts from the basic (ending up in the documentation of packages like NumPy and pandas) to the cutting-edge (Transformers, BERT, GPT-3, Stable Diffusion). Jay is also a co-creator of popular machine learning and natural language processing courses on Deeplearning.ai and Udacity.

Maarten Grootendorst is a Senior Clinical Data Scientist at IKNL (Netherlands Comprehensive Cancer Organization). He holds master's degrees in organizational psychology, clinical psychology, and data science, which he leverages to communicate complex machine learning concepts to a wide audience. With his popular blogs (*https://newsletter.maartengrootendorst.com*), he has reached millions of readers by explaining the fundamentals of artificial intelligence—often from a psychological point of view. He is the author and maintainer of several open source packages that rely on the strength of large language models, such as BERTopic, PolyFuzz, and KeyBERT. His packages are downloaded millions of times and used by data professionals and organizations worldwide.

Colophon

The animal on the cover of *Hands-On Large Language Models* is a red kangaroo (*Osphranter rufus*). They are the largest of all kangaroos, with a body length that can get up to a little over 5 feet and a tail as long as 3 feet. They are very fast and can hop to speeds over 35 miles per hour. They can jump 6 feet high and leap a distance of 25 feet in a single bound. The position of their eyes allows them see up to 300 degrees.

Red kangaroos are named after the color of their fur. While the name makes sense for the males—they have short, red-brown fur—females are typically more of a blue-grey color with a tinge of brown throughout. The red color in their fur comes from a red oil excreted from the glands in their skin. Because of their color, Australians refer to male red kangaroos as "big reds." However, because females are faster than males, they are often called "blue fliers."

Preferring open, dry areas with some trees for shade, red kangaroos can be found across Australia's mainland except in the upper north, lower southwest, and east coast regions of the country. Surrounding environmental conditions can affect reproduction. Because of this, females can pause or postpone pregnancy or birth until conditions are better. They often use this ability to delay birth of a new baby (joey) until the previous one has left their pouch.

The cover illustration is by Karen Montgomery, based on an antique line engraving from *Cassell's Popular Natural History*. The series design is by Edie Freedman, Ellie Volckhausen, and Karen Montgomery. The cover fonts are Gilroy Semibold and Guardian Sans. The text font is Adobe Minion Pro; the heading font is Adobe Myriad Condensed; and the code font is Dalton Maag's Ubuntu Mono.

www.ingramcontent.com/pod-product-compliance
Ingram Content Group UK Ltd.
Pitfield, Milton Keynes, MK11 3LW, UK
UKHW050133200225
455329UK00001B/1